DIRECT CINEMA

Nonfictions is dedicated to expanding and deepening
the range of contemporary documentary studies.
It aims to engage in the theoretical conversation
about documentaries, open new areas of scholarship,
and recover lost or marginalised histories.

General Editor, Professor Brian Winston

Other titles in the *Nonfictions* series:

The Image and the Witness: Trauma, Memory and Visual Culture
edited by Frances Guerin and Roger Hallas

Projecting Migration: Transcultural Documentary Practice
edited by Alan Grossman and Àine O'Brien

Films of Fact: A History of Science in Documentary Films and Television
by Tim Boon

Vision On: Film, Television and the Arts in Britain
by John Wyver

Building Bridges: The Cinema of Jean Rouch
edited by Joram ten Brink

DIRECT CINEMA

OBSERVATIONAL DOCUMENTARY AND THE POLITICS OF THE SIXTIES

Dave Saunders

WALLFLOWER PRESS
LONDON & NEW YORK

First published in Great Britain in 2007 by
Wallflower Press
6 Market Place, London W1W 8AF
www.wallflowerpress.co.uk

A catalogue record for this book is available from the British Library

ISBN 978-1-905674-15-2 (pbk)
ISBN 978-1-905674-16-9 (hbk)

Book design by Elsa Mathern

Printed by Replika Press Pvt. Ltd. (India)

CONTENTS

ACKNOWLEDGEMENTS

As most readers will be aware, books that have gestated for long years as on-going, evolving doctoral theses are never the work solely of the nominal author. Those who have influenced (and periodically amended) this erstwhile PhD – and to whom thanks are profusely extended – include Stella Bruzzi, Barry Langford and all at Royal Holloway, University of London's Department of Media Arts, John Izod, Brian Winston, and my undergraduate film tutors Dave Green and Jim Hornsby of the University of Luton. Naturally, the direct cinema filmmakers them-selves deserve praise, not only for the information and opinions they offered via correspondence, but also for a remarkable legacy that has inspired (and is surely yet to inspire) much art and many a disquisition. My untold appreciation goes to Yoram Allon and his colleagues at Wallflower Press for getting the book you now hold into the public domain.

My family and friends, of course, warrant sincere indebtedness for helping me always and offering unconditional sustenance. Thanks to my father, David, my brother, Thomas, my sister, Isobel, Steve Taylor (a partner in crime for four years) and particularly Sadie Eaton, who bore the brunt of countless bad tempers and personal crises played out in the Grottage! Especial gratitude goes to Jacob Leigh, whose diligent supervision, patient guidance and moral support saw this project through to completion. Lastly, and by all means mostly, I should like to thank my lovely mother, Jill, who died shortly before work on this book was completed. Though it is inadequate recompense for three decades of unconditional love and support, I dedicate this book to her.

Thanks, Mum.

INTRODUCTION

'THIS IS THE ACCOUNT OF A CRISIS':[1] DIRECT CINEMA IN CONTEXT

A time of extraordinary domestic discord and, as one optimistic critic wrote, the harbinger of 'a collective identity that will be blacker, more feminine, more oriental, more emotional, more intuitive, more exuberant – and, just possibly, better than the old one' (William Braden quoted in Patterson 1996: 442), 'the Sixties' was a tumultuous period in American history. Remembering the 1960s, now an impossible process for younger people seeking to grasp their significance or understand them within a broader cultural canvas, must now largely be relegated to the evaluation of contemporary evidence. Although for many years a mainstay of American studies, the 1960s' creative nexus has only relatively recently begun to be commonly understood as the product of a historical condition worthy of commensurate exegesis (see, for instance, Farber 1994; Cavallo 1999; Gosse & Moser 2003). The academic field of film studies has not been slow to acknowledge this development or take up associated lines of enquiry; yet non-fiction forms – and especially the still-influential synchronised-sound observational documentary, which came of age in the United States of the 1960s – have received scant attention in this regard.[2]

The present study endeavours to address this deficiency by hermeneutically and historically re-evaluating the canon of American *cinéma vérité* – or, as coined by Albert Maysles, *direct cinema* – as symptomatic in essence. Like any other expressive works, these celebrated yet politically underappreciated films, rather than representing disinterested, technologically determined singularities, constitute historically contingent testimonies that are rich in both subjective creativity and discursive potency: the shifting discourses of the 1960s affected all who were acute to them, including the observational school. This study thus posits the early films of the Drew Associates, Michael Wadleigh and Frederick Wiseman as inexorably bound to a broader political and artistic diachrony. In contrariety to what is almost a critical consensus, the direct cinema genus represents more than a surface account of events played out whilst those 'flies on the wall' (a term the filmmakers would come to loathe) looked on with apparent dispassion; rather, it engages in a substantial and compelling dialogue *with* America, *about* America, in an epoch beset and defined by upheaval. The pioneering and novel union of portable equipment with self-effacing, classically cinematic continuity facilitated, *but did not circumscribe*, direct cinema's transitory intellectual flowering.

Part One, 'Furthering Film', examines afresh the historical and cultural factors that led to direct cinema's emergence from its journalistic heritage at Time-Life, and the pioneering Drew Associates' evolving responses to these stimuli. Part Two, 'Counter-Cultural Commentaries', offers close readings of four music- and musician-orientated documentaries inspired by the counter-culture: D. A. Pennebaker's *Dont Look Back* (1965) and *Monterey Pop* (1967), Michael Wadleigh's *Woodstock* (1970) and the Maysles brothers' *Gimme Shelter* (1970). Part Three, 'Frederick Wiseman's Sixties', considers the esteemed filmmaker's best-known 'institution' films, *Titicut Follies* (1967), *High School* (1968), *Law and Order* (1969), *Hospital* (1970) and *Basic Training* (1971), and seeks to emphasise their timely import as overarchingly reformist statements.

In part, my aim is to demonstrate that the seemingly nebulous inventive impetuses and meanings that inhabit these often oblique filmic statements can be delineated by a close examination of their cultural and socio-political backdrop; by extension, I have sought to suture direct cinema to American history and provide a unifying, comparative overview of the major works. This volume does not attempt a rewriting of factual history, but instead highlights hitherto overlooked but nonetheless pertinent connections to external motivators and culturally sympathetic events. Where thorough background exposition is needed to provide sufficient context, the study digresses from filmic analysis, and, in the process, from received readings. This is necessary to expand upon existing conceptions of direct cinema, most of which reduce the movement to an uncommitted aesthetic mode whose realist conceits, performative naturalism and procedural effacement preclude orientation; in other words, there is usually a denial of socio-cultural specificity. Worse, critics too frequently espouse the fallacy that American reactive observationalism, hamstrung by a 'persistent pretense of impartiality' or 'a posture of objectivity' (Waugh 1985: 235), perpetually occupied a craven, politically purposeless vacuum of its own making: both of these prevalent views, this book aims to show, are far from accurate.

PART ONE | FURTHERING FILM

1 | BRINGING *LIFE* TO THE WASTELAND: THE BEGINNINGS OF DIRECT CINEMA

> To see life; to see the world; to eyewitness great events; to watch the faces of
> the poor and the gestures of the proud ... things hidden behind walls and within
> rooms ... and to take pleasure in seeing; to see and be amazed; to see and be in-
> structed; thus to see, and to be shown, is now the will and new expectancy of half
> mankind.
>
> – Henry Luce (quoted in Doss 2001: iv)

> The breakthrough in candid filmmaking that took place in 1960 has been described in
> the history books in strange ways, with many errors ... The biggest misconception
> so far is that these films were a result of some coming together of forces and people
> which was sort of accidental. The fact is that this was not spontaneous, this was
> thought out and planned over a period of years by someone who worked his butt
> off to do it, and that was me.
>
> – Robert Drew [1]

In the prosperous West, and nowhere more so than in the United States, those
with sufficient means have long enjoyed looking at the wider world via photography. Delight in visually apprehending the unreachable, the socially disparate, people in peril or the fallen in battle, disasters, celebrities, adventurers, statesmen,
criminals and indeed the gamut of a vast nation's experience is a predilection ingrained in modern American consciousness. Photographic mimesis, together with
the contemporaneous proliferation of steam-powered printing, telegraphy and the
railroad, would make ephemera seem finally graspable and transform American
aesthetic and intellectual life from the mid-nineteenth century onward.[2] 'The very
things which an artist would leave out, or render imperfectly', eulogised jurist
Oliver Wendell Holmes, 'the photograph takes infinite care with, and so makes its
illusions perfect' (1859: 746).

As the twentieth century loomed, photographs became a staple of the American press. Newspaper magnate William Randolph Hearst, who had realised early
in his career that photography perfectly complemented the text column, stressed
the market value of this communicative strategy and its usefulness in aiding 'the
comprehension of an unaccustomed reader ... that class of people which the *Examiner* claims to address' (quoted in Orvell 2003: 79). The continual development
of high-speed, portable cameras allowed ever greater mobility and spontaneity
on the part of the photographer, who was newly free to shoot transient events at

short notice; by the first years of the 1900s, the picture 'scoop' was ubiquitously appearing alongside fashion spreads, sports pieces and celebrity portraits. Concurrently, 'muckraking' photojournalists such as Jacob Riis and Lewis Hine came to prominence in an unequally wealthy America whose middle-class conscience was pricked by images of slums, child workers and oppressive, dangerous factories. 'The wish', said Riis, 'kept cropping up in me that there were some way of putting before the people what I saw [in the New York slums] … I wrote, but it seemed to make no impression' (quoted in The Editors of Time-Life Books 1970: 48). When Riis gave his written account of tenement overcrowding to the New York health board, his arguments yielded no results until his 'negatives, still dripping from the darkroom came to reinforce them' (ibid.). Riis' book *How the Other Half Lives* (1890) and Hine's innumerable later studies commissioned by the National Child Labor Committee bear stark testament to the Progressive age's reform impulse; the new visuality of print media could be employed to effect societal palliation, as well as to provide entertainment. Humanitarian crises were common subjects in which photojournalists traded, but when the Great War in Europe came, the English and French governments strictly proscribed coverage.

Following the economic buoyancy generated by World War One (and the subsequent predominance of modernist experimentation), another social documentary movement flourished during the Great Depression. The government-endorsed Farm Security Administration (FSA) provided magazines and newspapers, free of charge, with prints by future luminaries including Dorothea Lange, Ben Shahn, Russell Lee, Jack Delano and Walker Evans. Evans' collaboration with the writer James Agee, *Let Us Now Praise Famous Men* (published in 1941), is the most celebrated 'photo book' to come out of the FSA initiative and the epitome of the then popular genre, a mix of pictures and text that usually comprised a remedial sociological study of an American town or downtrodden rural populace. Corporate and bourgeois disillusionment with Roosevelt's New Deal commitments to welfare, loan assistance and the empowerment of labour unions, however, would shape the way such photographs were employed. Picture magazines, emerging in the mid-1930s, became the primary carrier of documentary images, which in their new context affirmed the correctness of free enterprise and cautious reform: cheery advertisements celebrating the American ideal were juxtaposed with studies of the poor drinking in ramshackle bars or enjoying anarchic jamborees. This type of publication was paradoxically capable of acknowledging America's problems and fears (the Dust Bowl crisis, organised crime, foreign totalitarianism) whilst simultaneously working to build a 'consensus culture' (Orvell 2003: 117) that would see its own increasingly consumption-orientated way of living as naturally superior to any alternative.

Launched in 1936, *Life* magazine was the brainchild of Henry Luce, head of the Time, Inc. media empire and already owner of the news magazine *Time*, the business periodical *Fortune*, and the radio (and latterly cinema) newsreel *The March of Time*. Luce pledged, in his investors' prospectus, to 'edit pictures into a coherent story – to make an effective mosaic out of the fragmentary documents which pictures, past and present, are' (quoted in Elson 1968: 278). Alfred Eisenstaedt, Margaret Bourke-White, Carl Mydans, John Phillips and Peter Stackpole were some of the first to take pictures for Luce's new organ, a would-be arbiter of national identity (among the comfortable classes) that ambitiously aimed, as Terry Smith notes, to become 'the primary vehicle through which Americans would, literally (in the literal sense of taking-up something to read), get "to see life"' (2001: 29). Tapping in to the visual means by which Americans were increasingly perceiving their world, *Life* almost always transmitted an apparition of middle-class humanism's ability to unify American society and heal domestic problems – an advantageous ethos given the demographic that had leisure and money enough to subscribe.

Aesthetic and technical standards were usually high, but rarely did *Life*'s 'photo-essays' imply incurable disunity or accentuate the moral inconsistencies of corporate internationalism; advertisers valued the magazine's 'pass-along factor', ostensible innocuousness and highly commercial diversity of features. *Life*'s appeal lay in its blending of Luce's pleas for a democratic American Dream (that might be realised via his principles of a capitalist elite shepherding the masses towards a mollified, Americanised world) with tidbits, show business, glamour and trivia. Stories about 'parlor games and pet elephants' (*Life* correspondent Loudon Wainwright quoted in Baughman 2001: 46) ran alongside photographs of famine victims, portentous Nazi rallies and didactic textual expatiations on political affairs. Although the editors considered that 'truth was visible and made to be documented' (Morgan 2001: 140), Dwight MacDonald, Luce's foremost critic, saw a fault in *Life*'s miscellany of articles designed to attract 'thumbers' and casual intellectuals alike, complaining that 'the crowd-catching, circulation-building formulae [of Luce] make truth almost impossible' (1974: 271–2).

Despite its famous, controversial images of World War Two casualties (that recalled those of Matthew Brady and likewise elicited a mixed response from a public equally repulsed by violence and galvanised by hatred of the enemy), *Life*'s enduring purpose was to pull America together. In its post-war heyday, and until confronted with the divisive social conflicts of the mid-1960s and the various quandaries they would pose for a populist, centrist magazine, *Life*'s more serious editorial content focused on domestic issues that its editors felt would posit 'the seamless and integrated, independent and yet united American middle class that Luce and *Life*'s editors imagined, solving the problems of inequity, poverty, racism, and alienation by simply imagining a better country' (Doss 2001: 12). Across big-business print media in the mid-twentieth century, the moral and ideological forces of growth liberalism held sway. Strong, fair leadership was advocated and celebrated, as were the wealth and glamour notionally attainable by any who acquiescently enjoyed the benefits of interest-led democracy. Concerned Americans were continually shown what was wrong with non-Western, non-Judaeo-Christian values, partly so that they might better recognise all sources of radicalism, collectivism and uprising as inherently foreign to their nature, and partly to encourage potentially friendly countries to support regimes amenable to trade. *Life*, unperturbed by reports of privation amongst the ethnic and elderly, seized upon the supermarket as an emblem of post-war profusion, venerating shopping trolleys as 'cornucopias filled with an abundance that no other country in the world has ever known' (Farber

1994: 13). The visual hegemony *Life* and other picture magazines exerted in the living room, however, would dwindle (along with radio's once immense popularity) in the face of the cathode-ray tube.

Television, by the early 1950s, began to supplant cinema as a carrier of current affairs programming and challenge the popularity of the photographic press. *The March of Time* and its imitator *This is America* would survive only until 1951, when television's continuous plethora of diverting material was fast becoming a national creature comfort. *Life*'s circulation dropped 21 per cent over six months in 1954, as 'the moving images that flickered inside most American homes made its famous photographs seem anachronistic ... Potential customers were no longer implored to "read all about it" when "it" could be seen and heard – and updated – on the tube at home' (Whitfield 1996: 154). Most quality television programmes were, though, escapist in nature, and factual scheduling suffered from inadequate production values and political emasculation. News teams, briefed to prioritise spectacle over story, spent their time 'hopscotching the world for headlines' (Barnouw 1990: 169) that would provide agreeable images; in-depth analysis was sacrificed to bland coverage of instantly visual domestic customs (beauty contests, society events, the occasional campaign oration) that were frequently staged for the camera. Television, in other words, had become a ubiquitous symptom of America's perceived dearth of inspiring ideals – or what many anxious Cold War commentators were calling 'the missing purpose' – in the mid- to late 1950s (see Diggins 1989: 350). 'More than anything else', wrote Henry Luce in 1960, 'the people of America are asking for a clear sense of National Purpose ... What is the National Purpose of the USA?' (quoted in Jeffries 1978: 451). Looking to diversify into the lucrative television market in a fashion that would reflect Luce's ethos by investing the news schedules with his publications' famous blend of social melioration and aspirational guidance, Time, Inc. sought the input of an ambitious picture editor at *Life*: ex-fighter pilot and World War Two veteran Robert Drew.

Life had first hired Drew in 1946, after the 22-year-old's chance participation in a story about P-80 jet planes (see Drew 1946: 104). Having initially intended to go to the University of Chicago to train to become a writer, Drew instead found that he could not resist the offer of a reporting job in California. A decade of journalistic experience followed during which Drew was 'a cog in a large, corporate machine' (O'Connell 1992: 11),[3] yet he nevertheless began to think of how he might improve upon Edward R. Murrow's probing but limited *See It Now*, at the time virtually the only alternative to the stilted 'newsfilm items threaded by an anchorman' (see Barnouw 1990: 168) that comprised the majority of telecast current affairs output. Following much deliberation about his professional options and several futile experiments conducted to discover fresh methods of newsgathering, Drew decided in 1955 to study at Harvard on a Nieman Fellowship. During this period, he developed an exploratory blueprint for a documentary format by which he might bring a sense of candid intimacy and the vivacious aesthetic evinced in the *Life* photo-essay to television. Studying the art of storytelling (through the fictions of Proust, Conrad, Fitzgerald, Hemingway, Shaw, Dreiser and Zola, among others) on a supplementary course, Drew proposed, in his research paper 'See It Then', a new form of programme that would improve on the earlier methods of Robert Flaherty and John Grierson:

> Grierson's documentaries were instructional in nature. That is, he, as a teacher, which he viewed himself [sic], would come up with a thesis for information people ought to have ... And Grierson's school of documentary filmmaking on reality, I thought, was propaganda ... And propaganda doesn't work, for real people ... If Grierson was at heart a sociologist and a propagandist, then Flaherty was at heart a naturalist ... and his aim was to discover. [Nanook of the North, 1922] was a strange cross of realism and naturalism, of form from the novel, but more than that, from real life. Grierson remained cut off from real life on one hand and the great currents of storytelling on the other ... I know that Flaherty set up and posed ... but as a theoretician it was to me a compatible, better way of viewing the potential of film for enlightening people ... drama would be the spine and strength and power of this particular reporting medium. (Drew quoted in O'Connell 1992: 35) [4]

Drew wanted to combine Flaherty's engaging style – a marriage of cinematic narrative conventions to footage based on 'discovery' – with the unobtrusive recording methods of which his charges (above all the revered veteran Eisenstaedt) had availed themselves at *Life*.

The customary non-fiction genealogy is, says Drew, erroneous when applied to his own, uniquely hybridised brand of observational drama: '[Dziga] Vertov had no influence on me, and I never heard of Jean Rouch. The guy who had the influence on me was Alfred Eisenstaedt. And it was the candid photography in *Life* magazine that inspired me.'[5] Whilst the contemporaneous *cinéma vérité* exponents in France were avowing their artistic lineage by paying tribute to Vertov's strident *Kino-Pravda*,[6] Drew sought not to follow this self-reflexive tradition but to focus on the potential of discreetly obtained footage; if filmic subjects and situations were chosen judiciously, thought Drew, then unstaged life in an America becoming accustomed to the camera's presence and function might yield up its own mode of truth. Aware that subjects may, as *Life*'s Wilson Hicks opined, be 'inclined to think of the photographer as a gross fellow ... who drives nice folks to distraction by his bedeviling insistence on "just one more"' (quoted in Evans 1997: 19), Drew proposed instead to lessen the television cameraman's intrusion into unfolding events. Leaving Harvard, he envisaged a new, more perceptive type of broadcast journalism with a 'capacity for mobile reporting on real life in the un-public situations that make up most of what is important about the news' (Drew quoted in O'Connell 1992: 41). As Drew recalled in 1962:

> What I found out was that real life never got out of the film, never came through the television set. If we could do that we could have a whole new basis for a whole new journalism ... It would be a theatre without actors; it would be plays without playwrights; it would be reporting without summary and opinion; it would be the ability to look in on people's lives at crucial times from which you could deduce certain things, and see a kind of truth, that can only be gotten from personal experience.[7]

'Voice of God' narration by a sonorous, guiding commentator, at the time a staple of established American current affairs shows, was to be minimised in favour of 'picture-logic'; there would ideally be no directorial interference, interviews, prompting of or interaction with pro-filmic subjects; and available light, natural sound and locations were to be used whenever possible. One obstacle to bringing about this 'theatre without actors', however, would be the restrictive, prohibitively bulky film technology of the day. Drew had previously failed, before going to Harvard, to convince his employers of the long-term viability of a project called *Key Picture*. The five-show series, utilising then-standard recording equipment, did not successfully transpose the *Life* essay to television; reality, as Drew found out, had to be rehearsed and replayed to meet the demands of the filmmaking process. If the basic philosophy was in place, then the technical means were not. Providentially, Drew would assemble upon returning to the *Life* office a team of talented cameramen and engineers with a shared interest in freeing the camera of its fetters: lightweight, synchronous recording facilities would prove the key to Drew's artistic ambitions.

M.I.T. graduate Donn Alan Pennebaker was a young, technologically skilled filmmaker who had previously made non-synchronous, short observational films such as *Daybreak Express* (1953), a kinetic sequence of New York locations set to Duke Ellington's eponymous tune, and *Baby* (1954), in effect a superior home movie following his toddling daughter around a zoo. While editing *Baby*, Pennebaker experienced a moment of epiphany: he became aware that he should not direct or impose a story upon his material at the production stage, but rather let the story and rhythm emerge later, in the assembly. Richard Leacock, a friend of Pennebaker and Drew who had worked with Robert Flaherty on *Louisiana Story* (1948), would also join the group. Leacock, in a similar vein to Pennebaker, was at this time experimenting with hand-held cameras in unrehearsed situations; *Jazz Dance*, which he filmed with Robert Campbell for Roger Tilton in 1954, features Leacock's frenetic depiction of a dancehall session.[8] Although lacking synchronised location sound, the film gives an illusion of synchronal audio and visual events due to its untamed visual style and carefully timed, sympathetically musical sequencing of shots. The filmmaker revelled in mobility, but saw room for improvement: 'I was all over the place having the time of my life, jumping, dancing, shooting right in the midst of everything ... But you couldn't film a conversation this way. It gave us a taste, a goal' (Leacock quoted in Tobias 1998: 47). All the associates agreed that they must depart from the 'yak, yak, yak, one cigarette after another' approach of Murrow and others and strive to evoke a feeling of 'being there' with the action (Leacock quoted in O'Connell 1992: 67).

In 1959, the still freelancing Leacock and Pennebaker, under Robert Drew's aegis, would devise an umbilical contrivance connecting a modified 16mm Auricon camera to a suitcase-sized, shoulder-strapped tape recorder. By no means perfect, the cord at least allowed crews latitude to rove and the capacity to record the words of those on camera, wherever they may be and whatever they might be doing. 'It was freedom! Screw the tripod! Screw the dolly!' declared Leacock.[9] A small breakthrough had been made: all that was now needed was a bankable subject in a dramatically workable situation that would suit Time, Inc.'s needs. In January 1960, Drew found his first big story.

JFK: THE GESTURES OF THE PROUD

> [Jack is] the greatest attraction in the country today … Why is it that when his picture is on the cover of *Life* or *Redbook* that they sell a record number of copies? You advertise the fact that he will be at a dinner and you will break all records for attendance. He will draw more people to a fund-raising dinner than Cary Grant or Jimmy Stewart and everyone else you can name … That is why the Democratic Party is going to nominate him. (Joseph Kennedy, on his son, Senator John Fitzgerald Kennedy, quoted in Hersh 1997: 89)

Senators Hubert H. Humphrey of Minnesota and John F. Kennedy of Massachusetts were among those contesting the 1960 Democratic Party nomination for presidential candidate. Astutely, Drew saw in their competition both a dramatic crisis (which would lend his prototypical filmic formula a ready-made narrative structure) and the potential to exploit a celebrity whose political career was evidently in the ascendant.[10] As Drew subsequently remembered apropos his choice of theme: 'this attractive young senator [was] running for president … And Humphrey was an interesting character too. And my idea was that the camera would live with each of these men throughout the period of the primary and tell their story' (quoted in O'Connell 1992: 62). The Wisconsin primary would be a closely-fought battle (in a territory Humphrey, a champion of the agricultural working class, would normally be expected to carry easily) that would be waged as much on terms of image as policy; with this in mind, Drew's gravitation to the 'attractive young senator' is not hard to fathom.

Kennedy and his family had been stalwarts of *Life*'s pages for years, not only because of their striking physical appearance and glamorous connections, but due also to a press relationship fostered by Kennedy's wealthy father, a vicarious 'one-man political brain trust' who would stop at almost nothing to further his eldest surviving son's political career (Hersh 1997: 89).[11] 'Jack', the handsome war hero and urbane easterner, had *savoir-vivre*, a beautiful wife, inexhaustible funds, cosmopolitan yet humane charm and a practised understanding of the proliferating medium of television. If Eisenhower was somewhat grandfatherly, then Kennedy seemed an ideal (if Roman Catholic) fillip for America as the decade turned – a 'male symbol of regeneration and hope' (Maitland 1988: 2). Economic prosperity in the post-war period had left many longing for spiritual, existential satisfaction. Kennedy was young and astute enough to realise, as Hugh Brogan notes, that 'there was a feeling that the country had lost its way under this elderly, prudent rule; was perhaps too comfortable, too somnolent; [and] had lost its sense of purpose' (1996: 7).[12] Downplaying past failures to take in hand either family friend Joseph McCarthy's fanaticism or issues of civil rights, Kennedy's catch-all pledges to push the country forward along economic, technological, military and reformist lines differed little from his rivals': JFK, recalled a student at the University of Nebraska, was simply 'exciting' (see Maier *et al.* 2003: 925).

Norman Mailer, an existentialist and exponent of the radical New Journalism (something the Luce press could never convincingly embrace), disparaged Kennedy's charisma and its disproportionately potent, superficial allure:

> The life of politics and the life of the myth had diverged too far ... It was a hero America needed, a hero central to his time ... He is a consummate politician, and has a potentially dictatorial nose for the manipulation of newspapers and television. He is a hero. And yet he is a void. His mind seems never to have been seduced by a new idea. He is the embodiment of the American void, that great yawning empty American mind which cannot bear any question which takes longer than ten seconds to answer. (1963: 55, 199)

Void or otherwise, Kennedy knew very well that, as David Halberstam claims, '*Life*'s power in Washington for some twenty-five years had been awesome, a dominant national vehicle'; for those in show business, and increasingly politics, '*Life* was king' (1979: 361). Drew, therefore, faced few problems in convincing Kennedy of the historical worth and potential promotional usefulness of his proposed film. 'What's in it for me?' asked Kennedy of Drew. 'I don't know, maybe nothing', replied the hard-working editor from Time-Life, 'but if you happen to win and you look good, it might be useful to you. At the very least, it will be part of the – it will be good history [*sic*]' (quoted in O'Connell 1992: 63). Kennedy, naturally desirous of cachet, agreed; Humphrey, having learned of his rival's assent, unhesitatingly granted permission for a crew to follow him also. With virtually unlimited access to campaign proceedings from the canvassing tours to the eventual ballot declarations, Drew had a persuasive proposal. Enlisting the help of cameramen Albert Maysles, a one-time psychologist from New York, Terence Macartney-Filgate, a Canadian National Film Board alumnus, and freelancer Bill Knoll, the nascent collective, given generous funding from Time, Inc.'s Broadcast Division, went ahead.

The 1960 election in Wisconsin is now perceived as the beginning of a period of change in the public face of American political administration; Drew's first major project, with twofold appositeness entitled *Primary* (1960), would fittingly usher in a new means of conveying and recording events. After years of quiz show rigging scandals, desperate or stilted political addresses,[13] the excessive paranoia of McCarthyism, HUAC hearings, scanty news broadcasts and supposed 'moral flabbiness' (John Steinbeck quoted in Whitfield 1996: 177), America's contrast with the Soviet Union seemed less pronounced. To reaffirm the values and processes of Free World democracy was thus a timely undertaking: to do so through a medium that had been dubbed a 'vast wasteland' (Federal Communications Commission chairman Newton Minow, speaking in 1961, quoted in Curtin 1995: 7) would require not only appropriately innovative technology, but also Drew's compliance with contemporary journalistic propriety.

PRIMARY: THE SELLING OF A MYTH

The flow of ideas, the capacity to make informed choices, the ability to criticise, all the assumptions on which political democracy rests, depend largely on communication. And you are the guardians of the most powerful and effective means of communication ever designed.

> – President Kennedy in a speech to the National Association of Broadcasters delivered in 1961 (quoted in Barnouw 1990: 29)

I know nothing grander, better exercise, better digestion, more positive proof of the past, the triumphant result of faith in human kind, than a well-contested American national election.

> – Walt Whitman, 'Democratic Vistas' (1871) (in Whitman 1982: 954)

In *Primary*'s first few minutes, the contestants' personal styles are contrasted and the notion of total journalistic access is efficiently evoked. Humphrey's everyman appeal, as he amiably chats with a lone farmer outside a campaign venue and waves from inside his quaintly emblazoned bus, is apparent; consecutively, Kennedy's stellar presence is summarised by the adoration he receives as he enters – filmed closely from behind – a hall full of cheering, crowding supporters. Meanwhile, the two Senators' theme songs, which stress quite different qualities, accentuate this character differentiation for both the candidates themselves and Drew's film. First we hear Humphrey's down-home mantra (set to the tune of 'Davy Crocket' and dubbed over footage of the Humphrey bus receding down

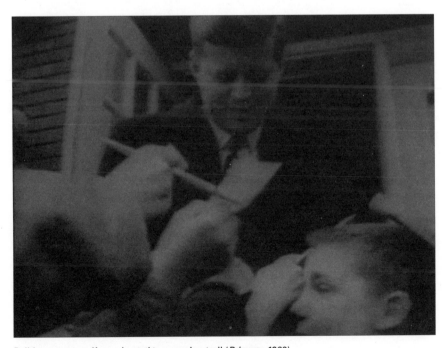

Politics goes pop: Kennedy on the campaign trail (*Primary*, 1960)

the highway) declaring that its subject is 'the president for you and me': the Minnesotan's musical appeal to the farming proletariat's needs, however, is jarringly interrupted by Kennedy's entrance, accompanied only by worshipful applause. *Primary*'s introduction, through visual and aural apposition, suggests that if Humphrey is an earthbound man of the arduous road, then his opponent has conversely appeared from nowhere, or descended avatar-like from the skies.[14] Kennedy's campaign song, 'High Hopes' (as recited by the assembly in *Primary* as he takes to the stage), boasts with unintentionally connoted chutzpah that, 'Everyone is voting for Jack, 'cause he's got what all the rest lack', and, more presciently, 'Oops there goes the opposition, ker-plop!'

Kennedy, before addressing a multitude and signing autographs, is mobbed by teenage girls who act as if the Harvard alumnus were a rock 'n' roll pin-up; a mother tells him that the speech was 'a big thrill for my kids at school'; and he indefatigably shakes the hands of and smiles at potential supporters, using 'that great Kennedy asset; a row of movie-star teeth' (Bradford 2001: 162), as they file past. Drew, again differentiating the two campaigners, cuts to Humphrey's entrance to a scantily attended rally. He is hailed by a group of accordionists (their rustic instrument being one of local popularity) who play his anthem; he thanks his hosts for an unpretentious dinner of ham and mashed potatoes; and he gives a radio interview during which his bonhomie (and tiredness) is obvious. The interviewer, when Humphrey has left, predicts that the more charismatic Kennedy will win in Wisconsin; Drew responds by highlighting Humphrey's eagerness to take his message to the people, cutting to a sequence in which the Senator is followed by a crew around streets and small shops whilst he hands out cards and charms the working-class electorate. Humphrey, as the film expresses, incessantly repeats himself in the course of duty, but the sentiments articulated in the sparse sync-sound material seem heartfelt,[15] and his ingratiating tics are, like Kennedy's, always revealing (despite – and because of – their strained nature). Copious non-synchronised bridging shots of Humphrey's shoes treading the pavement are effective in conveying peripatetic urgency (a trait the filmmakers shared with their subject), but this aesthetic approach might equally represent, as P. J. O'Connell opines, 'a cliché in its own time' (1992: 69), and a means of assembling a sellable television hour from mediocre footage. The spoken introduction outlining the programme's 'behind-the-scenes' mission, which serves today as a reminder that Drew had not fully escaped the 'lecture-logic' he found so stilting, is a cliché as well, and an unconscious admission of *Primary*'s failure to make total sense as a journalistic story told by the camera alone.

Veteran political correspondent Theodore H. White, whose book *The Making of the President 1960* covered the Wisconsin primary, wrote of Humphrey's leftish philosophy:

> [He had a] romantic, almost quaint faith in ordinary people. We passed a shopping centre, and he hated it, and the facts tumbled out – only the big firms, the Sears Roebucks and the Montgomery Wards and the Piggly-Wigglys could lease space in these big new shopping centers; the little merchant was being squeezed out, as

his father had been squeezed out ... the government ought to take care of the little merchant. (1962: 87)

Principally, according to White's *précis*, Humphrey wanted to 'keep the big man from crushing the little man' (1962: 88), a trope that succinctly illustrates the ex-chemist's struggle against Kennedy's financial might and sex appeal. As several critics have noted, White conveys better than Drew the machinations behind the elections and policies of a pivotal year, irrespective of his obvious (especially in later chapters and in relation to Richard Nixon) pro-Kennedy leanings.[16] Henry Luce's erstwhile favourite writer was able, in the printed word, to achieve a novelistic balance of drama and factual information that was, as Joyce Hoffman notes, 'simultaneously a civics lesson and an adventure story ... seasoned with the flavours of fiction' (1995: 111).[17] With shorthand, Kennedy's long-term collusion and detailed dispatches from his *Time* colleagues, White was both more privy and more fluent than Drew, who could, in *Primary*, only hint at contextual details that lay beyond the reach of his sought-after picture-logic. Nonetheless, the enthusiastically competitive rush of the 'too folksy' (White 1962: 90) presidential bidder provides a counterpoint to Kennedy's laconic manner and fits well a film whose guiding technology is so suited to extemporised roaming: though Drew could not yet supersede White's prose, he could certainly point out inadequacies in the entrenched artifices of conventional visual recording.

Drew derides outmoded technology in two scenes that are remarkable for their celebratory impudence. As Kennedy sits down to pose for an official photograph, an assistant tweaks his cuffs and tells him to 'intertwine the fingers a little' – the 'perfect' portrait is composed; from this, Drew cuts to the formal portrait adorning the back of Humphrey's bus, which shows the affable contender smiling with unbecoming rigidity. The promotional photographer thus condenses the real-life personality, or so the film implies, into an artificially designated *pars pro toto*, packaged for maximum appeal and bussed, mailed or broadcast around the country in reduced form – a simplified, consumable icon. *Primary* reiterates this suggestion of its own superiority when Humphrey dictates to a television crew how they should treat his address and phone-in session. Leacock pans slowly between Humphrey and the unwieldy, static camera set up to capture him, accentuating both the difference in capability between the two cameras and the gulf between Kennedy and Humphrey's media awareness. Kennedy, as *Primary* makes increasingly clear, knows when to state a case or obviously to perform (for Drew's candid crew as well), and when merely to be quiet and allow his image to exude. Humphrey, with the best intentions, tries to manipulate the broadcast to reiterate specific campaign issues, as would an old-fashioned orator who, wrote Max M. Kampelman,

grew up before television in the tradition where political speechmaking was an event in the community. How else other than by talking and teaching and explaining could there be an understanding of the issues by the electorate and how else could democracy function? ... The formula was simple: 'You tell them what you are going to tell them; you then tell them; and then you tell them what you told them'. (1978: 228)

15

Humphrey was passionate about getting his policies across at every opportunity, but incorrect in assuming that this gift for sermonising would win him enough urban votes in what Guy Debord would call a 'society of the spectacle', a culture in which the 'simulacrum', the visual representation of the physical thing, would supplant the thing itself as the more potent germ of desire (see Jappe 1999: 133).

When Kennedy is seen signing autographs for some thrilled young fans – who in all probability were not especially interested in the Senator's political ideas – he efficaciously avoids preaching in favour of offering the excited devotees 'a picture, an autograph, and something about the Capitol', so that they may tell their voting parents of his radiance. The Humphrey campaign was indeed spoiled, as Drew suggests in *Primary*, by 'the underlying fact that this country, Democrats and Republicans alike, was unwilling to be evangelised in 1960' (White 1962: 88). Drew, of course, loathed this anachronistic 'talking and teaching and explaining' in the socialistic films of Grierson and others, filmmakers who had felt a need, like Humphrey, to educate and inform in the name of societal justice; the image and its attendant power to instil excitement led the public like never before, as Kennedy knew and Drew appreciated, towards opinion. 'There was no distance about [Humphrey], no separation of intrigue, none of the majesty that must surround a king', White continued; Humphrey was 'just like everyone else; and a President, unfortunately for Humphrey, must be different from everyone else' (ibid.).

After we have seen and heard Humphrey during his television phone-in and a lengthy talk about agricultural subsidy to a dour assemblage of farmers, Drew conveys the essence of Kennedy's regal appeal in unequivocal terms. Despite Humphrey's earlier assertion that the eastern mass media, and by implication Kennedy, 'wouldn't know the difference between a corn cob and a ukelele', the more urbane candidate (object of a burgeoning 'national press cult' (White 1962: 93)) had his Midwestern supporters in 1960. 'The hardest thing to do on a Kennedy campaign is to harness the enthusiasm he generates', says an aide by way of a prelude to his employer's key scene in *Primary*; 'Everyone that meets him likes him, and they all wanna help.' A voice-over tells us that Kennedy is entering a Polish-Catholic hall in Milwaukee, and the most remarked-upon sequence in early direct cinema begins, not, in fact, with the Senator himself, but with his wife, Jacqueline. Albert Maysles' eighty-second trailing of Kennedy pushing through a throng (a snippet of which had been used fleetingly in the film's introduction) is preceded by footage of the future First Lady, who walks demurely into the hall before her husband.[18] As the couple reach the stage to face the crowd, again to the strains of 'High Hopes', Drew depicts 'Jackie' in a number of lingering close-ups, a treatment that is not, in *Primary*, accorded Muriel Humphrey.

Muriel, admitted her husband, 'could not compete with the Hollywood celebrity glamour that some of the Kennedy women brought to Wisconsin ... Instead, she projected not an image, but what she was: a warm and loving woman ... [Jackie's] fragile beauty beguiled and entranced men and women and children in an almost mystical way' (Humphrey 1991: 153). Sarah Bradford, Jacqueline Kennedy's most recent biographer, summarises her subject's aura:

'Jackie', close-up and adored in *Primary*

> Glamour was a commodity singularly lacking in contemporary American politics and, indeed, in American life east of Hollywood. The image that Jack and Jackie projected, of beauty, sophistication, taste and intelligence, offered the public something new, something that satisfied the American desire for change. As politics entered the visual age, their image was in tune with the times. Jackie made no attempt to dress down or be ordinary ... Jackie was a star, an American princess, and it was that image the public wanted ... Remoteness and mystique were the principal ingredients of her appeal. (2001: 163)

The enthralled crowd indeed seems, in the words of Wayne Koestenbaum describing a photograph of the former Miss Bouvier in public, to melt away and become like 'background peasants in a Renaissance religious painting' awed by her 'almost mystical' glow (1995: 24). Moreover, the same author, an evident admirer of the first White House resident ever to appear on the cover of *Photoplay*, concedes that Jackie was 'a pure case of the star *qua* star, without the utilitarianism of art or politics' (1995: 18). She was not, however, devoid of political purpose or an awareness of what her public role entailed.

At a time when the obfuscation of gender identities was seen by many as 'the most dangerous of modern maladies [and] destructive to the American way of life, that is, democracy itself' (Solinger 2001: 216), Jackie assiduously combined the attributes of the pin-up (or 'babe'), the homemaker and the princess, a synthesis that appealed to a public wary of familial breakdown and the erosion of nationally redolent types. She contained within herself a measure of every feminine ideal accordant with the social rules of consensus pressure: empowered yet demure, sexy yet restrained, intelligent but not pushy, Jackie stood by her man as a totem of quiet, aesthetic distinction. Like many others, Drew saw the import of her 'full, flowering beauty', asking Albert Maysles to 'work Jackie over', and to 'shoot her eyes, shoot her mouth, shoot her body ... Just render Jackie in any way that you can.'[19] Kennedy's public image, recalls Herbert S. Parmet, 'drew strength from the timely marriage of technology and nature. The contrast of Jack and Jackie to Ike and Mamie [Eisenhower] was striking, especially in a world not yet accustomed to saturated television coverage' (1990: 33). Jackie was, in one unattainably thrilling package, an example to her female admirers of how best they might comport to shore up the notion of a concretely definable, *American* woman. In addition, the parading of the Senator's polyglot, decorous spouse was a complimentary and persuasive means of using anodyne visuality (and aristocratic European ancestry) both to engender aspirational enthusiasm and to offset John Kennedy's masculine, often bellicose rhetoric.

Contrary to posthumous repute, Kennedy, until his last year, thought domestic issues secondary in importance to loosening communism's global hold. Despite a charitable overture to the emigrant Poles in attendance, the campaign oration Drew includes in *Primary* may indeed be, as Leacock says, 'the most saber-rattling going to war speech he ever made':[20]

> It shall be possible, for surplus food and surplus things that we have in this country, to be made available to the people behind the Iron Curtain ... I run for the presidency because of my view. I have strong ideas about what this country must do. I have strong ideas about the United States playing a great role in a historic moment, when the cause of freedom is endangered all over the world, when the United States stands as the only sentry at the gate, when we can see the campfires of the enemy burning on distant hills, that's what this issue today [*sic*], that's what we are attempting to determine. In the coming months and years, all of us, as Americans, are gonna be called out of the rank, our courage is going to be tested, and I am confident that we are going to give the same affirmative answer.

Kennedy was looking for consensus, not debate, amongst those who wished for a 'National Purpose' as a 'sentry at the gate' of liberty. As he confided in a conversation with defeated electoral opponent Richard Nixon in 1961, 'It really is true that foreign affairs is the only important issue for a President to handle, isn't it? I mean, who gives a shit if the minimum wage is $1.15 or $1.25?' (quoted in Reeves 1994: 100). By Eisenhower's second term, misgivings had arisen in his constituents about their nation's hitherto absolute post-war superiority. When launched in 1957, Sputnik proved the symbolic bane of military commanders: the radio-audible Soviet satellite undermined American prestige and public confidence as it traced overhead, portentously upsetting what had, until then, been a favourable scientific disparity between the superpowers. Adding to this national disquiet, a precarious 'missile gap' between the United States and the Soviet Union had opened up, claimed nervous politicians and intelligence analysts. 'Suddenly, so it seemed to many', noted John W. Jeffries, 'history might be running the wrong way' (1978: 453).[21]

Kennedy embodied, as Norman Mailer lampooned in his essay 'Superman Comes to the Supermarket', a mythical saviour, a 'great box-office actor' (1963: 51) who might turn America's dormant initiative to dominance in the worldwide arena and promote all-American values by inspiring public pride in a 'larger-than-life figure ... the president as personality' (Hoffman 1995: 149). In *Primary*, Drew accents the candidates' different attributes (as far as his inadequate equipment and restrained methodology will let him), but ultimately seeks coherent, traditionally upright reportage of the kind favoured by Luce and White. This creatively undemonstrative endeavour is undertaken not in the name of absolute neutrality – something that Drew, like Luce, felt would not make for good reporting – but to present a fair, easily construed and edifying picture of reality, rendered accessible to a *Life*-reading demographic. Fairness and impartiality, long the ideals of twentieth-century journalism, were in 1960 still the chief tenets by which factual broadcasters abided.

As a conservatively-schooled chronicler and an innovatory filmic storyteller finding himself in something of an artistic quandary, Drew attempts to up both the dramatic and journalistic ante by including a series of interviews with voters on the street. Asked for whom they are going to vote and why, the interviewees' opinions are editorially balanced to give a plethora of positions divided equally between Humphrey's and Kennedy's stalls. This has the dual function of providing both an empirical account of public opinion and some negligible (given the film's long gestation) suspense. Again, *Primary* goes awry as an observational piece, falling back on expository convention to provide hard information where none can be gleaned through the nascent candid approach. (A charge that could also be levelled at Drew for his continual reliance on the filmed practices of, and recorded responses to, other journalists who plainly *had* to ask questions of their subjects; Drew's supposed 'picture-logic', in *Primary* at least, is therefore arguably a false conceit.) We are subsequently informed by a voice-over, when images alone would convey the situation's weight, that Kennedy is bestowing a 'factory gate' handshake on election eve. He looks considerably more awkward when undertaking this kind of perfunctory engagement with the proletariat than Humphrey, who felt at ease with such campaign rudiments. Drew – allowably, given his commercial obligations – could not let his audience, accustomed in early 1960 to 'lecture-logic', infer what it may, even from something so visually self-evident. With Humphrey, reminisced Norman Sherman, 'It was buttons – campaign buttons he could pin on people. He liked the one-on-one contact, the touching, the intimacy ... It would be hard to imagine John Kennedy doing the pinning, much less enjoying it' (1991: 332). Drew's tentative film has thus far set up, as best it can within communicative parameters laid down by the forces of consensus taste, a relatively basic filmic showdown between two men fighting as noble heroes: the slick, eastern-Catholic outsider and the down-home, rural idealist. In *Primary*'s protracted final act, Drew stresses the capability of his new tools to see and hear beyond the province of the printed word and the newscast.

On election night, and in hotel rooms with Kennedy's and Humphrey's retinues, Drew's teams follow the competitors as they await returns. For several minutes, as the numbers slowly come in via a radio broadcast (another, here perhaps neces-

JFK anticipates the election results in *Primary*

sary, use by Drew of hard, verbal information provided by other broadcasters), the film intercuts material showing the two groups' anxious activities without recourse to narration or intervention. This lengthy observational sequence, however, is impaired by perpetually inaudible or indecipherably overlapping dialogue; one is left with only photography at the point in *Primary* at which synchronised speech, in harmony with the visual, might convincingly have comprised the 'theatre without actors' for which Drew was looking. Garnered from this flawed material, though, is a sense of the candid filmmaker's growing reliance on Kennedy's taciturn, relaxed conveyance of personality and compelling 'non-performance'. Stella Bruzzi writes:

> The Humphrey material is much tighter, more formal and coldly edited, as if the crew are no closer to him now than they were at the outset. The Kennedy sequences are considerably looser, the editing is more relaxed, the camera focuses on him not only doing things, but also observing and listening to others. Far from coming across as 'uncontrolled', the relaxed quality displayed in this footage serves to establish control with the subject, in this instance John Kennedy, whose responsive and engaged style mirrors that of observational documentary itself. (2000: 131)

Whether consciously or not, Drew finds Humphrey's reactions less interesting here than his opponent's; Kennedy, reclining in an armchair with quasi-insouciant grace, warrants more coverage than do the exhausted Humphrey and his clearly enervated wife. Drew's technique parallels the methodology of White, who had similarly asked to spend the evening in Room 320 of the Hotel Pfister, assuring

Kennedy that he would be 'quiet as Boswell's mouse in a corner' in his task of bearing witness to 'those human episodes in this campaign which mark its turning points' (quoted in Hoffman 1995: 123). As his obsequious notes attest, White was becoming ever more, like Drew, enchanted by Kennedy: 'Jack is sprawled with utmost grace on his couch in the corner, in his dark black suit, affecting to read a newspaper, not a single bone or muscle moving and exquisitely handsome and powerful looking' (ibid.). Whilst he was not (at this stage at least) overtly committed to the Kennedy cause, it may well be that Drew nonetheless found it easier to centre his coverage on a politician who was amenable to journalistic needs, and a man whose star shone more brightly than the rest at a moment in history when people were seeking such leadership. *New York Times* reporter Howell Raines spoke for many when he observed that Kennedy was 'alarmingly successful in turning journalists into cheerleaders' (quoted in Hoffman 1995: 150), and this talent was no doubt effective in beguiling Drew and his cohorts. Even Leacock, a self-proclaimed 'leftover communist' (quoted in Roth 1982: 28) (though a child of the English colonial planter class), was not immune, saying: 'I started out with a strong preference for Hubert Humphrey because of my left-wing political views, but I had also been completely charmed by Kennedy and by Jackie … and I rather converted from admiring Humphrey to loving him putting his foot in his mouth.'[22]

When the election results are made clear, and we hear that Kennedy has won by a narrow margin due to the 'big-city' vote, Drew closes his film by telling us that the candidates will fight on in West Virginia to secure by consent the backing of American Democrats before the Los Angeles convention. *Primary*'s final shot, echoing the film's introduction and likewise set to Humphrey's now faintly comedic campaign jingle, is of a dilapidated car bearing the Humphrey insignia, trundling away from the camera down a dusty road towards (or so we might infer) anachronistic redundancy. The man of the future – the general at the forefront of the as-yet un-named New Frontier – was already well on his way, as maybe Drew had sensed, to spearheading the United States' battle for worldwide liberty in the early 1960s.

CONCLUSION: STYLE OR SUBSTANCE – WHAT DOES AMERICA WANT?

Heroes are created by popular demand, sometimes out of the scantiest materials.
   – Gerald White Johnson (quoted in Smith 1986: 573)

Primary is an important film in the documentary canon, but it is not an especially good one. It stands today as a curate's egg that might well have been lost to posterity were it not for its pioneering but ultimately ineffective graspings at an alternative to didactic factual programming. The technology at Drew's disposal was not yet refined enough to permit comprehensive, synchronised-sound recording; the film is a brave but stultifying period piece, not the kind of engagingly dramatic reportage Drew originally envisaged. Due partly to its prolonged post-production, only a handful of channels, those owned by Time, Inc., broadcast *Primary* in 1960. The networks, mindful of its less than topical content in the wake of many other films that had covered the Wisconsin contest with less tardiness and in more conventionally satisfying ways, rejected it as a tedious muddle. 'You've got some nice footage there, Bob', said NBC news vice-president and former *Life* correspondent, Elmer Lower, of Drew's labour of love, the first, half-realised product of an eight-year period of preparation (quoted in O'Connell 1992: 70). *Primary*, conceded Leacock, 'was a breakthrough, but in no way, manner or form did *Primary* achieve what we set out to do, which was to show what really goes on in an election' (quoted in Mamber 1974: 39). P. J. O'Connell calls the film a 'confusing, meaningless ... mish-mash of inadequacies and trials and errors' (1992: 69), before sweetening his justifiable criticism by explaining Drew's aversion to standard newscasts and their unambitious nature. Critical discussion of *Primary* and its shortcomings has thus far largely been voiced within discourses around innovation, reception and aesthetics, rather than those of journalistic imperative or historical context. Although all these issues are undoubtedly important, there is reason to explore Robert Drew's motivation more fully.

When evaluating *Primary* from a historical standpoint, what matters most is Drew's choice of subject. If Stuart Symington, Estes Kefauver, Henry Jackson, Joseph Clark, Lyndon Johnson or any other Democrat had fought the primary in Kennedy's stead, it is doubtful that Drew would have been so keen to become involved. Despite the film's disingenuous voice-over that downplays any timely gravitation ('This could be any year – it happens to be 1960'), the combination of Kennedy and Humphrey was irresistible to Drew for several reasons. It allowed the journalist to hinge his visual story on contrasts between the two candidates; his minimising of explanatory material therefore was partly facilitated by obvious, notwithstanding poor-quality sound, character distinctions in the way of style and persuasive method. Kennedy, an already famous man who saw television as a means by which America could further democratic ideology, was very amenable to all reporters who he felt would not betray his trust; the consequences of such perfidy were sure to be dire for anyone brave enough to criticise the influential family's underhand dealings (see Hersh 1997: 109–10). Drew, like White, eagerly sought Kennedy's approval of his coverage of the Wisconsin election, screening *Primary* in a private consultation with its glamourous subject, who found nothing of which to disapprove in what is essentially and deliberately a film without obvious bias or message. *Primary* does nothing to upset the longstanding images of Kennedy and Humphrey already disseminated by the press and on television, those of a 'famous athlete or popular movie star' (Hersh 1997: 89) transposed to the normally dour world of party politics and an 'admirable but doomed' traditionalist competing for a prized mandate (Hoffman 1995: 122).

'In America', wrote White, sustaining a popular delusion, 'power is open to all who have the will and imagination simply to try' (1962: 27). Exalted by the same reporter as 'America's most original contribution to the art of democracy' (ibid.), the state primary crystallised for Drew's peers the essential nobility and decency of their country's 'exceptional' mission to lead by example and with vigour. The choice in Wisconsin – and *Primary* is ultimately about the process of free, informed choice – was in reality between men who each represented one side of the American liberal coin during the Cold War, a struggle that both considered worthy but that found a more focused vent in Kennedy's oratory than in Humphrey's prolixity.[23] Decisive in determining the candidates' destinies would be the younger Democrat's formidable synthesis of steely determination and innate 'coolness', a captivating attribute that for many observers and voters represented 'freedom from the stereotyped responses of the past [and] hope for spontaneity' (Schlesinger 1965: 104–5). An air of upward political thrust and empowering emancipation undeniably swathed Kennedy in 1960; moreover, this same aura surrounds Drew's stated rejection of didactic broadcasting conventions and goes some way to explaining the mutual affinity between Drew and his heroic subject. As Kennedy projected the vague but stirring notion that 'he could redeem American politics by releasing American life from its various bondages to orthodoxy' (Schlesinger 1965: 116), so Drew strove for a sympathetic, and arguably just as superficial, break from his own stylistic forerunners.

At the heart of *Primary*'s weakness is a compromising truth: Drew wanted to court the favour of high-profile subjects, and to do this in 1960 he had to remain innocuous in his coverage for fear of being ostracised from a clique that was defending national interests. There are few revelations in *Primary*, a film whose apparent aim was to capture the drama inherent in real-life situations and to 'show what really goes on'; rather, its producer, in wishing to avoid Griersonian 'propaganda' and slant, makes a trade-off that renders his film impotent in various artistic respects. As Joyce Hoffman observes:

> No censor had to draw a line for journalists in the 1950s and early 1960s: the journalists had already drawn it for themselves, and in doing so they joined an alliance in which they were the acquiescent partners in their relationship with political authority. With 'the national security' as their overarching concern, the nation's leaders and the journalists who reported on their activities took up arms against the perils of communism. They never publicly questioned the validity of those perils or what our constant preoccupation with military preparedness did to us as a society. (1995: 167)

'In practice', writes Daniel C. Hallin, 'the function of objective journalism was generally to transmit to the public the government's perspective on the world' (1984: 13), an irony not lost on Bernard Cohen: 'The more "neutral" the press is – that is, the more it tries faithfully to transmit a record of "what transpires" … the more easily it lends itself to the uses of others' (1963: 28). Drew, therefore, is only 'fair' in the respect that he offers no great depth of personal analysis, and 'truthful' only in his allegiance to an ethos of simple, disengaged visual storytelling, wrought without the potentially controversial imposition of subjective judgement or rhetorical application.

As is demonstrated in *Primary*, Drew was a catalysing superintendent (if a cinematic tyro) who in some measure succeeded in freeing the camera-sound crew from a physical tether; he did not, however, unburden the documentary form of consensus journalism's insidious prevarication with regard to government policy. Bound to a remit from Time, Inc. (to 'further film as a journalistic medium') and his own ambitions to become an insider in the Kennedy retinue, Drew did not in 1960 consider comment an important part of his work. He was a journalist whose living depended on access to those individuals who could sell the related stories in *Life* to middle-American consumers, suburbanites who wanted nothing of scrutiny or dissent. More palatable to consensus taste was affirmation that the USA was working as well as it could to bestow an example of Free World effectiveness upon lesser unfortunates – the 'gestures of the proud' casting light and hope upon the 'faces of the poor', as Henry Luce would have wanted and as Drew obligingly provided.

2 | THE NEW FRONTIER AND BEYOND: DIRECT CINEMA'S SEARCH FOR A SUBJECT

It is now possible to film with a simplicity that has been little more than a dream in the past. Taking the camera off the tripod is like being cured of a paralysis.
　　– Ian Cameron & Mark Shivas (1963: 12)

What American cinéma-vérité undertakes to acknowledge is not the necessity of death, but the reality of life, the life of reality, the real possibility of spontaneous expression, in the present. Freedom is the "truth of cinema" that television in America was – is – busy denying.
　　– William Rothman (1997: 124)

John Kennedy assumed office on 20 January 1961, delivering an inaugural speech that provided a contrast with Eisenhower's rhetoric by dint of its enjoinings to planetary crusade: 'We observe today not a victory of a party but a celebration of freedom ... Now the trumpet summons us again [to] forge against these enemies a grand and global alliance'; 'Ask not what America will do for you, but what together we can do for the freedom of man' (Kennedy 1962: 6, 10). Melding fervent optimism to the invocation of un-American demons, Kennedy's first oration in tenure was persuasive political theatre. The State of the Union Message, coming shortly afterwards, contained overtures aimed at placating pacifists, militarists, liberals and conservatives alike; but, as William L. O'Neill remarks, 'in the real world one must choose between opposites, and President Kennedy had already done so' (1971: 30).

In his forswearing of pro-filmic manipulation, interaction, didacticism and political advocacy, Robert Drew paradoxically imbued his vision of reality with an auspicious sense of national purpose. The short-lived television documentary boom of the 1960s (which was quietly heralded by *Primary*'s observational breakthroughs, although not prompted by them) must, writes Michael Curtin, be 'understood within the larger agenda of Kennedy's New Frontier, which sought to forge an alliance of reform factions behind an invigorated and interventionist U.S. foreign policy' (1995: 7). Television, the newest of America's weapons in the Cold War, accommodated Drew's endeavours as appropriately democratic in spirit; *Primary*'s de-emphasised rhetorical perspective and visual dynamism thus piqued the interest of networks and affiliated sponsors, who, despite manifold initial misgivings, would conduct a transitorily fruitful relationship with its producer.

The markedly dispassionate nature of Drew's subsequent early 1960s documentaries, which were largely produced under the patronage of both Time, Inc.

and ABC-TV, was suitably compliant with what would become known as the 'Fairness Doctrine', a series of rulings that encouraged programmers to air differing (but never too insolent) perspectives on issues of national importance. This manifesto was part of a broader initiative, formulated by the Kennedy administration, which sought an explicit connection between foreign and television policies (see Curtin 1995: 24). Federal Communications Commission chairman Newton Minow, in an inaugural address made in spring 1961 to the National Association of Broadcasters, expressed the aims of his appointer and the nature of what amounted to a personal role as moral superintendent of the 'tube':

> [In] today's world, with chaos in Laos and the Congo aflame, with Communist tyranny on our Caribbean doorstep and relentless pressure on our Atlantic alliance, with social and economic problems at home of the gravest nature, yes, and with technological knowledge that makes it possible, as our President has said, not only to destroy our world but to destroy poverty around the world – in a time of peril and opportunity, the old complacent, unbalanced fare of action-adventure and situation comedies is simply not good enough. (1964: 50–1)

Minow's speech ended with a paraphrasing of Kennedy's appeal to national courage in the face of perceived menace: 'Ask not what broadcasting can do for you – ask what you can do for broadcasting. I urge you to put the people's airwaves to the service of the people and the cause of freedom' (1964: 64). Whether or not Drew calculatingly opted to join his fellow correspondents (who, as Theodore White admitted, were 'marching like soldiers of the Lord to the New Frontier' (quoted in Hoffman 1995: 142)), direct cinema's infancy was spent in a network broadcast environment that would nurture its ostensible dispassion.

Drew, after *Primary*, went on to make many syndicated television films (sold under the name 'The Living Camera') with some or all of his original, core crew of Leacock, Pennebaker and Maysles. These include *On the Pole* (1960, sometimes called *Eddie*), featuring the racing driver Eddie Sachs in his bid to win the Indianapolis 500, a contest between alpha-male protagonists reminiscent of *Primary*;[1] *Yanki No!* (1960), constituting a daringly even-handed examination of Castro's revolutionised Cuba, to which was added (by ABC and to Leacock's lasting chagrin) a 2,000-word voice-over that made clear to viewers the left-wing totalitarian's 'messianic', and hence hypnotic, appeal to the impressionable proletariat;[2] *The Children Were Watching* (1961), which reported on the integration of New Orleans' schools and that was, for many, the first conveyance of overt racism seen on television; *Football* (1961, alternatively known as *Mooney vs. Fowle*), featuring two clashing Miami school teams in another example of Drew's fascination with the idea of noble competition; and *The Chair* (1962), a typically crisis-based film centred around a black man, Paul Crump, convicted of homicide, and his lawyer's attempts to secure a commutation to life imprisonment.[3]

Drew returned to his favourite subject, JFK, three times after the President's narrow electoral victory over Richard Nixon. *Adventures on the New Frontier* (1961) reconstituted material from *Primary* and spliced it with new footage of Kennedy at home, garnered from candid sessions granted to the filmmaker by a statesman now unafraid of betrayal by his foremost filmic adherent. Historian Dan T. Carter denigrates the film as a 'puff piece' accentuating 'the informal and "personal" attractiveness of Kennedy as decisive president and doting father. Fluid camera angles, obviously unrehearsed dialogue and occasionally poor technical quality gave viewers a sense that they were watching the raw materials of history' (1995: 143). American non-fiction programming in the early years of the 1960s habitually evoked a sense of faith in the nation's rectitude. News media rarely censured the country's broadest aims, or seriously countered a hypothesis underlined by Michael Curtin: that a society 'enlightened by unbiased information and expert commentary could muster the necessary willpower to take on the great issues confronting the Free World' (1995: 153). Stories that reinforced confidence in the ability of elected leaders to perpetuate and disseminate freedom were commonplace; items criticising those in positions of corporate or political power – to whom the networks deferred – were not. The presidency, the most visible nucleus of the United States and its goals, was sacrosanct in a time before Woodward and Bernstein's Watergate revelations made cynicism about government almost a default stance.

Ensuring that Drew and his team could not even accidentally expose any weaknesses in the administration was in any case an easy task for aides, who more often than not simply turned the producer away. Although Leacock's annoyance at what he regarded as 'total censorship at the source' (quoted in Levin 1971: 206) is understandable, so too is the rationale behind such denials of access. One meeting Drew was prohibited from filming was a discussion between Kennedy and his cabinet about the eventually disastrous April 1961 Bay of Pigs invasion of Cuba, a fiasco during which the President, fearing Soviet reprisal, failed to support CIA-trained exiles with any worthwhile military backing.[4] Likewise, Drew could not cover talks on the subject of Berlin or anything related to the Cuban missile crisis of the following year; international emergencies were out of bounds for all reporters, in spite of Drew repeatedly asking to film his head of state during a truly critical situation, one that might genuinely have shed some light upon the internal workings of government. Ostensibly, as regulators maintained, the public had a 'right to know'; in effect, all but the most trivial machinations of those in power remained invisible. The President, in an address to newspaper publishers in 1961, denied any wish to impose censorship in the shape of an 'official secrets act', but nonetheless asked his audience to ensure that what it wrote was not only newsworthy but also 'in the national interest' (see Dallek 2004: 375).

As Leacock admitted, he was often faced with insurmountable obstacles when trying to express himself or make the most of his new equipment: 'There was no chance of our being privy to the real discussions that took place. No one has ever got that on film. There is much more chance of getting somebody fucking on film than of getting politicians being honest' (quoted in Levin 1971: 206). That Leacock or someone like him might eventually be privy to either act was one of the philandering President's concerns, and he was keen to keep the media on his side. Throughout his term, Kennedy felt secure that he had successfully controlled his media image through a series of televised press conferences and a policy of selective restriction; he circumspectly offered rewards (access to mundane scenes in the Oval Office, tours of the White House given by Jackie) for those who remained within 'traditional limits', whilst chiding the few who criticised his actions or sought to publicise his clandestine romances (see Dallek 2004: 477–8). These affairs were an open secret in newsrooms, but the mainstream press, out of loyalty (and perhaps a sense of hypocrisy), always resisted exposing Kennedy's continual indiscretions. Nobody wanted to upset a friend, and if they did they could expect to be harassed, at Robert Kennedy's behest, by J. Edgar Hoover's FBI.

Complete journalistic integrity, which Leacock sought more fervently than Drew, was unattainable when following high-office subjects. There would always be issues of creative constraint and pro-filmic disingenuousness (the career politician is by nature a performer), but there would also always be secrets that must remain absolutely so. Four weeks after the Bay of Pigs, according to the subsequently unearthed Pentagon Papers – the government's classified history of the Vietnam conflict – Kennedy sent four hundred Special Forces members to Indochina. 'Vietnam', insisted aide Walt Rostow, 'is the place where [we] must prove we are not a paper tiger … We have to prove that Vietnam and Southeast Asia can be held (quoted in Hersh 1997: 220). Having learned a valuable lesson from the botched invasion of Cuba (for which he publicly accepted responsibility), Kennedy ensured that there would be more discretion around his new adventure: he and his brother Robert, the Attorney General, would take it upon themselves to see that the South prevailed against Northern insurgency, whatever the eventual price. 'The quagmire', notes Seymour Hersh, 'was forming' (1997: 221)

Civil rights, however, was a matter of increasing concern to liberals in office, most of whom wanted their cause promulgated in the media, and a subject – already addressed in The Children Were Watching – that would lend itself to Drew's 'crisis' template. A domestic, progressive issue such as the racial desegregation of Southern schools required no vetoing from Washingtonian officials in 1963; indeed, the promotion and depiction of liberal reforms at home was seen as a desirable means of demonstrating Kennedy's resolve with regard to contentious domestic policies (see Barsam 1992: 312). When the President took office, he had failed to accept the potentially seismic challenge that issues of race offered him, preferring instead to concentrate on international concerns. Eventually, 'Jim Crow' endangered America's global image to such a degree that it had to be confronted on television, lest Communists abroad and at home seize upon what appeared to be white apathy about incendiary black concerns (Curtin 1995: 169–70).

Crisis: Behind a Presidential Commitment (1963) centres on Alabama Democratic Governor George Wallace and his attempt, literally and illegally, to block the enrolment of two black students, Vivian Malone and James Hood, by standing in the door of their college. Wallace, who after losing a gubernatorial election to overt racist John Patterson vowed that 'no other son of a bitch will ever out-nigger me again' (Anon. 1996/97: 67), was an ideal foil for Drew's Hyannis Port heroes, a 'sleazy, strutting Alabama redneck' (Carter 1995: 142) whose parochial style and squat physique could not have contrasted more appreciably with the Kennedy brothers' poise. To many, Wallace did not come across well in Crisis. This was

Malone and Hood wait for justice in *Crisis: Behind a Presidential Commitment* (1963)

partly due to Kennedy's rebound into public favour after his astute brinkmanship during the missile affair of October 1962 (and recent implementation of popular tax cuts), but also because Drew's film functions as a public relations vehicle for the media-literate President and Attorney General, who are depicted apparently unaffectedly inhabiting both patriarchal and professional roles. Second only in direct cinema lore to *Primary*'s follow-shot of JFK is a shrewdly filmed telephone conversation between Robert Kennedy and his imposing deputy, Nicholas Katzenbach, who had been sent south to face Wallace. Kennedy's infant daughter is put on the phone to 'Uncle Nick', and the filmmakers capture both sides of what is a cordial and politically symbolic adjunct about the hot climate in Alabama. Wallace, however, looked awkward trying to project what he imagined would pass for Southern affability. The Governor was plainly acting up for a medium about which he was still unsure, and disquieted in the presence of 'Yankee' journalists whom he innately distrusted. 'I know what they'll do', he remarked to aide Earl Morgan: 'They'll have Bobby Kennedy looking like an eloquent statesman, and they'll have me picking my nose.' He was not far wrong. 'They did leave out the nose-pickin'', laughed Morgan later on; Drew had had to settle instead for images of Wallace 'slurping his food' (quoted in Carter 1995: 144).

Malone and Hood are fairly and sympathetically represented in *Crisis*, atypically for a time in which, so Michael R. Winston asserts, 'television had more to say *about* blacks in American society, but very seldom was any of this said *by* blacks' (quoted in Curtin 1995: 175). Positioned for a liberal, middle-class audience, the two prospective students – who are anodyne, good-looking emblems of a righteous, white cause – nevertheless occupy a decentralised narrative space quite outside the clash over their futures: the political suppression of a high-profile segregation-ist thus comprises the thrust of the film (as is repeatedly conveyed by the at-times otiose voice-over, something upon which Drew was still reliant). The fight between Robert Kennedy and Wallace – the titular crisis – itself orbits a bigger issue: pro-gressive governmental reform versus intransigent parochial opinion, or the popular indignation of the conservative South (as embodied by the strutting Wallace) ver-sus a newfound federal morality (as embodied by the Kennedys). Somewhere on the periphery of this filmic wrangle lie Malone and Hood, necessarily aggrieved but placidly reasonable beneficiaries of a long-overdue privilege only granted them by the White House one hundred years after the Thirteenth Amendment.

Wallace, even with huge public support from Alabamans, could never win in Tuscaloosa. His physical blockade was eventually no more than a courageous but pathetic protest in the face of Katzenbach and the federalised National Guard. 'I am not interested in a show', Katzenbach tells Wallace at *Crisis*'s climactic confronta-tion, momentarily looking to Leacock's camera as if seeking accordance: 'I don't know what the purpose of this show is.' In the end, Wallace had his moment of defiance, and Hood and Malone were unceremoniously escorted through a back door. That night, 11 June 1963, Kennedy addressed the nation on television to call for the passage of a comprehensive civil rights law, one of the most important and far-reaching decisions of his presidency. The crisis in Alabama had convinced him that executive action alone would not work any longer; he had, for the first time, conceded a moral duty to rid the United States of unconstitutional inequality. Drew ends *Crisis* with Kennedy's ardent speech, a plea for civic progressiveness that brings the narrative to an optimistic close and bodes well for an integrated future in which Wallace and his like are consigned to permanent redundancy. In reality, the emergency had not resolved itself with such neatness.

Only a few hours after the President had gone on air, a tragic event saw that news of his oration was relegated from several of the following morning's front pages. Mississippi Field Secretary of the National Association for the Advance-ment of Colored People, Medgar Evers, was gunned down by a white suprema-cist: he bled to death within an hour of being shot.[5] Outside the Kennedys' urbane 'universe of eloquent words and noble deeds' (Carter 1995: 155), Wallace's stand in the schoolhouse door looked, to both realists and ideologues, like the act not of an anachronistic monster but of a popular spokesman. 'Wallaceism', proclaimed black activist and Kennedy ally Martin Luther King Jr, 'is bigger than Wallace' (quot-ed in Carter 1995: 196). The administration, or so some maintained, was pushing for too much, too soon.

Crisis was to be the last effort by Drew that held any prospect of bringing about a formal revolution in current affairs broadcasting. The innovations inherent to Drew's work were no longer novel, and many of his aesthetic techniques and storytelling devices were being appropriated piecemeal by more conventionally informative productions. Equally frustrating for Drew was the growing wariness amongst his peers regarding the observational style's cinematically influenced ef-facement of recording processes. *Crisis*, said the *New York Times*' Jack Gould, had taken place in a 'circus atmosphere', amid manipulation by its arch and illusory subjects, collaborators in a dangerous, high-office 'peepshow' (1963a: 75). That Drew should be considered a security risk because of the apparent candidness of his approach is not a little absurd. Given Drew's deference to Kennedy and the President's own endeavours to ensure America's standing (and Drew's exclusion from every genuinely important meeting), the New York Times' affronts were as ironic as they were damaging.[6] Gould, one of America's foremost critics, fervently damned Drew's most ambitious film as 'thoroughly ill-advised' and liable to 'tarnish national dignity' (1963b: B13). Audience response to Crisis was generally favourable, but not sufficiently so to ensure Drew a secure tenure on television. A fad having passed, networks grew less interested in independent factual productions, as did the sponsoring companies. Viewers were not familiar enough with the observational approach to understand that it could not deliver on whatever promises may have been imagined of total, non-invasive fidelity to the putative world. Trusted presenters such as Walter Cronkite henceforth appeared in hybridised productions influenced by early direct cinema but uncommitted to its ambitious, visually dependent narrative approach.[7] Once again reassured of the camera's inherent truthfulness, audiences were didactically guided by familiar faces and sonorous commentaries, interspersed with 'on-the-fly' footage to imbue at least an element of what Drew had laboured for – a sense of real life 'getting out of the film'.

Thirty-three days after Crisis was first transmitted, a terrible reality in Dealey Plaza, Dallas, transfixed the world via television and robbed Drew of his most illustrious subject. Vice-President Lyndon Baines Johnson was sworn-in on Air Force One, declaring, 'Let us continue', as a token salute to Kennedy's 'Let us begin'. But 'Continue what?' was the consensual retort amongst assiduous commentators, who remembered only a mediocre administration that had passed few significant bills (see Isserman & Kazin 2000: 103). Most were too dazed, however, to deride a man so unexpectedly lost. A radical student – whose views could not have been governmentally endorsed – expounded of Kennedy's murder: 'For me, the assassination has made all other acts irrelevant and trivial; it has displaced time with paranoia, good with evil, relative simplicity with incomprehensibility, and an ideal with dirt' (quoted in Diggins 1992: 191). Even Abraham Lincoln and Franklin Roosevelt's deaths did not impact as hard on their constituents or arrive with such abruptness as the Dallas atrocity. Kennedy was only 46, and America was at peace, prosperous and (mostly) happy. 'Besides', notes Jon Margolis, 'those earlier presidential deaths might as well have taken place in another country. They were pretelevision [sic], and television, by bringing the president into almost every living room almost every day, had transformed the relationship between him and the people' (1999: 10). Thanks to the ubiquitous invention that had become the 'comforter of first resort' (1999: 11), anyone who wanted to join in the mourning could. All normal broadcast schedules were dropped: during four days in November 1963, a stunned America virtually shut down, its populace letting the events as reported unfold in their homes.

Television crews did not capture the President's killing, or his wife's frantic attempts to retrieve a chunk of his brain. Abraham Zapruder's accidentally horrific amateur footage, upon its release into the public domain (first via selected stills in

Life and much later in its uncut entirety), would forever inform popular discourse on film's potential truly to bear witness. Endlessly scrutinised for a myriad reasons, the Zapruder film remains to this day a paragon of non-fiction filmmaking as evidence and objective record. Drew, like many others, set to work conveying not the impact of a bullet, but the sadness of a nation now without its young figurehead. The filmmaker decided to express himself by looking back at Americans as they experienced an outpouring of grief – to 'watch the people watching the funeral' (Drew quoted in O'Connell 1992: 200).

The short film *Faces of November* (1963) is poetically unreserved in its photography, poignantly revealing of its producer's feelings and uncharacteristically spiritual. Beginning and ending with the bare branches of a tree silhouetted against a harsh white sky, the narration-less piece is Drew's lament for a modern martyr. Shots of mourners parading past Kennedy's coffin (we might here infer a tragic echo of *Primary's* handshaking scene) are set to the Funeral March. Those in attendance seem equally black and white, male and female. Jackie and Robert Kennedy, she tearfully behind a veil and he with solemnity, look on, and it is easy to empathise with all those who are bereft of a husband, father or leader. As the corpse lies in state in the Capitol, the camera slowly tilts up to the Rotunda's dome to show long rays of winter sunshine pouring down upon the flag-draped coffin and the catafalque whose presence asserted a Catholic's religiosity.[8] All this imagery, its unfussy composition and sympathetically dignified editing never effacing an emotional heart, makes for a persuasive, if at times slightly hackneyed, piece of work; 'documentary filmmaking at its simplest and best', is how P. J. O'Connell describes it (1992: 200). Drew had successfully exemplified, as never before, the

Robert Drew laments a martyr's death – and finds poetry amongst the *Faces of November* (1963)

Life essay on film. For the first time also, no one was interested in broadcasting his efforts.

Faces of November was lost amid a torrent of reportage, hard information and fervent eulogising. There was no place on television for Drew's award-winning requiem, whose awkward twenty-minute length exacerbated scheduling difficulties.[9] Only later would the enduring myth of 'Camelot', authored by Theodore White at Jacqueline's request, seize the public imagination and create a vast market for romanticised Kennedy nostalgia. To sustain a moderately successful relationship with the networks, Drew, as he later conceded, would have to compromise some of his hard-won principles.[10] This, indeed, he did, continuing for many years to produce a modest number of invariably acclaimed (though now mostly forgotten and unavailable) broadcast films.[11] Leacock, Pennebaker and Maysles, however, had already had enough of what they saw as a restrictive purview. After *Crisis*, Leacock and Pennebaker (Albert Maysles had left earlier to form a production company with his brother, David) decided to go their own way.

HAPPY MOTHER'S DAY: LEACOCK BREAKS THE NEWS

> Those who labor in the earth are the chosen people of God … [in] whose breasts He
> has made His peculiar deposit for substantial and genuine virtue.
> – Thomas Jefferson (1787) (quoted in Peterson 1984: 290)

Robert Drew was at heart a reporter, and his choices of subject matter and methodology have always been in the tradition of a newspaperman beholden to market forces. Leacock, by contrast, was inclined towards leftish reflection and averse to the rhetorically void stories proffered by his former employer: 'In my opinion, it is the nature of broadcast television, that "cultural wasteland", that posed a problem for Bob Drew … Drew's dream, to put twenty to fifty, whatever, hour-long shows on broadcast TV was our nightmare' (O'Connell 1992: 238, 236). Joining with Pennebaker to form Leacock-Pennebaker Films was thus a natural progression for Leacock, especially given Pennebaker's sympathetic if extreme distaste for Drew's 'prosaic, predictable bullshit' (quoted in Levin 1971: 236). The pair now had independence to express themselves as they saw fit, and concomitantly much less security in the knowledge of guaranteed mass exhibition.

On 14 September 1963 Mary Anne Fischer, of Aberdeen, South Dakota, gave birth to America's first set of healthy quintuplets and her own reluctant celebrity. Media operatives began to circle the rural family, and Leacock, with Joyce Chopra as sound recordist, was among those sent to provide coverage of what remains a rare event.[12] *Happy Mother's Day*, Leacock's first production subsequent to his split from the Drew Associates, gives both a critique of the tendency of conventional journalism to invade, reduce, commoditise and exploit the province of those who have no possible redress or alternative, and a response to the formal demands of national television. Its sponsor, the *Saturday Evening Post* (a long-time publisher of Norman Rockwell's anodyne cover paintings that romanticised rural and working-class life) was consequently and predictably displeased with what it saw. Echoing Henry James' mid-nineteenth-century appraisal of the sensationalist press as 'so ubiquitous, so unprecedentedly prosperous, so wonderful for outward agility, but so unfavourable, even so fatal, to development from within' (quoted in Reynolds 1988: 566), Leacock, in *Happy Mother's Day*, subverts twentieth-century textual conventions to challenge materially pervasive forces of consent.

Happy Mother's Day begins with a deadpan voice-over whose dispassionate intonation hints at a subversive intent. Immediately, Leacock rejects tradition – and the dictates of Drew – by incorporating a hated device paradoxically to undermine its formal standing. The most crucially informative introductory line, 'Mrs Fischer has just become a mother of quintuplets', is drawled with such disdain for the affected ardour or gravitas (what Ernest Callenbach called the 'Voice of Doom' (1961: 38)) evinced by most mainstream documentary narrators of the time that its sarcasm is striking. We see the Fischer babies in hospital incubators, name-checked in turn by the narrator, but there is an uncomfortable dissonance between picture and sound; his voice is almost mordant, too uninvolved in what it describes to sit easily with our expectations. 'Aberdeen South Dakota', continues the narrator over an aerial shot, 'is a prairie town. The land around it is flat.' This, as William Rothman wryly notes, is plainly 'speaking the obvious' (1997: 128), and the film does so quite simply because it is not the obvious that concerns Leacock; rather, *Happy Mother's Day*, so the filmmaker admits, 'has nothing to do with having quintuplets' (quoted in Levin 1995: 207).

As Mary Anne leaves the hospital, the first close shot we see is of her crowded by many intrusive microphones before she wearily gets into a car to go home. 'I don't have many feelings', she says, battered by a physical ordeal yet still acute to the pressures of civic obligation. Her husband, Andy, seems bewildered by the sudden rash of attention. 'Mr Fischer', says the deadbeat narrator, 'keeps live-stock, to help cut the food bill.' We see shots of the fecund parents' five previous children playing with various animals on their farm (which is rented so that the children may have 'space to grow' away from the city in which Mr Fischer works); a local dairy, so we learn, has donated a year's supply of milk to cater to the numerous new children's needs (and to reap the publicity); and 'five little kittens' are cuddled by their juvenile owners in a banal equivalence that speaks of a universal human pleasure in taking care of the vulnerably appreciative.

Into this frugal but apparently happy situation comes the first of many old-school press reporters, John Zimmerman of the *Saturday Evening Post*. Zimmerman asks the obliging family to pose in their ramshackle car, photographing Andy (along with his wife and older brood) in his 'only luxury', a hand-cranked Model-T Ford, as it trundles noisily around the yard. The Fischers have sacrificed material goods – the Model-T was, by 1963, superannuated for thirty years – to an abundance of children; the journalist hence seeks to construct a quintessence of small-town pastoralism for the modern age, a romanticised image of make-do homeliness that might concretise, in middle-class readers' minds, the American rural family as a 'font of virtue' happily immune to the charms of post-war consumption. (The picture magazines, which families like the Fischers could not afford, were a significant means of displaying such temptations.)[13] But, for Students for a

Democratic Society (SDS) leader Tom Hayden, such complacency represented a distraction from uncomfortable realities. As he declared in the seminal 1962 Port Huron Statement, or what amounted to SDS's (and the entire New Left's) early manifesto: 'Some would have us believe that Americans feel contentment amidst prosperity – but might it not better be called a glaze above deeply felt anxieties about their role in the new world?' (Students for a Democratic Society 1970: 165). The then recently opened Disneyland, notes James T. Patterson, cursorily 'managed to have things both ways, celebrating Main Street (à la Norman Rockwell) as well as Tomorrowland. Main Street evoked nostalgia for traditional smalltown styles of life, while Tomorrowland appealed to the still strong yearnings of Americans for the new' (1996: 342). If the affluent classes felt guilty about any technological and economic disparities between suburban and agricultural communities, between those who 'chose' to buy into the American Dream and those who did not, the mainstream news media's Capra-esque presentation of families such as the Fischers helped assuage it. What is more, even the poor might sample the 'outright, thoroughly vulgar joy' (1996: 317) of material possession, so long as they could perform a newsworthy trick.[14]

Leacock cuts to a scene featuring Mary Anne in a local department store, being shown sundry gratuitous dresses she might wear for upcoming civic occasions. 'Mrs Fischer', the narrator says, 'has not had a store-bought outfit since her marriage.' She is allowed to try on a mink coat, but is not allowed to keep it: 'Take it, quick', she laughs, looking simultaneously uncomfortable and desirous of something beyond her means. We then see Zimmerman atop a stepladder, photographing 'a representative selection of the gifts that the Fischers have been offered'. Strewn across a lawn lie all manner of chattels. 'Automobiles, wading pool, high chairs, bathroom fixtures, washing machines, TV sets, toys', recites the now gratingly aloof narration, as Leacock slowly pans his camera across the items, which indeed are, as Rothman suggests, 'absurdly lifeless and soulless when viewed en plein air in this way, divorced from their everyday use and from the glamorous aura with which magazines, ads and television commercials invest them' (1997: 135). Perhaps a more obvious problem with these only temporarily displaced 'manifestations of generosity and public interest', as the narrator puts it, is 'invasion of privacy'.

Andy is interviewed by Leacock and Chopra, in a camera framing that shows his wife's obvious ambivalence towards her new role as town mascot. She looks on glumly at left-of-frame as her husband says what he thinks he should:

It's something that don't happen every day of the week here ... It's always been a quiet town, it's bound to liven it up tremendously ... Anyone within a hundred miles of Aberdeen will drive in just to say they've been in the town ... You're gonna have to let 'em in to see [the quintuplets].

Mary Anne reflexively responds by saying, 'They're never going to be on display to anybody as far as I'm concerned.' Chopra asks, incredulously, 'Anybody?' The reply is, 'To anybody.' Leacock has here ingratiated himself beyond all reasonable expectation. His camera, as far as its most important subject is concerned, sits apart from those of the pressmen as a gratefully privileged, benevolent presence whose reason for existence somehow transcends journalistic praxis. Mrs Fischer may have sensed that Leacock was not after a 'scoop', but a tale with greater and more lasting import: the story of how a place like Aberdeen pursues its own economic wealth within the American system.

After a meeting of the town council, which decides there is nothing wrong with 'money coming in' regardless of the Fischers' right to privacy, and a scene featuring a mayoral decision in favour of a celebratory parade, we again see the babies in hospital. They are weighed and checked for health: everything is agreeable – there is no financial liability, so Leacock suggests by juxtaposition, or risk that one child may die and bring consequent doom to the prospects these five siblings have bestowed upon a community. The narrator again speaks, with extraordinary haughtiness, over a number of shots showing the extended Fischers preparing themselves: 'The morning of the parade honouring the one-month birthday of the Fischer quintuplets. Relatives have come from as far away as Oregon and California. The Fischer house is crowded to the walls – as a matter of fact it's jammed.' There is a rehearsal of the parade, staged, as the voice-over says, 'for the benefit of the newsmen, whose ... [there is a rhetorical pause] *deadlines* can't wait.' Looking suspicious and bored, the Fischer children greet an awkward congressman, who seems resignedly enjoined to the cause of self-promotion. The youths are then posed for agents of the local press, who, according to their time-honoured remit, once more condense and display humanity for material gain.

A bemused Native American, decked in full tribal regalia, is asked to squat in front of the children for a picture: 'Come on, turn around and look at 'em, Chief – turn around and *look at 'em*', demands a peremptory photographer. The 'Chief' does not know which way to look or how to act for the camera, but there is little sense that anyone in the film is feeling sympathetic discomfort for his embarrassment. Presumably the elder is one of a remaining few Indian Dakotans who could still earn a living as a bygone curio, for hire to municipal parties so they may disavow their ancestors' pogroms. He is thus brought forth as a noble savage, a representative of peoples long subdued by the Hotchkiss gun but still invoked as a triumphant reminder of who the white Europeans displaced to make way for settlers such as the Fischers. South Dakota's historical relationship with the aboriginal 'Redskins' is crystallised by the 1890 battle at Wounded Knee, a much-documented atrocity during which at least 150 Sioux men, women and children were massacred; a less notorious truth, however, is that L. Frank Baum, the usually placid editor of South Dakota's *Aberdeen Saturday Pioneer* and later the author of *The Wonderful Wizard of Oz* (1900), advocated the annihilation a week before it happened:

> The Whites, by law of conquest, by justice of civilization, are masters of the American continent, and the best safety of the frontier settlements will be secured by the total annihilation of the few remaining Indians ... Their glory has fled, their spirit broken, their manhood effaced; better that they should die than live the miserable wretches that they are. (Quoted in Stannard 1992: 126)

If Baum had called into question popular stories of 'Indian uprisings', as a responsible editor should, then the slaughter may never have ensued. As subsequently reported by the *Pioneer*, one of the scanty survivors – a young girl named Lost Bird – was taken in and exhibited for profit by a General Colby, before ending up in Buffalo Bill's Wild West Show and dying at age 29. Disturbing parallels with the Fischers' own situation can of course here be construed; moreover, it is the quietly pernicious propensity at the heart of consensus journalism that is most pertinent to Leacock's agenda in *Happy Mother's Day*.

At a function in the Fischers' honour, the mayor gives a grandiloquent speech calling for the town to respect the family's privacy. Yet the event is clearly contrived to expose and totemise they who are the community's novel 'responsibility'. Much as the kittens on their farm are kept, the Fischers here find themselves cosseted pets of Aberdeen, a place at least temporarily 'dedicated to their welfare' because of a statistical anomaly. A soprano performs a twee rendition of a Grieg folk dance, and Leacock looks for facial reactions with his camera, along the way finding Mary Anne, who gives a very fleeting smile directly to the lens. William Rothman describes this glance as transfiguratively epiphanic, and an inaugural declaration of the sync-sound camera's freedom: 'It is at this moment that *A Happy Mother's Day* [*sic*] is born. It is at this moment that [direct cinema] itself is born, or reborn as a movement of independent film' (1997: 142). Rothman's assessment not only avows the rhetorical importance of Mary Anne's partiality to Leacock, but also goes further in arguing for the existence of a 'secret bond between Mrs Fischer and Leacock's camera' (1997: 141), a putative relationship that intellectually cuckolds Andy – the 'decent man' without mental recourse to ironical comment.

It is, though, difficult to be sure of the philosophical nature of this 'bond', or even whether factors other than the filmmakers' affable personalities and long-term presence are at play. There is intimated, in Mrs Fischer's to-camera smile, an irreverent sympathy with the cameraman that lends the film a qualitative sensitivity to the ridiculousness unfolding; yet there is also a sadness in Mary Anne's acquiescence to what she obviously considers absurd, and this may be equally significant to Leacock's thinking. She knows she can never become empowered enough in her own right to escape the literal and metaphorical boundaries of Aberdeen, as Leacock had so easily escaped the strictures of clichéd reporting and corporate remit; she will, unlike the sync-sound camera and despite her happiness in motherhood, perhaps never be free. What Rothman indisputably gets right, though, is that films such as *Happy Mother's Day*, 'dispossessed from network television and thus compelled to discover or create their own audiences as *films*', marked the 'true birth of cinema-vérité in America' (1997: 121). Without ethical or financial obligation to sponsors, Drew's more left-wing, left-field alumni could be as impudent as they dared. The climactic street parade, notwithstanding its stoical majorettes, is depicted as a washout. Leacock focuses on the older Fischer children's miserable faces, and this cheerless sentiment is echoed by the narrator, who emphasises in a sarcastic drawl – while rain falls upon everyone, including the doctor who delivered the quintuplets – that it was 'a typical day of celebration in Aberdeen, South Dakota, USA'.[15]

After protracted legal disputations and the *Saturday Evening Post*'s censure of the initial cut, ABC bought the rights to Leacock's raw footage, subsequently shaping an innocuous and now forgotten version for network broadcast.[16] His cherished original remains a canonical work, mostly because it represents the first significant move by one of direct cinema's instigators to challenge the staid condition of televised non-fiction. Although Leacock found it hard to incorporate reflexive acknowledgement of his own presence among the journeymen reporters, something he admits he 'did want to bring up – the pretence of our not being there' (quoted in Levin 1971: 204), we nonetheless witness in *Happy Mother's Day* what amounts to a giant leap towards direct cinema's potential. No longer 'lodged in the bosom of the mass media' (James 1989: 213) at Time-Life, Leacock took the opportunity to formulate a contemptuous retort.[17] In filming the Fischers, downhome folk who had not chosen to be held aloft as town mascots nor committed any transgression or entered into any competition, Leacock departed from the Drew norm by seeing no crisis other than perhaps the one most crucial to the observational documentary's survival: whether or not that form could be applied usefully to bring about a change in our apprehension of the often stultifying modern condition and its principal architects.

Baby-boomers, however, born into prosperity and reaching an age – a 'teenage' – at which they exerted spending power, were, in the early 1960s, beginning to alter the mass marketplace and notions of conservative accord. Thanks to their parents, they had pocket money to spend on what they wanted: vigour, excitement and rejection of the pervasive authority that had allowed America to become vastly rich but concomitantly entrenched in prudery. For some years, white pop music and youth culture in general had produced no torchbearers capable of upsetting this comfortable stasis. Marlon Brando had grown up, and James Dean, the most potent symbol of the short-lived teenage rebellions of the mid-1950s, was dead; the 'kids' now found amusement in beach movies, surf music, bobbysoxer pin-ups and tail-finned cars. 'A generation raised on crew-cuts, teeth-braces, hot rods and Coca-Cola', asserts Ian MacDonald, 'knew nothing of blues or R&B and had forgotten the rock 'n' roll which had excited their elder brothers and sisters only five years earlier' (1994: 8). Elvis Presley, since his army service and digression into lightweight musical film appearances, was no less a legend than in his heyday; yet he bored his public by repetition, continually reprising lucrative but colourless roles arranged around increasingly sub-standard songs. Folk music offered a conscientious, if sometimes dour, objection for those of a different bent, but its devotees were not of appropriate number or inclination to bring about a national craze.

In the sad months after Kennedy's death, America felt in need of a tonic, a happy displacement of national grief upon something overwhelmingly life-affirming yet not explicitly sexually dangerous or politically earnest. What arrived from across the Atlantic, however, hyped and heralded by radio and television, would divide parents and children as never before over what could be considered morally, principally, aesthetically and artistically decent. 'The lads that will never be old' (A. E. Houseman quoted in Goldsmith 2004: 179) were signalling a change in generational attitudes that would impact upon popular culture for four decades or more. 'Beatlemania', to be sure, 'struck with the force, if not the conviction, of a social movement' (Ehrenreich *et al.* 1997: 524).

WHAT'S HAPPENING!: THE MAYSLES BROTHERS MEET THE BEATLES

> The boys and girls of this age are young men and women looking for something in life that can't always be found, a *joie de vivre*. Life is changing all the time. We are all looking for a vision of the ecstasy of life.
> – Leopold Stokowski (quoted in Goldsmith 2004: 157)

> It's [easy] to understand the hostility of the Establishment: on some level, it knew it was doomed.
> – Martin Goldsmith (2004: 178)

David Maysles convinced his more experienced brother of the Beatles' worthiness as subjects for a documentary.[18] Unlike Albert, he had heard of the jovial Liverpudlians, liked their music and sensed that their first visit to the United States might represent, for the nation's youth, an unusually potent exciter. On 7 February 1964 (or 'B-Day', as the media had christened it), the Beatles' plane touched down at the recently renamed John F. Kennedy International airport to be met by thousands of screaming (mostly) young women and over two hundred press correspondents. A pop group whose joyful music simultaneously evoked and reinvented the stateside rock 'n' roll that had come before, and whose 'mop-top' hairstyles infuriated parents and captivated teens by the million, set foot on American soil expecting a warm reception but quite unprepared for the anomalous hysteria they encountered. 'We've never seen anything like this before', said an airport worker to the *New York Times*, 'not even for kings and queens' (see Gardner 1964a: 25–6). John Lennon was astutely circumspect even as he was overwhelmed, asking photographer Harry Benson, before stepping off the plane, 'Where are all the Freedom Riders?' (quoted in Goldsmith 2004: 133).[19] The Beatles were not politically active, college-educated 'longhairs' of the sort hated by the Establishment; they were, to middle-class suburbanite elders, something far more confusing: they extended an invitation simply to 'let go' and enjoy the feeling of 'protest against the adult world' (sociologist David Riesman quoted in Ehrenreich *et al.* 1997: 527), without commitment to specific issues or conventional ideologies of dissent.

The Maysles arrived at the airport to begin shooting a film that would be the first direct cinema production entirely to eschew voice-over. This was an inestimably significant development, and one made possible in large part due to the puckish Beatles' assiduously constructed public personalities. Though certainly they worked to an internalised script of sorts, the Beatles were openly too far at odds with prescribed devices (specifically 'lecture-logic' via the 'Voice of Doom') to sit easily within media formats unsympathetic to their irreverent repartee. Always within Drew's favoured 'crisis' narratives was an imperative quest for justice or valour that often required verbal elucidation and dramatic emphasis; the Beatles, however, had already won over their young constituency (the chief audience that the Maysles sought) and saw no need to change tack in the wake of unprecedented attainment. Vivacious celebration was self-evidently the crux of the function of the Beatles as torchbearers for the 'kids', and the group knew exactly how to play at being 'John, Paul, George and Ringo' when on promotional duty; everybody thus thought they knew the Beatles, because the Beatles made sure nothing sullied or complicated their image. This awareness suited the Maysles brothers' urge to escape Drew's conventional impositions, as well as offering a means of allowing the pro-filmic world to avow itself – without pretensions to omniscience or anthropology – as an independently valid hypothesis for the first time.

What's Happening! The Beatles in the USA (1964) begins with New York disc jockey Murray 'the K' Kaufman, the Beatles' foremost early champion in America, espousing the band's greatness on air. 'Here's what's happening, baby – The Beatles!' shouts Kaufman, before playing 'She Loves You', which had been a breakthrough hit in the UK, replete as it was with an Americanised 'yeah, yeah, yeah!' refrain that so annoyed elders and thrilled teenagers. The directors cut to an excited female crowd at the airport, who sing the same song, wear t-shirts emblazoned with the 'Fab Four''s smiling faces, and flaunt cheaply-produced Beatle 'wigs' on top of their shoulder-length hair. Placards are raised on the concourse. Most are friendly, but two declare hostility: one reads, 'Beatles Unfair to Bald Men', but another is more serious – 'England Get Out of Ireland!' A screaming crowd rushes to greet the plane as it lands, before we see a television press conference – something John Kennedy had popularised – that demonstrates the group's intelligence and softly cynical, Goons-influenced charm:[20]

Reporter:	Prove to us that you can sing!
Lennon:	No, we need money first…
Reporter:	Don't you get a haircut at all?
Harrison:	I had one yesterday.
Starr:	It's no lie; you should have seen him the day before…
Reporter:	How do you account for your great success?
Lennon:	If we knew, we'd form another group and be managers.

The film's titles then run over 'I Saw Her Standing There', a paean to dance-floor libido in which the narrator conspiratorially implies lust for the underage but sexually willing: 'Well she was just seven*teen*, you know what I *mean*.' As Ian MacDonald extols, the song 'socked avid young radio-listeners in the solar plexus. With the authentic voice of youth back on the airwaves, the rock 'n' roll rebellion, quiescent since 1960, had resumed' (1994: 60). Murray the K exultantly dances around his radio studio, and a close-up of a promotional picture of the Beatles, with two-dimensional wobbling heads simulating their stage act, provides a light-hearted comment on the band's reflexive transposition of sexual urges to the upper body: a commercially efficacious relocation away from Elvis's crotch and its 'animal gyrations' (Congressman Emanuel Celler quoted in Guralnick 1994: 384). More explicitly, the group's tonsorial verdure represented a mocking of gender distinctions.

Paul, in the eye of the storm – *What's Happening!* (1964)

Partial androgyny – as expressed musically in their Little Richard-style falsettos, trilled as they simultaneously shook their heads – was threatening to parents because it offered children a quasi-perverse means of aesthetic divorcement: the Beatles did not appear bestially licentious, but mystifyingly feminised. Naturally, boys copied the look to appeal to girls. 'In thousands of living rooms, kitchens, and dens', writes Jon Margolis, 'parents pleaded, urge, cajoled, bribed, and finally commanded their sons to get a haircut' (1999: 140). The Beatles offered no firm political stance, yet the media cited them, positively and negatively depending on financial imperatives, as a challenge to the status quo. Regardless of obscurantists' protestations, continues Margolis, 'beneath millions of [short-haired] skulls, a rebellion brewed' (ibid.). There was *in utero* an uprising by both sexes (though what shape it might ultimately take was uncertain), and the Maysles brothers captured its initial stirrings with sympathetic enthusiasm.

McCartney, Starr and Lennon ride in the back of a limousine, while Albert Maysles films them from the front seat. The two songwriters are evidently performing for the camera, but, as with Kennedy, this is part of their professional lives, a learned response to a medium whose power was symbiotically growing, especially in America, with corporate forces. McCartney listens on a portable radio, emblazoned with a Pepsi-Cola logo, to reports that his band will be reading some of their poetry, 'tomorrow night from seven to eight'. The bassist affects an obtuse, 'hillbilly' accent, mocking the speciously jovial presenter ('We ain't *writ* no poetry') and a promotion of Kent cigarettes, whose 'exclusive, micro-lined filters … really satisfy!' The Kent theme tune, its asinine rhymes amusing the three Beatles, contrasts with the Britons' affable (although real) cynicism and musical vitality. Law-

41

rence Laurent of the *Washington Post* underestimated the younger generation when he opined that 'our adolescents don't know the difference between parody and the real thing' (quoted in Goldsmith 2004: 147). Rather, they were enjoying the novelty of release from conservative strictures that the Beatles, who according to Laurent looked 'like sheep dogs and sound[ed] like alley cats in agony' (ibid.), provided in their public personas and their art. Upon stopping for only a moment, the car, despite an escort of mounted police, is besieged by hysterically high-pitched young women. When they get moving again, Albert Maysles – in an acknowledgement of his own privilege – films a man holding a cine camera, who runs alongside in an attempt to glean some footage of the thrilling new celebrities. When they reach their hotel, a crowd is waiting to mob them. 'Get in, quick', says Lennon, with a trace of fear in his voice.

The foray by English 'beat' groups into the land of their spiritual forefathers had begun with an unpredictably resounding success; the Beatles were the vanguard of what would be a mutually beneficial spate of transatlantic pop-cultural (and especially musical) exchanges spanning the next decade. In their suite, the seemingly chain-smoking quartet sits rapt in pride and bewilderment watching news reports on the television. 'The British invasion this time goes by the name of Beatlemania', intones a presenter; '"B-Day" has been common knowledge for months, and this was the day.' Again, swollen with justifiable feelings of conquistadorial victory, the band satirises the American media, sending up the portentous Huntley-Brinkley Report on television by irreverently mimicking its sincerity. McCartney, with the heartfelt righteousness of youth, sarcastically criticises the newspapers for condensing the Kennedy Airport press conference and thus not getting across the nuances of Scouse wit: '"How about your hair?" Answer: "We're really bald." *Funny.*'

We cut back to Murray the K in his WINS studio (complete with the wobbling, cardboard heads), announcing, 'This is the Beatles' station! They've taken over – they're telling us what to play! I got one week of this and I'm gonna become the fifth Beatle, baby!' In a scene that becomes an *à la mode* parallel to the groundbreaking telephone conversation in *Crisis*, Kaufman calls the group and invites them to give on-air requests. McCartney chooses Marvin Gaye's 'Pride and Joy', possibly to enhance his group's standing amongst the black community and effect cachet with aficionados of more 'authentic' musical genres and performers. It is not a song that can be seen as analogous in many ways to the Beatles', yet it provides the basis for a joyous montage, as the Maysles brothers celebrate 'what's happening, baby!' in a New York milieu far removed from Washingtonian politics. A young, black woman, dressed and made-up in the style of Motown singing groups, dances alluringly behind the middle-aged but effervescent Murray the K; the film cuts between the studio – in which the undulating young woman is the main focus of filmic attention – and the band enjoying the song in the hotel as it emanates fuzzily from the Pepsi-Cola transistor. This is a short but exciting thirty seconds of filmmaking, and one of the first instances of true revelry amongst the direct cinema founders in the looseness of their bonds to journalistic duty: here one art form delights in sympathy with another, feeling the thrill of the new. Later, at the

Fig. 7 A night off for the Beatles in the Peppermint Lounge – *What's Happening!*

famous Peppermint Lounge, the Maysles brothers would take even greater pleasure in filming the Beatles 'twisting' on a night off, with results that bring to mind Leacock and Tilton's *Jazz Dance* (1954), an aesthetically similar blend of mostly unsynchronised sound and flailing bodies. Here, though, the vibrant camerawork and montage add to a sense that the famous Beatles, intoxicated and inaudible over the music, might for a moment have forgotten their collective concern for the maintenance of a public image. They are purely having fun, away from any psychological pressure to keep up the drollery that the fans and record companies found so easily sellable; the band flirts on a face-to-face level with self-assured women, not infatuated girls, and for once we infer a sexual physicality beneath the libidinous group's commercially acceptable veneer and coded lyrics of wanting to 'hold your hand'.

There is yet more teenage hysteria, as the filmmakers present further evidence that 'the vision of a suburban split-level, which had guided a generation of young women chastely through high school, was beginning to lose its luster' (Ehrenreich *et al.* 1997: 531) in the face of alternatives, however fantastical or idolatrous. Dozens of young women chant, 'We want the Beatles! We want the Beatles!' and gaze up at the hotel's windows, periodically gasping upon the sight of any movement therein. But the objects of their adoration are heading not for suburban romance but for a press call in Central Park, to fulfil promotional obligations. The foursome again demonstrate their pleasure in parodying the media ('Hey, *Bea*dles! Hey, *Bea*dles!'), whilst simultaneously providing the assembled photographers with what they want – posed shots of the band in affectedly spread-limbed action, playing on a reputation for fun-loving, neotenous displays of 'spontaneous' exuberance. The

Maysles brothers, like Leacock during *Happy Mother's Day*'s creation, were outside looking in at these repeated demands with amusement, knowing that what they had was something more, despite the band's unwillingness ever to drop its act; their subjects, all the while doing their performative duty, doubtless shared the joke, as an emerging affinity between the filmmakers and the band serves to illustrate.

'Can you do it once more?' asks a photographer. 'I thought I hadn't stopped', replies Ringo. Paul breaks off from an interview about what he did last night, something the viewer of *What's Happening!* already knows ('Watched TV. Listened to the radio. We're lazy.'), to connect proactively with the filmmakers' future narrative: 'In fact, ladies and gentlemen, for the continuity of the film, I'd like to reintroduce the radio.' He holds the Pepsi radio aloft, and he and Ringo dance to what they think might be 'Breakfast at Tiffany's'. The pressmen do not ask for a repeat performance, and it is clear that the Beatles have always been, though very politely, one step ahead in their comprehension of marketing devices (if not the protocols of candid documentary). This scene, and the many other nods to mutual camaraderie in *What's Happening!*, suggest an evolving approach to direct cinema's hitherto cardinal rules about interference, exchange of ideas and disavowal of the camera's presence. There is a soulfulness in evidence that would be quite incongruous in *Primary*, or any of Drew's subsequent observational films. What the Maysles brothers have discovered is that Drew's 'theatre without actors', an idea whose initial austerity was giving way to fresh invention, need not pretend always to be without responsiveness, humility or *joie de vivre*.

By way of comparison, we briefly see Brian Epstein and his haughty female assistant, who has trouble with an American's continual mispronunciation of his name as 'Epsteen'. That the Beatles had got to America at all was largely down to 'Eppie', an astute manager whose professional guidance was in part facilitated by his reserved, English charm. A gay man in an epoch when even in show business such proclivities were still frowned upon (and illegal), he was tortured by his sexual identity and by an abiding addiction to prescription drugs. Seeming slightly detached both in and from the film (and very aware of his comportment), Epstein's clipped accent and equally subdued hairstyle certainly mark him out from his charges; his reaction upon hearing that his 'boys'' record has entered the charts at number seven is to proclaim it 'marvellous … I think it may go to number one, actually'. Yet it was he who had struck a deal to give free Beatles t-shirts to anyone who turned up at JFK Airport to greet the band, and he who appreciated the power of hysteria, keeping Lennon's wife, Cynthia, in the background (she is occasionally glimpsed in *What's Happening!*).

Paradoxically, the Maysles brothers' approach tells us everything and nothing about the enigmatic manager. Whilst in New York, Epstein enjoyed a clandestine affair with a construction worker: as a result he fell victim to an attempt at extortion (see Guiliano 1986: 56). No facet of this intriguing, secretly conducted life could ever have been a part of *What's Happening!*, an exemplar of direct cinema's intrinsic inability to explore forbidden provinces. But, by dint of Epstein's reserve, a truth (and importantly a truth quite distinct from Drew's dramatic vision) nonetheless emerges from the documentary's facility. 'Brian', remembers Geoffrey Ellis, 'wanted to keep the fans' enthusiasm for the Beatles at fever pitch ... He knew he had a world-beating act. He knew he could get virtually anything for the Beatles' (quoted in Geller 2000: 77). The world would indeed fall at his and his charges' feet, yet he had no idea what direction the musicians would eventually take to transcend the limits of teen pop and confront concerns beyond love, lust and the pitfalls of hyperactive fame. All that mattered, in 1964, was the selling of his cherished phenomenon; indeed, it seems likely that the band's lampooning of product endorsements and advertising slogans in *What's Happening!* was partly a means of voicing frustration about its economically determined profile without offending Epstein.

A legendary 9 February appearance on *The Ed Sullivan Show*, brokered well in advance by Epstein, secured the Beatles a place in popular history as the working-class English group that conquered America by sheer force of vivacity. 'The Presleyan gyrations and caterwauling of yesterday are but lukewarm dandelion tea in comparison to the 100-proof elixir served up by the Beatles', effused the New York *Daily News* on 10 February (quoted in Guiliano 1986: 51): 73 million people had watched the previous night's performance, during which the Maysles brothers were banned from the production floor (ibid.). In lieu of shooting the *Ed Sullivan Show* from the wings, Albert Maysles propitiously decided instead to go to the nearest tenement building and follow the sound of music to an apartment door. Sure enough, two generations were inside gazing at the television, the children in adoration, their parents in bewilderment, and the resulting scene is charming, revealing and emotionally potent – an illustration of direct cinema's potential. Without the excitement of the quartet's stage act, however, *What's Happening!* henceforward palls. After the tangible exhilaration of its first scenes, the impish but laboured charm exuded by the film's subjects wears thin, giving way to vignettes that substantiate the band's reputation for telegenic adeptness but ultimately ring hollow. A number of similar situations (on trains, in hotel rooms, in corridors) that should have been wonderful moments become grating minutes, as the band largely refuses to drop its guard and allow subcutaneous humanness to sully the 'Fab Four' myth; put simply, there are only so many variations on an inherently limited theme.

John, Paul, George and Ringo are indeed 'what's happening', but what we see via the Maysles brothers is a vaudeville act stretched beyond its limited promise into something that begins to look like simple mugging; the Beatles gave up touring in 1966, and it is not hard, on this evidence, to see why. At first the youthful musicians revelled in adulation, but nonetheless grew quickly jaded with playing caricatures of themselves, ostensible cartoons in serfdom to marketing devices. As Philip Norman remarks, by 1964 the appetite for Beatles-related ephemera was so great that the 'vaguest representation of insects, of guitars or little mop-headed men, had the power to sell anything' (quoted in Neaverson 1997: 8).[21] In *What's Happening!* the Beatles do little to counter establishment accusations that they are merely commoditised playthings, indifferent to being drowned out by shrieking acolytes. What is conveyed, rather than a portrait of four genuinely distinctive personalities, is an impression that the wobbling heads in Kaufman's studio efficiently impart the band's quintessence.

'The bigger we got', remarked Lennon in 1973, 'the more unreality we had to face. It was all just a bad joke to me. One has to completely humiliate oneself to be what the Beatles were, and that's what I resent' (quoted in Guiliano 1986: 51). For the time being, the 'bad joke' (along with some superbly-crafted pop music) was engaging enough to captivate a nation, but not sufficient to sustain an hour-long, unscripted film. Richard Lester drew inspiration from *What's Happening!* when making *A Hard Day's Night* (1964), and offered, arguably, a more entertaining, satisfying and astute commentary on the nature of stardom than the Maysles brothers' protracted documentary. The Maysles' influential but flawed effort was consequently driven out of distribution by Lester's homage, about which Albert is magnanimous: 'Imitation, after all, is the sincerest form of flattery.'[22] Lester was able to build a more cogent narrative around the group's media personalities, fusing character distillation with set pieces accompanied by several new songs. Despite the semi-underground, *ad hoc* tone of *What's Happening!* and its several charming scenes, it does not provide frequent enough relief from the band's adept press routine. The Beatles may have shared a distaste of journalistic fakery with the filmmakers, yet they were unable to give profoundly even to people whose trust was implicit. (In 1968, the Maysles brothers would form the elusive bond for which they were looking, with a group of Irish-American Bible salesmen pitching in Boston and Florida. The resulting film, *Salesman*, is one of direct cinema's most celebrated achievements; it is, however, an almost timeless account of the 'drummer' and his travails in a marketplace inured by mass promotion. Owing more to Eugene O'Neill and Arthur Miller than to Robert Drew, *Salesman* draws on the formal traits of dramatic fiction to mourn the lot of commercial actors less fortunately endowed than the Beatles (see Barsam 1992: 330–2; also Spears 1995).)

What's Happening! does succeed, though, in conveying its directors' impetuses. David Maysles reflected: 'I was trying to show how they typify a great part of American youth. I feel that there is a sort of restlessness. They want to find out what's happening in town. Where are they going to go? It's like *Marty* [1955]. They're always looking for something – for a "beat"' (quoted in Macdonald & Cousins 1998: 263). The Beatles, in 1964, amounted to a talented novelty act, evincing no hint of the true greatness that would arrive with the sonic depth and lyrical scope of their latter work. They represented simple, hormonal abandon, in particular through the repackaging of standard American rock 'n' roll in unusual harmonies, Anglo-centric humour and iconoclastic fashions. Two years later, the group would look back on their jocular behaviour with embarrassment, as they now lived 'X-rated lives' (Richard Lester quoted in Neaverson 1997: 35) that might have shocked conservative America into apoplexy had these proclivities been evident in 1964. But, even in their early-1960s guise as the 'lads from Liverpool', they were a threat to the older generation: 'four erotic divinities' (Carlin 1964: 37) arriving on their shores from the Old World to sweep away newly and undesirably orgasmic daughters, feminise sons and debase long-held values. Moreover, the Beatles' 'invasion' of the United States, notes Christopher Booker, was 'the first time that any country had fought back against America's domination of twentieth-century mass-culture since the first craze for *Alexander's Ragtime Band* in 1912. And the irony of it was, of course, that America's rout had been achieved with what were almost entirely her own weapons' (1969: 225).

America would soon respond in kind with a musical retort. In the meantime, more ominously subversive elements of the nascent cultural rebellion were quietly conducting their own radically experimental rituals. Aiming to reject paradigms engendered by the 'final stages of a sick society' (Leary 1999: 11) and to expand the mind with chemistry, this was the 'new religion' of LSD-25, and Dr Timothy Leary was its prophet.

YOU'RE NOBODY 'TIL SOMEBODY LOVES YOU: PENNEBAKER TURNS ON

> Any action that is not a conscious expression of the turn-on-tune-in-drop-out rhythm is the dead posturing of robot actors on the fake-prop TV studio stage set that is called American reality ... Never underestimate the sacred meaning of the turn on.
> – Timothy Leary (1999: 3, 5)

After making the short films *Lambert & Co.*, about the singer Dave Lambert attending an audition, and *Michèlle et Michèlle* (both 1964, the latter unreleased), D. A. Pennebaker decided to accompany his friend, outré cabaret entertainer Monti Rock III, to Leary's wedding. Held in a Millbrook, New York mansion belonging to stockbroker William Mellon Hitchcock (that Hitchcock rented to Leary and his followers for a nominal fee), the ceremony was to sanctify the twice-married ex-Harvard professor's union with Swedish model Nena von Schlebrugge. Since the curtailing of his tenure at Harvard – ostensibly for missing classes, although in reality for subjecting undergraduates to drug experiments – Leary had used Millbrook as a haven in which to conduct the psilocybin, mescaline and LSD 'trips' he was sure would provide insight into the human mind's untapped potential.

Together with long-term academic collaborator Richard Alpert, Leary extolled 'higher consciousness, ecstasy, and enlightenment through hallucinogens', publishing his findings in an evangelising journal, the *Psychedelic Review*. Sitting amongst incense-swathed statues of Buddha and Shiva, Leary reiterated his hopes: 'It's only a matter of time until the psychedelic experience will be accepted ... We're simply trying to get back to man's sense of nearness to himself and others, the sense of social reality which civilized man has lost. We're in step with the basic needs of the human race, and those who oppose us are *far out*' (quoted in Lee & Shlain 1985: 96). When not in the kitchen observing one of radical psychiatrist R. D. Laing's 'mystical ballets', or riding a horse that had been painted pink and blue, Leary immersed himself in a saturnalia: 'Jesus Christ', he complained, 'do I have to fuck every girl that comes into this place?' (quoted in Margolis 1999: 38). Chemist Albert Hoffman's accidental 1938 discovery was giving a small but growing band of dedicated American followers not only a reason to feel that they were pioneering a new era of love and philosophical lucidity, but also the chance to exult, before the inevitable legal clampdown, in a 'party with a purpose' (Margolis 1999: 129).

You're Nobody 'Til Somebody Loves You was the result of Pennebaker's weekend with Leary and his retinue, and it is a film that reflects its subjects' and maker's shared desire to abjure the statutes of traditional reporting. As Martin A. Lee and Bruce Shlain note, Leary 'realized that the press was not an organ for disseminating truth; no matter what one said, it would always be distorted by straight journalists' (1985: 115). Likewise, the much-disdained Vast Wasteland was dismissed, at least by those who were 'hip' to the Establishment's pervasive media presence, as irredeemably beholden to corporate cryptarchs (a suspicion borne out by ABC's subdual of *Happy Mother's Day*). Pennebaker, in the months following his acrimonious separation from Drew and network television, was obviously no emissary of reaction; rather, it seems likely that he enjoyed, with Leary, a sense that the 'subliminal message – LSD could take you to extraordinary places – would come through between the lines and young people would turn on in greater and greater numbers' (ibid.).

Echoing *Primary*'s ending, Pennebaker begins *You're Nobody...* with a shot of a car receding down the road. We do not yet know where the vehicle is going, and nor do its bohemian occupants, who appear to be cheerfully if concernedly off course in their excursion to visit a 'great scientist', who, says Monti Rock, 'looks like Dr Jekyll'. An up-tempo soundtrack announces a celebratory intent, but there is no title, no voice-over narration, and indeed no background exposition or provision of information other than the sign on the back of the car reading 'Monti Rock III'. *You're Nobody...* thus takes up the story of American observational documentary from where *Primary* left off; this time, though, the passengers' destination is not democratic rejection but spiritual refreshment. Unlike the Beatles (and even Hubert Humphrey), Pennebaker's subjects herein are not sufficiently famous as to require no introduction for a largely unfamiliar audience. What is evinced is total renunciation, a more committed extension of *Happy Mother's Day*'s sarcastic commentary and *What's Happening*'s reliance on the Beatles' recognisable, predefined identities; *You're Nobody...* is the start of an adventure for Pennebaker and those who were unafraid of 'dropping out', personally and artistically, of the 'sick society'. Theodore Roszak argued that 'ingenious rationalisation', or 'the total *ethos* of the bomb' (1971: 47), suffused the dovetailing mainstream discourses of efficiency, progress, welfare and warfare in the mid-1960s; affluent, democratic civilisation, so R. D. Laing contended, might for this reason benefit from a 'dissolution of the normal ego, that false self competently adjusted to our alienated social reality' (1967: 119). Postulating an omnipresent psychical exertion of authority, Leary was more forthright in condemning American orthodoxy, which he labelled damaging to 'internal freedom': 'Politics today is a disease – it's a real addiction' (quoted in Roszak 1971: 168). Governmental liberals, unconvinced of the efficacy of such radical notions, promoted technocracy's ultimate fulfilment through educational and civil equality as the means by which apotheoses of freedom and happiness could be attained. Global collectivism, in their view, remained the most persistently intractable moral concern.

Whilst Lyndon Johnson worked to implement social reforms and to honour his predecessor's best intentions, he was equally committed to managing a tough yet not perceptibly reckless approach to the Cold War. Remembering Munich's concessions, Johnson knew that a weak hand abroad could have dangerous corollaries; all the same, he remained wary of a course that was taking him 'further and further out on a sagging limb ... I don't like it, but how can I pull out?' (quoted in Dallek 1998: 243). Total disengagement in Vietnam, especially since the removal of Ngo Dinh Diem, sanctioned by Kennedy, was not an option without a degree of concomitant humiliation; despite Congressional voices urging him to withdraw, Johnson felt bound by both duty and conviction to attain at minimum a pyrrhic triumph that might appease anti-Communist voters and grant him tenure to effect domestic melioration. All-out war, however, proved an unpopular prospect. Even as no regime stable or independent enough to defeat the North emerged, it became clear that hawkish rhetoric would not win the forthcoming presidential election. The incumbent would eventually defeat right-wing Republican Barry Goldwater, largely because of the latter's pledge to escalate activities in Vietnam and Johnson's television adverts seizing upon his rival's casual attitude to nuclear weapons. Both men realised the need to pursue victory with determination, but Goldwater's heated pronouncements were misjudged: anything short of avowedly belligerent prosecution represented, to the electorate, preferable moderation. Democrats propitiously maintained in the public mind a fear of Goldwater as 'ridiculous and a little scary: trigger-happy, a bomb-thrower, a radical [who] will cancel Social Security' (Jack Valenti quoted in Dallek 1998: 169). Consequently, Johnson's electoral mandate, as even supporters acknowledged, was the product of anti-Goldwater rather than pro-administration feeling. 'We must love each other, or we must die', intoned Johnson during his notorious 'Daisy' advertisement spot, over images of a young girl picking petals from a flower: 'The stakes are too high for you to stay at home' (quoted in Dallek 1998: 175). A close-up of the girl's startled face then fades to black and is followed by footage of a mushroom cloud.

By 1964, reportage of the kind favoured by John Kennedy, although still prevalent, was out of touch with the epoch's creative mettle. 'Underground' magazines and films espousing uninhibited sex and reinvented religiosity as weapons against the 'spiritual bankruptcy which begat the bomb' (Nuttall 1968: 175) were becoming vehicles of popular expression. Three films released in 1964 – Stanley Kubrick's *Doctor Strangelove or: How I Learned to Stop Worrying and Love the Bomb*, Sidney Lumet's *Fail-Safe* and John Frankenheimer's *Seven Days in May* (which incorporated, as had John Cassavetes' off-Hollywood dramas, the hand-held aesthetic of direct cinema) – appeared in high-street movie houses; all these dealt with atomic-age nightmares and concordantly inspired intellectual debate vis-à-vis American culpability. Kurt Vonnegut's novel *Cat's Cradle* (1963), with its first chapter entitled 'The Day the World Ended', similarly encapsulated the growing undercurrent of dissent amongst commentators worried about America's moral rationale: across all media, the 'flimsy stupidities of life' (Gitlin 1987: 206) were being called to account. On the gallery circuit, Andy Warhol's transgressive silk-screen rendering of several *Life* photos featuring Jacqueline Kennedy immediately before and shortly after her husband's death was a crowd-drawing exhibition; Warhol's joyfully postmodern exorcising of a national ghost superseded, by virtue of acuity,

Drew's heartfelt but trite eulogising of a fallen saint. Impulses of dissatisfaction permeated as far as the *Saturday Evening Post*, for which Norman Rockwell began painting black people, and in which Malcolm X's autobiography was soon to be serialised. 'The old swimming hole', noted one critic of the era's shifting nature, 'was polluted' (quoted in Whitfield 1996: 240).[23] As a young folk singer proclaimed, the times were changing, and all who wished to remain above this dirtied water had 'better start swimming'. Metaphors like these took precedence over denotative statements, the better to seek oneness amongst the 'with-it' by simple encryption. All the same, actions spoke as loudly as words. The Free Speech Movement, responding to the political suppression of campus activities, succeeded in shutting down the University of California's Berkeley site; the Mississippi Summer Project (of which three members were murdered by the Ku Klux Klan) registered new black voters; and, for the first time, draft cards were publicly burned. Millbrook, however, was a relative oasis of calm; Leary was holed-up in the mansion not to avoid engagement but to contemplate his own purpose as an intellectual maverick in a confusing world.

After Cuba, Berlin and then the shock of Kennedy's murder, existential insecurity, in the anxious era of the Bomb, seemed timely. Lewis Mumford called for a 'new myth of life' in order that 'a passionate religious faith in man's own capacity to transform and perfect his own self' might be achieved (quoted in Henrickson 1997: 380). As Leary was giving up mental acquiescence to the 'fake-prop TV studio', Pennebaker sympathetically renounced any sense of duty to convey anything other than what simply felt human, instinctive and good: the 'new myth of life' was infusing direct cinema with extempore characteristics quite distinct from those manifest in its early incarnation as a 'sub-species of journalism', or *Life*'s inferior, televisual loss leader.[24] *You're Nobody...* thus represents both a confident divorcement from previous formal requisites and a congruity to trends defiantly at odds with dramatic archetypes; Drew's material crises yield to a numinous means of portraying humanity without obligation to storytelling, consensus or logic.

When the cars arrive at Millbrook for the wedding of 'Mr and Mrs Swing', as jazz singer Cab Calloway called them, Pennebaker cuts to the bride-to-be having her hair arranged. The director relishes what is an atmospheric scene, filming candles, baroque windows and von Schlebrugge's classically beautiful profile. An Indian raga plays in the background, typically for a house in which the aesthetic setting was contrived to aid the LSD experience by using Eastern culture to counter Judaeo-Christian pre-eminence. More so than blues, pop or rock 'n' roll, the sound of Asia bespoke progressive ideological distantiation from American guilt; slaves had created blues, and rock 'n' roll was arguably a trivialising bastardisation of what in its generative phase was a protest-based idiom born of oppression. After a brief shot of Charles Mingus improvising jazz at the piano (jazz was suitably free-form, and Mingus' blackness an affiliative totem of 'hipster' credibility), we then cut to Leary, who is attempting to put his suit on with the help of several friends. 'Richard, do you know how to operate this?' asks Leary of Alpert. Leary, since leaving Harvard, had usually worn diaphanous gowns, and seems bewildered by his Victorian-style waistcoat. 'This is the closest I've ever been to a straitjacket!' jokes

Leary. Cross-cutting between the bride and her groom's preparations, Pennebaker lavishes close-ups on von Schlebrugge, who lounges with her bridesmaids in the dimly-lit house, wearing sunglasses and smoking. We see a close-up of Leary's daughter Susan, just out of prison for marijuana possession, reclining on a sofa, stroking a cat and obviously stoned. Pennebaker has entered into the spirit of the event, and ingratiated himself entirely. 'I filmed [You're Nobody...] as a kind of pageant and edited it as a mystery' (quoted in Levin 1971: 229), said the director of his first fully-realised experiment in completely extemporised filmmaking. The mystery is certainly in place, as is a sense of pageantry, but what is perhaps most important is that Pennebaker was taking steps towards a new appreciation of musical, counter-cultural forms as transposed to film. 'Sometimes I think it's beautiful, sometimes I wonder why I did it' (ibid.), he remarked; he did it, one might conclude, because he had made a decision, conscious or otherwise, to stay in tune with artistic fashions. 'All art aspires to the condition of music', wrote Walter Pater (quoted in Iser 1987: 56); by the same token, the old aphorism ut pictura poesis rings true. For Leary, 'all political systems were equal oppressors and power-trippers. Political news was game-playing, a bad trip, a bringdown, a bummer' (Gitlin 1987: 208). Pennebaker, it follows, was moving away from such 'bummers' by stylistic assimilation, infusing his work with a dynamic mimesis that fed off his impulsive need to reject archetypical triteness: in short, he wanted to stay young.[25]

The von Schlebrugge-Leary wedding is never shown. At the point of the ceremony's commencement, Pennebaker cuts to Monti Rock on stage, singing the title song at the reception: the filmmaker thus repudiates any closure or dénouement as something best left to reporters working to a template set down by corporate interests. You're Nobody 'Til Somebody Loves You operates outside these limits, finding for itself a modish niche as a film more inclined to explore new aesthetic perspectives than old narrative paths. It is a fleeting piece of work, but is indicative and predictive of Pennebaker's and direct cinema's overall trajectory in the mid-1960s. Where once Drew optimistically supposed that the sync-sound camera's unprecedented access might precipitate a means by which everyone with a television set could see into the real lives of the bold and the brave, there was now a more interesting avenue to explore: the colourful politics of upheaval.

CONCLUSION: FROM JFK TO LSD – LEAVING THE 1950s BEHIND

Everything went young in '64.
– Andy Warhol (Warhol & Hackett 1980: 69)

The notional 'Sixties', which do not of course exist as a decimally discrete entity, began perhaps not with JFK's election, but with his death, a moment in which America's providence changed and a political inheritance was bequeathed its new chief-by-proxy. It was a time for vivified action against the prospect of doom brought on by America's decapitation, and against those who had denied Kennedy's mooted civil rights, medical and anti-poverty bills passage. 'Everything I had ever learned in the history books', recalled Lyndon Johnson, 'taught me that martyrs have to die for causes ... I had to take the dead man's program and turn it into a martyr's cause' (quoted in Dallek 1998: 63). While trying to build a harmonised nation that he labelled the 'Great Society' (in deference to JFK's New Frontier and Walter Lippman's *Good Society* (1937)), Johnson was soon, however, distracted from his ambition to go down in history as the world's greatest reform leader by a 'bitch of a war on the other side of the world' (Johnson quoted in Anderson 1993: 89). Kennedy's least agreeable legacy, the 'limited' anti-Communist war in Vietnam, would be escalated by his flamboyant successor after the precipitous Tonkin Gulf Resolution of August 1964, for which renowned liberals Edward Kennedy, Eugene McCarthy and George McGovern voted. Vietnam, more than any other experience, subsequently came to shape the 1960s as a decade of fractious domestic conflict. The liberal consensus of the post-war 1950s began to break down by the time of the Drew Associates' dissolution; visual art reflected this antagonism by attempting to free itself from institutionalised preconceptions and obligations.

Susan Sontag, in a 1965 article entitled 'One Culture and the New Sensibility', made a case for the non-typographic media's germane vibrancy. She called for film, 'the most alive, the most exciting, the most important of the art forms right now', to join with other media and create an 'erotics of art' with a 'much cooler mode of moral judgement' (2001: 11, 14, 298–9). In the films made by Leacock, the Maysles brothers and Pennebaker immediately after their split from corporate control, we see an emerging ideological alignment with anti-establishment impetuses. They did not, however, wish to endow their work with political fervency; rather, these filmmakers tried to detach direct cinema from its hitherto customarily journalistic vocabulary – a strategy Sontag would have commended – so that a more emancipated form of expression might be attained. Drew's steadfast preoccupations, moreover, helped set his former employees apart as fashionable mavericks gradually bringing the promise of a genre's merits into both a new age and a new forum.

While Drew's erstwhile colleagues were making friends with the Beatles, consorting with Timothy Leary and creatively renouncing all that the Time-Life veteran valued, Drew himself remained committed to the cause his training had espoused. His natural domain was a technological wonderland of jet-planes and racing-cars, of spaceships and limitless possibility, rooted in a sphere predicated on ballot-box ideals, masculine figureheads and the economic optimism engendered by World War Two's favourable outcome. But his was a world being superseded in many ways. Programmes like *Assault on LeMans* (1965), *Men Encounter Mars* (1965) and *On the Road with Duke Ellington* (1967) pleased their sponsors, yet there was no such phenomenon as 'Dukemania': audiences were by then seeking other kinds of pleasures in a transformed cultural climate. Drew was unresponsive to America's fracturing psyche, and unable to deduce that the 'end of ideology' was an assumption whose perspicacity, as the decade wore on, would be tested.[26] He was a product of Eisenhower's 1950s, which were, according to some accounts 'the happiest, most stable, most rational period the Western world has ever known since 1914' and 'the dullest and dreariest [epoch] in all our history' (historian Eric Goldman and an un-named source both quoted in Diggins 1989: 178). Well-meaning, prodigious but out of touch with discriminatingly attuned consumers, Robert Drew was already an anachronism.

Sontag continued: 'Because the new sensibility demands less "content" in art, and is more open to the pleasures of "form" and style, it is also less snobbish, less moralistic – in that it does not demand that pleasure in art necessarily be associated with edification' (2001: 303). A new era of popular rebellion, birthed by recent historical events, existential uncertainty and government policy, was beginning; the novel outlook of this new age found reinforcement through its adoption of fresh, culturally and politically functional means of expression, infusing all who were keen to the spirit of the times. 'What *I* think was happening at this point', noted Andy Warhol, 'was that commercial moviemakers were learning and incorporating from underground movies but that underground movies weren't developing their narrative techniques as much as they might have ... Commercial moviemakers had always known that a movie couldn't make it big without a coherent story line, but now they were starting to do the narrative things with a freer style' (Warhol & Hackett 1980: 139). Within this crucible of stylistic osmosis lay Pennebaker, Leacock and the Maysles brothers. Though they were not interested in overt confrontation (and were still against anything approaching *agit-prop*), they nonetheless were sufficiently cognisant of which aesthetic and narrative devices were at variance with the cultural undercurrent of progression towards an idea of cinematic maturity; after Drew's influence declined, American observational cinema found an appropriate artistic locus.

The Beatles came back to America, in August 1964, for a second, frenzied tour, ending their run on 20 September with a charity concert at the New York Paramount Theatre. During the show, a skinny, curly-haired young man repeatedly invaded the stage and was escorted away several times by security men until he was eventually recognised as an acquaintance of the band. The supposed interloper turned out to be Bob Dylan, a poetically-inclined protest singer of cult repute whose perceptive, melodic albums were talking points amongst cosmopolitan aficionados. When the concert finished, Dylan accompanied the band back to their hotel rooms to talk about music and enjoy philosophical discourse over alcohol, cigarettes, and – most crucially – pot. Earlier in the tour, at some undetermined yet decisive moment, Dylan had introduced the British band to marijuana, a gesture that would impact upon pop music's future with immeasurable weight.[27] The Beatles went home feeling inspired to diverge from what they knew in the way of generic pop and to explore symbolism as a route to potential fulfilment. In the few months that followed, Dylan's American and international following grew; he was no longer just a curio who set intelligent verse to song, but a figurehead for adherents to the growing 'counter-culture'. The world's first 'spoilt generation' was about to challenge prevailing mores, and direct cinema, emancipated from the strictures of network commission, concomitantly established an affinity with the youth movement that would yield its most celebrated films.

PART TWO | COUNTER-CULTURAL
COMMENTARIES

3 | LOOKING FORWARD (FROM AN AMERICA PAST TO THE AMERICAN MODERN)

In October 1955, in the North Beach district of San Francisco, writer and Columbia alumnus Allen Ginsberg held a poetry reading at the Six Gallery, a converted body shop. The flyer promised: 'Wine, music, dancing girls, serious poetry, free satori. Small collection for wine and postcards. Charming event.' For the last decade, Ginsberg's life had been one of deviation from post-war American normalcy. A drug-user, homosexual, political radical and freethinker, he befriended college football player Jack Kerouac, later author of the *roman-à-clef* and apotheosis of the 'Beat Movement', *On the Road* (1957). Kerouac coined the term 'Beat' in joking tribute to his Catholic upbringing, spuriously claiming that it was an abbreviation of 'beatitude' (in fact it is an amalgam of the terms 'deadbeat' and 'downbeat'). Media attention propagated their notoriety for excess and outrage, and, after Ginsberg's first public recital of the free-form poem 'Howl', the public *en-masse* knew exactly who the Beats were, and what stance they had adopted:

> I saw the best minds of my generation destroyed by madness,
> starving hysterical naked.
> dragging themselves through Negro streets at dawn looking for an
> angry fix,
> angelheaded hipsters burning for the ancient heavenly connection
> to the starry dynamo in the machinery of light. (Ginsberg 1956: 9)

Ginsberg and the rest of the Beat writers, including William Burroughs, Lawrence Ferlinghetti and Gregory Corso, were vehemently opposed to America's cultural and economic systems (as Ralph Waldo Emerson, Henry David Thoreau and Walt Whitman had been a century earlier), lamenting the damage they perceived them to be inflicting on the individual. Homogeneity, indoctrination and spiritual compromise, according to the Beats, were the true ends of Western, capitalist orthodoxy; Ginsberg bestowed the epithet 'Moloch', after a Semitic deity said to eat children alive, upon his nation's dominant ethos.

The Beats' influence spread, resonating within the nation's young who for the first time yearned for guidance of a kind removed from the organised religion and dogma to which their parents had adhered. Mainstream US media on the whole advocated the status quo, dismissing mass, governmentally unsanctioned escapism of this type as misconceived, fanciful and bound only to cause harm. Sensational stories crossed the Atlantic became the basis of tabloid exposés in England, where incendiary headlines ('This bizarre new cult', 'This is the Beatnik Horror',

'Dope Fiends') incited outrage in parents whilst inspiring their children to join the 'road to hell' (Green 1999: 37). Psychotropic drugs were becoming popular means of 'self-transcendence' (Huxley 1959: 64), or simply getting high whilst abjuring the older generation's vices (see Young 1997). Inside the university system, anti-establishment partisans coalesced into newly prominent and politically viable organisations. Mostly seeking to undermine mercantile principles without recourse to totalitarian bureaucracy, such groups pursued ideals based on individual autonomy, equality and freedom from remote authority. Knowledge for knowledge's sake was espoused, as was the importance of uninhibited carnal experience to countering the 'repressive' technocracy. The Pill, arriving in 1960, furthered sexual liberation and sparked the youth culture's imminent embrace of 'free love'. In addition, a renaissance of the women's movement effected widespread feminist indictment of entrenched gender roles and domestic servitude; 'the problem that has no name', as Betty Friedan called it (1992: 13). Suspicion of elitism, media dominion, orthodoxy and governmental commitments intensified in the young, who increasingly looked to rock performers for both arousal and cogitative inspiration. The Beat poets had heralded, with radically cynical poetry, a movement that would eventually announce itself with much wider resonance through osmotic musical forms. An unknown English guitar band, early in its career, paid homage to the founding fathers of the counter-culture by changing its name from 'The Quarrymen' to 'The Beatles'. The band would not, however, embrace ideas beyond the banal concerns of frivolous pop until exposed to the reinvigorated American poetry of Bob Dylan, a lexically inventive *oeuvre* that not only questioned authority, catalogued injustice and championed freedom of speech, but also came, by mid-decade, to effect pop music's intellectual rebirth.

Robert Zimmerman grew up in the 1950s in Hibbing, Minnesota, part of America's agricultural Midwest. An admirer of Allen Ginsberg, James Dean and protest singer-songwriter Woody Guthrie,[1] he changed his name to the less Jewish (and thus less categorisable) Bob Dylan, relocating to Greenwich Village – the Mecca of bohemian and Beat life – in 1961. Dylan and Ginsberg became friends as the enigmatic folk singer's career took-off in the wake of his well-received third album, *The Freewheelin' Bob Dylan* (1963). In August 1963 Dylan appeared at the Washington D.C. Demonstration for Jobs and Freedom, where Martin Luther King Jr recited his 'I have a dream' speech.[2] Integrated though the attendant throng were, Dylan remained sceptical. As the event drew to a close, he turned towards the Capitol and said, 'Think they're listening? No, they ain't listening at all' (quoted in Isserman & Kazin 2000: 97).

D. A. Pennebaker's 1965 film *Dont Look Back* follows Bob Dylan on a promotional trip – and what transpired to be his final acoustic tour – to England. Made shortly after Pennebaker had ceased operating under the aegis of Time-Life and Robert Drew, the film constitutes the first act of a quartet that William Rothman (among others) sees as a coherent whole: 'The arrival of the counter-culture that Dylan prophesied and helped goad into existence was announced in Pennebaker's landmark *Monterey Pop* [1967] … the counter-culture's mythical high-water mark was registered in Michael Wadleigh's *Woodstock* [1970] … Its violent Death was prematurely reported in *Gimme Shelter* [1970]' (1997: 145; see also Ehrenstein & Reed 1982: 75–83).

Dylan was the perfect focus for a documentary, and the embodiment ('the Zeitgeist streamed through him like electricity', in the words of pop star Marianne Faithfull (Faithfull & Dalton 1995: 54)) of an epoch in which direct cinema, and almost all creativity, would flourish: a new American Renaissance.[3] Rothman continues:

> The counter-culture, evidently one of American *cinéma vérité*'s great subjects at
> this historical moment, was a political movement that turned half my generation of
> Americans into rebels with a cause (ending the war in Vietnam). At the same time,
> it was a utopian attempt to transform America by achieving a new philosophical
> perspective (it was also a perspective older than classical American cinema, as old,
> indeed, as the transcendental philosophy of Emerson and Thoreau), not by traditional
> political means. (1997: 145)

Part Two of this study asks, in the light of Rothman's brief but insightful claim, if there is indeed an epic cohesion – a grand, symptomatically replete counter-cultural narrative – evident in the four celebrated rock music documentaries that span half a decade of youthful rebellion: *Dont Look Back*, *Monterey Pop*, *Woodstock* and *Gimme Shelter*. In this chapter we shall take a closer look at the first of these.

DONT LOOK BACK

'An American bard at last ... his voice bringing hope and prophecy to the generous races of young and old'.[4]

The renowned prologue of *Dont Look Back* depicts Bob Dylan holding up and then nonchalantly tossing aside a series of prompt cards upon which are written words abstracted from 'Subterranean Homesick Blues', which backs him on the soundtrack. Standing in an alleyway (the side of the Savoy Hotel, London), Dylan occupies the right of the frame, dominating the composition with a virile, James Dean-like poise; Allen Ginsberg is on the extreme left. Clearly staged and in no way interpretable as anything other than contrived, this prelude introduces Dylan as collusive in the filmmaking process and confident enough to look directly out of the frame; he is looking forward, at us watching him in the future, and setting out his terms from the outset. Ginsberg's peripheral presence aligns Dylan with his beloved Beats – a seminal movement of the past – but, unlike Ginsberg, he is directly engaging with the transience of artistic creation. Dylan's blasé dismissal of his own, provocatively misspelled words underscores not only his contempt for orthography, but also his archetypically poetic desire to highlight the disposability of literal meaning; formalism, in his world, is a redundant stricture.

Pennebaker too exhibits a typically counter-cultural disregard for formalised language (the apostrophe was omitted from the film's title on Pennebaker's suggestion)[5] and sees no need for explanatory voice-over or subtitling. As Paul Arthur

Dylan announces the arrival of the counter-culture – and the passing of his old self – in
Dont Look Back (1965)

notes, Pennebaker takes 'solace in not having to label events … The implied aversion [in direct cinema] to language in its ordering, or depleting, of sensory impres-
sions is a pervasive – and quite powerful – facet of the anti-authoritarian program
of Sixties counter-cultural and political opposition' (1993: 119). *Dont Look Back*,
from its earliest moments, thus constitutes an extension of *You're Nobody 'Til
Somebody Loves You*'s experiment in formal emancipation. When Dylan's lyric
invites us to 'duck down the alleyway', to look for a new friend, he is asking us
to seek something other than the obvious, to explore hidden routes, not just the
figurative – and literal – main streets and highways of the dominant cultural and
political mainstream.

'Subterranean Homesick Blues' exemplified Dylan's new, electric sound influenced by the Beatles. Performed by a full band on record, the song was a depar-
ture from both traditional instrumentation and the attitudinal pitch of his past, as
William Rothman explains:

> The singer in 'The Times They Are A-Changin'' addresses listeners who already know
> what he is telling them; he is not *informing* them they'll sink like a stone if they don't
> start swimming, he is calling upon them to 'admit' this. The singer in 'Subterranean
> Homesick Blues' is addressing a listener who already knows which way the wind is
> blowing, already knows change is necessary, but has not yet taken the leap … the
> singer is cajoling, provoking, shaming his listeners into repudiating the lies society
> tells them, into aligning their lives with the truth they know in their hearts. (1997:
> 150)

Since his professional separation from Robert Drew and Time-Life, Pennebaker (as *You're Nobody 'Til Somebody Loves You* had previously hinted) was as eager as Dylan to denigrate didacticism, narratorial guidance and over-simplification, bluntly saying of such things, 'You don't need any of that shit' (quoted in O'Connell 1992: 224). Evidently it was time for both artists to explore less familiar territory and follow a course befitting their mutually progressive natures. Dylan, through this introduction, makes a virtual declaration of intent: 'Catch this while you can – I'm moving on.' Pennebaker, whose working relationship to Dylan in *Dont Look Back* has been described (by William Rothman (1997) for example) as that of a 'co-conspirator' sympathetically attuned to his subject's motivation, is obviously going with him. '[The film] throws away almost all its information', the director has subsequently iterated, 'and becomes purposefully abstract and tries to be musical rather than informational' (ibid.). Arthur Marwick's claim that the 1960s' key artefacts depended in large part on an 'obliteration of boundaries between different art forms: between painting and sculpture, between music and speech, between film and drama' (2000: xiv), is a germane explication of the impulses informing Pennebaker's distinct contribution to an epoch's cultural character. 'Subterranean Homesick Blues' – the sound of a mythical 'spokesman for a generation' yearning to stand upon a higher podium – effectively acts as a condensation of *Dont Look Back*, a celebratory snapshot of the mid-1960s' intellectual legitimation of expressive individualism (see Bellah *et al.* 1985).

ALL I REALLY WANT TO DO...

We cut to a close-up of Dylan's face; a harmonica is braced around his neck, and we hear a guitar sounding in the familiar style of Dylan's early, unaccompanied work. Several other people are present in what turns out to be a backstage dressing room area, and the unspoken code of 'candid' direct cinema – that one must not look at the camera – is in effect. Dylan exits up a flight of stairs, to the strains of audience applause, and enters a spot-lit stage, whereupon there is a cut to the film's titles, as the song 'All I Want to Do' begins:

> I ain't looking to compete with you,
> To beat or cheat or mistreat you,
> Simplify you, classify you,
> Deny, defy or crucify you.
> All I really want to do-oo,
> Is baby be friends with you.

This verse, which is in equal measure pledge and caveat, establishes a benchmark of moral reciprocity behind which Dylan positions himself for the duration of the film. Despite the singer's assurance that all he really wants to do is be friends with us, such friendship is not unconditional. He does not *wish* to beat, cheat, simplify, classify, deny, defy or crucify the lover (or the listener) to whom he sings, although he may, under provocation or impulse, *have* to. 'I do not wish to treat friendships

61

daintily', wrote Ralph Waldo Emerson in 1841, 'but with the roughest courage ... Should not the society of my friend be to me poetic, pure, universal, and great as nature itself?' (n.d.: 152, 155). To simplify, classify, defy or crucify would hence be at odds with Dylan's Emersonian beliefs in the absolute inviolability of personal autonomy; 'Trust thyself', exhorted Emerson in 'Self-Reliance', 'Nothing can bring you peace but the triumph of principles' (n.d.: 98, 114). Whoever would simplify Dylan would be party to reductionism, ignoring Pennebaker's titular admonition and thus rejecting Dylan's *idée fixe*. According to Wilfred Mellers, Dylan 'seeks escape from any human relationship that threatens his personal integrity. These songs are not really cruel, because he is asking the other person not to fear self-knowledge' (1984: 133). As we shall see, Dylan is capable of evasion and cruelty, especially when others seek to understand or penetrate his identity.

The *dramatis personae* scrolls upwards, with 'Bob Dylan' rendered as if a hand-written autograph to ascribe greater status, individuality and co-authorship to Dylan than his typographically denoted co-stars: manager Albert Grossman, 'road manager' Bob Neuwirth, singer Joan Baez, Animals keyboardist Alan Price, music agent Tito Burns, singer-songwriter Donovan and banjoist Derroll Adams.[6] The song abruptly fades after only one verse; thereafter we see Dylan, accompanied by Grossman and Neuwirth, striding through an airport bus terminal. Smoking a cigarette, which he dangles louchely from his lips, Dylan meets some male fans, who ask him what has changed since his last visit and why he is 'so big this time?' Dylan replies (in *faux naïveté*) amid the bustling attendees, 'I have absolutely no idea – I don't even know about it if it is [if I am?]. I figure I'll just go out and do the same thing I did before.' His disingenuous revision, 'I don't even know about it', is a concession that humility is an attribute well suited to the camera's nature – an internal acknowledgement, perhaps, that he is not only under unmediated scrutiny, but, for the length of the shoot, his byzantine ego too is entwined in the filmic processes at play.

THE TALL TALES OF AN AMERICAN SUBVERSIVE

Dylan enters a press conference and begins toying with an outsized light bulb. The first question we hear from a reporter is, 'How long since you were last in London?' This is answered (if laconically) – 'about a year' – but a question concerning his eccentric prop is more readily entertained. 'I usually carry a light bulb', says Dylan. 'Somebody gave it to me, you know? It was given to me by a very affectionate friend.' A female journalist enquires, 'What *is* your real message?' to which Dylan smilingly responds, 'Keep a good head, and always carry a light bulb.' With an offbeat surreality evoking the Beatles' routine in *What's Happening!*, Dylan only answers the questions he feels worthy. He is happy to talk about the light bulb, an object cunningly utilised to interpolate and disrupt the conference, but not to explicate his 'real message', for to do so would be pandering to those he feels have been superseded by the counter-culture's luminaries and their growing influence upon critical thought. Pennebaker acknowledges Dylan's mischievous attitude:

It was showing off. He liked the idea of being an intellectual youth. It intrigued him, because most newspaper reporters of the ilk that he would run into were buffoons to some degree … Occasionally, they were smarter than that. But it was all part of the picture he wanted to create of himself, as a kind of young Tartar … very much influenced by Kerouac and Ginsberg. (Quoted in Hogenson 1984: 3)

A young, attractive woman (framed in a big close-up), and a man, both with World Service Received Pronunciation, interview Dylan:

Woman: Do you think that a lot of the young people, who buy your records, understand a single word of what you're singing?
Dylan (drawled): Sure.
Woman: You reckon they do?
Dylan: Sure.
Woman: Why do you say they do?
Man: How can you be so sure?
Woman: I mean, they're quite complicated songs, aren't they?
Dylan: Yeah, but they understand them.
Woman: How do you *know* they understand them? Have they *told* you that they do?
Dylan: They told me. Haven't you ever heard that song, [sung] 'She said so?'[7]
Woman: Would you say that you cared about people particularly?
Dylan: Well yeah but, we all have our own definition of all those words: care; people…
Woman: Well, surely you know what people are?
Man: You sound angry in those songs. Are you protesting against certain things that you're angry about?
Dylan: I'm not angry. I'm delightful!

The singer's uninterested response to these questions is no surprise given his interviewers' vapid repertoire and stiffly British doggedness. Nearly every question is deflected, either with perplexing philosophy reminiscent of Protestant theologian Horace Bushnell – Dylan now sees cognitive plurality and irreducibility in the words 'care' and 'people' – or sarcastic indifference.[8] The woman further enquires, leaning towards Dylan and almost whispering:

Woman: Have you ever read the Bible?
Dylan: Have I … Um. No. I'm Jewish.
Woman: Because a lot of the things you say…
Dylan (interrupting): I haven't read it.

Nonetheless, many of Dylan's early- to mid-period songs contain biblical allusions or directly referential lyrics.[9] One explanation is that Scriptural myth so permeated the Midwest in which Dylan grew up that he could not help but assimilate its imagery, stories and tenets into a lyrical gamut already steeped in folklore and frontier legend. Another is that he is lying to denigrate organised religion, but this seems

63

an unlikely wile for an intellectual who would surely wish to be seen to have read the Bible to validate his secularism.

A majority of Dylan's fellow countrymen and women were, in the mid-1960s, affiliated with a church or synagogue. Billy Graham's use of television as an evangelical platform had become a powerful means of converting those who sought such guidance to his brand of Americanism and Christian rectitude, a reinforcement of Eisenhower's 1954 'one nation under a God' amendment to the Pledge of Allegiance.[10] Dylan evidently did not approve of formal designation or conformity to creeds dictated by others, especially the staunchly anti-Communist and right-wing Church.[11] 'Have you ever read the Bible?', a worthwhile and perceptive attempt to derive the influences on Dylan's oeuvre, elicits an uncharacteristic response in its addressee. There is no deflection or philosophical obfuscation, just an answer, if a tellingly curt one. However limiting Dylan may consider a comparison of his songs' imagery and themes to those of the Scriptures, he does not deny that the interviewer is right, and seems more vulnerable, or at least more openly contemplative here than before.[12]

We see another beautiful woman in close-up, this time the folk purist Joan Baez, until recently Dylan's lover and muse, who has joined the tour – though not, to her reported chagrin, to perform.[13] For the first time, Dylan, then in the initial throes of his romance with Drew Associates secretary Sara Lownds, had not invited the staunchly generic folk singer to join him onstage. A zoom-out reveals that Baez is being photographed, and asked to pose in a coquettish manner. She repeatedly says that she 'can't pose' (the folk movement abhorred artifice), and eventually feels compelled to grimace and gesticulate, rendering all the shots useless to any contemporaneous, mainstream publication. Dylan explains to another journalist that on tour, he does not write, and that he does not turn himself 'off to it', or try to fight it (the media circus), because if he did, he would 'go insane'. Fight it, he does not; resist its psychological intrusion, he does. Dylan knows where his contractual and personal obligations lie, and is aware of the moral division between the two; he must make an appearance, but he is not bound to supply perfunctory copy. Baez dislikes posturing for the photographic press' convenience, and pulls faces to demonstrate her displeasure innocuously; Dylan's façade, however, is more contrivance than diffidence, the act of an ascending celebrity cultivating an enigma.

For thematic continuity, Pennebaker cuts to Dylan reading a newspaper aloud: '"Dylan, puffing heavily on a cigarette – he smokes eighty a day…"' Following incredulous laughter, Dylan drawls, 'I'm glad I'm not me.' This epigram, one of the most pertinent in *Dont Look Back*, self-reflexively summarises both Dylan's attitude to the mainstream media and his own, astute affectation of a prophylactic 'Dylan'. As a child Dylan was secretive and a loner, prone to self-mythologising and the telling of tall tales:

He was an inveterate storyteller, fabricating myths about himself so vividly that he hardly knew whether he spoke truth or falsehood. Central among these myths was his pretence that he was an orphan. This, and his repudiation of his Jewish ancestry,

> may have been a rebellion against the smalltown business world his father repre-
> sented ... Furthering his rebellion he became a greaser or motorcycle maniac, pursu-
> ing the James Dean legend. Yet he belonged no more to a jet set than he had done
> to the kids he consorted with as a child. His true identity he sought, from the age of
> ten, through poetry and music. (Mellers 1984: 111)

Dylan's outlandish invention falls squarely in the tradition of storytellers or novelists
like Mark Twain (see, most notably, the *Adventures of Huckleberry Finn* (1884)),
whose incorporation of frontier legend celebrates the roughness of American ter-
rain and rejects the 'staidness' of English, aristocratic style (as Dylan rejects the
staid, English questioning, and Pennebaker sympathetically abjures his own restrictive heritage): in the virgin New World, anyone had the potential to reinvent
independently or to divorce themselves from old-fashioned origins. Noah Webster saw an American duty of 'honor' in the invention of a national dialect; Robert
Hughes likewise asked, 'Why should we permit the survival of the curious notion
that our language is a mere loan from England, like a copper kettle that we must
keep scoured and return without a dent?' (both quoted in Bryson 1994: 92). Wild,
digressive hyperbole, structurelessness and the 'telling of tall tales' are all native
to the American literary psyche, and perhaps exist, according to David S. Reynolds,
as personal means to further or 'exaggerate democratic individualism' (1988: 451).
As a musician and writer Dylan follows this course, an informal approach of discon-
tinuity and peculiar juxtaposition that Reynolds labels the 'American Subversive'
style (1988: 202). Dylan is, moreover, the embodiment of Robert Butler's 'American Adam', standing proudly and heroically alone without community or constan-
cy. As Ian Johnston explains, 'the American Adam answers to no traditional faith,
no system of moral absolutes; he carries with him no divine prohibitions ... He
answers only to his conception of himself, even when he is put into a world that
does not live up to those expectations' (1997: n.p.).

As Dylan revealed in his recent memoir, he was 'intrigued by the language
and rhetoric of [the 1800s]': 'The age that I was living in didn't resemble this age,
but yet it did in some mysterious and traditional way ... Christian piety and weird
mind philosophies turned on their heads ... It's hard to find any of the neo-clas-
sical virtues ... I crammed my head full of as much of this stuff as I could stand'
(2004: 84, 86). Nineteenth-century Democratic America was a kind of 'carnival
culture', a melting pot of idiomatic dislocation from proper English usage in which
the writer brought together the 'high' and the 'low', the sacred and the profane, in
a new atmosphere of personal and social freedom.[14] If Dylan's poetry is, in form,
carnivalesque, then his persona is analogously typical of the democratic imagination's 'rascal heroes'; in his brash self-confidence he resembles Herman Melville's
Ishmael, the humorous narrator of *Moby-Dick* (1851) who both consorts with ren-
egades and expounds philosophically. In American novels and plays, the 'b'hoy',
the 'swaggerer, swearer, boaster, idler' (Whitman 1982: 50), or Whitman's boister-
ous mystic in *Leaves of Grass*, seem almost prototypical of Dylan. The Dylan we
see can only be the machinated, pro-filmic construction he wants us to see, but
this may not be far from his fundamental nature as a 'b'hoy', or trickster, a man

65

whose spoken words reveal his purpose to be as quintessentially literary and as archetypically American as Ginsberg and Kerouac, or Whitman, Melville and Twain before them. 'The positive elements of nineteenth-century and contemporary transcendentalism', wrote Martin Schiff, 'all centre around the concept of man as a unique, spiritual being whose individuality must not become stifled, no matter how great the political, economic, social and technological pressures for conformity. In a materialist age [this can] function most effectively as the soul and conscience of America' (1973: 142). In other words, to paraphrase Whitman, we hardly know who Dylan is, or what he means, but he shall endeavour to be good for our spiritual health nevertheless.[15]

ONLY A PAWN IN THEIR GAME

A personable BBC reporter interrupts Dylan, who is lounging with a newspaper. Dylan's attitude to this particular interviewer is apparently one of reverence: he is black, hence in a minority whose rights Dylan has championed, and he has been assimilated totally (down to his RP enunciation and regulation suit), a phenomenon that must have piqued the singer's curiosity, unused as he would have been to black broadcasters being at ease within large corporations.

> Something that will certainly interest our listeners, in Africa, Bob, is your deeply humanitarian attitude to a number of public matters, for instance, you are quoted as saying, 'People talk about Negroes as if they were objects.' Now, does this sort of compassion, on your part, present any problems for you, in America? ... How did it all begin for you, Bob? What actually started you off?

Dylan respectfully considers his answer, but instead of showing it, Pennebaker cuts to found footage of an appreciably younger Dylan performing 'Only a Pawn in Their Game' to a group of blacks and civil rights activists in Greenwood, Mississippi. The sequence does not show us how it all began for Dylan, or whether the Africa Service reporter educed from his interviewee what others could not: a measure of truth. It does, however, reiterate Pennebaker's lack of interest – that continually chimes in with Dylan's – in expository provision (an approach, of course, favoured by Robert Drew). The film, rather than staying with Dylan's answer in a journalistic fashion, arbitrarily looks away, creating its own response.

Casual interpretation here begs a fallacious inference: that Pennebaker, in suggesting that Dylan rode the rails and worked the fields with the impoverished black underclass of the Deep South, is heroising his subject, rather as Dylan mythologises himself. But, in the light of the film's overall thrust, the cut represents Dylan and Pennebaker's shared personal and artistic progression, not hagiographical falsehood: it is where Dylan is *now* that is important. In singing forthright songs of topical, political importance, Dylan felt restricted by the high ethical expectations engendered by such protestation, and frustrated by the folk genre's narrowness of purpose; Pennebaker likewise resented his prior subordination to network priorities and the reporting tradition exemplified by the journalists in *Dont Look Back*.

'Only a Pawn in Their Game' confers Dylan's cherished quality of individuality upon its primary subject – Medgar Evers, black victim of a 1963 racist shooting[16] – and relegates the murderer to the status of mindless (and consequently blameless) automaton, manipulated by the white establishment and the Ku Klux Klan's insidious credo:[17]

> Like a dog on a chain,
> He ain't got no name,
> But it ain't him to blame,
> He's only a pawn in their game.

One could also, however, accuse Dylan of being a pawn in a game. In 1963, CBS refused to allow Dylan to perform 'Talkin' John Birch Society Blues' on *The Ed Sullivan Show* (see Adams 1963: 61).[18] Amid the controversy surrounding the song, Dylan had been telling his friends, 'They'll kill that song over my dead body! That song's going on the album!' (quoted in Harker 1980: 120). CBS, to which Dylan was beholden, inevitably had the final say, and the song was vetoed. Dave Harker addresses Dylan's quandary:

> It is meaningless to blame Dylan for truckling. Either he accepted censorship, and so got criticised for selling out to showbiz and to capitalism, or he lost access to the channel which guaranteed him an audience amongst those young people he wanted to reach, and resigned himself to cultural impotence for the rest of his life. He faced the same decision as Johnny Otis, or as the hillbillies. So, the head went down. (ibid.)

Jonathan Eisen notes that 'there is no consensus in the industry other than to sell, and they will sell antiwar songs and good poetry just as easily as they will sell the schlock' (1969: xii). Yet this market strategy depends on the content of these songs and poems not offending the sensibilities of the corporations' core customers, the relatively prosperous whites who, to appropriate Harold Macmillan's phrase, had 'never had it so good'.[19] Financial exploitation of blacks was the norm within the record industry of the mid-twentieth century. None of the major companies paid black artists any royalties whatsoever; indeed they were lucky even to get composer credits (Harker 1980: 105). Rolling Stone Keith Richards was also, perhaps naïvely, shocked to discover that

> all the bread we made for Decca was going into making little black boxes that go into American Air Force bombers to bomb fucking North Vietnam. They took the bread we made for them and put it into the radar section of their business. When we found that out, it blew our minds. That was it. Goddam, you find out you've helped kill God knows how many thousands of people without even knowing it. (Quoted in Fong-Torres 1972: 292)

He was, though, a multi-millionaire by the time of this exclamation, the early 1970s.

THE ADMIRERS

There is a cut from appreciative clapping in Greenwood, 1963, to the cavern-ous Sheffield City Hall in the 'present' time of *Dont Look Back*. The camera tilts down from the ceiling after scanning the roof-lights, and settles on Dylan, alone in the blackness amidst the resounding applause. He sings 'The Times They Are A-Changin'', which Pennebaker edits for brevity, and begins his next song, 'To Ramona', pausing partway through to tune his guitar. A journalist in a booth tel-ephones his copy to *The Manchester Guardian*:

> Sentence. He is not so much singing as sermonising. Colon. His tragedy, perhaps, is that the audience is preoccupied with song. Paragraph. So the bearded boys, and the lank-haired girls – all eye-shadow and undertaker make-up – applaud the songs and miss, perhaps, the sermon. They are there. Colon. They are 'with it'. Sentence. But how remote they really are from sit-ins and strikes and scabs, and life. Paragraph. 'The times they are a-changing', singeth Dylan – they are when a poet, not a pop singer, fills a hall.

Echoing the young woman's previous refusal to accept that Dylan's fans 'under-stand a single word' of what he is saying, this punctilious journalist, though obvi-ously stirred by Dylan's oratory, likewise betrays an inability to appreciate youth culture as a *Gemeinschaft* (a spontaneously arising organic social relationship). Responsive fashionability need not connote mass ignorance; rather, precisely due to the means of their delivery, Dylan's lyrics engaged with a generation as no other writer's could, consolidating a shared devotion whose cosmetic manifestations were only the most obvious signifier of a gleeful yet newly serious defiance. With a formal restraint precluding genuine empathy, the Fourth Estate attributed such surface phenomena to a timeless need for pubescent bonding experiences. Yet unlike the Beatles' relatively uncomplicated, sexually potent commodity, Dylan's records and performances also inspired critical uncertainty as to the root of his paradoxical appeal. Teenagers were turning away from the easily construed mu-sic enjoyed by their elder siblings towards chimeras of less restricted expression – something that perplexed all who were unprepared.

Poetry was crossbreeding with politics and pop to create a ritualistic discourse of ambiguity that many in the older demographic struggled to understand. 'Sit-ins and strikes and scabs', terms of quotidian reportage, protest and clarity, bore the burden of traditional (and hence reductive) ideology more heavily than Dy-lan's evolving approach to songwriting. He was becoming the nexus for a cultural revolution, swiftly acculturating amenable followers of the folk genre (and winning new fans in the process) by setting mischievously untamed linguistic amalgams within reassuringly wonted chordal schemes. Dylan's mid-1960s work simultane-ously delighted like that of the Beatles, bristled like that of the Beats and critiqued, chronicled and enjoined like Guthrie; his 'real message' lay within a multiplicity of vivid personal qualities that transcended his idols' limitations, facilitating a mythic rebirth of the stranger-hero whose power was such, for a time, that market values

An icon faces the future (*Dont Look Back*)

could be pre-empted. After the early, Kennedy-era albums of hopeful and mostly explicit reform ballads, Dylan, despite a deeply individualistic bent, accurately presaged the (anti-)intellectual bearing by which America's youth would plot a course towards its climactic decadal encounters of later years.

Dave Harker, a teenage Briton at the time, describes his first experience of listening to Dylan's *Freewheelin'* LP:

> Amongst our group of adolescents, the record came to exercise a significant degree of influence. Doubtless, in part, there was the customary ego-tripping of those who felt they'd latched-on to something important well before anyone else. But there's no denying the sheer power of the lyrics – Dylan's marvellous ability to juggle with words to form striking images and phrases – finally converted at least three of us, made us admirers (fans being too ignoble a status). In spite of the rudimentary musical frameworks, each new Dylan LP was eagerly awaited. Dylan had created in us expectations that only he was capable of fulfilling. (1980: 121)

To aver, as does the man from the *Guardian*, that Dylan's music generates an excitement that resonates most amongst stylishly attuned youth is not to devalue his songs; they are not calls to arms in a proposed workers' revolution, but provocative musings indicative of the epoch's diversifying linguistic and existential perspectives. Stand-alone poetry had failed to find the mass appeal and outlets of popular song, a medium that was beginning to define the 1960s irrevocably. 'The minute I heard Bob Dylan with his guitar', Taylor Mead told Andy Warhol, 'I thought, "That's it, that's what coming in, the poets have had it"' (quoted in

69

Warhol & Hackett 1980: 38).[20] Dylan's acolytes may, for the most part, have been remote from scabs, strikes and sit-ins, but they were far from unmoved by his message, explicitly political or otherwise. 'Something is happening here/And you don't know what it is, do you, Mr Jones', taunted Dylan in 'Ballad of a Thin Man' (1965). The song, in its railing against institutionalised intellectualism, decries not only structural assertion, but also by implication pours scorn on elder pressmen whose 'too hasty judgements on Dylan's work', as Roger Lewis observes, 'often turn out to be catastrophically wrong' (1972: 97). It was, however, not just the intransigent 'Mr Jones' who had difficulty adjusting.

Some young women – 'all eye-shadow and undertaker make-up' – wait outside Dylan's Liverpool hotel and gaze longingly up at his window, hoping to catch a glimpse of their hero. They whistle to try and get the attention of whoever might respond, and eventually Dylan (or someone like him, we cannot tell) appears, whereupon they hysterically giggle: 'Isn't he gorgeous! Pinch me! Pinch me! All me dreams have come true!' The young women shout for Dylan to 'Come down!' and flatten their wayward hairstyles to look like 'Joanie'. After some time has been elided, they realise their ambitions and meet Dylan, who signs autographs for them before his show:

Girl: Are you gonna sing 'The Times They Are A-Changin''?
Dylan (resignedly): You want me to sing that, huh? You really *like* that song? What do you like about it?
Girl: I don't like 'Subterranean Homesick Blues'.
Dylan: Oh, okay, you're that kind of ... I understand right now...
Girl: It's not you; it doesn't sound like you at all.
Dylan (as if addressing a small child): But my friends are playing with me on it, I have to get some work for my friends, playing the guitar and drums. You don't mind that, huh?
Girl: It just doesn't sound like you; it sounds like you're having a good old laugh.
Dylan: You don't mind me having a good old laugh, do you?
Girl: No! No! But some people might not take it seriously, and say it sounds commercialised.
Dylan: You know different, though, right?
Girls: Yeah.

Dylan is kinder (at once flirtatious and avuncular) to the star-struck trio than he might have been, given their refusal to accept his new phase. The film's opening song did not yet occupy a place in Dylan's fans' hearts – they had not yet 'taken the leap'.

Music of an identifiably (if illusorily) pre-capitalist bent was still seen, by Dylan's admirers, as more historically resonant, more authentic and less subject to 'capital discipline' than the rock and pop modes Dylan was readying to embrace. Devotees thus found themselves addressing a predicament whereby putatively auratic folk music, its links to coffee-house Socialism and working-class experience made vestigial by mass marketing, was put forward against a notionally invalid, arbitrary converse: escapist frivolity of the sort the Beatles had exported. Chiding Dylan for a supposed betrayal of ideals as he switched creative focus from 'the romance of politics to the politics of romance' (Marc Eliot quoted in Frith 1981: 163; see also Stratton 1983: 143–56) was easily done, yet one must also credit consumers with a degree of autonomy, and the writer of 'The Times They Are A-Changin'' with more nous than the majority of contemporary pop acts. Dylan would be called 'Judas' for going electric, but he was not betraying a cause so much as taking up a new, irreverently empowered mantle. A poet, not a pop singer, had decried the 'rapidly fadin'' order, but to fulfil his own prophecy (that 'the first one now will later be last') Dylan, as he had been preparing to do for some time, broke loose: 'Come writers and critics, who prophesize with your pen', sang Dylan, untamed by linguistic convention, 'keep your eyes wide the chance won't come again.' Pop singers and poets, heeding Dylan's counsel, were by the end of 1965 no longer ossified in mutual exclusivity. Mainstream critical opinion was slow to resound with this development, but Pennebaker saw very clearly a chance to broaden, sympathetically, the horizons of his own art from liberal salubriousness to a filmic approximation of rock 'n' roll's seductive charge. 'Not in his goals but in his transition man is great', remarked Emerson, lauding a plasticity denied by literary praxis: 'Whoever lives must rise and grow' (quoted in Albanese 1975: 325).

Around the time of *Dont Look Back*, Dylan pronounced protest songs 'vulgar – the idea that somebody has to say what they want to say in a message type song. It's a stagnation type thing … worse than being a pregnant dog' (quoted in Mellers 1984: 138). Whatever the beliefs behind a person's choice of youth tribe and their concomitant musical affiliation, every sub-cultural, cultic motif is eventually co-opted (and thus stripped of its original signification) by capitalist forces. Even if purists saw Dylan's electric music as a surrender to corporate homogeny, it marked an artistic upturn from protestation and didacticism in terms of Dylan's lyrical breadth, and distanced him from the commoditisation of folk music and iconography.[21] *Dont Look Back* would itself eventually become the template for numerous imitations that lack *jouissance* as much as originality. Yet in 1965 it was incontrovertibly a step ahead of stagnant, television bygones. Pennebaker was, in congruence, 'going electric' – revising Drew's blueprint to fit with the quickening nature of his own, lived authenticity at the vanguard with Dylan: a world *Life* and its analogues were too diffident to accommodate.

The camera frames the front page of a copy of *Melody Maker*, with its bold headline, 'DYLAN DIGS DONOVAN'. Pennebaker zooms out to reveal that it is Dylan who is reading an article inside, sitting on the back seat of a car, in transit with Baez and an unidentified English man (the blues singer John Mayall) who sits between them. A disdainful looking Baez eats a banana and recites, sarcastically, Dylan's 'It's All Over Now, Baby Blue', a 'part poignant, part patronising, goodbye/fuck you to the folk revival' (Thurschwell 2002: 261). Ostensibly, Baez's mischievous substitution (of the word 'banana' for 'fire') and deadpan delivery all but rob Dylan's verse of its original effectiveness. In the context of Dylan and Baez's separation, though, Baez's irreverent reading reveals more her heartfelt sorrow than her need to debase this song and its timely exhortations: 'Strike another match, go start anew … Leave your stepping-stones behind … Forget the dead you've left, they will not follow you.' To prove that she no longer need worship Dylan's artistry, Baez picks one of his most haunting laments, a 'story of the disintegration of a woman's world' (ibid.) that, according to biographer Paul Williams,

> can be sung and performed a thousand ways – can be sung a thousand ways by the same singer – without ever losing its power and essential identity. This is a triumph for the songwriter as well as the singer. And for the listener, it is an opportunity to discover the endless possibilities for beauty and truth that can be coaxed from a seemingly limited construction of rhymed couplets and minor chords. (1994: 139)

Baez has yet coaxed another meaning, another beautiful truth, from 'It's All Over Now…', a truth about fractured relationships, or so it is tempting to speculate, that Dylan – the lover-poet departing to find a new muse – has internally accepted.

Dylan straps on his guitar and heads from another anonymous dressing room into the spotlight, to audience applause and encouragement from one of his entourage, 'Do good!' We can be sure that Dylan did 'do good', as by all accounts his performances were consistently engaging during this tour,[22] but we do not see even a tiny part of it, as Pennebaker again cuts, accentuating the increasing weariness of repetition he must have detected in his subject. Williams quotes:

> 'After I finished the English tour', Dylan told Jules Siegel in February 1966, 'I quit because it was too easy. There was nothing happening for me. Every concert was the same: first half, second half, two encores and run out, then having to take care of myself all night. I didn't understand; I'd get standing ovations and it didn't mean anything. The first time I felt no shame. But then I was just following myself after that. It was down to a pattern.' (1994: 141)

As Emerson complained, 'When a man rests, he stinks' (quoted in Albanese 1975: 325). For Dylan, as for his forebears, 'transition was the condition of nature, myth, and all of life' (ibid.). The adulation that made Dylan 'feel good' was becoming meaningless as he sought to break with the sacraments of his past; moreover, this sense of treading water goes some way to explaining both Dylan's artistic exasperation and increasingly brusque manner.

BOB DYLAN VERSUS TERRY ELLIS

Backstage at Newcastle City Hall, Dylan and his entourage receive a visit from campus journalist Terry Ellis, a thickly bespectacled science student. The conversation between Dylan and Ellis is charged; clearly in combative mood, Dylan does not suffer gladly Ellis' attempts at conciliation or musings on why musicians do not appear to like him. Dylan repeatedly strums his guitar over the intimidated and naïve Ellis's replies, each one doomed to derision in an increasingly personal attack that shows Dylan at his most vituperative:

Dylan: Why should I want to know you?

Ellis: I don't know – that's what I'm asking.

Dylan: Well I don't know, right? Ask me another question! Just give me a reason
why I should want to know you.

Ellis: Um … I might be worth knowing.

Dylan: Why? Why? Tell me why. What good is it for me to know you? Name me
one thing I'm going to gain.

Ellis: You might learn something from my attitude to life.

Dylan: Well, what is your attitude to life?

Ellis: I can't explain that in two minutes!

Dylan: Well why are you asking me to explain in two minutes?

Increasingly, it emerges that Ellis might indeed never have considered why people
may find him tiresome; the very fact that he is obviously drawn more to himself
as a subject than those he has come to interview ironically precludes the ingratia-
tion he desires. Though seeking solutions to this personal crisis, he is unable to
articulate even the most basic of helpful answers, instead implying (with some
justification) that these problems are those of the musicians, contemptuous of the
'square' in their presence. Sociologist Howard Becker describes this inter-tribal
tension in relation to the jazz scene of the 1950s:

'Squareness' is felt to penetrate every aspect of the square's behaviour just as its
opposite, 'hipness', is evident in everything the musician does. The square seems
to do everything wrong and is laughable and ludicrous. Musicians derive a great deal
of amusement from sitting and watching squares. Everyone has stories to tell about
the laughable antics of squares. Every item of dress, speech, and behaviour which
differs from that of the musician is taken as new evidence of the inherent insensitiv-
ity and ignorance of the square. (1997: 60)

In *Dont Look Back*'s febrile backstage social situation, an atypical, inverse hierarchy thus establishes itself with Darwinian efficacy. There is unquestionably an
element of victimisation within this overturned microcosm; however, it should be
Ellis to whom at least some blame is apportioned.

Dylan, having given Ellis plenty of time and many chances to explain his social
neuroses (and to ask some questions – which Ellis never does), suddenly becomes
totally engaged: he stops strumming and fixes Ellis with a flinty stare, exposing the
student's weakness:

Dylan (in close-up): What's a deep friend?

Ellis: Somebody who you're almost on exactly the same plane with them. Somebody you can communicate with very well.

Dylan: Somebody just like you. Looks like you?

Ellis: No.

Dylan: Talks like you?

Ellis: Umm.

73

Science student (and 'square') Terry Ellis learns a hard lesson in *Dont Look Back*

Dylan (now remonstrating loudly): How do you know if you like somebody – some-
one who *thinks* the same way?
Ellis: Someone who thinks the same way…
Dylan (interrupting loudly): Are you gonna ask your first question? Go ahead, have
you got a question to ask?
Ellis: No.

This is the only time Dylan solicits questioning, perhaps safe in the knowledge that Ellis has by now been enervated beyond composure enough to pose the type of journalistic query Dylan abhors. Friendship and devotion conditional upon conform-ity to preconceived patterns of acceptable behaviour and thought are, to Dylan, invalid. As he declaimed in *Tarantula*, under a rascal-hero pseudonym: 'it's every man for himself – are you a man or a self? be different – dont be a conformist … everybody will get the message … your benefactor, Smoky Horny' (1971: 81). All Ellis really wants to do is be friends with Dylan and Price and all his other 'hip' inter-viewees, but under the proviso that they 'think the same language' as he does. To see Dylan as a friend, Ellis must simplify and classify: Dylan, as his song continues, must in turn resort to beating, cheating and mistreating this man who has not yet learned to 'communicate well' with people who do not consent to a subjective ideal, or believe it to be necessary.

The attentive camerawork suggests that Pennebaker is more than usually ab-sorbed throughout this dialogue, judiciously framing and zooming to accentuate the emotional vicissitudes playing out through his viewfinder. This, according to

the filmmaker, is purely instinctive:

There's absolutely no concept in my mind of aesthetics, about how to tilt the camera or where to stand. My feet do that, and I don't think about it. You just watch, like an audience watching, with this ridiculous thing in front of your eye. (Quoted in Adams 2001)

William Rothman sees Dylan's question, 'Do you ever just be quiet, and just watch, and you don't say one word?' as implicitly referring to the tacit function of Pennebaker/the camera, as well as to Ellis's oblivious self-importance (1997: 180). It is hard to view this as an 'all but explicit' reference *by* Dylan, as Rothman emphatically does, but it is nonetheless an interesting empathetic association between Pennebaker, a 'master of the requisite spiritual discipline' (ibid.), and his subject. Dylan called Pennebaker 'The Eye' (see Sounes 2002: 209), perhaps with a nod to one of Emerson's most famous passages, a flight of fancy that succinctly anticipates the unattainable aspirations (invisibility, omniscience) of early direct cinema: 'uplifted into infinite space, all mean egotism vanishes. I become a transparent eyeball; I am nothing; I see all; the currents of the Universal Being flow through me; I am part or particle of God' (n.d.: 529). Terry Ellis may have typified, to Dylan, the kind of malleable young man upon whom it was worth expending not a little effort in order to effect a spiritual conversion.[23] The other journalists featured in *Dont Look Back* did not warrant such passion, attention and assessment as this untrained undergraduate, who went on not to become a scientist, but to manage rock stars.[24]

DYLAN MEETS 'THE *OTHER* FOLK SINGER'

Dylan takes the train north on the way to another concert, looking pensive behind sunglasses as nondescript conurbations fly past. We do not see the Manchester performance, only the tour party's dash along labyrinthine corridors and staircases to their waiting transport.[25] The group find their cars amidst the commotion, and the film cuts to the Newcastle City Hall's bill, prominently featuring the name 'DONOVAN'. After a protracted drunken argument over a smashed glass, we see Donovan, object of the film's running joke, in person. He looks timorous in the company of more worldly elders and much younger than his inspiration, though there is only a few years' difference in their ages. Donovan begins making overtures on the guitar that he has picked up, and sings:

When the night has left you cold and feeling sad,
I will show you that it cannot be so bad.
Forget the one who went and made you cry.
I'll sing a song for you.
That's what I'm here to do,
To sing for you.

After this verse, Dylan spurs Donovan on to play two more by exclaiming, 'Hey, that's a good song, man!' Lyrically, the song's intention is to be as anodyne as a lullaby in its reassurance of devotion – hardly Dylan's objective. Chordally and melodically, although Donovan proficiently explores similar territory to Dylan, he lacks Dylan's gift for seizing the imagination, as Donovan admits: 'It was hard when people said I was copying Dylan. It wasn't so much that he created a new sound – he had a new way of looking at life. I was inspired by Dylan in the same way that he was inspired by Woody Guthrie' (quoted in Anon. 1988: 25). It would have amused Dylan to see, in Donovan's early publicity shots, the Scotsman holding a guitar emblazoned with the words 'This machine kills', a prevaricatory neutering of Woody Guthrie's original slogan, 'This machine kills fascists'. Jonathon Green observes that, for British members of 'youth cults', 'the stimuli were strictly American. Like other imports, the British version would be relatively anaemic, a diluted version of the real thing, but nonetheless sincere' (1999: 26).[26] As a juvenile copyist, Donovan has overlooked, in favour of bland serenading, the vigour and vehemence essential to folk music's effectiveness. Donovan is a personable apprentice, but he is not in the league of a Woody Guthrie, a Hank Williams, or a Dylan.

'To Sing For You' is received politely by all, and Dylan now takes the guitar from Donovan to sing 'It's All Over Now, Baby Blue'. Dylan occasionally looks up at Donovan, and, to a lesser degree, others as he plays, making sure everyone in attendance knows the song's import on this occasion: 'The vagabond who's rapping at your door/Is standing in the clothes that you once wore.' This performance is not Dylan's most engaging – it might be a pedagogical demonstration for Donovan's benefit – but the song is intrinsically better than Donovan's, and on the verse's final line, Pennebaker pans to Donovan, who is transparently worshipful: Donovan is now the baby being lulled, or, more likely, gently taught the realities of life in the shadow of a superior talent.[27] Nobody feels the need to buoy Dylan with a 'well done'. A shot of Donovan's overawed expression fades to black.

THE MAN FROM *TIME* AND THE ALBERT HALL: THERE'S JUST THESE FACTS...

The tour party surveys the Albert Hall, Dylan (and Pennebaker) seeming taken by its grandiosity: 'This must be a very old theatre, huh?' A woman erroneously replies, 'Sure. Victoria died in 1894', and Neuwirth adds, 'Queen Victoria built it for her ... dude.' Backstage, Dylan tests his harmonica and plays the piano, as earlier essaying a chordal passage founded on gospel traditions. This is a strangely reserved style for a person who used to play

> great, great piano. Very great – I used to play the piano like Little Richard style. Only I used to play, you know, an octave higher, and everything came out. When he played, he had [*sic*] a big mistake. His records were great records, but they could have been greater records. (Quoted in Williams 1994: 38)

Dylan's adolescent interest (here expressed in 1961) in emulating and 'improving' upon the rapid 'boogie-woogie' style of Little Richard had clearly waned by the mid-1960s – or is this another 'tall tale' performed for a journalist in lieu of the unexceptional truth about a middle-class shopkeeper's son from Hibbing?[28] Certainly, Dylan's more impassioned performances for the press had evolved by the time of

Dont Look Back from embellished autobiographical yarns to what Terry Ellis would call 'knocking'.

There is a cut to Dylan, who faces the esteemed *Time* correspondent Horace Freeland Judson. Judson is immediately berated by Dylan:

Dylan: Are you going to see the concert tonight?

Judson: Yes.

Dylan: Are you going to hear it?

Judson: Yes.

Dylan: Okay, you're gonna hear it and see it, and it's gonna happen fast – you're not going to get it all, and you might even hear the wrong words, ya know? … 'Cause, ya know, I've never been in *Time* magazine, and yet this hall's filled twice. I've never been in *Time* magazine. I don't need *Time* magazine, and I don't think I'm a folk singer. You'll probably call me a folk singer, but the other people know better, the people that buy my records don't necessarily read *Time* magazine…

Dylan continues, offering a critique of media influence on conceptions of national identity and a tract on corporate journalism's lack of radical nous. Ginsberg had lambasted *Time* in his poem 'America' a decade earlier, and, as photographer Nan Goldin remarks, Time-Life's general approach 'was a challenge to my generation … to overthrow *Life* magazine and [its] whole system of communicating with America' (quoted in Hainley 1995: 97). William Burroughs, another of Dylan's favourite Beat writers, regarded Time-Life and *Fortune* as 'a vast control system … some sort of police organisation whose sole mission was to dupe a nation' (quoted in Tanner 1971: 127). These sentiments echo (albeit more fervently) those of both Pennebaker and Dylan: Pennebaker in his recent divorcement from Drew and Time-Life so that he might free himself of an artistically constraining journalistic remit, and Dylan in his equally restless desire to overthrow staid or remote value systems of the kind propagated by the press. Dylan's stance with regard to journalistic verity may not be especially original, but it is nonetheless a tenable rhetorical position. In 1960, a *Time* cover story, 'Those Rush Hour Blues', audaciously claimed that city commuters enjoyed their trip to work: 'In modern [middle-class, the 'certain class of people that take the magazine seriously', according to Dylan] society, there are few opportunities for the breadwinner to endure personal hardship in earning the family living, such as clearing the forest or shooting a bear' (Anon. 1960: 75). For blue-collar members of the American labour force – a high-risk employment sector with which Dylan sympathised – the reality was of course different. 'If I want to find something out', says Dylan to Judson, 'I'm not going to read *Time* magazine, I'm not going to read *Newsweek*. They've just got too much to lose by printing the truth. You know that.'

Dylan, however, in his interviews and in his everyday dealings, was an inveterate liar, and had much to lose personally (his nurtured mystique) by speaking the truth. A highly critical piece in the 4 November 1963 *Newsweek* exposed Dylan as a middle-class suburbanite (rather than, as he had claimed, an orphaned, part-

Indian hobo), prompting him to retreat temporarily from the public eye in acute embarrassment (see Hajdu 2002: 193; Sounes 2002: 77). Meanwhile…

> Judson: What kinds of truth are they…
>
> Dylan (interrupting): They'd go off the stands in a day if they printed really the truth.
>
> Judson: What is the truth?
>
> Dylan: Really the truth is just a plain picture of, let's say, a tramp vomiting into the sewer, man. And next door to the picture, Mr Rockefeller or Mr C. W. Jones on the subway going to work. Any kind of pictures. Just make a collage of pictures, which they don't do. There's no kind of ideas in *Time* magazine. There's just these facts.

Dylan makes a simple rhetorical juxtaposition to illustrate social inequity, and the hierarchies or castes perpetuated by the mainstream press to the end of safeguarding the status quo. Both Dylan's collage-like lyrics and Pennebaker's filmmaking utilise the informal juxtaposition of evocative imagery or uncaptioned pictures (though of course the recorded 'natural' dialogue has replaced its forbear, the intertitle of the silent film) as potentially more truthful, or at least more sophisticated devices ('ideas') than textually 'clarified' or augmented visuals ('just these facts'). In 1843 New Yorker Mike Walsh launched a radical magazine, *The Subterranean*, which carried a sloganeering headline, 'Independent of Everything, Neutral in Nothing', the rhetoric of which, like the publication's title, Dylan would approve. Walsh's organ championed the working class, specialised in satire and sarcasm, criticised the 'ultra-dishwaterness' of conventional magazines and included early works by unconventional poet Walt Whitman.[29] It did not, however, in the face of libel suits and poor sales, last long. For *Time* to eschew print conventions and ignore marketplace demand would be unrealistic; formal macro-mutations are commercially and artistically risky ventures, but creative progression within a given idiom in which one is well versed, as Dylan knows, is safer.

Dylan continues to orate of his recondite wisdom and musical originality:

> You see, I know more about what you do … than you'll ever know about me … I could tell you that I'm not a folk singer and explain to you why, but you wouldn't really understand. All you could do, you could nod your head.

For the last five years of his performing career, Dylan had been asserting this point continually, as an interview with Billy James (a publicist from Columbia Records) from 1961 demonstrates:

> Dylan: I'm not a folk singer.
>
> James: Is Woody a folk singer?
>
> Dylan: Woody was a folk singer…
>
> James: Why do you say you're not?
>
> Dylan: Uh, Woody was a folk singer to the point – Woody was a glorified folk singer. Woody was a man that went back – don't print this on record – but

Woody was a man who dwelled on simpleness [*sic*] because he was get
ting attention for it. (Quoted in Williams 1994: 38)

So Guthrie went back, or looked back, therefore he could be 'pigeonholed' as a folk
singer by Dylan in 1961 with little compunction. In *Dont Look Back*, Judson asks
Dylan, 'Would you be willing to try [to explain]?'

Dylan: No, because it would be, you know, there are certain things which …
          Every word has its little letter and big letter.
Judson: 'Pigeonhole'.
Dylan: That's not the word at all … You know, the word 'know', 'k-n-o-w'?
Judson: Yes.
Dylan: Like, we all know things. But we really know nothing.
Judson: But you're saying you know more about what I do…
Dylan: No, I'm saying that you're going to die … So am I. I mean we're just going
          to be gone. The world's gonna go on without us. You do your job in the
          face of that. And how seriously you take yourself, you decide for yourself,
          okay? And I'll decide for myself. Now you're not going to make me feel
          unhappy by anything you print about me … You couldn't offend me. And
          I'm sure I couldn't offend you … So all I could hope for you to do is, uh,
          you know, all your ideas in your own head, somehow, wherever they are.

Dylan again questions the reporter's moral principles, this time by directly challeng-
ing Judson's own, personal conscience – even though he 'has to eat and live', in
Dylan's words. After a brief moment of consideration, the reporter responds with,
'Do you care about what you're saying?' This incenses Dylan:

Dylan: How can I answer that if you've got the nerve to ask me? You've got a lot
          of nerve asking me a question like that! Do you ask the Beatles that?
Judson: I have to ask you that because you have the nerve to question whether I
          care…
Dylan (interrupting): I'm not questioning you because I don't expect any answer
          from you. Do you think someone wouldn't go see somebody if they didn't
          want entertainment?
Judson: Of course not.
Dylan: Who wants to go and get whipped? And if you do want to go and get
          whipped … Aren't you into being entertained?
Judson: Yes.
Dylan: Right, so, do you think anybody who comes to see me is coming for any
          other reason than entertainment?

In relegating himself to the status of showman, Dylan again deftly avoids any
comparative discourse. Dylan *is* a great entertainer, a great performer and a great
melodist, but he is more than these alone and he *does* have a message, however
couched (or often explicit); his inimitability for a pop musician of his time is an im-

portant factor in *Dont Look Back*'s effectiveness in conveying a sense of transition and anticipation. Donovan is an entertainer; the Animals are entertainers; even the Beatles had not yet transcended their 'Love Me Do' 'simpleness', an intellectual transmogrification (influenced by Dylan) that would not be complete until *Revolver* (1966), with its groundbreaking audio collage 'Tomorrow Never Knows'.[30]

Dylan is offended by Judson's charge of apathy, but this accusatory ploy is the journalist's only resort when faced with his interviewee's exasperating abjuration. It is now Dylan who simplifies and denies his own painstakingly wrought back catalogue, classifying – pigeonholing – it under 'entertainment' simply because he does not want to talk about it to a representative of Time-Life. After a pregnant pause during which he appears ashamed of the harshness of his tone, Dylan thankfully defuses the situation, and brings the interview to a less charged close:

Dylan: First of all I'm not even a pop singer…
Judson: Caruso, he's appealing to a popular, you know…
Dylan: He's a pop singer. I'm just as good a singer as Caruso. Have you heard me sing? I happen to be just as good as him. You have to listen closely, but I hit all those notes. [Tentative laughter] And I can hold my breath three times as long if I want to.

Some self-effacement here conceals a genuine desire to be held in regard as a singer warranting the attention (but not the fawning adulation) of critics who would lionise Enrico Caruso. The purpose of this almost comedic deflation must, however, be primarily one of mercy to Judson, who has been admirably restrained.[31]

We see the crowds gathering outside the Albert Hall, and Dylan asks whether Donovan is here. 'I don't know', says Neuwirth, 'people like Donovan look just like ordinary people.' We learn that the Beatles are in attendance, and we see Dylan adjusting his jacket in the mirror. To great applause, he takes the stage and sings 'The Times They Are A-Changin'', 'Talking World War III Blues' (in which he says 'I looked in my closet – there was Donovan!' – to laughter and jeers), 'Beneath the Gates of Eden' and 'Love Minus Zero/No Limit', with its final refrain that again (as Rothman (1997: 195) has observed) evokes Baez:

The wind howls like a hammer,
The night blows cold and rain.
My love she's like some raven,
At my window with a broken wing.

Pennebaker zooms out to frame Dylan, tiny and humbled in the bottom left of the screen, the spotlight beaming down upon him from the opposite corner like a sunbeam through a cloud. Dylan faces this spiritual and physical climb towards the light as he looks towards his future and the unknown, with certainty only of one thing: there is no going back. Dylan, Grossman and Neuwirth leave the final concert and the tour behind, in a car. 'I feel like I've been through some kind of … thing', ponders Dylan, as if caught in a split second of his own momentary transcendence, 'there's something special about that'. 'They've started calling you an anarchist', Grossman informs Dylan, 'just because you don't offer any solutions.' 'You're kidding! Anarchist! Gimme a cigarette! Give the anarchist a cigarette! They couldn't say "Communist". I don't think it's cool to be an anarchist, though...' The words 'DONT LOOK BACK' appear on the screen, and the credits run.

CONCLUSION: FIVE PHASES OF FANTASY – (1) THE ANTICIPATION STAGE

'Do your own thing. Be what you are. If you don't know what you are, find out. Fuck leaders.'[32]

Bob Dylan is a talented man of hypocrisy and contradiction, and an impenetrably private individual whom *Dont Look Back* does not attempt to lay bare. Inarguably one of the most important songwriters of the twentieth century, Dylan has consistently explored intellectual precincts that colour our thinking about songs, poetry and life; our arbitrary bifurcations between sense and nonsense, tradition and the modern, structure and disorder, and which propel his art. Dylan largely eschews a formal niche carved by others, and *Dont Look Back* correspondingly rejects dramaturgical procedure, offering few conventional *coups de théâtre* or spectatorial pleasures. The film does, however, anticipate a time of change: it portends an exciting future, taking us *with* Dylan's mind (but not into his mind) on a spiritual journey into modernity.

Christopher Booker identifies this expectant ardour as consistent with what he calls the 'vitality fantasy' underpinning the epoch's hunger for rejuvenation, in particular the nascent 'Anticipation Stage', of which *Dont Look Back* (though Booker's Anglo-centric chronology begins earlier) is redolent:

The fantasy cycle has five stages ... the first is the *Anticipation Stage* – of 'vital' energy, sensing constraint, looking for a dream-focus, a cause, a release ... The bubble of excitement welling up in England over the years after 1956 was nothing more nor less than a gigantic 'vitality fantasy', of which the rise of the teenage sub-culture, the cult of youth ... and the sense of being carried into a modernistic future, were all different individual symptoms. (1969: 79)

Booker also recognises the young English public's desire to formulate an American prototype for modern living and to draw inspiration from American culture, noting that: 'the American Dream has grown up throughout the twentieth century into the most powerful "vitality image" in the world – and it is therefore the example of America which any country wishing to escape into the modern must follow' (ibid.). More than a century earlier, Alexis de Tocqueville claimed of the American people a disregard for history: '[Americans] do not bother at all about the past, but they gladly start dreaming about the future, and in that direction their imagination knows no bounds, but spreads and grows beyond measure' (1966: 485). De Tocqueville's observation not only underscores an abiding American preoccupation with the promises of the New World and its vistas of hypothetical opportunity for all; it also facilitates the positing of Dylan's psyche within his homeland's cyclical, periodically regenerative national character: a frontiersman ethos of alternant bravery, hubris and prudence. If Dylan looks back, it is inevitably to those – both good and bad – who entertained the possibility of selfhood, of 'doing their own thing' unchecked by moral or ethical custodians.

In the mid-1960s Dylan crystallised the nebulous intellectual, artistic and political strains of the emergent counter-culture (and embodied the 'vital', American fantasy hero) better than most. He was at once a meticulous professional, expressive individualist, poetic satirist, peaceful protester, masculist libertine and neo-Romantic.[33] Though he sought to progress to avoid 'vulgar stagnation' (and to acquire vast personal wealth), his young followers understandably wanted only the Dylan they felt served them best: the sub-Woody Guthrie folk singer or the Hank Williams impersonator of his first two albums. Ironically, those who desired and, in many cases, actively fought for change in their respective constitutions and legislation did not gladly accord Dylan the blessing to evolve personally in the way he would like. When Dylan asks us not to follow leaders – whether they be deities, protest groups or the government – he is asking us to deny the basic human urge to delegate responsibility to a putative superior, and, in so doing, paradoxically reinforcing his own credentials as a spiritual leader to those who cannot turn inward for guidance as he can. He realises that anarchy is 'not cool', though his capricious mind could change tomorrow, but offers no alternative, no solution, no 'real message' that the journalists and fans in *Dont Look Back* desire so continually (and for Dylan, infuriatingly) to derive from his mysterious, often quasi-Scriptural verse. 'I was sick of the way my lyrics had been extrapolated, their meanings subverted into polemics', recalled Dylan in 2004; 'I had been anointed as the Big Bubba of Rebellion, High Priest of Protest, the Czar of Dissent, Archbishop of Anarchy ... All code words for *Outlaw*' (2004: 120).

At times Dylan's songs address factual events creatively, much in the way that Pennebaker ('The Eye') does – just quietly watching, tacitly absorbing. Often they evoke sadness, pathos, anger or laughter as the best artists can, but always, to a varying degree, they provoke independent reasoning: never do they *purely* dictate, entertain, prescribe or inform (as did contemporary television documentaries in the current affairs mould). America would be saved from its divisions, said Walt Whitman, 'only by a race of "bards" who would register the multitudinous facets of modern life, link them together, and infuse into them a religiosity they had lost in the "dry and flat Sahara" of American society' (1982: 939). Dylan, of course, suggests no such potential antidote; yet this serves only to accentuate an affinity with human nature as unbound by rules, determinism and organised religion. Renunciation of obligation – a guiding principle that Pennebaker clearly admired in his subject – became *Dont Look Back*'s key theme and the catalyst for a new, neo-transcendental approach to cinematic documentary filmmaking by which precepts could be sidelined in favour of existential poesis. Dylan and Pennebaker's mutual, serendipitous attitudes of progressiveness hence not only consolidated observational cinema's transitory fascination with ascendant pop performers (that had falteringly begun with *What's Happening!*), but also represented the first entirely assured break within the originators of the school from Time-Life's aesthetic and narratory demands.

Jeanne Hall calls *Dont Look Back* a 'systematic critique of the value of conventional reporting methods' (1998: 235), and sees the film as a logical rhetorical consolidation of the 'unproductive interviews and forced photo sessions scattered throughout many early Drew films' (1988: 226) that accentuate the contrasting mobility and dynamic vitality of direct cinema.[34] This insightful reading, however, misapprehends Pennebaker's criticism as not applicable to Drew. *Dont Look Back*, like *Primary*, is indeed a celebration of creative liberation, but it is also a rejoinder: the fixities of corporate journalism ultimately applied as much to Pennebaker's former colleague (beholden as he was to profit-driven networks, and reliant upon classical storytelling techniques) as to Horace Judson. 'More and more', laments Pennebaker of his latter times on Drew assignments, 'we were becoming like *Life* photographers; just story, story, story, story. That didn't seem like a helluva lot of fun' (quoted in O'Connell 1992: 167). The 'dry and flat Sahara' of the affluent postwar years, along with a pervasive fear of 'formlessness' and change, was being challenged by the 1960s' youth culture, a movement to which Pennebaker would grow increasingly attracted. 'Would you care if I told you it was all fake?' Pennebaker asked writer G. Roy Levin, in a diatribe more redolent of Dylan: 'What if I told you it was only a script?' (quoted in Levin 1971: 240). As Levin noted: 'No one considered a serious playwright writes straight, realistic plays now. Nobody paints straight, realistic paintings, makes straight, realistic sculptures' (1971: 242). In the field of documentary filmmaking, Robert Drew (like Ellis and Judson, a 'square') represented all that was becoming distasteful to Pennebaker. '*Dont Look Back*', explained the director, 'has a kind of responsiveness to Dylan, born of Dylan coming very close to things that I've been thinking about for a long time. It's sort of an epiphany that took place' (quoted in Levin 1971: 262).[35] A story of sorts has been told, but there is no *dénouement*, closure or resolution, just the beginning of Dylan's (and direct cinema's) journey into the future.

Back in an America whose embrace of youth culture was now nearing its peak, D. A. Pennebaker's next film – this time shot of necessity in colour and with multiple cameras – captured the first, ecstatic throes of the 'Summer of Love', as the fantasy entered the 'Dream Stage'.

4 | DANCING ON THE BRINK OF THE WORLD[1]

MONTEREY POP

'There's a whole generation, with a new explanation.'[2]

Held on 16–18 June 1967, the Monterey Pop Festival introduced America to what would become a regular cultural experience: the three-day rock concert. Conceived as a counterpart to the annual Monterey Jazz event and staged upon that festival's Californian site, Monterey Pop's inception stemmed from an emerging belief that popular music (due in part to Dylan's poetic influence on rock lyrics) was now worthy of respectful attention. Both industry showcase and benefit concert, Monterey Pop gave the counter-culture's musical figureheads critical legitimacy and exposure whilst helping also to invent the 'Summer of Love' by founding the Sixties' first shrine of mass pilgrimage: the biggest 'love-in' to date.[3] D. A. Pennebaker was immediately enraptured by the concert's *au courant* quality, and a euphoric – if illusive – aura of delivery from his country's troubles: 'Everyone was going to California … There was a new sense of freedom in the air and that was reflected in the music, in the drugs, in everything … What happened at Monterey was I found myself in the middle of this cyclonic thing … We just had to turn on the cameras' (quoted in Arnold 2001).

Monterey Pop, after some psychedelically-inspired titles set to Big Brother and the Holding Company's 'Combination of the Two', opens with a zealous young woman extolling, 'Haven't you ever been to a love-in? God! I think it's going to be like Easter and Christmas and New Year's and your birthday all together, you know? … the vibrations are just going to be flowing everywhere.' There then follows a montage sequence set to Scott McKenzie's 'San Francisco (Be Sure to Wear Some Flowers in Your Hair)':

> If you're going to San Francisco,
> Be sure to wear some flowers in your hair.
> If you're going to San Francisco,
> You're gonna meet some gentle people there.
> For those who come to San Francisco,
> Summertime will be a love-in there.

Most of the shots during this segment present these 'gentle people', the young, predominantly middle-class, college-educated and white 'hippies' who were gravitating towards America's West Coast (particularly San Francisco's Haight-Asbury district) in the mid- to late 1960s.[4] Though they shared the student Left's anti-war stance, most hippies were essentially apolitical hedonists who had chosen to shun conventional employment and pursue instead a lifestyle of art, music, sex and drugs. They sought freedom from authoritarian control, the right to attain personal satisfaction (both physical and spiritual), and to avoid the draft to Vietnam – much to the annoyance of more conventionally patriotic and conservative Americans, of whom many had lost sons to the protracted campaign in Indochina. One such parent, although tired of the bloody war, succinctly summed up the feelings of her generation: 'The college types, the professors, they go to Washington and tell the government what to do ... But their sons, they don't end up in the swamps over there, in Vietnam. No sir' (quoted in Patterson 1996: 670).

Such was the hippie movement's predication upon nonconformity that men's hair was worn long (and frequently at such a length that the Beatles seemed like paragons of restraint). Both sexes ostentatiously combined ethnic or anachronistic clothes with gaudy, cheap jewellery, a look that further disturbed intractable adults in both the public and private sphere. Californian Governor Ronald Reagan memorably called a hippie somebody who 'dresses like Tarzan, has hair like Jane, and smells like Cheetah' (quoted in O'Neill 1971: 670), but in truth hippies were more inventive (though they also visibly belonged to their own clan) than the highly conservative Reagan could have appreciated. Rejecting the subdued colour schemes and Brylcreemed dreariness of their parents with flamboyance and imagination, the demographic born of record-breaking post-war natality anathematised the middle-aged and scorned every 'far out' symbol thereof. 'Don't trust anyone over thirty', ran an SDS slogan, whose intention was to provoke campus dissidents into revitalising politics in an age of failing liberalism. The hippies had no need of such a mantra, but they likewise saw seniority as a handicap – if sometimes for no other reason than a hatred of everything aesthetically demure.

This rejection of one's older contemporaries was not, however, a novel phenomenon. Transcendental philosopher and civil reformist Henry David Thoreau, in his influential 'call to a new nationhood' (Cavell 1992: liner notes), *Walden* (first published in 1854), held no regard for his elders' opinions either: 'Practically, the old have no very important advice to give to the young ... I have lived some thirty years on this planet, and I have yet to hear the first syllable of valuable or even earnest advice from my seniors' (quoted in Cavell 1992: 8). The Beat poets – most notably Ginsberg – had drawn heavily on Thoreau's tract for better living and the free verse of Thoreau's contemporary, Walt Whitman, who often celebrated what he viewed as a holistic correlation between man, nature and the universe. More than a century after Whitman's 'Song of the Open Road' first appeared, a new nation of acolytes found truth in its sentiments of physical and spiritual questing:

Afoot and light-hearted I take to the open road,
Healthy, free, the world before me,
The long brown path before me leading wherever I choose... (1998: 120)

Yearning for a glimpse of Mark Twain's 'dreamy, exquisite fairyland' (1984: 838), the latest in an unending line of optimistic migrants were converging upon the Western seaboard to celebrate their own emancipation from stymieing demands. From the Gold Rush prospectors of the nineteenth century, through spiritual seekers and cult leaders, California's inhabitants relished 'the freedom to create their own version of America ... liberated from the country's Puritan heritage' (Cavallo 1999: 105–6). With its harbours, sunshine, flora, mineral wealth and legends of golden opportunity, the United States' West Coast is still a land of promise and new beginnings: a symbolic Outer Limit at the very edge of the world. 'We go westward', wrote Thoreau in 1863, 'as into the future, with a spirit of enterprise and adventure' (quoted in Bode 1947: 604). But, as author Joan Didion cautions, 'The mind is troubled by some buried but ineradicable suspicion that things had better work out here, because here, beneath that immense bleached sky, is where we run out of continent' (2001: 150).

The many pretty, diaphanously adorned young women who have come to Monterey seem of especial interest to Pennebaker, who devotes a great deal of his first sequence to their effervescent expressions and whimsical behaviour. Indeed, the theme of physical beauty, of naïve youth in happy abandon, encapsulates the apparently uncritical and sometimes unreservedly favourable stance the film adopts. One shot in this montage comprises some police officers, seen laughing along with some concertgoers: here is harmony even between the square and the hip.[5] On the lyric, 'Be sure to wear some flowers in your hair', Pennebaker – in a literal illustration of the kind normally avoided in direct cinema – cuts to a girl blowing bubbles, who has flowers in her hair. It is as if a concession has been made to the wonder and simplicity of this 'cyclonic thing' by which Pennebaker is mesmerised, and to his joy upon discovering that in California (not actually San Francisco – Monterey is eighty miles to the south), in this New Age Tir nan-Og, people really do wear flowers in their hair.[6]

The Mamas and the Papas' 'Creeque Alley' – lyrically a virtual Who's Who of mid-1960s folk-rock – accompanies another, similarly composed (though perhaps, at times, even more surreptitiously filmed) montage, the underlying theme of which is physical movement, or, figuratively, collective 'progression'. Movement, in Thoreau's essay 'Walking', symbolises freedom from organised society and the divorcement of the New World from the Old; why not, asks Thoreau, 'live free', like 'a child of the mist?' (quoted in Bode 1947: 623–4). According to Dominick Cavallo: 'The freedom to move might sever ties between children and parents. Equally important, it could shatter the symbolic connection between the idea of family and its relationship to tradition and personal continuity ... Movement meant [to the writers of the American Renaissance] perpetual youth, a new start for every generation' (1999: 85). Moreover, movement (McKenzie's 'people in motion') called attention to the shifting, 'cyclonic' counter-culture, and not the static or stolid past.

Again, Pennebaker includes a clip demonstrating affability between the police and the hippies, and again, Pennebaker fixates upon nubile women: this time with more attention paid to young women's legs strolling in time to the overdubbed

'People in motion': an obvious attraction for Pennebaker throughout *Monterey Pop* (1967)

music.[7] One shot finds the Mamas and the Papas' Michelle Phillips, resting front-of-stage. As the cameraman tilts up her body from her boots and frames her waif-like face nodding to some unheard diegetic music, Phillips gestures with her palms held vertically towards the camera for him to move away or to stop filming her. This display of unbridled, somewhat aggressive sexuality lends the camera (and, of course, Pennebaker and his crew, which included Richard Leacock and Albert Maysles) a slightly insalubrious, voyeuristic and highly masculine aspect: at one point a young woman, sitting on the ground, looks up with disdain, meeting the gaze peering down at her. Bill Nichols states, with reference to such proxemic violations, that

> the documentary viewer's subjectivity shifts according to whether a politics of sexual or special representation is predominant. The indulgence of fantasy is blocked to some degree not simply by the invocation of a desire to know, but by an awareness that the views given originate from the encounter between social actors on either side of the lens. The viewer's relation to the image, then, is charged with an awareness of the politics and ethics of the gaze. (1991: 77)

The visual approach of *Monterey Pop* unquestionably colours our perception of the filmmakers' 'relation to the historical world' (ibid.). As Pennebaker says, 'It's possible to go to a situation and simply film what you see there, what happens there, what goes on ... And what's a film? It's just a window someone peeps through' (quoted in Levin 1971: 235). Although beautiful, sexually 'liberated' women were naturally attractive to Pennebaker, the nature of this unobtrusively obtained material brings to mind Jonathon Green's appraisal of John Crosby's 1965 *Telegraph* eulogy to 'Swinging London': 'Like some ageing medallion man, leering over a disco floor on which he's no longer young enough to dance, [Crosby] positively salivates over "a frenzy of the prettiest legs in the whole world ... a gleam of pure joy on their faces ... all vibrating with youth"' (1999: 71).

In *Dont Look Back*, the filmmaker's position of privilege and consensual acceptance (he definitely belongs, therefore so do we) tempers the spectator's attitude toward the filmic gaze: Pennebaker's occasional indulgences (there are fewer in *Dont Look Back*, and those are certainly less objectifying) do not possess the seamy quality detectable in *Monterey Pop*. Pennebaker's adoration of women, and, consequently, that infatuation's projected relationship to the fragmented bodies represented on screen, is now more scopophilia than yearning – a spatial perspective more akin to telescopic observation than respectful portraiture. Impersonal, zoom-lens photography is Pennebaker's preferred approach for the majority of this film's offstage content, an arm's-length methodology that allows panoramic physical vantage but precludes critical expatiation. Much of the music, however, remains an effective force: *Monterey Pop* is, unlike *Don't Look Back* and *What's Happening!*, foremost a concert movie.

'SOMETHIN' GRABBED A HOLD OF ME, DARLIN'...'

The Mamas and the Papas perform their hippie anthem 'California Dreaming', after which we see a ticket-taker, who says, 'Once you leave, you may not re-enter. But you won't want to leave!' and some Hell's Angels taking their seats. During Canned Heat's lively 'Rollin' and Tumblin'', Pennebaker inserts reaction shots exclusively of attractive women enjoying the set. After Hugh Masekela's 'Bajabula Bonke' (mostly uninterrupted by inserts), a blonde-haired woman says, to camera, 'Like you kind of have to wait for a new wave to come, and then a whole new set of rock 'n' roll bands comes with it, which creates all the other ... bullshit'. We cut to singer Grace Slick and Jefferson Airplane, against an oil-projection and slide-show backdrop, performing 'High Flyin' Bird'. It is difficult to deduce whether the stoned-sounding woman is referring, as Pennebaker implies, to Jefferson Airplane and the similar 'acid rock' bands emergent in the area, or the more visceral acts (Jimi Hendrix, Janis Joplin, The Who) on which Monterey Pop's subsequent repute is founded; by all accounts the latter were the stars of the show.

The Janis Joplin song included in *Monterey Pop* is 'Ball and Chain', a searing interpretation of 1950s rhythm 'n' blues singer Big Mama Thornton's original:

Sitting down by my window,
Looking out at the rain.
Down by my window, baby,
And all around me,
I said suddenly I felt the rain.
Somethin' grabbed a hold of me, darlin',
Honey, it felt to me, honey like, yeah, a ball and chain.
Oh honey, you know what I mean,
It just hurts me.

Janis Joplin revamps the blues (and gives the performance of a lifetime) in *Monterey Pop*

Wearing a gold lamé trouser suit and Cuban-heeled boots that she had bought especially for her set, Joplin renders 'Ball and Chain' with passion, taking the extemporised vocal nuances of the blues (regarded as a black idiom until popularised and mass-commercialised by the British Invasion of the mid-1960s) and endowing them with a soulful, guttural roar all of her own. The show Joplin put on at Monterey was an all-or-nothing gambit, a showcase that sometimes traverses the fine line between coruscation and showboating. Her voice strains at the edges, but in pushing herself she at least transcends the limiting strictures of Big Brother and the Holding Company's somewhat approximate backing: she literally cries out for a more solid musical foundation.

William Rothman writes of Joplin's physicality and sexual dynamism; he describes the 'audience in ecstasy witnessing her ecstasy' (1997: 201), and it is true that she is communicative and unrepressed in this respect. However, Joplin's art at this time may have been more about sublimation than consummation. According to biographer Alice Echols, 'Janis became a lot more attractive to men in the wake of the festival ... Janis had long made a conversational staple out of her inability to "get fucked"' (1999: 178). Simon Frith states, with germane relevance to Pennebaker's camerawork:

> As long as female attraction is defined by the male gaze, girls are under constant pressure to keep control of their appearance; they can't afford to let their performance go. A drunken, raddled woman remains a potent image of ugliness; a haggard Keith Richards retains a far more glamorous appeal than a haggard Janis Joplin or Grace Slick. The irrational elements of the counter-culture – in other words, the sex

and drugs and rock 'n' roll – could not be appropriated by girls as they were boys without affecting their self definitions, their relationships, their lives. (1983: 242–3)

Naomi Wolf has observed our culture's proclivity to reduce women to either 'beauty' or 'heroine' (1990: 59), and although Joplin obscures this bifurcation, insecurities about her looks remained with her always. Cynical about newly interested men's motives, in 1970 a 'bitter and desperate' (Isserman & Kazin 2000: 162). Joplin lamented, 'I used to ask guys I was balling, "Do I ball like I sing? ... Is it really me or am I putting on a show?"' (quoted in Echols 1999: 180). The cameras are respectful of Joplin's highly individual presence, and concentrate on capturing the eurhythmy – stomping heels, wildly gesticulating arms – of what is an empowered (emotionally vulnerable though Joplin may have been) physical display. Joplin's self-presentation suggests a necessarily defensive yet compelling spectacle: her music, along with its driving, destructive intoxicants, is her life force, and it is towards this force that both audience and spectator gravitate. At the end of the song we see a close-up of 'Mama' Cass Elliot, mouthing 'Wow!' in admiration. Pennebaker here not only alludes to Elliot's deference to Joplin's sheer vigour (Elliot possessed a more traditionally pleasing voice), but also to his own enthralment by an unconventional, tragically heroic beacon of the Sixties' intrinsic dissonances.

FIVE PHASES OF FANTASY – (2) THE DREAM STAGE

Over the violin introduction to Eric Burdon's Animals' rather contrived arrangement of the Rolling Stones' 'Paint it Black',[8] Pennebaker inserts a rapidly-sequenced series of jump-cut framings showing a young woman's face and its constituent features in various expressions of simulated excitement or joy. Though reminiscent of avant-garde meditations on close-up objects and faces (particularly Fernand Léger's cubist *Ballet mécanique* (1924); see Rees 1999: 45), the fast cutting and suggestive fixation upon the open mouth are more in keeping with the highly sexualised (but often, with the aim of critical elevation from 'artless' pornography, abstracted) imagery of 1960s psychedelia. Christopher Booker sees a connection between the experimental, fragmentary nature of this aesthetic and the counter-cultural vitality fantasy (by 1967 well into its 'Dream Stage', a period of 'rising excitement, when, as in a day-dream, everything seems to be going right' (1969: 72)):

> Whatever the form of vitality fantasy ... we find the same story: that the essence of the sensations on which it feeds is that they are, in some way, violations of order or the image of order ... It may be a violation of aesthetic order: providing visual thrills derived from unusually angled photographs, speeded up or slow motion film, the visual tricks and unusual juxtapositions of Surrealism, the optical illusions of Op Art or the suggestively disordered glimpses of *collage*. (1969: 67–8)

Pennebaker repeatedly incorporates stylistic elements associated with the hippie movement's iconography, and in so doing locates *Monterey Pop* in the bounds of a generic visual scheme. *Dont Look Back* is documentary film as concomitant form to Dylan's music; in *Monterey Pop*, Pennebaker's cinema has mimetically taken on the characteristics of a movement it wishes to honour.

The customs of the apolitical counter-culture largely emphasised a negative rather than a positive, an absence not a presence; a hippie's accoutrements and behaviour asserted, 'I am *not* The Man; I am *not* the Establishment.' *Monterey Pop*, by means of Pennebaker's self-proclaimed beguilement and artistic mimesis, seconds this sentiment (this film is not square; it is not Establishment; it has assumed its subjects' hip mindset), immersing itself in a 'happening scene', in what Herbert Marcuse called the 'Great Refusal – the protest against that which is' (1964: 63), but not that hybridised and diverse scene's essential complexity. Many specific, politically problematic elements remain only vague, remote intimations. Country Joe and the Fish's 'I-Feel-Like-I'm-Fixin'-to-Die-Rag' (a sardonic anti-Vietnam War anthem, of which more in Chapter Five) was excluded in favour of their less politically incendiary 'Section 43', a sprawling instrumental. David Crosby astutely presaged, 'I want to say this anyway, even if it's edited out of the TV film', before voicing his pacifistic views and decrying John Kennedy's assassination. The Hell's Angels' ominous presence, although repeatedly acknowledged, is not discussed; nor is the issue addressed of the growing numbers of mentally disturbed and physically ruined individuals taking up residence in the area who had already begun to taint California's abiding reputation as a sunny, bohemian utopia. 'Rape', said San Franciscan Digger Chester Anderson in 1967, 'is as common as bullshit on Haight Street ... Minds and bodies are being maimed as we watch, a scale model of Vietnam' (quoted in Didion 2001: 86).

It was necessary for those who wished to make known personal allegiance to a particular cause for reform or agitation to wear badges, wield placards or sing songs of dissent; Pennebaker, though, proffers a broadly adoptive affirmation of belonging to the counter-culture's most benign bloc. Although America was in a state of unprecedented polarisation – its citizens were either hip or square, either with or against the state – neither pole had claim to a harmonious unity of spirit. In short, there is a parochial, partisan selectivity evident in *Monterey Pop*, a binary simplification that is central to the film's romanticised tenor.

THE JIMI HENDRIX EXPERIENCE

The counter-culture's failings were yet to become so manifest as to demand filmic coverage: the fantasy was still, just about, effectual. *Monterey Pop*'s longest look into the shadows, into the equal and opposite Yin that must follow the daydreaming, is Jimi Hendrix's elemental performance, a set that redefined existing notions of how the electric guitar could be used.[9] Though a black man, Hendrix, like Joplin, had few black fans; most derided him for selling-out to white ideals (and employing a white rhythm section in Noel Redding and Mitch Mitchell), and Joplin for her mimicry of a black vernacular – the blues. Another cover version, the song included in *Monterey Pop*, 'Wild Thing', was Hendrix's closing number. Previously recorded by English band The Troggs (but written by Chip Taylor), 'Wild Thing', as appropriated by Hendrix, becomes a suitably feral rock dirge – a dramatically distorted three-chord retort to those blues artists who merely copied their idols:

Wild Thing,
You make my heart sing,
You make everything ... groovy.
Yeah, Wild Thing!

Hendrix abounds with bestial, onanistic or explicitly carnal gestures quite atypical of contemporaneous performers, going so far as to wield his decorated Stratocaster as if it were a (his) giant phallus, pluck the strings with his teeth and mime intercourse with a loudspeaker. His mid-song guitar solo (played effortlessly with one hand as if to accentuate the melody's plainness) mocks Kaempfert and Snyder's 'Strangers in the Night', a middle-of-the-road hit for Frank Sinatra in 1966, before descending again to exhilarating depths of debauchery and animalism evoked by howling, orgiastic feedback and vibrato. Hendrix surely would not be so coy when 'exchanging glances': this is not easy listening, nor is it supposed to be. Hendrix was forcefully reclaiming the blues, wrenching it away from the pop groups who had diluted its power by learning the basics in homage but ignoring the primal instincts, born of frustration, behind its creation in the cotton fields and the chain gangs. The Who's Pete Townshend was in no doubt as to Hendrix's intention: '[It was as if Hendrix was saying] you've taken this, Eric Clapton and Mr Townshend, you think you're a showman. This is how we do it ... when we take back what you've borrowed, if not stolen' (quoted in Shaar Murray 1989: 91). Hendrix's Monterey 'Wild Thing' revamped the Troggs' whining paean to teenage lust and showed exactly what years of pent-up artistic dissatisfaction touring in backing bands had led to, a cathartic explosion that critic Nelson George calls, 'the revenge of the R & B sideman' (1988: 109).

Hendrix's home crowd, fellow Americans who had never experienced such an unabashedly masculine routine, were impressed enough to make him an enormous star. Despite his love of drugs and flamboyant attire, ex-paratrooper Hendrix was never a hippie *per se*, but nor was he aligned with radical factions or political extremes:[10] he was an accepting and accepted ally of the largely white 'flower children', who saw in him both unassailable talent and an almost instinctive 'coolness' – here was an unthreatening Negro, dressed like a hippie, and playing the most effusive music they had ever heard. Not everyone was so taken. *Esquire* critic Robert Christgau called Hendrix 'terrible', and, more cuttingly, a 'psychedelic Uncle Tom' (quoted in Perry 2004: 47), after antebellum writer Harriet Beecher Stowe's graphic religious stories of a black preacher showing whites how, in Stowe's terms, 'the Negro mind, impassioned and imaginative, always attaches itself to hymns and expressions of a vivid and pictorial nature' (1967: 83). At the end of the song, Hendrix sets fire to and smashes his guitar amid a cacophony of amplifier noise and Mitchell's aggressive, Elvin Jones-influenced drum soloing; the docile audience seems shocked and bewildered. Pennebaker too does not apparently know how to respond to this climactic thrill, other than to cut to Mama Cass singing, 'Got

Hendrix steals the show (and destroys his guitar) in *Monterey Pop*

a feelin' that I'm wastin' time on you, babe...' William Rothman concurs: 'I always find myself thinking, "Truer words were never spoken"' (1997: 204).

Though Rothman's remark (in concordance with Pennebaker's implicit purpose) is a permissible sideswipe at Elliot's less than revolutionary oeuvre, Hendrix himself is not beyond reproach for perpetuating a male ideal of hippie womanhood: the submissive, nameless, 'thing' of which he sings. Ostensibly, the 1960s gave women sexual freedom, emancipation from domesticity and escape from inevitable pregnancy; this was, arguably, an entirely illusory transposition manufactured by social vicissitudes to a male's biological advantage. Simon Frith proffers an eloquent summary of female servitude within the 'bachelor sub-culture':

> The ideal bohemian woman is the 'innocent' prostitute – anti-domestic and a symbol of sex as transitory pleasure. The prostitute can be treated (as rock stars treat groupies) with a mixture of condescension and contempt, as someone without an autonomous sexuality. Sex as self-expression remains the prerogative of the man: the woman is the object of *his* needs and fantasies, admired, in a way, for her lack of romantic hypocrisy but despised for her anonymity. (1983: 242)

Former Ealing art student Pete Townshend described his onstage 'auto-destruction' as a trans-media extension of Gustav Metzger's violent exhibitions: Metzger once destroyed a guitar during a lecture attended by Townshend, but the explanation nonetheless seems, as Frith and Howard Horne opine, rather post-hoc (1989: 100). Townshend's demolition appears more obviously to signify the momentary, immediate and impermanent nature of creative performance, the drawing of a one-off event to an absolute close and the empowering (for the band) preclusion of an encore. With Hendrix (who, in his early career, self-admittedly copied the Who's chaotic finales), there is another perceptible dimension to his guitar's immolation. Hendrix's numerous, anonymous Stratocasters, like his 'wild things', his 'transitory pleasures', are disposable vessels to be loved and left, used and discarded – the shards distributed amongst anyone who will take them.[11]

If men could not – or did not want to – marry their newly 'liberated' (from the 'restrictive' sphere of marriage) sweethearts, they could certainly now consume or purchase them freely. Perhaps Mama Cass' expression of doubt was highly insightful; her declared belief that she might be wasting time on her hippie lover spoke saliently of a counter-cultural irony, a sub-surface disparity that threatened an epoch's perceived (in the eyes of its defenders) moral tenability. 'When you're looking at that era', notes *Creem* journalist Roberta Cruger, 'men definitely used the burgeoning feminism as an excuse to get whatever they wanted. It was like: "Why won't you have sex with me? Aren't you sexually liberated?" ... There was a double standard, but there was lip service being given to feminism' (quoted in DeRogatis 2000: 79).

In the 1950s the young, male rebel sought to escape the 'bondage' of female family (whether mother, sister or girlfriend: all were seen as potential domesticators whose natural imperative compelled them to stability) and to be a loner, to move on and not, to remember Dylan's Hollywood hero James Dean, look back at the four walls of orthodoxy. By the mid-1960s those women who had chosen the counter-culture's 'empowering', permissive lifestyle, remained effectively subordinate: not to an individual, but to many men, who wanted not to settle down but to roam.

THE HIPPIE TRAIL: RAVI SHANKAR

The film's most prolonged montage sequence is cut to Ravi Shankar's 'Raga Bhimpalasi', a sub-continental sitar and tabla composition. This contemplative segment, which befits the underlying music's microtonal drone, is more sedate in pace and meter than the previous montages. An elegiac shot of a neatly aligned pair of black shoes (pointing 'east', or to the right of the frame), abandoned in the middle of a car park, opens the sequence on a stimulating, evocative note. Perhaps somebody in a state of spiritual enlightenment has symbolically 'parked' their shoes, removing the encumbering footwear to facilitate closer contact with nature, or perhaps, as William Rothman speculates, Pennebaker is evoking the removal of shoes before entering a Hindu temple (1997: 205). As the soundtrack takes a turn eastward, so the concurrent images (of tranquil people wandering and awakening) follow suit, leaving behind the comfort of Western tonality and aesthetic convention for the meditative, introspective philosophy of India: Pennebaker loses his own metaphorical shoes and follows the 'hippie trail'.

Many hippies longed to travel, and, for them, these voyages of geographical- and self-discovery were a large part of the 'dropping out' process, as Jonathon Green writes:

Barefoot and hitting the 'hippie trail' – at least for a few days – with Pennebaker in *Monterey Pop*

> For most it was a phenomenon that long-preceded their wanderings, that clichéd but still potent 'lure of the East'. For the more reflective hippies, underpinning the myth of self-discovery was a turning against the Judaeo-Christian ethic, so laden with guilt and work ethics, and a belief that the religions of the East, however diluted, might be more what the seeker required. One could stay at home and immerse oneself in these new, ascetic disciplines, but how much more exciting to head out East, following one's Karma. (1999: 226)

Though asceticism in the strictest sense – abstinence from drugs, amongst other gratifying indulgences – was not what most had in mind, the romantic notion of an exotic East held mass appeal as an alternative source of inspiration to those who had gone to the States' most westerly point. In the tie-dye and face painting of hippie fashions, this inspiration was plainly implicated; it was thus inevitable that Eastern musicians also would find a place, however short-lived, in the seemingly uncongenial locale of the counter-cultural United States.

George Harrison's rudimentary use of the sitar on the Beatles' 'Norwegian Wood', and the group's subsequent dalliance with Transcendental guru Maharishi Mahesh Yogi's professed method of attaining 'higher consciousness' through mantra and meditation, encapsulated and promulgated this brief fascination. Renowned sitar player Shankar, who was delighted with the attention and fame this new interest had brought him, was nonetheless anxious that his music's deep-rooted, traditional purposes were not forgotten by frivolous and superficial hippie consumers:

> There is more to it than exciting the senses of the listeners with virtuosity and loud crash bang effects. My goal has always been to take the audience along with me

deep inside, as in meditation, to feel the sweet pain of trying to reach out for the supreme, to bring tears to the eyes, and to feel totally peaceful and cleansed. (1999)

If Hendrix reaches for more corporeal sensations, and Joplin evokes the heartbreak of love, Shankar's 'Raga Bhimpalasi' endeavours to attain a state of spiritual perfection.

The camera now wanders as if lost but unafraid, and awestruck by the colourful mass of humanity enveloping it. We now see images of naked feet (in contrast to Joplin's and Phillips' heels and adding to the discarded shoes' symbolic import), balloons, face-painting, a monkey with 'LOVE' daubed on its forehead, a man with a painted scalp, psychedelically customised cars and the Hell's Angels' jackets (but not their faces, and filmed from afar). A subjective, travelling shot then tracks along a row of people leaning against a wall – some of them acknowledge the camera, but most remain oblivious. Fingers caress a fur coat; a lone dancer 'freaks out'; the young woman from the introduction with the flowers in her hair has now fallen asleep, but Pennebaker finds some other friends in two smiling, flaxen young boys. There is now no apparent sexual preoccupation (in keeping with the peak phase of a hallucinogen trip, and in empathy with Shankar's stated beliefs) or suggested hostility by subjects to those filming them. Pennebaker now wants to explore the *whole* festival – the whole 'cyclonic thing' – in all its component detail, colour, shape and texture. He has been taken along, and wants the viewer to be taken along, sympathetically, with Shankar and his mesmerised audience. 'As Simon and Garfunkel say', noted Robert A. Rosenstone, 'one has to make the "moment last", and this is done best by those who open themselves up to the pleasures of the world' (1969: 141).

The 18-minute performance gradually intensifies in terms of both rhythmic definition and melodic density. Frenzied motifs repeatedly emerge, recur and recede, as Shankar's face is framed, contorted in application to his music. Next, his hands take priority, then his bare, tapping feet – every extremity moving in concert, as every individual attendee becomes part of a greater whole, part of Monterey Pop as immortalised in *Monterey Pop*. 'Raga Bhimpalasi' reaches its climax, to a standing ovation and longer and much louder applause even than was accorded Joplin or Hendrix, who sits rapt in the audience: a master of raw musical physicality admiring a master of elevated musical spirituality. An aerial shot pans over the elated, but curiously (for an era that retrospectively evokes total lack of inhibition) regimented and polite crowd, who shout and whistle for an encore. The end credits run.

CONCLUSION: LOOKIN' FOR FUN AND FEELIN' GROOVY [12]

'The ideas of the time are in the air, and infect all who breathe it.'
    – Ralph Waldo Emerson (1983: 627)

There is entrenched, within *Monterey Pop*'s joyous worldview, an unswerving rejection of critical discussion. Emerson's notion that, 'Life is good only when it is magical and musical, a perfect timing and consent, and when we do not anatomise it' (1882: 147), is a sentiment clearly echoed in Pennebaker's own philosophy. One is reminded of *The Tempest*, in which Miranda, bestowed with the gift of awe, exclaims upon first seeing the court party:

O wonder! How many goodly creatures are there here!
How beauteous mankind is! O brave new world,
That has such people in't! (V. I)

To which, retorts Prospero, "Tis new to thee...'

Pennebaker's spellbound diminution of inconvenient, malignant or troublesome factors (the attendant Hell's Angels, Black Panthers and every politically dissenting performance) keeps the pro-filmic whimsy of Monterey safely away from its putative shadow: the 'unquietness' that may pierce the air at any moment (Marx 1964: 27). When *Monterey Pop* transcends its own, demonstratively wholesome *raison d'être*, as it sometimes does, there is epiphany: Hendrix fucking his guitar, or Joplin's exhilarated, possessed incandescence. For the rest of the time, its purpose is clear – a confrontational aspect allowed sufficient shrift could pollute or obscure.

Monterey Pop co-cameraman Albert Maysles is highly critical of this 'we've got the Flower Generation and everything is just hunky-dory'outlook (quoted in Bell 1999: 255–6), saying:

I react strongly against the so-called 'point of view' documentary because I think that it limits the outcome to the point of view that you start out with, no matter what that is ... I feel that in a documentary film, which has one obligation above all, it has to be factual. For me, it has a second obligation, that is, to be fair so if there's a judgement to be made, it should come from the viewer. And, the viewer should have a good deal of information from which to make the judgement. (Quoted in Bell 1999: 255)

In considering a vista such as the Monterey Pop Festival, contemplative evaluation, as opposed to enraptured reverie, is the most rational methodology with regard to Maysles' professed ideals of historicity and fairness; yet rationality, in *Monterey Pop*, has been unreservedly subordinated to sensualism: 'as in a daydream ... every need is gratified' by a euphoric self-immersion into the vitality fantasy's 'bubble of excitement' (Booker 1969: 72, 79). Pennebaker's empirical 'obligations' to the viewer, such as they are, are not fulfilled. In looking for fun, or in looking to sanctify and sanitise an event – or in this case an entire ethos – a film can be little other than synthetic propaganda, a benignly intended *Triumph of the Will* (1934) in which not Adolf Hitler, but Eastern avatar Ravi Shankar entrances and incites the masses to exaltation.[13]

Despite the numerous misgivings that arise from Pennebaker's assenting treatment, *Monterey Pop* relays a message we perhaps want to receive, a spectral postcard from a past that can never be relived – not least because many principal players, including Jimi Hendrix, Janis Joplin, Keith Moon, John Phillips and Otis Redding are dead, eventual victims (however directly or indirectly) of the carefree lifestyle espoused by *Monterey Pop*. The summer could not, and did not last forever: as the real estate developers (the intrusive 'Machine') had ruined the undulating beauty of the landscape (the Happy Valley, or the 'Garden'), enterprising pushers and cynical corporations moved in to turn the counter-culture to their capital advantage, and the drugs, with devastating insidiousness, got harder and deadlier.[14] Nevertheless, the vision of oneself as a youth in California circa 1967 is an attractive fantasy. The compound, contemporary discourse of 'flower power', to which *Monterey Pop* has contributed extensively, suggests a harmonious life of endless sun, artistic fulfilment, happy sex without jealousy or disease and a human condition enhanced by striving quixotically, as Pennebaker strives, for an impossible, romantic idyll. The California Dream excited Pennebaker like thousands before him, instilling in him a sanguinity and optimism shared by the artists, pioneers, poets and Puritans who had made their way to the brink of the world in search of rebirth and renewal, a romantic American myth expressed in Robinson Jeffers' 'Continent's End' (1924):

I gazing at the boundaries of granite and spray, the established sea-marks, felt behind me
mountain and plain, the immense breadth of the continent, before me the
mass and doubled stretch of water. (Quoted in Hicks *et al*. 2000: 408)

Somehow, the idealist movement with a 'new explanation' survived to forge what has become its defining moment in history: a congregation so epic in scale that it would come to label a generation.

5 | IN SEARCH OF ELYSIUM

WOODSTOCK

> The general human condition – war, peace, the generation gap, human rights, our re-
> lationship with the Earth – can all be looked at within a kind of metaphorical construct
> called Woodstock. Max's farm is not the important thing; it's about going back to the
> Garden, wherever the Garden is.
>
>   – Michael Wadleigh (quoted in Anon. n.d.)

> This thing was too big. This thing was too big for the world … When they see this in
> the moving pictures they'll really see something.
>
>   – Sidney Westerville (extract from introduction to *Woodstock*)

In July 1969 President Richard Nixon's NASA beat the Soviets to lay claim to Earth's
satellite, fulfilling Kennedy's 1961 promise to put a man on the lunar surface by the
end of the decade; Americans had conquered space itself, planting their flag alongside a plaque reading, 'We came in peace for all mankind.' Back on Earth, for the
USA's grounded populace, it had been a turbulent two years since Hendrix sung
of kissing the sky at Monterey Pop. The Vietnam War was going disastrously – to
the disbelief of aghast patriots[1] – and looking as if it would end in stalemate. The
Tet Offensive[2] of January 1968 saw fighting and casualties escalate dramatically,
with 80,000 Viet Cong guerrillas launching assaults on every city in South Vietnam
following an audacious attempt to capture the US embassy; America would win
this particular battle, but at the cost of much public support. The government's
Middle-American mandate began to ebb as consensus turned gradually against
continued escalation.

   Vivid filmed and photographed coverage of retaliatory executions brought home
to many the butchery with which the protracted conflict in South-East Asia was destroying young men. In Saigon, cameramen filmed the national police chief shooting a captured Cong guerrilla at point-blank range; bloody pieces of cranium were
freeze-framed spurting from the exit wound. On patrol in Quang Ngai Province on
6 March, American soldiers entered the town of My Lai seeking to ensnare enemy
troops. When villagers refused to cooperate and yield up the guerrillas, the GIs
murdered more than 350 of them by burning, shooting, bayoneting and explosion.[3]
Anti-war protestors and moderates alike seized upon the mounting moral outrage,
citing incidents like these as proof of America's incompetence and culpability in
an insane struggle. President Lyndon B. Johnson tacitly conceded that continued

escalation would not work, whilst simultaneously stepping up the blanket bombing campaign against the enemy's towns and hamlets; peace seemed further away than ever. Hundreds of US troops, and hundreds of Vietnam's civilians, were losing their lives every week; the 'unbridgeable chasm' (Isserman & Kazin 2000: 261) between the generations grew wider as Johnson's political reputation fell apart.

On 31 March, with the election looming, a tired Johnson decided not to accept the imminent party nomination (that as an incumbent he would have received, in spite of national difficulties and competition) and to stand down. By moving aside he hoped to remedy some of the racial, ideological and political discordance that lay behind the civil unrest of his tenure's latter times. On 4 April the non-violent and greatly revered black rights activist Martin Luther King Jr was shot dead by a sniper, fuelling many black citizens' rage at years of white oppression. That night, regardless of pleas for calm by the President, rioting erupted in Washington, D.C., prompting turmoil in 130 other cities. In Haight Street, San Francisco – until recently the Mecca of the 'Love Generation' – every shop window was smashed; Chicago's impoverished West Side experienced arson and looting on a massive scale. 'Now that they've taken Dr King off', exclaimed black rights leader Stokely Carmichael, 'it's time to end this non-violence bullshit' (quoted by Isserman & Kazin 2000: 227). Radicalism was globally ubiquitous in 1968. In Paris, left-wing students took over the Latin Quarter, inciting a walk-out by ten million workers and ultimately bringing down de Gaulle's government; riots, most of which were student-led, took place in Berlin, Tokyo, Bologna, Milan, Mexico and Czechoslovakia, provoking often overly aggressive repression from police. There were, in 1968, 150 violent demonstrations (plus many more non-violent showings of dissent) on US university campuses alone. American liberalism took a further blow when Robert Kennedy – a champion of the underprivileged – was shot dead in a hotel lobby whilst celebrating his victory in the key California primary; his killer was a deranged Arab nationalist.

Narrowly defeating Democrat Hubert Humphrey, Republican candidate Richard Nixon assumed office on 20 January 1969, requesting during the swearing-in ceremony that the customary Bibles be opened to Isaiah 2:4: 'They shall beat their swords into plowshares, and their spears into pruning hooks: nation shall not lift up sword against nation, neither shall they learn war anymore' (see Nixon 1978: 366). Seven months later, courtesy of four wealthy young men who at least shared Nixon's enthusiasm for inculcatory self-promotion, a pop festival took place on a farm in Bethel, New York. Promising 'Three Days of Peace and Music', the Woodstock Music and Arts Fair was the brainchild of Michael Lang, Artie Kornfeld, John Roberts and Joel Rosenman, the oldest of whom was 26. Beating the Maysles brothers, Pennebaker and Richard Leacock[4] to the commission, filmmaker Michael Wadleigh withdrew $50,000 from his personal and business accounts to pay for film stock, promising his crew double time if the movie of the festival was a success – on the understanding that they would receive nothing if it was not. During the weekend of 15–18 August roughly half a million people (as many as were US soldiers in Vietnam) converged upon Max Yasgur's pasture in upstate Sullivan

County to create a counter-cultural mini-nation, and one of America's worst-ever traffic jams.

Woodstock begins with local publican Sidney Westerville's straight-to-camera remembrance, a homage that portends the multitudinous enormity of the event and praises the young visitors' respectfulness to their rural elders:

> I was here when this crowd really came. We expected fifty thousand a day and there must have been a million … And the kids were wonderful. I had no kick, it was 'sir' this and 'sir' that, and 'thank you' this and 'thank you' that. Nobody can complain about the kids.

The amiable landlord's awkward cadence and austere appearance indicate that he is neither a practised performer nor a hippie; Wadleigh thus forwards him as an apparently non-conspiratorial and reliable herald of (and witness to) the film's vista. Westerville attempts to give what he feels is an appropriately considered performance for the camera, but his stilted delivery highlights an indifference to the rhetorical conventions of contemporaneous documentary: direct cinema's contingent naturalism is normally more dependant upon spontaneity (and those serendipitous accidents that then necessarily occur) than planning. By including Westerville's naïve tribute as an introduction, Wadleigh acknowledges his parochial subject's persuasive charm for both cineastes and the broader public alike, and imbues *Woodstock* with an egalitarian dimension. Consequent to this short preamble and its use of the past perfect tense, the film in main is presented as a flashback: a remembrance and record of a fleeting time when the 'wonderful' kids 'really came' to the idyllic meadows of Bethel.[5]

'GOING UP THE COUNTRY': THE INVASION OF SULLIVAN COUNTY

We dissolve to a series of images depicting the farm just before the festival. Crosby, Stills and Nash's wistful 'Long Time Gone' underscores the sequence of bucolic scenes featuring hippies on horseback, rolling fields, swaying grass, the local farmers tending crops and the huge, wooden stage being erected:

> It's been a long time comin'.
> It's goin' to be a long time gone.

David Crosby's words (written in despair on the night of Robert Kennedy's assassination) have an obvious import in this new context: what is happening, or what is about to happen, is a momentous climax to a sadly transient age – a one-off. Michael Lang, the festival's hirsute and shirtless co-organiser, gives an on-site interview to a conservatively turned-out reporter for television network ABC:

Lang: I guess the biggest hassle is dealing with politics, you know?
ABC: Is there a lot of politics involved, you mean with the cities? And you've got that solved?

Lang: Looks that way…
ABC: How long did it take you to put it together, about two or three months?
Lang: About nine months…
ABC: Where are you gonna go from here? Are you gonna do another one?
Lang: If it works.

The reporter repeatedly rubs his short hair as if willing it to grow, as if by becoming a 'longhair' his foundering rapport with Lang might improve through instant spiritual cohesion. Irrespective of this mainstream journalistic attention, the young venture capitalist appears desperate to ride off on his motorbike to attend to more pressing concerns. Unlike Dylan, he bears no real malice, but he is nonetheless singularly uninterested in disclosure.

Another montage is cut to 'Going Up the Country', by Canned Heat:

I'm gonna leave the city, got to get away,
I'm gonna leave the city, got to get away,
All this fussin' and fightin',
Man I just can't stay.

Although singer Bob Hite introduces the song by bemoaning the lack of toilet facilities ('This is the most outrageous spectacle ever, but there's only one thing I wish … I sure gotta pee!'), his lyric's sentiments seem sincere, and redolent of the era's harking for simplicity. One theme more prevalent in *Woodstock* than in *Monterey Pop* is that of returning to the 'Garden', to a pre-industrial, pastoral ideal far removed (or as far as was possible) from the 'hassle', and the 'fussin' and fightin'' of the cities.

Agrarian idealism has, historically, been a common reaction against technology's encroachment upon the land and lives of the New World. As the railroads pressed further west, signalling and contributing to the expansion of America's commercial and industrial infrastructure, many sought withdrawal from 'civilisation's growing power and complexity', and to find a naturally harmonious alternative (see Marx 1964: 9). Author Washington Irving, writing in 1842, expressed a longing to 'blow up all the cotton mills … and make picturesque ruins of them all'. 'If the Garden of Eden were now on Earth', he complained, six years later, 'they would not hesitate to run a railroad through it' (quoted in Maier *et al.* 2003: 411). Michael Wadleigh avers that this yen finds its precedent in the Old World:

Everyone thinks of it as sort of the seminal event of the Sixties generation, indeed, we're called The Woodstock Generation after the festival. But the other interesting thing is that it's like *The Canterbury Tales*, or *Pilgrim's Progress*. It's really a timeless idea where you see kids streaming out of the cities that are so dirty and complex and pollution-ridden and crime-ridden, coming to the countryside. You know, back to the land, back to the Garden, to sort of this pristine natural setting that has the lakes and trees and so on, and the innocence of nature. (Quoted in Bell 1999: 11)

NASA had just expended untold resources putting a few men on the Moon, but a vast number of people wanted instead to get closer to the still fecund Mother Earth, to regress to a time of opportunity and peace when the virgin wilderness could be tamed, but not raped.

Allied to this abiding and well-meaning urge was an irrational, hedonistic abandon, which, at Woodstock, knew almost no bounds:

> I'm going, I'm going where the water tastes like wine,
> I'm going where the water tastes like wine,
> We can jump in the water,
> Stay drunk all the time.

An ebullient young man (yoga instructor Tom Law), framed in close-up with a wide-angle lens,[6] pulls open a can of beer and guzzles it down, spilling froth on himself and the camera; there is a slow pan along some stoned 'freaks', one of whom appears narcoleptic; eccentrically modified buses form psychedelic encirclements within which camps have sprung up; and children dance with adults, silhouetted against the blue moonlight. These shots comprise an absorbing portrait of the 'Love Generation' similar in purpose and composition to Pennebaker's montages in *Monterey Pop*; but the hair is now wilder, the clothes more outlandish, the air hazier and the light more diffused – it is altogether more otherworldly.[7] Some smiling nuns stroll through a group of hippies, one of the sisters affably throwing a 'peace' sign to the camera, a gesture that is freeze-framed for a short time to heighten the essential human congruity (and the humour) of two seemingly disparate factions displaying at least a superficial unity.

For the first time, the film now deploys its flamboyant split-screen technique, forcing the spectator to decide where to look at any one time in a given composite.[8] Wadleigh engenders an even greater sense of overwhelming enormity, and an inference, perhaps, that if Woodstock is 'too big for the world', then it is surely too big for a single frame of film. Images come thick and fast in two adjacent framings as the stage is readied at night, and hundreds of abandoned cars clog the roads, bumper to bumper. A middle-aged couple are interviewed about their reaction to the influx of hippies:

[*Woodstock*] Crew: What do you think about it?

Woman: Well, we were standing on the curbs watching them come in last night, and all the townspeople. It was just like an army invading the town – it's hard to believe!

Crew: Do you live here?

Woman: No, we're here for a vacation.

Crew: Oh, are you! Are you having one?

Woman: We did up until last night. They kept us up for a while.

Crew: Who's 'they?'

Man: The freaks. [to hippie] Is that what you call yourselves?

Hippie: Sure. That's what everybody else calls us.

103

Man:	What do you call yourselves that for?
Hippie:	We admit it. Compared to everybody else we're freaks.
Man:	As long as you behave yourselves, there's nothing wrong.
Hippie:	I'm not putting bad connotations on the word 'freak'.

Central to this section is the notion (motivated by Sidney Westerville's introduction) of a benevolent invasion. The townsfolk reiterate their cautious yet accepting view of a financially valuable, harmless in-pouring of 'freaks': 'It's a great shot to Sullivan County, business-wise'; 'They're beautiful people, beautiful people'; 'It's been kind of overwhelming ... I'll say one thing for the young people, they've been very nice, all of them. So far anyway.' Helicopter shots emphasise the scale of the convergence upon the congested town, as the Grateful Dead's Jerry Garcia gives his own, awestruck perspective: 'It's really amazing. It looks like some kind of biblical, epical, unbelievable scene ... The cars look like jackstraws from the helicopter; there's just a continual flow of people.' It becomes apparent that the boundary fence will not be ready in time, and that Woodstock will be a free festival. Promoter Bill Graham suggests blocking the New York State Thruway: 'There has to be some control ... There has to be some way of stopping the influx of humanity.' But, the incursion still swells exponentially.

Michael Lang concedes to the returned ABC reporter that he may not break even: 'The point is that it's happened ... It's working. That's enough for now.' Trying to comprehend the motivation behind such a massive assemblage of young people (and how it could possibly be 'working' on a financial loss), the journalist asks:

ABC:	What is it that musicians have that they can communicate so well to the kids?
Lang:	*Music.*
ABC:	But there's always been music.
Lang:	Music has always been a major form of communication, but now the lyric and the type of music is a little bit more involved in society than it was.

We see some bands brought in by Marine helicopter (not a vehicle most at the festival ever hoped to see), Jerry Garcia holds a joint aloft ('Marijuana: Exhibit A'),[9] a nervous Janis Joplin worriedly exclaims, 'Look at all those people!' and the music begins with black folksinger Richie Havens' 'Handsome Johnny':

Hey look-a-yonder tell me what's that you see,
Marching to the fields of Concord.
Looks like Handsome Johnny with his flintlock in his hand,
Marching to the Concord war,
Hey, marching to the Concord war...[10]

Robed like an African magus, soaked with sweat and with his eyes screwed shut, the imposing Havens passionately delivers his message of the sad inevitability of intra- and international conflict. Wadleigh shoots Havens' insistently swinging foot, which heavily pounds the stage to demarcate the beat, in a framing that recalls Joplin and Shankar in *Monterey Pop*. Though Havens does not mention Vietnam by name in this rendition, he does not have to; the song summarises the collective attitude of the more politically attentive audience members towards all war, and starts the concert on an appropriate note of protestation – one man addressing world apathy, voicing publicly what Dylan had said at the 1963 March on Washington: 'What's the point of singing this song? Some of you are not even listening.'

Massed revellers trample the chicken-wire fence to the ground and pour onto the pasture, as co-organiser Artie Kornfeld professes that this is 'at the point where it's just family, man'. Producer John Morris is less amused, and waves the camera away so that he may confer with Lang and Kornfeld in private. 'You are now giving the world's greatest three-day freebie.' 'That's the way to do it, man', replies Kornfeld. The camera pulls back and shoots the huddled trio from afar, as the PA system broadcasts that, 'It's a free concert from now on ... The people running this thing are going to take a bath – a big bath.' Woodstock's optimistic architects, or so it appears, have lost all control over the fate and consequences of their scheme.

All kinds of 'freaks' wander the site, some inebriated, some, like legendary hippie personality Wavy Gravy (alias Hugh Romney, occasional Woodstock emcee, Merry Prankster[11] and member of the Hog Farm commune[12]), by nature enthusiastic. Romney roams, dressed in a floppy hat and wielding a tambourine on a stick, looking for people with whom to talk or share his kazoo. He chats to a shaven-headed policeman, the camera craning down to frame the solemn law officer's pistol (on which he assertively rests the ball of his thumb in the manner of a Hollywood western gunfighter) and Romney's sceptre-like tambourine stick, the incompatible symbols of their respective vocations. Two extremes of cultural expression are juxtaposed, with the straight lawman facing the 'Wavy' jester, or more accurately, the lawman facing someone whose thinking operates at variance to the concept of the need for law. We receive a quite different picture than Pennebaker's approbatory, 'everything is hunky-dory' affirmation of unity between two opposites – there is instead an appreciable tension.[13] A warning about a bad batch of LSD is broadcast by Wavy Gravy ('It's not poison, it's just badly made') and a distressed-looking Tim Hardin slurs some improvised lyrics.[14]

The camera encircles Hardin as he ambles, adding to a sense of disquiet. Noise builds up on the soundtrack to a cacophonous and suitably panic-stricken combination of a helicopter, the 'Earth Lights' men and women chanting, 'He loves me, he loves me not...' and 'Explosive, explosive, explosive', the tuning of a guitar and a motorcycle's droning engine: this is an interesting collage, but not a pleasant experience. 'Much of what is greatest in human achievement', expounded Bertrand Russell in his *History of Western Philosophy*, 'involves some element of intoxication, some sweeping away of prudence by passion. Without the Bacchic element, life would be uninteresting'; but, he maintained, 'with it, it is dangerous. It is not a conflict in which we ought to side wholly with either party' (1996: 26). As a means by which to negate the suggested effects of the drugs and the consequent paranoia, Wadleigh introduces a familiar, comforting presence: the scorned female protagonist of *Dont Look Back*, now venerated as the hippies' deific Earth Mother – an Artemis to counter Dionysus.

DREAMERS AND DOERS: 'NO DICE, SON, YOU GOTTA WORK LATE'

The film cuts to some homely snapshots of Joan Baez and her husband David Harris (who was then in prison for draft refusal), followed by the pregnant Baez onstage at night, picked-out by a spotlight:

> I'd like to sing you a song that is one of my husband David's favourite songs. And let me just tell you, he's fine … and we're fine, too! [Baez pats her stomach] And David was just shipped from the county jail, which is very much of a drag, to a federal prison, which is kind of like a big summer camp after you've been in county jail.

We cut away to Baez offstage, who outlines the bad treatment and threats Harris received while in the county prison: 'The first time he felt afraid was when a couple of guards started talking very loudly [saying] "we're gonna get you, motherfucker", and he prayed a little bit harder…'. Back on stage, Baez tells us that Harris organised a hunger strike, before she commences a song on her guitar:

> I dreamed I saw Joe Hill last night,
> Alive as you and me,
> Says I 'but Joe you're ten years dead',
> 'I never died', said he…
>
> From San Diego up 'til Maine,
> In every mine and mill,
> Where working men defend their rights,
> It's there you find Joe Hill,
> It's there you find Joe Hill.

Written by Earl Robinson in 1938, 'Joe Hill' concerns the legacy of the eponymous union organiser and folksinger, executed (on circumstantial evidence) for murder. On the eve of his death in November 1915, Hill sent a telegram to the Industrial Workers of the World (or 'Wobblies') leadership, saying, 'Don't waste any time in mourning. Organise' (see Hardy & Laing 1995: 426).

'Joe Hill', like Havens' 'Handsome Johnny', is a statement of general advocacy employing specific, historical examples; the former promotes solidarity, the latter peace.[15] Both songs express contemporaneous relevance also: 'Joe Hill' to David Harris's anti-draft hunger strike and peaceful lobbies, 'Handsome Johnny' to the ending of lives in the jungles. Folk music, moreover, inherently complemented the Woodstock philosophy of returning to the Garden, as David Hajdu observes:

> A music historical by nature, it conjured distant times … celebrating the past rather than the 'new' and 'improved', those ostensibly synonymous selling points of the

post-war era. It was small in scale – a music of modest ambitions easy to perform alone, even *a cappella*, without a big band or orchestrations – when American society, with its new supermarkets, V-8 engines, and suburban sprawl, appeared to be physically ballooning. Folk music was down to earth when jet travel and space exploration were emerging. (2002: 11)

Baez, shot reverently from a low-angle, also sings, *a cappella*, 'Swing Low, Sweet Chariot', a traditional Negro spiritual in which she demonstrates not only her ability to diversify from the chiefly rock- and pop-based scope of Woodstock's music, but also her disciplined, operatic mezzo-soprano's commanding presence on a big stage. As the archetypal hippie Earth Mother (or New Age Virgin Mary – the 'Madonna of the disaffected') (Didion 2001: 40), Baez is Woodstock's iconic crux, the embodiment of benevolence.[16]

In distinction to the mannerly articulation of Joan Baez, the Who use volume to drive home their abrasive message from the opposite pole of the counter-cultural axis. A shout of defiance to American hippies from four English rock 'n' rollers, 'Summertime Blues' is a cover of Eddie Cochran's original holler of teenage despondency. Guitarist and *de facto* bandleader Pete Townshend wears a white boiler suit, the uniform not of a rock star or sub-cultural eccentric, but a sanitary worker or civil authority employee: he removes himself from the throng by adopting a sartorially converse look. Importantly, though, it is not a tailored ensemble denoting Establishment affiliation, but a working-class outfit; Townshend is asserting sympathy (unlike Baez, who is concerned with heartfelt but detached sermonising) to the *working* man, the proletarian demographic that sought partial escape through the 'hops' and dances at which white rock 'n' roll was first promulgated. He is doing a job, not promoting an ethos or affecting a stance.[17] 'Young Americans', admitted Townshend, years later, 'were concerned about being blown to bits in Vietnam ... I [just wanted to] make my fortune and bring it back to Britain. And I didn't really give a fuck about what was happening to American young men. I really didn't' (quoted in Denselow 1990: 108).

Singer Roger Daltrey's lengthy tassels and luxuriant hair are a concession to the hippie aesthetic, but it is Townshend who governs the group's image, sound and attitude. The filmmakers emphasise his authority, working in support of the musician through concomitant visual construction and meter.[18] Split-screen cuts mimic the song's metrical suspense and release, freezing and reanimating Townshend upon his fervent power-chords' re-entrance, enhancing the performance and lending the guitarist a supernatural command over gravity (and Wadleigh a command over Townshend).[19] Cochran's lyrics put a 'downer' on the summer as the frustrated narrator's work commitments preclude romance: 'Sometimes I wonder what I'm gonna do/But there ain't no cure for the summertime blues.' No such blues preoccupied the accretion of middle-class dropouts at Woodstock, and, as if to drive a point home, Townshend ends his band's set not by wantonly destroying the tool of his trade (as he and Hendrix did at Monterey, and as the crowd must have expected), but by hammering it down with punishing force onto the stage and disdainfully throwing it to the concertgoers. Baez employs sedentary mollification to persuade with sweetly sung words of support for the miners and millers of 'Joe Hill'; Townshend prefers strident physicality and dynamism: raw, surly anger unleashed with aplomb on the quixotic but increasingly forlorn 'love crowd'.

FIVE PHASES OF FANTASY – (3) THE FRUSTRATION STAGE

> As the straining for an unattainable resolution increases … the heady delights of anticipation are flecked more and more with frustration, which eventually leads to the *Frustration Stage*…
>> – Christopher Booker (1969: 72)

As we have seen in *Monterey Pop* (and more obliquely in Bob Dylan's infidelity to Joan Baez), the Sexual Revolution was something of a poisoned chalice in terms of women's liberation. To the maturing 'baby-boomers'[20] who had consensually embraced polygamy (or 'free love'), Woodstock was the perfect, annexed testing ground for the libertine ideas of Herbert Marcuse, among others,[21] who criticised advanced capitalism's 'repressive desublimation':

> The unsublimated, unrationalised release of sexual relations would mean the most emphatic release of pleasure as such and the total devaluation of work for work's sake. The tension between the innate value of work and the freedom of pleasure could not be tolerated by the individual: the hopelessness and injustice of working conditions would strikingly penetrate the consciousness of individuals and render impossible their peaceable regimentation in the social system of the bourgeois world. (Quoted in Robinson 1972: 49)

In the following dialogue, two young and insightful attendees describe their open relationship and philosophical outlook to an unseen interviewer from Wadleigh's crew:

Boy: There's a lot of girls here, and they're probably a lot freer than other places. I'm sure there's gonna be a lot of balling! [laughs]…

Crew: Are you two going together?

Boy and Girl: No!

Crew: But you come up here together?

Boy and Girl: Yeah.

Crew: And you like that?

Boy: Yeah. I like her; I love her. I enjoy her.

Crew [to girl]: What do you think about all that?

Girl: Well, the way I look at it, I've known Gerry for four, five, six months now, when he moved in to the family group that I already knew for quite a while. In that time I got to know him real well, and I learned to love him. Like, you know, we ball and everything, but, it's like a pretty good thing, because I have plenty of freedom, because we're not going together and we're not *in* love or anything like that, you know?

A young and extremely perceptive couple of hedonists in *Woodstock* (1970)

The young woman goes on, somewhat melancholically, to explain that she cannot communicate with her parents because they do not understand her and her mother is sure that she will go to hell, a place the young woman feels does not exist. In their stated rejection of parental control and value imposition, the two conform wholly to the stereotypical hippie mindset, but seem nonetheless prematurely world-weary, dismissing the taking of drugs as 'almost contrived' (though whilst smoking a joint), and the idea of popular revolution as 'mass insanity'. Perhaps they have been looking for a panacea they now know can never be found: as the boy says, 'I just want to be myself, and find some place where I can maintain some kind of balance within myself.' The tenets they have turned against (family order, discipline, monogamy, religion) in search of an alternative represent for them the impedimenta of an abhorrent, repressive regime, but the consequent disillusionment and spiritual disquiet appear to have affected their psyche. As the 1960s drew to a close, it was becoming apparent that the 'new explanation' held no more promise than the old one. It was more than ever an existential quest with no obvious answer: 'The Hamlet trip – to be or not to be?', as the boy ruminates.

The 'beautiful people' at Woodstock had made a choice of sorts: Nixon and Kissinger were bad; Vietnam was bad; conservatism, the Old Guard and parents were wrong – but what was good and who was right? Whilst these sentiments of dissent are worthy, there is something contrite about the young couple's realisation of their once promising ethic's impending, ignominious dwindle to powerlessness. Indiscriminate sex without committal love had led not to a new state of enlightenment, but to the ultimately frustrating pointlessness of sybaritism, a placebo of which, like drugs and unidentifiable objectives, the more cerebral were already growing tired:

Boy: It's like, people that are nowhere, are coming here 'cause there's people
        that they think are somewhere. Everybody's looking for some kind of an-
        swer, when there isn't one … People don't know. They don't know how to
        live, and they don't know what to do … People are very lost, I think.

In a London *Evening Standard* report of 1961, 'Teenage Morals and the Corruption
of Society', judge Mr Justice Stable is quoted as saying, 'Girls are now getting to
have no sense of responsibility. They do not know right from wrong and they [only
talk about] sex. They think that it is part of their lives' (quoted in Comfort 1963:
98). This archaic tirade from the decade's beginning prophesies the fall of civilisation due to lax female morality and young women attaching 'as much importance
to the fact of sexual intercourse as they do to ordering an iced lolly' (ibid.). By the
decade's de-censored closure it was apparent that the end of the family was not
nigh, and equally so that injunctions issued by the middle-aged – perhaps born
out of jealousy, as Dr Alex Comfort (1963: 95) suggests – against casual sex held
no sway with adolescents seeking enjoyment (as they always had) and escape
from societal norms. More steadfast adherents to the alternative lifestyle with its
concomitant openness could influence, but never entirely replace, that which they
sought to supersede. 'Back then', claims festival attendee Jesse Slokum, 'many
people growing up saw how much cheating was going on, and how much divorce
there was, and thought "what's the point of limiting sexual relations to marriage
if it's not going to be honoured?"' However, Slokum's beliefs, expressed with
hindsight in 2002, tend markedly toward conformism (notwithstanding a certain
reticence): 'My impulse now is to say I was young and foolish then … eventually
seeing through the presumptions of the times … one makes adjustments … it's
like building a foundation for a house … you don't start the walls until the baseline
is plumb.'[22]

With no defined goal, the Woodstock Generation's dream could not be realised, and the infrastructure of the United States' intrinsically familial foundation
would prevail as the most stable national framework even in the face of unusually massive youth rebellion. Woodstock, beneath its commendable, benevolent
endeavours – to bring about a global shift in consciousness; to usher-in the Age
of Aquarius; to end the Vietnam War – could not escape its primal nature as the
1960s' Bacchanalian climax.

GETTING HIGH AT THE HOP WITH SWAMI SATCHIDANANDA: WHAT'S HAPPENING IN AMERICA?

The aim of all Eastern religion, like the aim of LSD, is basically to get high.
    – Timothy Leary (quoted in Turner 1995: 62)

Yoga master Swami Satchidananda's homily at the festival is not without a touch
of absurdity. He declares (to great applause) his desire that America, which 'leads
the world in several ways', should now lead the world spiritually.[23] It would seem
that the love crowd, with their promiscuous, acquiescent and malleable natures,

appealed to the 'Woodstock Guru' as potential global leaders; equally, his ethnicity and genial persona attracted the Woodstock Generation to him. An authentic, Indian Sannya monk (whose bushy, white beard and saffron robe Wadleigh savours), Satchidananda's address speaks volumes of a duality central to the counter-culture's ultimate ineffectiveness: hedonism paired with ersatz spirituality in an often poorly considered quest for New Age cachet.

1950s' nostalgia-act Sha-Na-Na's incredulously-received 'At the Hop' is deceptively anachronistic. The simplicity and truth in a lyric advocating nothing more than abandonment to dance is closer to the real heart of Woodstock's purpose than the lauded protestation of Baez or Havens. The decade was ending, the revolutionary optimism fading fast and the hyper-political New Left groups with which the hippies noncommittally intermingled had splintered or dissolved: why not just cast aside transcendental, reformist or pastoral pretensions and hold a saturnalia for its own sake, where the 'water tastes like wine'?

> Well, you can swing it you can groove it,
> You can really start to move it at the hop.
> Where the jockey is the smoothest,
> And the music is the coolest at the hop.
> All the cats and chicks can get their kicks at the hop.
> Let's go![24]

At the town hop of the late 1950s as evoked by Sha-Na-Na, the music is merely cool, not far-out. At the hop, you can drink, dance, perhaps have sex and then go home to your parents in a cherished car – without any desire for existential lucidity. This simple, suburban means of adolescent release (and the superannuated 'doo-wop' genre) was not enough for progressive partygoers: there had to be something else, something more meaningful.[25]

The motivation behind the secondary and often superficial desire for metaphysical fulfilment expressed by the hippies of the 1960s lies partly in the cyclical patterns of industrialised America's historical self-destruction, and partly in a belief that entrenched white, Judaeo-Christian intolerances were still holding sway over the nation a century after the Thirteenth Amendment. Following the Gold Rush came the ghost towns; the illicit alcohol-fuelled fever of the Roaring Twenties gave way to the Wall Street Crash, the Great Depression and Fitzgerald's fabled Gatsby, literary embodiment of America's Jazz Age, floating dead in his own pool; after the frivolity, so said history, must come the Hoovervilles.[26] Doo-wop and rock 'n' roll, like Jelly Roll Morton's 'Doctor Jazz' ('He's got what I need, I'll say he has!'), had brought only momentary respite from the worries of humanity and its economies' boom-and-bust tendencies. At the dawn of the Age of Aquarius,[27] thought the hippies (inspired by Timothy Leary), by looking elsewhere for their kicks – to the more novel stimulants LSD and marijuana, and to the ancient wisdom of the East – a spiritual infusion would provide the syncretistic impetus for lasting transformation. 'We're not on the Christ trip', evangelised Leary. 'That's been done, and it doesn't work. You prove your point, and then you have 2,000 years of war. We know where that trip goes' (quoted in Wolfe 1971: 173). If God-fearing Mississippian Elvis Pres-ley had 'stolen' rock 'n' roll from its oppressed, black progenitors, then now was the time for young, white Americans to assuage their religious guilt and become closer to divinity through a new, hybridised form of musical and physical release:

> Blue suede shoes were left behind in favour of blue onyx sea, gamma rays, vibrations and astral planes. Instead of riding along in your automobile, you were now 'speed-ing through the universe' or 'taking a place on this trip...'. There was confusion as to whether you were getting blissed out or ripped on acid... (Turner 1995: 73)

(Pennebaker, we remember, chose to climax *Monterey Pop* with Ravi Shankar, not Jimi Hendrix, Otis Redding or Janis Joplin.)

When the hop became instead a 'be-in', physical thrills, given a quasi-mystical motivation, could be justified and reconciled with intellectual concerns, however weakly conceived. William L. O'Neill explains:

> At advanced universities social smoking of marijuana was as acceptable as social drinking. More so, in a way, for it was better suited to the new ethic ... And it helped further distinguish between the old world of grasping, combative, alcoholic adults and the turned-on, co-operative culture of the young. Leary was a bad prophet. Drug-based mystical religion was not the wave of the future. What the drug cult led to was a lot of dope-smoking and some hard drug-taking. (1971: 239)

Sha-Na-Na, stylistically incongruous though they are, belong amongst the 'freaks' as pan-stick-complected ghosts from a party long-ended, a reminder that Wood-stock, the greatest hop ever held, must eventually come to a parodic end itself, no matter how intellectually liberated or progressive its attendees. The youngsters at the festival aimed to demonstrate contempt for a proselytising culture of unfeel-ing capitalism and intransigent normalcy. In fact, 'Uncle Tim's Children', for that was what San Franciscans were calling followers of the 'Psychedelic Revolution', inadvertently paved the way for an even worse societal blight of chemical depend-ence. They disparaged their elders for drinking and tranquilising, yet their habits, to sceptics, seemed no different. Post-war America, as Satchidananda says, may indeed have led the world in several ways, but its more indolent youngsters – the 'supermarket hunter-gatherers' (Scully & Dalton 1996: 135) – were far from spiritu-ally convincing, or politically astute enough to inherit the Congressional mantle. Poet and author Jeff Nuttall makes this point emphatically:

> The significant difference between [hippie] culture and the [American] Indian culture (which it oh-so-consciously imitates) is that Indians balanced and supported their mo-bility with portable skills like hunting, riding and fortitude, whilst the West Coast hip-pies were utterly parasitic in that their whole self-maintenance relied on the excess material in the over-materialistic culture they purported to despise. (1968: 205)[28]

'Of such ironies', writes O'Neill, 'was the counter-culture built' (1971: 240).[29]

THE FATE OF OUR BABIES: WHAT ARE WE FIGHTING FOR?

John Sebastian begins his set with an ad-libbed monologue, the aim of which seems to be elevation of the festival organisers' public relations status: 'Just love everybody all around you, and clean up a little garbage on the way out and everything gonna be all right … And the fence, you have to look after the fence, man: the press can only say bad things unless there ain't no fuck-ups – and it's looking like there ain't gonna be no fuck-ups.' Emcee Chip Monck informs the audience that a woman has had a baby. 'Wow, this really is a city', ponders an observably high Sebastian, before launching into 'The Younger Generation', a folksy assemblage of ruminations on the generation gap.

Together with its accompanying montage, the song constitutes *Woodstock*'s only over-romantic moment. We see shots, slow-dissolved together, of naked babies frolicking, a breast-feeding mother and the clumsy attempts of small, cute children to play the drums. Wadleigh's visual approach, previously so urbane in its supplementing of events, now works to elicit wonder: analogously to Pennebaker's *Monterey Pop*, the employment of simplistic concatenations and agreeable imagery subordinates nuance to sentimentality. When Sebastian is interrupted by the noise of a helicopter's blades and the editors cut back to the stage by way of explanation, it is a moment of respite from this shrewdly placed, calculatedly mawkish presage.

A thrilling counterpoint follows. Country Joe McDonald, wearing an irreverently open-necked US Army shirt, rouses the crowd with his 'I-Feel-Like-I'm Fixin'-to-Die-Rag', a sardonic missive aimed directly at the patriotism of Vietnam advocates:

Yeah, come on all of you big strong men,
Uncle Sam needs your help again.
He's got himself in a terrible jam,
Way down yonder in Vietnam.
So put down your books and pick up a gun,
We're gonna have a whole lotta fun.

And it's one, two, three,
What are we fighting for?
Don't ask me I don't give a damn,
Next stop is Vietnam.
And it's five, six, seven,
Open up the pearly gates,
Well there ain't no time to wonder why,
Whoopee! We're all gonna die…

Well, come on mothers throughout the land,
Pack your boys off to Vietnam.
Come on fathers, don't hesitate,
Send 'em off before it's too late.

Be the first one on your block,

To have your boy come home in a box.

More openly public-spirited than the young Dylan's occasionally sour protestation and with a stirring lilt reminiscent of Woody Guthrie and Pete Seeger, the words successfully fuse a hippie's spontaneity to the measured rhetoric of a gifted topical songwriter.[30] Country Joe's ideal, appropriately (at Woodstock) rejecting the 'structured puritanism of the left wing', was 'music, fun and politics being all together' (Denselow 1990: 68–9). As Dylan turned to introspection, McDonald moved on to psychedelic performance and the student scene of Berkeley, becoming a 'protest rocker' *par excellence* on the West Coast, where political pop music had mostly degenerated into an addled mess.

The song's irony is skilfully communicated by a symbiosis of McDonald's satire and Wadleigh's treatment. A 'sing-along' lyric subtitle complete with bouncing-ball phrasing guide appears, and the absurdity of the Indochinese conflict is brought deftly to the fore; here is an ex-naval man, parodying 1920s dance-hall jazz, and in doing so making as effective a case for cessation of American involvement as Baez, Havens or the omnipresent placard-carrying demonstrators of 1969. By this point Nixon had no strategy that would guarantee American triumph: all he could do was stave off Northern victory for a few, bloodily destructive years (see Isserman & Kazin 2000: 268–9). The anti-war movement's radical factions (such as the newly formed SDS splinter group, the Weathermen, so-named after the Dylan lyric),[31] generated some negative publicity, but McDonald's send-up of governmental folly at the expense of the boys 'coming home in a box', struck a chord with GIs and civilians alike:

As a lad of 17 or so, the lyrics to 'I-Feel-Like-I'm-Fixin'-to-Die-Rag' brought into focus the wildly visceral, moral, hormonal, intellectual and political feelings and thoughts I

Country Joe McDonald's words working at one with Wadleigh's methods in Woodstock

was having at the time. And more importantly, it was about the funniest song I'd ever heard. That's probably what did it for me. 'I'll be skipping that routine', I remember telling myself at the time. Aside from the ethical arguments, it simply seemed like a really *dumb* idea. (Nyren n.d.)[32]

Wadleigh shares this effusion, declaring that, 'Someone should give him an award for that song. That is one of the greatest war songs there is' (quoted in Tiber 1994: 25). At the time of Woodstock, Country Joe McDonald was fast becoming the nemesis of high-office politicians, due mostly to this single, influential composition's Zeitgeist-epitomising zeal. Indeed, 'I-Feel-Like-I'm-Fixin'to-Die-Rag' has in no small part wrought the life of its author:

[The lyric] was blasphemous because it was, from a military point of view, essentially demanding the right to be empowered and make a decision on whether or not you're going to lose your life or not, and it dissed everybody that was important – Wall Street, the Commander-in-Chief, the generals, everybody ... so it made all the leaders mad, right? Of course ... I have become a living symbol of the Vietnam War, and now I'm a living symbol of not only the resistance to the Vietnam War, but of the veterans themselves. And almost all the veterans have come to love that song. (Quoted in Bell 1999: 223)

Wadleigh's apposition of Sebastian and McDonald presents us with a stark choice, and prompts the question of whether or not we should want our children to grow up to be Uncle Sam's 'big strong men'. When we can have the Garden, Wadleigh implores, why slaughter each other in the swamps? If we want to preserve the innocence of youth (and the lives of the typical young men presented throughout McDonald's opening 'F-U-C-K Cheer'),[33] so the film proposes, then we must work to change the system for the better, fighting for the things that matter, not for an arbitrarily superior ideology. 'The Rag' frightened the Establishment not simply because of its anti-war stance, but by virtue of its subversive take on the draft, and on those in Vice President Spiro Agnew's 'silent majority' who would wait 'sixty or ninety days' for the war to end the way they wanted (Nixon quoted in Hersh 1983: 79–80). 'I refuse to believe that a fourth-rate power like North Vietnam doesn't have a breaking point', fumed Nixon (quoted in Baritz 1998: 196), with hubris belying his lack of mandate for continuation. Young men would come home in boxes for another three years, despite the best efforts of a refrain that 'essentially said, "Fuck you, we're not going to Vietnam,"' but said it with irresistible panache (McDonald quoted in Bell 1999: 224). As McDonald leaves the stage to an embrace from John Morris, the crowd – having risen rapturously to its feet – applauds. Wadleigh underlines and seconds this appreciation by fading out the immense roar (the sound of which bridges the next splice between scenes) very slowly. We cut to a middle-aged couple attempting to mend their car:

Crew: Tell us how you feel about [the festival]...

Man: You want me to explain it in plain English? A shitty mess.

Woman: Our 150 acres were all … And we didn't rent it to them, they were all trespassing, every one of them.

Some young women approach (clearly expecting antipathy) and ask the woman, with trepidation, if they may use her telephone – a question to which she responds with maternal restraint:

Woman: This is a disaster area, we don't even have a phone – it's been out since the storm. Water I can give you. I'm sorry the phone is out …
Man (becoming harassed): It's a disgraceful mess, if you wanna know the answer … My fields are all cut up; our second cut of hay is gone; the milk truck couldn't get here, and the milk had to be thrown out.

So the invasion has not been entirely beneficial. Numbers have swollen so vastly that the townsfolk cannot cope with supporting the revellers' needs, nor confine them to Yasgur's land; the festival is 'working', but destroying its environs.

Traits more typical of the parent culture's acquisitive philosophy are already emerging. A man who runs an on-site stall selling cigarettes refuses to disclose how much money he has made (that would be 'too private'), but says he would like to see the event staged again the following year. 'Well, I can't say the farmers would', replies a more civic-minded off-screen voice. In the simultaneously displayed left-hand framing, a man flaunts the contents of his LSD 'baggie'; the cameraman's hand reaches forward, takes out an illicit pill and handles it for our perusal. Leering at the camera's wide-angle lens, a young man (wearing, very typically, a Che Guevara T-shirt)[34] rolls one on his tongue and swallows it. A colourful plethora of marijuana pipes, water bongs and chillums are on sale at another stall, a hip but nonetheless capitalistic venture operating at the heart of the Garden. 'What about the garbage?' 'Where there's people there's garbage', comes the cigarette seller's retort. 'You can't stop progress.'

PARADISE ON BETHEL POND: 'HOW SWEET THE PHENOMENA OF THE LAKE!'[35]

The townsmen of Bethel argue about whether or not the kids they have been feeding are 'on pot'. 'If pot makes them happy and there's no trouble, maybe we should put all the adults on pot', says an even-tempered citizen. 'A fifteen-year-old girl sleeping in a tent? Are you out of your mind? It should never have happened. They're all on pot', replies his ardent neighbour. 'If you took four or five hundred adults and gave them plenty of booze you know what would have happened? We had to feed them. There was nothing else we could do.' While the dispute continues in the town, Wadleigh uses the left of the composite to introduce the picturesque lake, gradually zooming in on some nude bathers enjoying what seems to be a conversely serene experience:

Male bather: About a year ago I wouldn't have believed it, but this is the way to swim. It's the way to go all the time actually.

Crew: Think that's gonna happen?

Male bather: It's gotta happen! Everybody's free, everybody's talking ... Every
body's really nude!

Girl in sunglasses: I think skinny-dipping's just beautiful if you wanna do it – if
you can do it. Some people can't because their environment made them
feel that it's wrong, even though they know in their subconscious that it's
right, good and normal and natural.

Public nudity was, for the hippies, both a rejection of puritanical, establishment
values and a statement of intent: they would go back to the Garden, a time of
innocent delight in the nature of themselves, and cast aside the neuroses of modernity. Open nakedness was proscribed by law, but nevertheless a significant part
of hippie, left-wing or counter-cultural life, extending to progressive urbanites as
well as retreatants. Naomi Wolf, a San Franciscan child of the late 1960s whose
father was arrested for hosting a nude ballet, remembers the proclivity of her social group to disrobe:

Everyone, it seemed, was divesting him- or herself of clothing ... Our moms and
dads went to Esalen on weekends, or Big Sur, and sat around naked in hot tubs with
other kids' moms and dads, and other kids. 'Take it off', purred an ad for shaving
cream; 'Take it *all* off.' That was what cool people did. (1998: 53–4)

Wadleigh's representation of unclothed bodies adheres to the style of fixed, me-
dium- or long-shot framing commonplace in nudist films of the 1950s, an austere,
cautiously detached visual approach revealing sensitivity to the difficult nature of
the subject, whatever the censorial climate.[36] The thorny issue of what Bill Nichols
(1991) calls 'axiographics' again comes to the fore, though this time as a part, centrally, of the production's ethos; how should Woodstock, in the midst of the sexual
revolution, appropriately portray the 'cool people', 'taking it *all* off'?

In 1960s' America, reacting to the moral sternness of the post-war decade, liberal intellectuals argued for the abolishment of censorship, fearing that such suppression might lead to people seeking 'unhealthy' sexual channels (see Isserman
& Kazin 2000: 150).[37] Subsequent to City Lights publisher Laurence Ferlinghetti's
trial and acquittal over 'Howl''s 'obscene' content, the publication or display of
non-sexual nakedness was not, by 1969, in itself a hurdle: in 1968 the blockbusting
quasi-alternative rock musical *Hair* had already brought full-frontal sensationalism
to Broadway (proving the cigarette seller's adage, 'you can't stop progress').[38] In
American literature, skinny-dipping and outdoor nudity feature in the works of Walt
Whitman, Mark Twain, Lincoln Steffens, William Styron, Anne Morrow Lindbergh,
Herman Melville, James Michener and Henry Miller, among others, yet nowhere
in these predominantly anti-establishment writings does the need arise for artistic
detachment or literary temperance; rather, the subversive imagination celebrated
the sexual gamut. In 'Song of Myself' (a libidinous work that faced attempts at
banning), Whitman has a voyeuristic woman observe, from afar, numerous male
bathers: 'Twenty-eight men bathe by the shore ... She owns the fine house by the

rise of the bank, she hides handsome and richly drest aft the blinds of the window … she saw them and loved them' (1998: 37). *Woodstock*'s cautious treatment of a potentially 'smutty' topic, however, demonstrates great understanding, on the part of its producers, of contemporaneous Middle-American disquiet regarding popular culture's supposed role in the moral corruption of the young. At a time when US customs were routinely seizing insipid, Swedish 'skin flicks', many of which concerned the amorous exploits of counter-cultural caricatures, any cinematic depiction of similarly bare flesh inevitably trod a fine line between 'cultural pretension' and 'exploitation' – at least in the minds of the 'silent majority' (O'Neill 1971: 222). As Bertrand Russell noted, 'Prudence versus passion is a conflict that runs through history' (1996: 26), and this conflict, of course, permeates the minds of both artists and ideologues.

Frederick Wiseman was still contending with insurmountable hostility and censorship for his depiction of naked mental patients in *Titicut Follies* (1967), a misconstrued account of institutional life that reactionaries were quick to brand 'crass', and 'excessively preoccupied with nudity' (Anderson & Benson 1991: 97). What the cameraman (Al Wertheimer) encounters in the bathing scene in *Woodstock* is a problem of identity that the observational filmic style renders particularly acute. He does not want his camera to be endowed with a gender, or an erotic slant: this should be a physical return to prelapsarian Eden, and nakedness should be presented routinely, not fetishised by the 'repressed', technocratic gaze. Wertheimer does 'seek-out' women in the process of undressing, but stops short of fragmentising their secondary characteristics: 'right, good, normal and natural', as the teenager says. It is inconceivable that Pennebaker would have shot the nudists in the salacious manner in which he photographed the young women of Monterey, and so it is true that Wadleigh is aware of the boundaries, which, as an empathetic filmmaker at the heart of the idealist *milieu*, he must not cross. If nudism was to be forwarded as a 'way to go all the time', then potentially disincentivising physical factors had, paradoxically, to be suppressed. Like Hugo Van der Goes before him, Wadleigh respects his epoch's paradigms of decency.[39]

Equal screen time is given to both sexes, and the crew do not shy away from directly addressing the bathers; in this way the crew present a balanced portrayal, put themselves in a morally defensible position and pre-empt accusations of voyeurism. Editor Thelma Schoonmaker wanted to include footage of a priapic nudist, but was told by a Warner Bros. executive, 'Thelma, one hard-on and you get an X' (quoted in Bell 1999: 83). Neutered by this understandable compromise to commercial interests, the bowdlerised scene retains an endearingly ingenuous but questionable aura of complete asexuality. The bodies on display are uniformly nubile, but effectively desexualised by the utilitarian mass-communality surrounding this natural resource – the divine *aqua caelestis*. A man shaves; a woman washes; a group sing 'Row, Row, Row Your Boat': the lake is the babies' baptismal font and balneotherapeutic spa, proof that Eden (as opposed to the Garden of Earthly Delights) will provide everything for the truly 'healthy' of body and mind. 'The people of this country should be proud of these kids', says a Chief of Police to the unrelenting ABC reporter. 'They can't be questioned as good American citizens.'

The prelapsarian bathers of *Woodstock*

THE PORT-O-SAN MAN AND THE KIDS' BENEDICTION: TWO FATHERS

After Wavy Gravy announces that the Hog Farm will be providing free food ('We must be in heaven, man!'), we cut to a scene featuring the on-site portable sanitation, the 'Port-O-San', and its stoically professional attendant, who is busy with a suction pump:

Crew: You're getting a little behind on this job, aren't you?
Man: It's not the idea of being behind. It's just you can't keep up – that's what it is.
Crew: You're using quite a bit of that stuff [deodorant bar], huh?
Man: Yah. That helps give you a little pleasanter, er, odour, you know…

Despite an unenviable job tending to the few, over-spilling units meant to serve a fraction of the crowd that have arrived, the Port-O-San man remains affable:

Crew: You're doing a good job here.
Man: Glad to do it for these kids. My son's here, too. I got one over in Vietnam, too. He's up in the DMZ[40] right now, flying helicopters.

His children are simultaneously involved in the major, antithetical events that have come to define the period. One is fighting a deadly war, the other a battle against mud and badly made LSD. As the attendant bids goodbye to the crew, a very stoned man exits a previously engaged cubicle:

Crew: How was it?
Man with pipe (misunderstanding): It was outta sight! [He offers his pipe to the soundman] You want some?
Crew: Thanks, not right now. How would you rate the facilities?
Man with pipe: Huh? Oh. Wow! It beats the woods! Are you doing a movie?
Crew: Yeah.
Man with pipe: About this? What's it gonna be called?
Crew: 'Port-O-San.'
Man with pipe: Oh. Far-out.

We have seen how *Woodstock* underlines the irony of the hippies' pseudo-independent existence, and how the infrastructure of the parent culture supported its dissident young. Never, though, has the essence of 1960s America's contradictory nature been bared as it is here. The Port-O-San man is 'glad to do it for these kids', kids that do not want to work, kids that profess to want the Garden but prefer the effluent toilet and deodorant bars of modern, industrial life. His own son faces death in Indochina, flying helicopters built by industry and empire to watch over capitalist interests; his other son enjoys the spoils. There is, in the sanitary worker, a familial compassion that speaks of an all-American patriarch's best qualities: faith in the future, a belief in hard work, and the need to endure a thankless task for the good of the children. The Port-O-San man (Tom Taggart) is, according to *Woodstock*'s associate producer, Dale Bell, 'a symbol of the universality of humanity' (1999: 120). Vocal acceptance of the counter-culture by a conventionally noble elder such as Taggart at least goes some way to ratifying hippie aims; moreover, for the viewer it is a tender vindication. 'To each one of us', writes Bell, 'he was a symbol of compassion' (Bell 1999: 121).[41]

Another, more prominent inter-generational spokesman was on hand to consecrate the arena: *Woodstock*'s true, bucolic father figure, Max Yasgur. Director Michael Wadleigh remembers, 'When we arrived and looked out over Max Yasgur's glorious farm, it was obvious that the stage was a cathedral in the wilderness',[42] and his words deliberately recall Bunyan's pilgrims' arrival at the Celestial City, 'come from the City of Destruction, for the love that they bear to the King of this place' (1987: 140). If Woodstock's stage was a cathedral, to which the faithful were coming from the oppressive cities, then the performers constituted the preachers and shamans whose messages of higher consciousness and unifying love reached out from the pulpit to the souls of the congregation. Max Yasgur, the logic follows, was thus the counter-culture's divinely appointed benefactor, the humble, middle-aged dairy farmer whose land became the Garden, and whose name evoked reverence. The crowd falls silent with anticipation as John Morris heralds the landowner's appearance:

Morris: We have a gentleman with us, it's the gentleman upon whose farm we are: Mr Max Yasgur…

Yasgur: I'm a farmer [quiet applause]. I don't know how to speak to twenty people at one time, let alone a crowd like this. But I think you people have proven something to the world … This is the largest group of people ever assembled in one place. We have had no idea that there would be this size group, and because of that you've had quite a few inconveniences as far as water and food and so forth. Your producers have done a mammoth job to see that you're taken care of … But above that, the important thing that you've proven to the world, is that half a million kids – and I call you kids because I have children not older than you are – half a million young people can get together, and have three days of fun and music, and have nothing but fun and music, and I God bless [sic] you for it.

Morris makes no attempt to adapt his diction, reverting to politesse in deference to Yasgur, the genial pontiff of Bethel. Conversely, to connect with his young audience, Yasgur holds his left hand aloft in the obligatory peace salute, while the camera slowly pans to show the enthralled multitudes. The farmer knows he is now part of history, and that what he says must be especially wrought for the occasion. Half a million people, as Yasgur says, had gathered on his farm, half a million people who had not rioted or run amok (to the immense relief of the organisers), but had enjoyed, above all, 'nothing but fun and music'.

That Yasgur does not quote the festival's promotional subtitle ('Three days of peace and music') verbatim is significant: Lang and company exploited fashionable hippie phraseology, concocting a marketing dictum based on fanciful notions; Yasgur speaks only of *fun* and music, and in doing so transmits the truth behind Woodstock's pretensions. Total 'peace', in the apprehensive Cold War era (as in all eras), was a pipe dream: the word itself became a totemistic mantra for idealists. 'Fun' implies no such internal denial – Yasgur sees a hop before him, not a love-in or an 'Aquarian Exposition'. As he exultantly raises both his arms to the concert-goers, we see that Yasgur's right hand, its third and fourth fingers missing due to a mechanical accident, is improbably frozen into a permanent peace sign, a lasting reminder to the grounded King of the Celestial City that without a little luck, things can, and do, go wrong.

JIMI HENDRIX (SLIGHT RETURN): BY THE DAWN'S EARLY LIGHT

Gypsys [sic], Suns and Rainbows, Hendrix's newly expanded band, took the stage early on the Monday morning, by which time the crowd had dwindled noticeably. Most had gone home either to jobs (many were 'plastic' or part-time hippies) or to escape the squalor and poor food. A tired-looking Hendrix saunters into view, and approaches the microphone: 'I see we meet again. Hmm!' Although Hendrix's lacklustre set lasted for hours, Wadleigh cuts straight to what is by far the most poignant piece, an apocalyptic rendition of America's national anthem that provides one of *Woodstock*'s few truly great political statements, and a fitting finale.

After a lengthy, indulgent display of directionless improvisation (the legacy, so his closest friends presumed, of heroin and frustration), Hendrix found the inspiration he was looking for, and struck up, solo on guitar, 'The Star Spangled Banner'. Using feedback, distortion, whammy bar and wah-wah pedal to augment his masterful fingering (Wadleigh films Hendrix's preternaturally elongated hands in close-up), Hendrix throws his whole body into a critique of contemporary America. Charles Shaar Murray describes the radically reworked composition's aurally evocative power as a (for him) putatively specific comment on Vietnam's desecration:

> The clear, pure, trumpet-like notes of the familiar melody struggling to pierce through clouds of tear gas, the explosion of cluster-bombs, the screams of the dying, the crackle of the flames, the heavy palls of smoke stinking with human grease, the hovering chatter of helicopters... (1989: 24)

In warping Old Glory (as opposed to burning the flag), Hendrix twists the principal symbol of American national identity, subverts a sacrosanct tune and extrudes it through a personally revisionist channel.[43] Hendrix, though a pacifist, was not completely anti-Vietnam in his beliefs, viewing hard-line Communism as a menacing threat to free will and expression. In his tenure as a non-engaging paratrooper of the 101st Airborne (or the 'Screaming Eagles'), he had learned to respect the soldier's duty and function as a defensive tool, the aim of which was to safeguard his nation's liberty. Many jingoistic Americans viewed the Woodstock reading of their national hymn as an insolent travesty, but Hendrix's intentions were to give an inherently triumphal song a more elegiac dimension suited to the conflicts of the time. When asked by a reporter why he performed 'The Star Spangled Banner' in such a way, Hendrix replied:

> We are all Americans, aren't we? When it was written it was very nice and beautifully inspiring. Your heart throbs and you say, 'Great, I'm American.' Nowadays we don't play it to take away any of the greatness America is supposed to have. We play it the way the air is in America today, and that air is [full of] static. (Quoted in McDermott & Kramer 1992: 282)

This is a more pensive and contemplative young man than had lasciviously revamped 'Wild Thing' at Monterey only two years earlier. The highly-sexed theatricality is gone, as are the flamboyant, crowd-pleasing tics (the tongue-lashing, the guitar-fucking) that made Hendrix front-page news and an overnight sensation. His mournful aubade for Woodstock's end is the soundtrack to a generation's collective awakening; nothing had changed, and the introspective hangover would last a decade. 'The ironies were murderous', writes Shaar Murray: 'a black man with a white guitar; a massive, almost exclusively white audience wallowing in a paddy field of its own making' (1989: 24).

The New American Dream was deconstructing itself: Hendrix saw that the threat of revolution was empty as clearly as any anti-establishment fanatic or cynical right-wing commentator. He distrusted stifling authority and fomenting radicalism alike, but could forward no means of realising a united States or discharging the 'static' air of the late 1960s. Hendrix chose to articulate this with a uniquely expressionistic, sonic treatise of disillusionment and cataclysm that, like Bob Dylan, offered no solutions: it had been a 'long, strange trip' that had ultimately led nowhere.[44] The sub-par versions of 'Hey Joe' and 'Purple Haze' that Hendrix sang perfunctorily at Woodstock saw him reluctantly look back to a time of optimism, only recently passed, when the 'long brown path' was open before him. As the national anthem – as alien as it was familiar – surged across Bethel's mud-covered dales of human detritus, it seemed a fork had been reached at which a new musical direction might be the only road to redemption. Eddie Kramer, Woodstock's sound engineer, sensed that all was not well: 'Knowing Jimi's capabilities, I never got a good feeling as I recorded the show. Later, when I saw the film rushes and listened to the recordings in Los Angeles, I distinctly remember worrying that Woodstock might be the beginning of the end for Jimi Hendrix' (quoted in Mc-

The party, and the dream, is over (*Woodstock*)

Dermott & Kramer 1992: 277). If even those exalted arbiters of musical taste, the Beatles, were on the verge of acrimonious dissolution, what hope was there? The guitarist himself conceded that an epoch's (*his* epoch's) end was upon him:

> I've turned full circle. I'm back where I started. I've given this music everything, but I still sound the same. When the last American tour finished, I just wanted to go away and forget everything. Then I started thinking about the future, thinking that this era of music, sparked off by the Beatles, had come to an end. Something new has to come and Jimi Hendrix will be there. (Quoted in McDermott & Kramer 1992: 351)

On stage at Woodstock, Hendrix drifts back into vague extemporisation, this time with a melancholy, flamenco-tinged progression, as Wadleigh, through a plaintive montage, conveys the devastation wreaked by the festival. Lost souls wander, picking up shoes (a finality to the barefooted freedom begun in *Monterey Pop*) to see if they might fit; people scavenge for food amongst the endless mud and debris; and the sad emptiness of the once teeming stage, the Cathedral in the Wilderness now forever abandoned, brings the tragedy home: the party is over.

CONCLUSION: WHICH GARDEN?

> The illusion of blessed peacefulness in that Garden endures only for as long as do our conditioned expectations of Eden. There are the new-made Adam and Eve in the foreground, naked and awe-struck ... The trees around them are heavy with appetising fruit; there is the fountain of life behind the trees ... It is more charming than anything else [in the Garden of Earthly Delights], if you keep your distance.
> – Peter Beagle (1982: 40)[45]

A commonly held opinion of *Woodstock* is that it is a finely composed memento, but otherwise little more than *Monterey Pop*'s sybaritic, elephantine double: a three-hour advert for the 'dropped-out' lifestyle.[46] Whilst a casual viewing might lend credence to these assumptions, if we look carefully we discover interwoven undercurrents that make it more than partisan persuasion, and more substantial than a simple concert film. For every depiction of utopian bliss there is an equal and opposite moment of dystopian misery; for every hard-won counter-cultural freedom we see on screen there is a sobering reminder that the binding chains of American conservatism still held fast and strong. If there is true and lasting heaven in *Woodstock*'s essayistic vision, then it remains tantalisingly beyond the hippies' ideologically immature grasp. When the Garden's limited resources ran dry, it was back to the dirty cities, back to the cold, conditional embrace of The Man, for the heavy-hearted pilgrims who had had their three, long days (or five or more years) of peace and music. The 1970s, for many of the Woodstock Generation, would be spent mourning this perceived loss of innocence, pursuing 'sensible' careers in orthodox vocations, or battling addiction and despondency: Woodstock, as the song says, had been a long time coming, and would be a long time gone. 'The dream is over', said John Lennon to *Rolling Stone* in 1970. 'It's over and we've got to get down to so-called reality' (quoted in Turner 1995: 109).

Woodstock almost certainly could not have happened – at least not on the same enormous scale – without two catalysing factors: the baby boom and the Vietnam War. A surfeit of young people, all of whom shared a dislike of the draft and of political posturing, saw that there was a compelling reason to congregate on Yasgur's farm, if only for what might be the party of a lifetime. The shrewd organisers capitalised on both the hedonistic and spiritual needs of their customers, marketed the concert perfectly, and, as fate would have it, stumbled upon an ideal, and in hindsight charmed, site for such an event. Astutely, Wadleigh and company sensed that this would be something bigger than a run-of-the-mill love-in and invested time and money to capture the whole, expansive fabula – not just the accomplished and mostly topflight stage acts. And we do indeed construe that we have seen the *entire* festival, including its repercussions for the immediate, put-upon community of rural shopkeepers, landowners and lawmen. It is variously a 'shitty mess'; a perfect community of 'wonderful kids'; a hellhole of the 'very lost'; a heaven in which people need and feed each other; and a free-loving commune bought by free enterprise. Wadleigh, Scorsese and Schoonmaker's sophisticated, empathetic and insightful collective worldview – coupled with a persuasive 'fusion of vision and technology' (Bell 1999: 57) – articulates their subject's inherent tension with style, impact and perceptive depth. The film is all the more convincing for its peeling away of an attractive complexion to reveal the subcutaneous maladies beneath – problems that exist whether or not we deny them or brush them aside, like Pennebaker, in the name of myth-making. In a hallucinatory Mecca of mud and confusion in which 'enemy' helicopters were dropping flowers, the manifest absurdities of America's second Civil War could not be ignored. The world in front of Wadleigh's camera was not a clearly-cut Manichean template (Vietnam or Woodstock; the Navy or the Peace Corps; Them or Us); rather, it was riddled with impetuous philosophical responses to what were, on the whole, unanswerable questions.

A rhetorical case, however, *is* set out in *Woodstock*. The documentary gathers together its vast body of evidence and presents it, narrativised and carefully formulated, for us to evaluate. Wadleigh is a sagacious filmmaker, and meditative enough to realise that the positive aspects of the New Age, beliefs he now unequivocally endorses (advocation of peace, civil and economic reform and the denunciation of intolerance and environmental harm),[47] were not entirely divorced from the negative and futile hedonism, self-absorption and crises of identity that eventually wrecked the more rational hippies' commendable ideals. But it is with the contemplation of inspiring possibilities, not discouraging actualities, that *Woodstock* is concerned; at its crux is the idea that mankind really could live together in harmony, if only we appreciate what we have got, while we have got it – or, in the words of Joni Mitchell's ecological fable, 'Don't it always seem to go, you don't know what you've got 'til it's gone.'[48] The fragility of the Garden is the film's core theme; the central message is that all this fleeting happiness is bought at a price to our conscience and morals, unless, that is, we work at making it last, and truly 'set our souls free'. Mitchell's elegantly wistful 'Woodstock', performed by Crosby, Stills, Nash and Young, closes the film on an insistent note:

> By the time we got to Woodstock, we were half a million strong,
> And everywhere there was song and celebration.
> And I dreamed I saw the bombers, jet planes riding shotgun in the sky,
> Turning into butterflies above our nation.
> We are stardust, we are golden, we are caught in the Devil's bargain,
> And we've got to get ourselves back to the Garden.[49]

It would seem that the Devil still cannot be cheated. Ever more commercially cynical and logo-saturated anniversary concerts (that regularly enjoy considerably less luck than their archetypal namesake) continue to sully the dream. Whilst a dwindling band of nostalgic 1969 veterans gather illegally every year on Yasgur's farm, plans are afoot to develop the original site, and thus instigate the ultimate phase of Woodstock's commoditisation. 'I think corporate America realised, "We can sell this"', laments Arlo Guthrie, 'and so we started seeing pictures of natural women washing their hair in streams ... We have sort of wrapped it up and been buying it and selling the image in various ways for the last thirty years' (quoted in Bell 1999: 262). Soon – all counter-cultural threat having long ago liquefied into marketable nostalgia – we really will have 'paved paradise', and put up a parking lot to ease the strain on the Thruway.[50] 'We do not ride on the railroad', despaired Thoreau in *Walden*, 'it rides upon us' (Thoreau 1961: 81).

6 | COMING DOWN

'Rape, murder, it's just a shot away.'[1]

With the 'explosion into reality' every fantasy, if pushed far enough, must inevitably bring about its own self-destruction; and … behind the glittering dream of life and vitality hides nothing less than the death wish.
    – Christopher Booker (1969: 72)

GIMME SHELTER

Woodstock had been, all things considered, remarkably successful in many ways – not least in its aleatory attainment of definitive counter-cultural status. Envying the cachet that the New York festival had bestowed upon those involved, the Rolling Stones, in a bid to turn the hippie phenomenon to their advantage, decided to stage a free concert in California, with themselves as the headline act. This event was proposed for December 1969 – a West Coast love-in with the potential to rival Woodstock – and would be the final date on the grandstanding Britons' 'Let it Bleed' tour, which Albert and David Maysles (whose independent breakthrough had come with *Salesman* (1968), an elegiac indictment of the conventional American Dream) had been commissioned to film. As fate would have it, the final product of the Maysles' time with the band became less an endorsement of Jagger and company's showmanship than a symbolically replete fable of the Love Generation's hubristic demise.

The Maysles open *Gimme Shelter* with the Stones (the *soi-disant* 'Greatest Rock 'n' Roll Band in the World') performing 'Jumpin' Jack Flash' to a jubilant New York audience. Then, in an atypically self-reflexive mode for direct cinema, the film cuts to a hushed editing suite in which the band and filmmakers are ensconced scrutinising a rough cut. 'It's really hard to see this together, isn't it', says drummer Charlie Watts to David Maysles. 'This gives us the freedom, all you guys watching it … We may only be on you for a minute and then go to almost anything', comes the reply, a declaration by the filmmakers of their editorial prerogative, and, moreover, a confutation of Bob Dylan's co-authorial assertion in *Dont Look Back*'s introductory routine. *Gimme Shelter*'s linearity is punctuated by periodic returns to this site of retrospective contemplation; thus we infer continually that the Stones are *not* in control, or, perhaps, that it is now the Maysles brothers who hold the prompt cards. Conversely to Dylan's trailblazing, transitional Old World epiphany, the English had now come to America, and would find themselves unwitting conspirators

Explosion into reality: Jagger confronts himself in *Gimme Shelter* (1970)

in the counter-culture's eventual implosion. Henceforth, the editing suite becomes a conscientious hall of mirrors, a means by which the Maysles brothers force an internal confrontation between their subjects and their subjects' pro-filmic egos.

On the editing machine, the film and its accompanying soundtrack are re-wound, and we hear a radio journalist reporting a catastrophe, the violent nature of which overshadows *Gimme Shelter* from this pre-title scene onward:

> Well, the Rolling Stones' tour of the United States is over. It wounded [*sic*] up with a free concert at the Altamont Speedway for more than three hundred thousand people. There were four births, four deaths, and an awful lot of scuffles reported. We received word that someone was stabbed to death in front of the stage by a member of the Hell's Angels … We want to know what you saw. What was the Altamont free concert like?

Sam Cutler, one of the British organisers, telephones the show to give his side of the troubling story, as the usually cocksure Mick Jagger looks on with a gloomy (though still aloof) countenance: 'The Angels did as they saw best in the difficult situation, as far as I'm concerned. They were people who were here, who tried to help, in their own way. If people didn't dig it, I'm sorry.' Cutler's opinion (that, even at this early point, seems flippant) does not assuage the room's air of nervousness. Sonny Barger, vociferous president of the Oakland, California chapter of the Hell's Angels and *de facto* nationwide figurehead, calls in to rail against the Stones with frightening vehemence:[2]

> I didn't go there to police nothin', man. I ain't no cop, I ain't never gonna ever pretend to be a cop, and this Mick Jagger, like, put it all on the Angels, man – he used us for

127

dupes, man, and as far as I'm concerned we were the biggest suckers for that idiot [Jagger visibly recoils] ... And you know what, they told me that if I sat on the edge of the stage so nobody would climb over me, then I could drink beer until the show was over, and that's what I went there to do. But, you know what, when [the concertgoers] started messing over our bikes, they started it. Ain't nobody gonna kick *my* motorcycle ... When they jumped on an Angel, they got hurt.

A saturnine Watts laments that before Altamont he had held the motorcycle gang in high esteem, and expresses his regret and surprise at the eventual tragedy: 'Oh dear ... What a *shame*...'. 'The violence at Altamont was completely unexpected', continues the radio presenter. 'The Rolling Stones had performed for overflow audiences without incident at major cities across the States.' The viewer now definitely *does* know what to expect, and it is on a note of foreboding that the film's dreadful momentum begins. The stark, capitalised words 'GIMME SHELTER' appear on the Steenbeck's screen, as the film cuts to the Stones striking-up their most famous song, 'Satisfaction (I Can't Get No)', live on stage in New York.

FIVE PHASES OF FANTASY – (4) *THE NIGHTMARE STAGE*

When the *grandioso* rendition of 'Satisfaction' has run its protracted course, the Maysles take us back (or chronologically forward) to the editing suite, and to a penitent but typically poised Jagger watching himself address a mid-tour press conference:

Reporter: Are you any more satisfied now, as far as your career is concerned?

Jagger [drawling theatrically with an affected glottal stop]: Do you mean sexually or philosophically? Yeah, we're more satisfied now, sexually.

Reporter: How about philosophically and financially?

Jagger: Financially dissatisfied, sexually satisfied, philosophically *trying*. [At which point we cut back to Jagger in the viewing room, who dismisses this as 'rubbish'.]

Reporter: I read in one of the papers that you'll be giving a free concert...

Jagger: We are doing a free concert in San Francisco, on December the sixth ... The location is not Golden Gate Park, unfortunately, but somewhere adjacent that's a bit larger ... It's creating a sort of microcosmic society, you know, uh, which sets an example to the rest of America as to how one can behave in large gatherings.

In lawyer Melvin Belli's 'bordello-style' (Pauline Kael quoted in Macdonald & Cousins 1998: 275) office, a tense parley with an equipment leaser is underway to see that Jagger's plans to set a behavioural example are realised without impediment.[3] The prophetic leaser is reluctant to comply: 'I see nothing but trouble. This whole thing is one pain in the ass.' Belli resembles a more baleful Albert Grossman, both in his aggressive business manner ('Don't turn me into a proctologist!') and grey, bespectacled appearance; correspondingly this scene, in which we learn that, by

Charlie Watts confronts the filmmakers of *Gimme Shelter*

Saturday night, 'at least a hundred thousand kids' will be at whatever venue is secured, echoes *Monterey Pop*'s negotiations but is both inherently and contextually ominous in tone. 'Don't scare off these people', says Belli to his aides: 'If I were advising *them*, I'd tell 'em to hide out.' The Maysles again cut to Jagger's muted facial reaction – a pair of eyebrows raised momentarily at the statement's duplicitous gall.

During a playback in Muscle Shoals studio of the Stones' most attractive and melodically realised composition, 'Wild Horses', Albert Maysles captures the musicians' awe of their own talent (here once more the Stones contemplate their recorded selves) in a continuous long-take. Scanning the room, the cameraman finds appeal in Richards' tapping, snakeskin boots, Jagger's burgundy pout, and then Watts' unblinking, brooding glare at the lens. Charlotte Zwerin, the film's co-director, sees a certain truth in the sequence's admission of direct cinema's artifice: 'There's such an honesty and frankness about it: "Yes, this is a movie, yes I'm taking your picture, you're aware of it, you're looking at me and I'm looking at you." And [Albert Maysles] doesn't stop. It's beautiful.'[4] It is the drummer's hangdog stare, not Richards' vampiric repose that, for Maysles, best incarnates the augury of *Gimme Shelter*'s opening events: 'Such an interesting face ... It reminds me of Charles Dickens' *Tale of Two Cities*. One of the opening scenes in the book, there's a bottle of wine that crashes to the street, exploding, and the wine flows. You know that it's a portent of the flow of blood that's to follow in the revolution.'[5]

Following a montage set to 'Love in Vain', tinted deep red (and edited in slow motion to evoke a bloodbath in which the beguiled masses are ritually baptised by Jagger's Luciferian persona), we see Belli on the telephone. A donor has been found: Dick Carter – impecunious owner of the Altamont Raceway, a bleak, eighty-acre plot near Livermore, California – has called to offer his site. 'It's on!' announced a thrilled *Rolling Stone* when the news became public. 'It will be a little Woodstock and, even more exciting, it will be an *instant* Woodstock' (quoted in Norman 1993: 383). Littered with burnt-out cars and shards of broken glass, Altamont, the diametric opposite of Woodstock's beauteous location, had long been on the verge of total abandonment. Doubtful about the outcome of such a hastily conceived and unorganised venture, Bill Graham, whose experience in such matters was vast, warned: 'They'll never do it. They should call it off or it'll explode in their faces' (quoted in Norman 1993: 384). As they had done before Woodstock, superstitious hippies consulted astrological charts. To their dismay they saw that on 6 December the Moon would be in Scorpio, heralding a period of violence and disorder (ibid.).

Michael Lang, involved in the capacity of co-organiser, is interviewed by television crews, who seek confirmation of the ostensible similarities between Altamont and its majestic precursor for reasons of journalistic *précis*:

Reporter: You were at Woodstock, and you've now been out to Altamont, right? How does it stack up? Do you have the room?

Lang: I think we have the room, sure. I think we can hold as many people as want to come.

Reporter: Can you change location that fast?

Lang: We had a much bigger operation to change at Woodstock and we did it pretty quick. I don't think we'll have many problems.

Reporter: Is this going to be Woodstock West?

Lang [grinning]: Well, it's gonna be San Francisco!

Jagger, stupefied by cannabis, is also questioned by the media, and answers with a confused observation delivered in an accent approaching self-parody: '*I* think the concert's an *excuse* … You know, because, like, thing is, like, everyone's coming and having a good time … The concert's not, uh, it's like the *proscenium* of a theatre … It's an excuse for everyone to get together and … get really *stoned*. Do you under*stand*?'

At a Stones concert, support act Ike and Tina Turner perform 'I've Been Loving You Too Long', a slow but vigorous blues enlivened by Tina Turner's protracted stimulation of her phalloid microphone. Though this tightly framed display is outrageous (and analogous in its *outré* flamboyance to Hendrix's enthralling behaviour at Monterey Pop), it is hard to forget the imminent tragedy and enjoy the music or the show – a trade-off the Maysles, through editorial construction, have sagaciously made. Turner's normally effervescent sexual presence is tempered by our awful foreknowledge, and hence imbued with a disturbing quality; the film intently communicates the failure of pop music, free love and permissiveness (the quest for 'satisfaction') always to make things right, or to cease an inexorable cultural trajectory – the death throes of the vitality fantasy – towards the end of an era:

Still the drive to climax continues – and as the fantasy craves for more and more violent sensation, so the Frustration Stage passes into the fourth, or *Nightmare Stage*, the reverse of the Dream Stage, in which everything goes increasingly and unaccountably wrong, and marked by a steadily more violent and shadowy sense of menace. (Booker 1969: 72–3)

Backstage, Jagger gets dressed for the show. Hung across his lean, ashen chest is a large wooden crucifix that he had taken to wearing under his shirt for good luck. The Maysles linger on the totem long enough to convey a bemusing dichotomy: Mick Jagger, the man who had 'made destruction cool and the Devil a rock star' (Norman 1993: 380), apparently sought protection from Jesus Christ.

In the darkness and cold, Altamont's stage – standing inexplicably at only chest height – is readied hastily by Sam Cutler and his associates, who are seen climbing scaffolds in shots that are almost identical to those in *Woodstock*'s opening montage, except for the vapour rising from mouths and noses. From a low-flying helicopter in greyly diffused daylight, the camera scans the hundreds of cars that line the road to the festival 'like jackstraws', but the sight is less than 'awesome', and biblical only in the sense that it is apocalyptically desolate. The barren landscape undulates towards an obscure, beige horizon, as tiny people shuffle lifelessly down the unpromising road: this is not, by any optimistic stretch of the imagination, another Garden. Alighting from their chartered aircraft, the Stones enter a miserable world of their own invention, a visibly perturbing dystopia inhabited by the insane and enraged. Jagger, immediately after stepping from his ride, is greeted with a punch in the face from a frenzied concertgoer, a gesture that would prove an apt welcome to Altamont.

'FAREWELL HAPPY FIELDS'[6]

The Stones are ushered into their trailer by Hell's Angels, who had been booked by San Franciscan Digger Emmett Grogan (allegedly for $500 worth of beer, though accounts differ) to act as security. 'Nobody'll come near the Angels, man', Grogan was quoted as saying. 'They wouldn't dare' (quoted in Barger 2001: 160).[7] Cheap drugs are already beginning to take a toll on the attendees, turning normally placid freaks into paranoid, raving madmen who claw at the air and scream inanities at their friends. A sober man makes a plea to Cutler and Lang for medical assistance broadcasts to be made. 'Tough shit', sneers Cutler, whose sour register when dealing with the public could not be more at variance to John Morris' amiable manner at Woodstock: 'If you lay successive numbers of bummers on this crowd, by the time six o'clock comes, they're gonna be in a real mood.' A white woman canvasses for donations to the Black Panther Defence Fund to free jailed activists: 'After all, they're just Negroes', she implores.

The sonorous roar of the Angels' 'hogs' builds as we see them arrive at the festival, to inserted glances of worry and apprehension. They take position around the stage, upon which a morbidly obese male has stripped to reveal pendulous, waxen breasts. During The Flying Burrito Brothers' set, the violence begins: Angels wielding sawn-off pool cues set upon some hippies directly in front of the stage.[8] Cutler decides that he should now risk 'laying a bummer' on the crowd, and, in a languorous voice laden with annoyance, asks for a doctor. Nobody (at least in the film) is concerned; the festival is rapidly losing any allure of the humanistic kind, and Jagger, for the first time in his ignominious cinematic career, momentarily loses his cool, banging his head whilst emerging from his trailer to sign autographs. Fighting recommences halfway through Jefferson Airplane's opening song, forcing them to stop playing and attempt to calm the fracas with platitudes that might have worked at Woodstock, but seem here like the ministrations of pathetic, incongruous mediators:

> Grace Slick [speaking maternally]: *Easy ... easy ... easy*, tiger ... It's kind of weird up here. [Marty Balin, Jefferson Airplane's other singer, joins the tussle]
> Paul Kantner [Jefferson Airplane's guitarist]: Hey, man, the Hell's Angels just smashed Marty Balin in the face and knocked him out for a bit – I'd like to thank them for that. [An angry Angel takes the stage and a microphone]
> Angel: Is this thing on? Are you talking to me? Let me tell you what's happening: *You* are what's happening.
> Slick [the beating with pool cues continues]: No! You've got to keep your bodies off each other unless you intend to love ... You don't bust people in the head for nothing. Let's not *keep fucking up.*

Slick, the festival's traumatic nature having already tested the most steadfastly *laissez-faire* players, is here reduced to a hippie mother hen, fighting to breach a communicative impasse. For the motorcycle outlaws, most of whom were from poor backgrounds, primal aggression was, and had always been, the only possible means of personal or group expression. They wanted to affirm their tribe's nobility and potency not by burning draft cards, but by existing collectively outside the parent culture, creating and maintaining an almost totally independent community based on disregard for anything (including human life) other than bikes – the symbols of their creed. To bring middle-class, fanciful hippies and proudly fearless bikers together in large numbers, especially where one side was assigned official marshalling status, was likely to cause friction. Largely because of this pernicious shift in power, Altamont would not enjoy the sunny atmosphere of Monterey Pop.

The organisers' misguided belief that a shared spirit of rebellion made the hippies and the Angels kin was disastrously naïve, given the numerous testaments of chapter members to the contrary, including this anonymous Angel: 'People will have to learn to stay out of our way. We'll bust up everyone who gets in our way' (quoted in Thompson 1967: 15). Journalist Hunter S. Thompson, who spent a year riding with the Oakland chapter, saw their savagery as an inevitable by-product of circumstance:

> They are out of the ballgame and they know it. Unlike the campus rebels, who with a minimum of effort will emerge from their struggle with a validated ticket to status, the outlaw motorcyclist views the future with the baleful eye of a man with no up-

ward-mobility at all ... instead of submitting quietly to their collective fate, they have made it the basis of a full-time social vendetta. They don't expect to win anything, but on the other hand, they have nothing to lose. (1967: 162)

'The adrenaline rush of combat', according to David Steigerwald's disquisition on the Vietnam War's reflection of contemporaneous cultural phenomena, 'was the ultimate experience in an age in which people were seeking intensified experience' (1995: 120). The Hell's Angels, happily antagonistic, were bringing that adrenaline to the home front, crushing determinedly those they considered weak, complacent or effete.

When the Grateful Dead arrive, Michael Shrieve (Santana's gifted teenage drummer, who is seen giving a virtuoso performance in *Woodstock*) warns Jerry Garcia of the escalating brutality: 'Hell's Angels are beating on musicians ... It's really weird, man, it's really weird.'[9] The Angels ride their bikes towards the stage, and the crowd parts as if in deference to rancorous gods. By the time the Stones take tardily to the boards, their audience, having been deliberately kept waiting for hours to build expectation, is indeed in a 'real mood'.[10]

JUST CALL ME LUCIFER

Uncharacteristically, Jagger begins the show by asking people to stay still, and to not 'push around'. His band-mates strike up 'Sympathy for the Devil', but get no further than a few bars into the first verse before a scuffle starts only a few feet in front of them. Jagger attempts to placate the crowd:

Hey, Keith, Keith! Will you cool it and I'll try and stop it. Hey, people, brothers and sisters, *brothers and sisters*! Come on now – that means everybody just cool out. Will you cool out, everybody ... Everyone all right? Okay ... Something very funny happens when we start that number.

The Stones attempt the verse once more, outwardly oblivious to both the Alsatian dog roaming at their feet and the strange, new appropriateness of 'Sympathy for the Devil''s lyric. Jagger wrote the song, after reading Mikhail Bulgakov's *The Master and Margarita*, as a genteel comment on the 1960s' murderous turbulence and the hypocrisy of religious dogma (a contradiction echoed in the lively samba beat chosen to accompany Jagger's Mephistophelean impiety). In Bulgakov's novel, the Devil, in the guise of an aristocratic stranger, makes an appearance in 1930s' Moscow to converse with two men who are debating the likelihood of Jesus' existence, announcing: 'Excuse me, please, for permitting myself without an introduction' (1967: 17). This literary overture would inspire the Stones' co-songwriter, who at Altamont found himself in the unusual situation of reciting his paean to Satan's supposed hip status whilst looking out over a very real hell:[11]

Please allow me to introduce myself,
I'm a man of wealth and taste.

Been around for a long, long year,
Stole many a man's life and faith…

I watched with glee while your kings and queens,
Fought for ten decades for the gods they made.
I shouted out 'Who killed the Kennedys?'
When after all, it was you and me.

As the band plays, the Maysles present what is – in thematic terms – the film's key shot: a gimlet-eyed Hell's Angel glowering contemptuously at Mick Jagger in a manner that is undeniably chilling. The strained alliance between the bikers and the Stones, the brutal 'one percenters'[12] and the 'sissy, marble-mouthed prima donnas' (Barger 2001: 163), is frighteningly and succinctly conveyed by this single, haunting image of taut, counter-culturally polar discordance and 'pure inexplicable hatred' (Pirie 1971: 227). (If Pennebaker was reluctant to confront the issue of the Angels at the relatively peaceful Monterey Pop, there is no such discretion here; Gimme Shelter's crews display remarkable – and perhaps unwise – bravery given the unruly circumstances.) A lone, nude young woman tries to rush the stage but is beaten back by several bikers in a display of unnecessary heavy-handedness.[13] Yet another fight breaks out, and Jagger is again forced to take on the role of a mollifying schoolmaster, charged with a disorderly class of reprobate bullies:

Jagger: People. People! Who's fighting and what for? Why are we fighting? We don't want to fight – come on! Every other scene has been cool … [A few people vainly make peace signs]

Richards [his voice lapsing into that of a chagrined middle-class schoolboy]: That guy there [pointing at an Angel], if he doesn't stop it, man … Either those cats cool it, man, or we don't play.

Jagger: I don't know what's going on, who's doing what, it's just a scuffle. All I can ask you, San Francisco, is, like the whole thing, this could be the most beautiful evening we've had for this winter, and we've really, you know, let's not [Jagger self-censors the word 'fuck'] it up, man. I can't do any more than just ask you to, to beg you, just to keep it together. Hell's Angels, everybody, let's just keep ourselves together. If we are all one, let's show we're all one. We need a doctor by that scaffold there.

The Stones start 'Under My Thumb',[14] during which, claims Sonny Barger, Keith Richards was put under not a little duress: 'I stood next to him and stuck my pistol into his side and told him to play or he was dead. He played like a motherfucker' (2001: 165). We see a prolonged shot of a bearded, drugged man in the throes of chemical madness, pulling at his face and gurning grotesquely to Richards' sinuous guitar solo, before being pushed off the stage by three Angels. Albert Maysles is to this day troubled by Altamont's air of desperate exasperation: 'There's one impression [of Gimme Shelter] that I have most of all – that is, oh my god, look at these kids with all that promise, with all that idealism that's lurking somewhere

The Angels rub up against the Stones (*Gimme Shelter*)

in there. You know, drugs, and whatever else, the energy just can't seem to express itself' (quoted in Bell 1999: 256). 'Oh baby, it's all right', the lyric incants ad nauseam, perfectly and absurdly encapsulating the chutzpah of its composers and the Woodstock vision of peace and love's souring premise. Amidst the insanity, a camera catches an arm's momentary swipe.

The Maysles cut back to the editing suite. 'Can you roll back on that, David?' asks Jagger, drawing his chair nearer to the monitor. It transpires that the murder has been filmed, and David Maysles points out a distressing detail evident in only one exposure: 'There's the Angel, right there, with the knife.' Jagger remains facially and vocally impassive. 'You couldn't see anything – it was just another scuffle. That's so horrible.' Meredith Hunter, a young black man (dressed conspicuously in a dapper, lime-green suit) who had brandished a gun, is seen being stabbed in the neck, frame by frame.[15] Back at the concert, a bloody paramedic details the casualty's injuries; Hunter's girlfriend is in hysterics ('They can't hear his heart – I don't want him to die'); and the Stones play 'Street Fighting Man', unaware of the killing and of Hunter's terrified last words to his attacker: 'I wasn't going to shoot you' (see Norman 1993: 399).[16]

FIVE PHASES OF FANTASY – (5) THE DEATH WISH STAGE: EXPLOSION INTO REALITY

They even look physically smaller ... they were really only infants, suddenly finding themselves completely helpless ... they didn't know how to put it into words, but what seemed to me the worst was the sudden awareness that their fantasy strengths were no use to them.

– T. R. Fyvel (quoted in Booker 1969: 77)

So describes T. R. Fyvel the 'extraordinary change in demeanour of members of teenage gangs when they have been brought up against the sudden "reality" of arrest by the police' (ibid.). The Rolling Stones, inextricable participants in the counter-culture's ill-fated search for the ultimate experience,[17] are suffering the equivalent of this punitive humiliation as we see them in the edit room. Jagger's incitements to pseudo-diabolical excess and Richards' experiments in skirting the line between dissipation and death had ended, for them, in a lucky escape – their feelings are cloaked in nonchalance, but this looks like a defensive façade born out of rock music's entrenched machismo. Here are five celebrated and intelligent embodiments of the vitality fantasy, witnessing its disintegration and being charged, tacitly, with effrontery; but, 'However hip or enlightened they are', writes Marianne Faithfull, 'Mick and Keith are also very English, and in England you just don't talk about emotional things ... Personal feelings and anxieties are taboo ... Hipness itself was part of the problem' (Faithfull & Dalton 1995: 224–5). Theatrically tossing his scarf over one shoulder, Jagger, with a glum look to camera, mumbles his slightly remiss farewell to the Maysles. This haunting shot is freeze-framed, and a certain sadness and helplessness in the singer's cultivated emotional inadequacy is implied. 'See y'all', is as much as he can say, though we feel certain that during the preceding ninety minutes of the film we have witnessed him, like Dylan in England, going through 'some kind of ... thing'.

The band and its retinue hurriedly cram themselves into a helicopter to make their getaway, and disquieting parallels with *Dont Look Back*'s equally transitional (but far less harrowing) limousine 'escape' are apparent: only five turbulent years have passed, but much has changed for the worse. In silence, and visible only by their moonlit outlines, stultified revellers crawl away from the concert – and, perhaps, away from the pleasant delusion of the hippie dream.

The revellers of Altamont crawl away from a decade's end (*Gimme Shelter*)

CODA: THE MAYSLES' DARK REFORM

Altamont was meant to be the last great festivity of the 1960s, but instead became, along with Charles Manson's transgressions, a shorthand index of the counter-culture's death. It is possible, as Christopher Booker argues, that the counter-culture could not sustain itself any longer under the weight of its own naïve impulses: 'all fantasies, all disturbances must ultimately long for and bring about their own destruction – in order that the steady flow of society and nature may be preserved' (1969: 76). Perhaps, more simply, the counter-culture succumbed to what Norman O. Brown called a 'Dionysian ego' (1959: 175), as thousands of young intellectuals turned from the frustrations of radical politics and vague dissent towards the more immediately gratifying thrills of 'narcissism and erotic exuberance' (1959: 307). If this is so, Altamont was merely a symbolically charged symptom of this cyclic self-obliteration, not a causal factor in the hippies' dissolution. The Angels, for all their problems, had been around on their own terms for a long time, and would survive the 1960s undaunted by the relatively brief rise to prominence of pacifist idealism. As Sonny Barger declaimed:

> All that shit about Altamont being the end of an era was a bunch of intellectual crap. The death of Aquarius. Bullshit, it was the end of nothing … As for me, with the 1970s on hand, I was headed for some wild times that would make Altamont look like a church picnic. (2001: 169)

Barger, who unequivocally blames the Stones for the debacle, had no political stance to maintain, no record-buying public to appease, and no need of cachet outside his motorcycling clique. 'Intellectual crap', as he puts it, had never factored in his life. For members of the British blues invasion, so instrumental in bringing black music to the white American masses through insinuation of radio playlists, the discomfiture in the wake of Altamont was a big deterrent; the Stones themselves would not tour the States again until 1972, and only then in a regimentally cosseted, insular world of groupies, hard drugs and increasing ennui.[18]

Until David Maysles had shown him Hunter's gun in arrested relief against a crocheted skirt (a peculiarly discordant and metonymic superimposition), Jagger was unaware that someone had been allowed so close to him with a firearm. In Britain, where to this day even most police do not carry guns, the singer had felt secure under the safeguard of the local Hell's Angels, innocuous part-time mimics of their West Coast progenitors. The Hyde Park concert of July 1969 had gone without major hindrance, so it seemed logical to concur with Emmett Grogan and let the bikers provide protection in California. Allen Ginsberg – in admiration of their defiant spirit – had sung the Angels' praises, as had Ken Kesey, who had once invited them to his Hog Farm commune for a protracted party. Even San Francisco's Human Be-In, prior to Monterey Pop the largest gathering of its type, had enjoyed relative calm under the Angels' guard (see Steigerwald 1995: 184). At some point, however, luck simply had to run out, and it took Altamont's ill-omened combination of unsuitable venue, abundant bad drugs, impromptu staging, procrastinating headline act, socio-political frustration *and* praetorian Hell's Angels to see that this eventually happened. 'They got exactly what they originally wanted – a dark, scary environment to play "Sympathy for the Devil"', remarks Barger (2001: 166). *New Yorker* critic Pauline Kael, in a column from December 1970, seconds this opinion, in the process erroneously implicating the filmmakers:

> The free concert was staged and lighted to be photographed, and the three hundred thousand people who attended it were the unpaid cast of thousands. The violence and murder weren't scheduled, but the Maysles brothers hit the *cinéma vérité* jackpot ... Musically Jagger has no way to cool it because his orgiastic kind of music has only one way to go – higher, until everyone is knocked out ... It's impossible to say how much movie-making is responsible for those consequences, but it is a factor, and with the commercial success of this kind of film it's going to be a bigger factor ... It doesn't look so fraudulent if a director excites people to commit violent acts on camera, and the event becomes free publicity for the film. (Quoted in Macdonald & Cousins 1998: 273, 276–8)[19]

Gimme Shelter was not 'lighted to be photographed', that much is certain. That the Stones' 'Let it Bleed' tour had ended in bloodshed was not the fault of its chroniclers; rather, it was a confluence of various, unforeseeable catalysts beyond their control.

As the filmmakers point out, their treatment of the Altamont catastrophe is far from either a simple admonition of Jagger or an embroidered, veiled 'snuff movie':

> We did not produce the event ... All the evidence [Kael] uses in her analysis of [the Stones'] disturbing relationship with their audience is evidence supplied by the film, by the structure of the film which tries to render in its maximum complexity the very problems of Jagger's double self, of his insolent appeal and the fury it can and in fact does provoke, and even the pathos of his final powerlessness ... Rather than give the audience what it wants to believe, the film forces it to see things as they are. (Quoted in Macdonald & Cousins 1998: 394)[20]

This dualism in Jagger's persona (his Dylan-esque 'double self': the godly diabolist who wears a crucifix and invokes the Devil; the cultured hedonist who reads Bulgakov and smokes marijuana) echoes both the ambiguous characters employed in 'dark reform' works of the American Renaissance period, and the contemporaneous, broader paradoxes of the latter hippie movement. Likewise, Kael's attack on the Maysles and what she construes to be their cynical, sensationalist exploitation of terror is not without an antebellum parallel. Herman Melville's *White-Jacket* (1850) – a dark-reform work graphically exposing the horrors of naval life – attracted criticism for its supposedly hypocritical or gratuitous descriptions of immoral behaviour and depravity. Some reviews, as noted in David S. Reynolds, accused the author of 'wallowing in the mud he pretended to be cleaning up'; a London paper disparaged *White-Jacket*'s 'disgusting details' and 'horrible wit'; and still another publication doubted 'the soundness and knowledge of such a wholesale reformer' (1988: 151). However, as Reynolds has noted:

> Significantly, the most common metaphor surrounding dark reform – tearing away veils – was applied to the novel in a favourable review in *Saroni's Musical Times*, which declared that Melville has 'lifted the veil which covers the ... "real life below stairs,"' as he remorselessly 'tears the veil of romance which has been cast over the "world in a man-of-war"'. (Ibid.)

'A man-of-war', wrote Melville, 'is but this old-fashioned world of ours afloat ... charged to the combings of her hatchways with the spirit of Belial and all her un-righteousness' (1966: 411). The Maysles brothers use this same, unflinching gaze and ambiguity of purpose to 'tear the veil of romance' from the face of a flagging, poisoned ideal; the 'drive to climax' was reaching its grim conclusion. Vaingloriously envisaged by its commissioners as a pre-emptive *tour de force* that would steal the still-gestating *Woodstock*'s thunder, *Gimme Shelter* instead immortalised the failures of an ethos in freefall and brought into question anarchic notions of personal license to indulge freely in the name of anti-authoritarianism. Much as Melville's compulsive Ahab chases his own destruction in the shape of the symbolic whale *Moby-Dick* (1851), the counter-culture, as depicted in *Gimme Shelter*, heedlessly pursues ultimate gratification, and, at the Altamont Raceway, 'dies' in so doing. 'The Beatles film we made in '64', recalled Albert Maysles, 'full of promise, energy and the innocence of youth, was like the start of something. [*Gimme Shelter*] marked the end, when everything fell apart' (quoted in Geller 2000: 74).

CONCLUSION: THE GREATEST NEED IN THE WORLD

> The greatest need in the world is to know the real world. If we know what's really going on, then we're in a better position to keep it as it is or make it different in ways that are specific to the films we see. It's my form of idealism, which I still find to be inspiring.
>   – Albert Maysles (in the audio commentary accompanying the Criterion DVD release of *Gimme Shelter*)

> Oh you youths, Western youths ... Fresh and strong the world we seize.
>   – Walt Whitman, 'Birds of Passage' (1998: 183)

Democratic idealism, an ethos intrinsic to the counter-culture, has by tradition informed American thinking. In the four rock documentaries discussed throughout Part Two of this study, this ameliorative urge is writ large: from the optimism of *Dont Look Back*, through *Monterey Pop* and *Woodstock*'s sanguine centrality, to *Gimme Shelter*'s sad apprehension of finality, the vitality fantasy of the 1960s has been etched in such a manner as to provide us with not only documents of, but testimonies to a great struggle's rise and decline. Throughout the decade the reformist American bards, in a custom ages old, exposed the paradoxes, tragedies and anguish of the 'most idealistic nation in the world' (Reidhead 1998: 928) and its continuing implication in collective sin. 'Rock', argues David Chalmers, '*was* the culture of the sixties' (1996: 94); furthermore, as Robert A. Rosenstone noted in 1969, rock as a political tool transcended the printed word's propagative limitations: 'Without reading Paul Goodman, David Riesman, C. Wright Mills, or Mary McCarthy, youngsters will know that life is a "rat-race", that Americans are a "lonely crowd", that "white-collar" lives contain much frustration, and that the war in Vietnam is far from just. And they will have learned this from popular music' (1969: 143). The filmmakers of the direct cinema school worked in harmony with the rock, pop and folk exponents they were compelled by acuity to scrutinise, built on the timely verve of their respective disciplines and effected a symbiotic union of cinema, music and message. Conflict was the central motif of the 1960s, and music the heart of peaceful protestation; pop, an exciting antidote to the solemnity of party rhetoric and the dearth of inspiring political figures since the murder of John Kennedy, offered up its own heroes to spearhead the popularly expected philosophical revolution. Similarly, the documentary form was transcending its roots in didacticism and finding new purpose in a world of change, disorder and unclear horizons. Though problems of racial inequality, the draft and territorial warfare were rife a century earlier, never before had a generation faced the threat of total annihilation, never had the desire to find a spiritual truth been so great, and never had the need for inventive – if retrospectively doomed – antidotes to man's inhumanity proved such a pivotal creative force.

The alternative methods of redress employed by the fleeting youth movement looked as if they might just work; free-thinking pacifist liberalism, for a time, could be mooted reasonably convincingly as a potential global ideology for the fourth quarter of the twentieth century and beyond. If one could 'know the real world', then one could set about changing it, but knowing the real world in a *milieu* increasingly distrustful of 'plastic-coated America' (Abbie Hoffman quoted in Cavallo 1999: 71) meant knowing oneself, and what better way to do this than by creating – with duly vital channels of communication – a fresh, potent discourse of linguistic and artistic reinvention. But, it is to the past that we must look (no matter what Dylan might say in contrariety) to understand more fully the ideological genea-logy of direct cinema. *Dont Look Back*, *Monterey Pop*, *Woodstock* and *Gimme Shelter* together comprise a poetic, idealistic legacy no lesser in ambition, insight and American specificity than the reform tracts of the American Renaissance composed a century before. Walt Whitman asks, in the 1855 edition of *Leaves of Grass*: 'Is reform needed? Is it through you? The greater the reform needed, the greater the Personality you need to accomplish it ... Rest not till you rivet and publish yourself of your own Personality' (1998: 302). Like Whitman, Country Joe, Jimi Hendrix and Bob Dylan, Pennebaker, Wadleigh and the Maysles brothers wanted only to potentiate an art form, and no longer limit themselves to a remit set down, in a 'staid' journalistic mould, by Robert Drew. Pennebaker sees his own, enterprising concept of expressive validity mirrored in Dylan's pluralistic view of an unfathomable 'reality' and total, Emersonian conviction in the righteousness of self-reliance when paired with individualistic expression; *Dont Look Back* is thus in essence a seconding of all its subject's beliefs, both in its dismissal of linguistic morphology's usefulness and a roundly subversive inclination towards ambiguity.

Monterey Pop, however, takes this absorption to a new level and finds Pennebaker situated in an ersatz heaven, trying only to extol and losing (deliberately) any critical distance to complete sympathy. That is not to say that *Monterey Pop* is somehow less valuable because it is not an impartial historical document; as it came to burgeon, direct cinema, like its musical stars, was involved necessarily as much in itself as in the world it surveyed. If the mid- to late 1960s alternative scene was indeed a 'cyclonic thing', of a significantly personal nature, then why could the films it inspired not be at once convincing political treatises and sympathetically implicated? *Woodstock* is both an impassioned, personally poetic plea for the realisation of a pre-industrial utopia and a vast, egalitarian cross-section of its makers' troubled nation, replete with pastoral sentiments beloved of Emerson and Thoreau. Entering the public domain just after Wadleigh's Academy Award-winning film, *Gimme Shelter*'s critique of the ultimately stultifying effects of hedonism demonstrates a contrapuntal, Melvillian approach to popular reform that recalls antebellum pro-temperance imagery and ambivalence towards idolatry, whilst still lamenting the death of an ideal from both literal and metaphorical intoxication. These personal visions – tracts for a new, modern-day United States whose citizens should look back only with discriminatory acumen – show us the means by which Bob Dylan and those who emerged from his shadow put aside what they saw as empty political posturing and sought a more philosophical vantage suited to a period of critical and cultural rebirth in America:

> The New Left and the counter-culture were more than rebellions against a repressive, boring Cold War culture. In addition they revived older, mostly pre-industrial visions of work, individualism, self-reliance, community and democracy. In effect, they pitted a somewhat mythic (though real enough) America of open spaces, adventure and unpredictability against the modern managerial, bureaucratic and (from their point of view) staid society that they inherited as they reached college age in the middle of the twentieth century. The fear and the furor created by the emergence of the sixties youth culture reflected an underlying struggle between two powerful, historically grounded yet contradictory versions of American life. (Cavallo 1999: 8)

The 'historically grounded' counter-culture of the 1960s engendered its filmic voice: a multipart entreaty for reform that resonates through American ages, expressing the troubled nature of a great but tragically flawed nation. 'The United States', wrote Whitman, famously, 'are essentially the greatest poem … the American poets are to enclose old and new for America is the race of races … The greatest poet … knows the soul' (1998: xxi, 441, 448). To aspire to know the soul, and hence the human race, is an admirable idealism that eclipses even those unattainable goals of omniscience, objectivity and invisibility with which direct cinema is (often wrongly) associated. If we could ever know beyond doubt 'what's really going on', as Albert Maysles says, then we would indeed be better positioned than our ancestors to effect a lasting change in the American way of life.

PART THREE | FREDERICK WISEMAN'S SIXTIES

7 | WISEMAN AND CIVIL REFORM: FOUR INSTITUTIONS

FREDERICK WISEMAN: A SHORT INTRODUCTION

Yale graduate and former lawyer Frederick Wiseman is the most steadfast adherent to the Drew-inspired template of formal austerity, and unquestionably the pre-eminent observational filmmaker of the last forty years.[1] Mostly eschewing non-diegetic supplementation and pro-filmic interaction with his subjects, Wiseman strictly observes a personally congenial, cinematically unadorned code he feels best suits his form of social commentary. A latecomer to direct cinema and the most volubly cynical amongst his contemporaries about early talk of *vérité*, he labels his films variously 'reality dreams', or 'reality fictions'. These terms, although glib, nonetheless appropriately update a truism attributed to John Grierson, 'the creative treatment of actuality' (see Eitzen 1995: 82), in their acknowledgement of the tendency on the part of documentarists to manipulate material for reasons of rhetorical or dramatic emphasis.[2] Typically working with huge shoot-to-edit ratios, Wiseman – who during production acts as sound-recordist and director – spends many months piecing together his 'arbitrary, biased, prejudiced, compressed and subjective' films (Anderson & Benson 1991: 279);[3] only well into the editing stage does it become apparent how a composition will take shape, and what elements are effective in apposition.

In distinction to the work of the Drew Associates and of Michael Wadleigh, Wiseman's works pivot not on the famous and urbane, but on the average, nameless (but not faceless) inhabitants of the quotidian world; rather than seek taut 'scoops' or charismatic protagonists, he sees import in, and wrings drama from, the mundanity and unpleasantness of the 'other' 1960s. 'The other America', wrote Socialist Michael Harrington, 'does not contain the adventurous seeking a new life and land. It is populated by failures, by those driven from the land and bewildered by the city, by old people suddenly confronted with the torments of loneliness and poverty, and by minorities facing a wall of prejudice' (1962: 17). This prosaic America, a class-divided homeland of dispossession and fear, is, as Barry Keith Grant (1992) has pointed out, Wiseman's backcloth. His aesthetic falls perhaps more squarely in the humanist tradition of Walker Evans and Robert Frank (the gentle and cruel American photo-documentarists of the 1930s and 1950s, respectively) than that of the Drew Associates; yet it harks back also to the disparaging agenda of Upton Sinclair in its illumination of the other America, a 'subculture of misery' (Harrington 1962: 9) in the world's wealthiest nation.[4]

Part Three of this study elucidates Wiseman's first five documentaries, all of which were filmed in institutions, and all of which thereby critique the wider soci-

ety: *Titicut Follies* (1967), set in the MCI-Bridgewater secure hospital for the criminally insane; *High School* (1968); *Law and Order* (1969), about a Kansas City police
department; *Hospital* (1969; first broadcast in 1970); and *Basic Training* (1971). As
Bill Nichols explains, Wiseman's works evince no progressive, causally contiguous
narrative, but utilise instead a 'mosaic' or 'slide-puzzle' assembly.[5] Framed by the
contextual locus of a particular institution,

> the supplementary or associational nature of Wiseman's mosaic pattern stresses
> goal-seeking and constraints more than determinism and causality. A later event
> does not occur because of a previous event as it does in narrative; rather any event
> occurs because of the constraints imposed upon all events (within a given system –
> in Wiseman's case, the system governed by the institutional code). (1981: 216–17)

Whilst the staffs of public institutions ('social actors' whose lives are intrinsic to
the behavioural system within which they function on a day-to-day basis) seek
to effect a prescribed remedial or didactic change, as is their professional duty,
Wiseman's self-proclaimed purpose as a filmmaker is not salubrious. It is true
that his ruminative films do not explicitly forward solutions to the problems they
depict; nor, for the most part, do they beg emotional participation of the casual
viewer or offer simple diatribes to satisfy the politically fervent. If, however, we
scrutinise Wiseman's early documentaries with a view to illuminating an ideological crux, the yens of an evolving mindset – a mindset thoroughly enmeshed in its
epoch – become clear. Belying Emile de Antonio's impetuous complaint that 'only
people without feelings or assumptions could even think of making *cinema vérité*'
(quoted in Beyerle 1997: 40), Wiseman's cultural perception and political beliefs
are the essence of his vocation. It is the aim of Part Three of this study to redress
a dearth of scholarly attention to Wiseman's place in history, and to seek a more
complete understanding of Wiseman's purpose as a filmmaker by assessing how
his chosen themes and content might reveal not only his motives, but also definable impetuses behind them.[6]

LOCI OF ANXIETY IN THE LAND OF THE FREE

> What is needed is a way to connect knowledge to power and decentralise both so
> that community or participatory democracy might emerge, to be connected with the
> problem of the individual in a time inevitably ridden with bureaucracy, large govern-
> ment, international networks and systems.
> – Tom Hayden (quoted in Cavallo 1999: 189)[7]

When we are admitted to any organisation whose purpose is to administer care,
instruct or evaluate, we entrust our wellbeing to professional operatives, and surrender our futures to their judgement. *Hospital*'s prelude – of a scalpel incising an
anaesthetised patient's abdomen – thus connotes more than the documentary
filmmaker's desire to penetrate; as a fragile human organism goes under the knife,
it surrenders all autonomy and submits itself to the greater body of the health-

care process. This arresting opening trope expresses, albeit with typical obliquity, one of Wiseman's chief aims: to confront us with discomforting truths about the Western condition of dependence upon, and uneasy faith in, regime-administrated systems. To the American individual, Howard F. Stein reminds us, personal submission is anathema:

> The core constellation of American values – which includes self-reliance or inner-directedness, autonomy, independence, mobility, privacy, individuality, and future orientation – is [in the healthcare system] systematically counterposed with such values as other-directedness, hierarchical authority, dependency, fixity, community, consensus or conformity, and past orientation ... Americans believe that they can master anything yet dread being mastered by anyone or anything. (1990: 33)

An important consequence of this deference, for Wiseman (and for many before him), is the resultant discursive dissonance between 'citizen' and 'professional', between the disparate voices of 'the lifeworld' (see Fairclough 1993: 143) and the structurally defined voice of a civically empowered occupation: he frequently asserts his fascination with 'the relationship between ideology and practice and the way power is exercised and decisions rationalised' (quoted in Halberstadt 1974: 25). Near the end of his 1849 treatise 'Civil Disobedience', Thoreau underlines his conception of the sacredness of individual liberty: 'There will never be a really free and enlightened State, until the State comes to recognise the individual as a higher and independent power, from which all its own power and authority are derived, and treats him accordingly'; but, 'in the century or so since Thoreau wrote these words', argues Peter Conn, 'the state has grown larger, and the individual smaller, than he could have imagined' (Conn 1990: 182).[8] Against a backdrop of worsening domestic crises, which, in the late 1960s, were alarming both the American electorate and those who served it, Wiseman examines the relationship of state to dependent individual within the modern, systematised civic institution – a system that did not, as Godfrey Hodgson writes, operate in isolation from the 'great national crisis of the 1960s: the disillusionment with rising federal budgets, the impatience of the white middle class with strident radicalism, the counterattack of organized interest groups, and the stubbornness with which conservative intellectuals have patched up intellectual defences of the free enterprise status quo' (1973: 60).

While the war in Vietnam raged on, matters of health, education, crime and welfare proved equally contentious domestic bugbears. For the ethnically and socially diverse low-income populace – a demographic to whom Woodstock was a dissolute irrelevance – urban malaise and the reality of physical decay were everyday concerns.

Wiseman's first documentary, *Titicut Follies* (filmed in 1966), devotes much of its time to showing the cruelty with which contemptuous warders treat their charges: the total institution indubitably serves here as a state-sanctioned conduit for the release of possibly innate, sadistic urges. Robert Jay Lifton, in his paper 'Medicalized Killing in Auschwitz', details several unsettling similarities between

Nazi concentration camps and modern America in the way custodial medicine is practised. He writes of Nazi operatives:

> SS doctors, in their literal life-death decisions, experienced a sense of omnipotence that could protect them from their own death anxiety in the Auschwitz environment. That sense of omnipotence, along with elements of sadism with which it can be closely associated, contributed to feelings of power and invulnerability that could also serve to suppress guilt and enhance numbing. Yet doctors could feel power-less, consider themselves pawns in the hands of a total institution. (Quoted in Luel & Marcus 1984: 29)

The warders and psychologists of the 'subversive' *Titicut Follies* are implicated personally in a scheme of self-perpetuating cruelty.[9] Even if they are beholden to a greater force, they are seen to sublimate their own sentient fears by exact-ing control over others deemed, by popular consensus, abnormal. The criminally insane – although quite reasonably incarcerated – become therapeutic quarries for men whose identities depend upon role-playing. Maintenance of a 'coherent, functioning world' (Stein 1990: 121) within Wiseman's Bridgewater is thus reli-ant on the victimisers' complete subjugation of their 'inferiors', problematic banes whom mainstream society would rather keep out of sight, mind and conscience.[10] Kennedy's optimistic 1963 reform act, which aimed to stamp out dehumanising methods of dealing with the mentally ill, had failed, largely because communities lacked the impetus to take care of them;[11] *Titicut Follies* is hence a reminder that 'snake-pit' asylums were neither sensible nor extinct. Wiseman's scathing com-mentary on Bridgewater evokes critical accounts of institutions in history from fellow observers such as Dickens, Melville, Upton Sinclair, James Agee and Mary Jane Ward,[12] but the prosperous 1960s was an ostensibly unlikely epoch in which to find a dungeon. Ken Kesey's asylum-set novel *One Flew Over the Cuckoo's Nest* (1962)[13] satirised the macrocosm through inmate relations and complained of American authoritarianism, but Wiseman's is a 'muckraking' broadside mostly without humour – if not without irony – ideally suited to the situation's anachronis-tic absurdity. Bridgewater's bureaucrats seem dedicated to procrastination and the misapplication of treatment; there are no advocates to mediate; and the doctors are flippant and apparently careless in the line of duty.

The film's first close-up, during the opening 'Strike Up the Band' stage per-formance, is of an inmate awkwardly attempting to keep in step with the stilted choreography of an ensemble dance sequence. Implying unity, cohesion and buoy-ancy, the Gershwins' title itself seems fanciful, as does the warder's compere, the incongruously affable host of a troupe (and an entire inmate/staff microcosm) isolated from one another through mental illness and regimented hierarchy. As a ceremonial practice typical of many institutions, the revue's purpose is simple: to bind together a fractured social order by temporarily fusing the superordinates' and the subordinates' roles in a performative ritual (see Goffman 1991: 102). In superficially changing the normal relationship between worker and inmate, the Fol-lies aims to demonstrate that perceived character and role differentiations within

Bridgewater are not as immutable as they may at first seem. Promptly, however, the film takes issue with this semblance of cohesion; Wiseman invites us to question the role of the 'lunatic' in relation to the asylum, and to ask ourselves who are the real madmen – the inmates or the guards.

An incestuous paedophile is quizzed by a nervously twitching, Teutonic psychiatrist filmed in unflattering close-up, while, in parallel montage, inmates are stripped naked to divest them of individuality (and means by which to commit suicide), and questioned: 'How many times do you masturbate? … [Your wife] must not give you too much sex satisfaction … Do you think you are a normal man?' The young and doe-eyed child-abuser, who obviously knows he is not normal, asks for help. 'You'll get help here, I guess', replies the psychiatrist – although we feel, as he is led away to solitary confinement, that he surely will not. In the film's most inflammatory scene, Jim, an obviously disturbed middle-aged man, is walked down a corridor and into a bare, concrete washroom, wherein he is shaved with slipshod force by a guard, who both verbally taunts him and, maybe even deliberately, cuts him. When Jim has been taken back to his unpleasantly spartan cell, after several minutes of goading, he stands naked and vulnerable in front of the camera, which peers at him as if through a Judas hole. As the guards – behaving alarmingly like cruel children – exhibit Jim for the crew, we wonder about his life outside of the total environment, and ponder the nature of his madness, as he himself, for a moment, appears to be doing. The guards ask Jim, for the benefit of the camera, if he used to be a schoolteacher, and if he passed 'with honours'. Jim says that he was a teacher of mathematics in Pittsburgh, that he played the piano, and that he did indeed pass with honours; but all that, as the guards know, was when he was a 'functioning' operative in society – a teacher in charge of a classroom, as the guards are now in charge of him after his decline into dependence. 'They figure they got the toys to play with', a politically fervent inmate (Kaminsky) shouts of the American government and its nuclear weapons, 'so they're gonna play with those toys.' On the micro-societal level of Wiseman's Bridgewater, the less empowered authoritarians (irresolute men born of a vast, unspecified folly to which the film's title alludes) have their toys, too.

The adamantly rational Vladimir, an emblem of the film's hopeless outlook and as close to a protagonist as exists in *Titicut Follies*, is doomed to frustration because of an impasse with the psychiatrist: 'Why do you say I am mad?' asks Vladimir. 'Because you've had a psychiatric assessment', replies the doctor, stubbornly. 'If I am wrong then you can spit in my face, you know?' Vladimir's response to this bizarre declaration is understandably incredulous: 'Why would I want to do that?' During his hearing later in the film, the young man passionately argues his case for release: 'Day by day, I am getting worse … I've been here for a year and a half, and this place is doing me harm. If you leave me here, that means that you want me to get hurt, which is an absolute fact.' Eventually, in pushing too passionately and too hard, Vladimir reveals the extent of his latent illness: he thinks his thorax has been poisoned. As Wiseman acknowledges: 'The situation is quite complex because Vladimir's critique is accurate and he is also quite sick. Once the label "paranoid schizophrenic" is attached to him the staff is satisfied. The fact that he has problems or has been convicted of a crime does not mean that he should be subjected to the kind of "treatment" he's getting' (quoted in Atkins 1976: 54). The panel is ultimately unsympathetic; they bandy some 'parody psychiatry' (ibid.) and opt to put him on a larger dose of medication.

Malinowski's suicide by starvation is a more obvious, irrevocable failure. The insouciant staff cannot save him, and do not give the impression of trying – a shortcoming underlined by Wiseman's infamously manipulative cuts between the emaciated patient's force-feeding and his cadaver's meticulous close-shaving (a counterpoint, also, to Jim's vicious grooming).[14] Irrespective of human dignity in life, the unbridled guards apparently afford the 'equalised' dead more respect than those living with the torment of mental illness. Cherished personal power, in the age of labour-division, comes with responsibility, and secular 'rites' performed for the deceased – so Wiseman seems to suggest – may bring at least imagined spiritual absolution. 'Remember, men', reminds the eschatologist as Malinowski is committed to the ground, 'that thou art dust, and unto dust thou shalt return.' Only a few men bear witness to Malinowski's interment, and they are staff from the asylum, such a place as to render all thought about God's charity hopeless for even the most ardent believer. The combined product of governmental negligence and innately American insecurities, Bridgewater, in *Titicut Follies*, is patently presented – in Wiseman's early 'Kino-fist' style – as a surrogate *raison d'être* for immoral functionaries, men for whom authority had perhaps always been synonymous with oppression.

Less harrowing but more insidiously respectable methods of abusing authority form the discursive core of *High School*. Emile Durkheim, in a 1922 essay on the power of education, compares the teacher's role with that of a hypnotist:

> The child is naturally in a passive state, one that is entirely comparable to that in which the hypnotised person is artificially placed. The child's consciousness still only comprises a small number of representations that are capable of fighting against those that are suggested to him. Thus his suggestibility is very easily aroused. For the same reason, he is very susceptible to the infectiousness of example, and very disposed to imitate. (Quoted in Giddens 1986: 182)

With a predominantly middle-class and relatively affluent student body, Northeast High School in Philadelphia could not, superficially, be a more different locale from Bridgewater; the inherent similarities, however, are exploited by Wiseman in a series of scenes whose (maybe overly) transparent effect is, as Wiseman concedes, to 'mock formal ideologies' that mirror larger trends in the United States' social system (quoted in Westin 1974: 61). According to sociologist Dan Dodson, the function of American schools is to 'take all the children of the community and teach them their place in the power order', so that 'all will understand their failures are their own. Otherwise they would react and blow the system apart' (quoted in Cayo Sexton 1967: 32). Durkheim's 'infectiousness of example', essentially the control mechanism by which this time-honoured propagation of orthodoxy in the nation's youth is effected, becomes, in *High School*, a malevolent force.

After the film's title flashes briefly up, there is a montage of travelling shots set to Otis Redding's '(Sittin' on the) Dock of the Bay', featuring nondescript sidewalks, fences, shop-fronts and houses – an implied morning's journey to school through an insipid townscape. 'Dock of the Bay''s presence on the soundtrack is a rare example of non-diegetic music in Wiseman's oeuvre, and has been read by Barry Keith Grant as a comment about alienation and the 'death of the American Dream' (1992: 58). 'It's about a guy who has left Georgia and gone to California in search of America', is Wiseman's interpretation of the song's pessimistic narrative. 'He's at the end of the continent. He's travelled all over and it doesn't mean a thing to him' (quoted in Rosenthal 1971: 73). Composed as a reciprocal but oddly backhanded gesture towards the concertgoers of *Monterey Pop*, who had given him a rapturous welcome and paved the way for his acceptance by a white audience, 'Dock of the Bay' sees the singer – a working-class black man – traverse the country in order to find happiness; he ends up, however, merely 'wasting time'. Pennebaker's late 1960s California, as presented in *Monterey Pop*, is an altogether more convivial locality. While the children of Keynesian economist J. K. Galbraith's affluent society gambolled in the sun, Wiseman was walking in the shadow of the Great Refusal and finding a culture of ennui still thriving across the land.

The first image of rhetorical significance, which comes only seconds into the film, is a close-up of the back of a milk truck emblazoned with the 'Penn Maid Dairy Products' insignia. The meaning of this metaphorical device will become clearer in time, but one instantaneous inference is that *High School* will concern itself with the 'production line' nature of secondary education in Pennsylvania (home of the Liberty Bell), as students coming of age in the midst of a supposed renaissance of existentialist individualism are 'churned out' like uniformly standardised tubs of butter. For all the heterogeneity and idealism on display, the nature of the United States, as Redding laments in 'Dock of the Bay', remained the same.

Soon, Northeast High School looms into view, its utilitarian architecture and towering chimneys giving it the look of a factory, a processing plant or, more ominously, a crematorium (Grant 1992: 53). Wiseman does not usually employ exterior establishing shots – almost certainly considering them trite – but this exception makes a point that left-wing existentialist Norman Mailer also articulates:

> Totalitarianism is a cancer within the body of history, it obliterates distinctions. It makes factories look like college campuses or mental hospitals ... It makes the new buildings on college campuses look like factories. It depresses the average American with the unconscious recognition that he is installed in a gelatin of totalitarian environment which is bound to deaden his most individual efforts. (1963: 201)

Once inside Northeast's 'totalitarian' environment, the students are given the daily bulletin and read the 'thought for the day', an aphorism contrived to inspire: 'Life is cause and effect. One creates his tomorrow at every moment by his motives, thoughts and deeds of today.' Following this, a glamorous Spanish teacher encourages her pupils to repeat, rote, the word '*Existentialista*'; the lesson is on Jean-Paul Sartre. A paradox becomes clear: the class's perfunctory, parrot-fashion response is quite at odds with the existential philosophy of Sartre, who stressed the importance of individual, creative power over religious or social authority, and advocated rebellion against controlling bodies as a precaution against loss of self. If one is to 'create his tomorrow at every moment', then one should not passively relinquish true freedom of choice – an absolute condition for human existence as Sartre imagined it – to the rote learning of any such philosophies. As Wiseman himself puts it:

> The ideology of the school is revealed in the daily bulletin ... The announced values are democracy, trust, sensitivity, understanding, openness, innovation – all the wonderful words we all subscribe to. But the practice is rigidity, authoritarianism, obedience, do as you're told, don't challenge. (Quoted in Atkins 1976: 54)

To emphasise further the stultifying nature of this process, Wiseman cuts to the percussion section of the school orchestra in rehearsal, an apparently uninterested group conducted by a bored looking music master, and a French lesson in which the students appear apathetically remote.

Wiseman repeatedly includes the school's militaristic senior administrator, who exercises, in an early sequence, what Thomas W. Benson and Carolyn Anderson call (after Gregory Bateson and others) the 'double bind' – a means by which to effect compliance by 'making nonsense of ordinary discourse' (1989: 119). Whatever choices the student makes in a double bind situation, he or she is continually foiled by conflicting verbal clues that lead inexorably to frustration. Michael, a boy who has been given detention for insubordination, is engaged in a dialogue with the administrator, who steers him towards an institutionally desirable but subsuming compromise:

Administrator: We're out to establish that you can be a man and take orders…

Michael: But, Mr Allen, it's against my principles; you have to stand for something.

Administrator: I think you should prove yourself. You should show that you can take the detention when given it.

Michael: I should prove that I'm a man and that's what I intend to do by doing what I feel is, in my opinion, is what I – is right.

Administrator: Well, are you going to take the detention or aren't you? I feel that you should.

Michael: I'll take it, but only under protest.

Administrator: All right then, you'll take it under protest. That's good.

So Michael has proven his manhood, by taking orders that are against his moral beliefs and losing a game of semantics and interpersonal power to Mr Allen.

Another of Northeast's teachers is seen patrolling the hallways. Upon his stopping to peer through a glazed door, Wiseman contiguously cross-cuts to a young women's calisthenics class in progress, somewhat unjustly implying that the member of staff is ogling their bottoms and hence unprofessionally prurient.[15]

(The spectator, it must be said, might also consider this prurience on the part of Wiseman and his cameraman on *High School*, Richard Leiterman.) The song the students are exercising to is 'Simple Simon Says', an asinine hit for the 1910 Fruitgum Company in the otherwise artistically progressive year of *High School*'s production; here, though, it is a dogmatic edict:

Put your hands in the air,
Simple Simon Says,
Shake them all about,
Simple Simon says,
Do it when Simon says,
Simple Simon says,
And you will never be out.

If you want never to be 'out', or a pariah, so the logic goes, you must do as you are instructed. A female teacher, shortly after the 'Simple Simon' scene, ineffectually recites Ernest Thayer's 'Casey at the Bat'. This comic poem of 1888 again promulgates an American obsession – winning – by depending for its impact on a sporting humiliation, as a batsman errs in a crucial baseball game, forfeiting respect and bringing misery upon his hometown:[16]

Oh, somewhere in this favoured land the sun is shining bright;
The band is playing somewhere, and somewhere hearts are light,
And somewhere men are laughing, and somewhere children shout;
But there is no joy in Mudville – mighty Casey has struck out.

Losing is thus equated with failure, and individuality once more subordinated to the following of instruction. If we recall *Titicut Follies*' opening routine, with its moribund performers and their confused dance moves, a parallel emerges through which Wiseman makes a comparison between the two institutions; the original cultural messages conveyed in 'Strike Up the Band', 'Casey at the Bat' and 'Simple Simon Says' may not be identical, but the idea behind the use of these widely enjoyed verses in Wiseman's first two films is plain: that those who are different, or 'out of step' with the system, can only ever lose in life. 'The most mortal of sins', lamented Theodor Adorno and Max Horkheimer of their adopted liberal democracy, 'is to be an outsider' (1997: 150).

At the rehearsal for the school fashion show, young women are taught how to carry themselves like 'attractive' women, and tutored in the ways of the all-American feminine aesthetic. Through awareness of contemporary fashion, the teacher seems to say, these young women will further conform to acceptable gender roles (and, consequently, find themselves 'suitable' men). Self-deprecatingly charming though she is, the middle-aged teacher extols a culturally ingrained physical ideal: 'If [that dress] were on someone with slimmer legs, I think it might look good. Could you find someone to model it Friday with real thin legs, honey?' The next mini-skirted model walks on stage to another unreserved critique: 'Now this young lady, she's got a leg problem too. If she did something about those stockings she might well look better.' Of a heavily-built young woman, the teacher comments: 'I think this young lady's done a lovely job of really putting some style into this particular garment ... This gal, she's got a weight problem – she knows it. And, um, she's done everything she can to cut it down ... This is what you do with fashion and design.' The class continues, and the young women are instructed to turn in a dainty manner ('You're not here to show your derriere!') and walk with a 'much more graceful' stride than the teacher's exaggerated, ungainly mimicry of the 'typical' Northeast student. 'These are the important things, girls', she tells the assembled participants, 'to walk with your shoulders high and proud.' 'Given the beauty norms set up in this society', remarks Pauline Kael in her contemporaneous review of *High School*, 'what are they to do? Cut off their legs? Emigrate? They're defeated from the legs up' (1969: 203).

To both radical feminists and less vehement participants in the sexual revolution, this type of homogenising practice was an infringement of newly-won rights to sartorial choice and satisfaction with bodily shape. At best, the fashion show looks like an amusing throwback to the 1950s, when popular notions of domestic bliss as the bedrock of American civilisation drew heavily on sexually-defined feminine ideals, epitomes that were reflected and propagated by the media in sitcoms such as *I Love Lucy* (1951–57) and in the commercials that paid for them. At worst, as is almost certainly Wiseman's purpose, the scene engenders a suspicion that, despite feminist author Betty Friedan's best intentions, the 'consciousness-raising' women's movement failed to permeate beyond its heartlands and influence provincial institutions. Speaking in hindsight of the 1950s, Friedan mourned women's collective enculturation by the 'feminine mystique', and saw that many (especially middle-class) wives had sacrificed their identities to the joys of homemaking and birthing as promoted by pamphlets written for female teens: 'You find yourself more completely a woman', gushed one, 'as, indeed, you are.'[17]

If homemaking was a positive thing, as far as Northeast High's conservative didactic policy was concerned, then the kind of promiscuity indulged in by the hippies in the name of 'free love', at least for women, was certainly not. After a class of boys has been given an affable but fundamentally hidebound lecture on the 'matriarchal', 'modern Jewish family' ('Once in while she's nice and asks your father if he wants to look at a new car they're going to buy'), the young women receive a talk on sex and the morality of the Pill: 'I think promiscuity is what any society cannot tolerate ... You've had to have practice at controlling your feelings and impulses, ever since you've been a baby. By the time you get to be a high school senior, you don't eat all the chocolate cake, because you don't want to get fat ... You have learned by now, as part of being human, that you can't have what you want, when you want it. The girls who haven't learned that – and the boys – are impulsive, and they never connect what they're doing today with what happens tomorrow.' The 'thought for the day' – 'One creates his tomorrow at every moment by his motives, thoughts and deeds of today' – seems apt, but this is a reconsidered seconding of that maxim's import; it is now an ominous warning about lack of abstentious self-restraint and the dangers of temptation.[18] Two teachers scold a young woman who wants to wear an 'inappropriate', short dress to a formal dance, one of them telling her that, 'It's nice to be individualistic.' The teacher then qualifies his statement, almost inevitably, by saying that, 'There are certain places to be individualistic...'. 'I didn't mean to be individualistic', says the young woman, unwittingly demonstrating for the viewer the school's success in its mission to reduce the sexually burgeoning students to undemonstrative products, ready for the adult world of self-possession, competition and functionality.

Simon and Garfunkel's 'The Dangling Conversation' forms the basis of a poetry seminar given by a young, polo-necked female teacher, whose appearance suggests a modicum of beatnik sensibility. Her reading is not as uninvolved as that of 'Casey at the Bat', but shows only reverence, not passion, for the wistful lyric:

> And we sit and drink our coffee,
> Couched in our indifference.
> Like shells upon the shore,
> You can hear the ocean roar,
> In the dangling conversation,
> And the superficial sighs,
> The borders of our lives.

The students do seem indifferent, and, 'like shells upon the shore', they can sense the wider world, with its promise of liberation, love and sex, but the school – the borders of their lives – stands in the way. The song, of course, is about a fading relationship, but Wiseman posits the class as a well-intentioned but ultimately otiose exercise in reducing poetry to science. If using a contemporary pop song is a commendable attempt to rouse the students' passions, then the regimentation of the classroom and the cold analysis (on the blackboard are written taxonomic categories: 'figurative language'; 'thematic words') has killed any enthusiasm for Paul Simon's enigmatic if sophomoric imagery. As the teacher turns on the tape player, Wiseman, over the music, cuts to a close-up of the spinning reels, perhaps to highlight the mechanical nature of teaching something that cannot be discussed in concrete terms and the contrast between the effects of recorded and live performances (we might remember Simon and Garfunkel in *Monterey Pop*, swathed in red light and adored by the crowd). Over the following verse, Wiseman composes an elegiac montage. From the students' faraway expressions that hint of internal escapism ('We are verses out of rhythm/Couplets out of time'), he moves out of the classroom and into the spartan corridor, where a solitary young woman leans against a wall; a prisoner of circumstance, she seems as stifled and unable to be alive within the buildings of Northeast High as the inmate-patients of Bridgewater. The truth is, of course, that she has never known the abject misery of the disregarded.

'We have, evidently, a great imbalance in American society', the well-meaning teacher who earlier read the daily bulletin explains to another class of students, who, in response, gaze silently at the walls and floor. 'On the one hand we have an affluent society, and that's one America', he continues. 'On the other hand

High School (1968): loneliness and isolation in a middle-class setting

we have another America – and by the way, that's the name of a good book by Michael Harrington, called *The Other America* ... and [Martin Luther] King was there [presumably Memphis, Tennessee] to try and uplift the other America.' A survey is conducted to ascertain how many among the classmates would join a club if other members were, in various proportions, 'Negro'. Most, it turns out, say they would join the club, but when a lone hand is tentatively raised to register a negative, the ostensibly prevaricating teacher steps in: 'Remember, there's no right or wrong answer, I'm just trying to determine what attitudes are.' He knows that the truth can never be determined under such circumstances. The white, middle-class children will, regardless of their feelings, demonstrate only what is expected of them in a time of racial and economic tension. Martin Luther King's assassination had just sparked rioting across America; his ambitious Poor People's Campaign, begun in January 1968, quickly dwindled to nothing because his advisers questioned the soundness of a plan that centred on swamping Washington with 'waves of the nation's disinherited' (Garrow 1986: 591–2) until Congress took notice. The system that King was trying to 'uplift' at the time of his death in Memphis seemed to reward the greedy and to punish the desperate of whom Harrington's book told, but whites simply moved to the suburbs in ever greater droves and ignored uncomfortable disparities. 'Poverty in the 1960s is invisible and it is new', wrote Harrington (1962: 21), and in *High School* – despite the best efforts of the teachers in this respect – the financially advantaged seniors appear to have no compulsion to change anything beyond hemlines. There was, says Wiseman, a tragicomic lack of appetite for reform at Northeast: 'A few days after Martin Luther King Jr was killed, there was a two-hour meeting of the student council. And a very serious debate about whether to send fruit or flowers to Mrs King. The decision was made in favour of fruit' (quoted in Atkins 1976: 53).

Those few who are seen to disparage the school's ideological practices do not come across as potential revolutionaries so much as self-consciously inchoate refuseniks. A student wearing sunglasses complains, during a seminar, that Northeast is 'such a cloistered and secluded place. The policy of Northeast is to avoid controversy completely … I think in its attitude towards education and in its relations with the world today, this school is miserable … It's completely sheltered from everything that's going on in the world, and I think that's wrong, it has to be changed. And I think that's our purpose here, and not to talk about films.' In his attitude, the student is admirably outspoken, and his critique is a ray of idealist – if politically schematic and juvenile – light; his sunglasses and not-yet-grown hairstyle, however, look as derisory as Mr Allen's ostentatious ring, another vain attempt to express uniqueness in a restrictive environment.[19] 'Mr Simon pointed me towards his office and said, "You don't look like a Northeaster, son,"' says the student, making plain his pride in ineffectual, cosmetic defiance. Anderson and Benson, harshly, call him a 'smug pseudo-rebel playing it cool', and 'another one of [the school's] products, groping unsuccessfully for a way to become fully human in a political situation that robs him of that opportunity' (1991: 35). In fairness, the seminar allows a venting of dissidence (if only to sublimate more considered disruption) that connects, however tenuously, to the turmoil of the macrocosm. Even though (or perhaps because) the teacher continually interrupts her class in order to quell overtly anti-authoritarian sentiment and stress that Northeast is far from the worst school of its kind, as was certainly true, the message is clear. 'Morally, socially, this school is a garbage can', opines a black student, 'let's face the facts.' Whether or not the viewer will ultimately agree with this statement is contingent upon the film's closing act, a series of rhetorical hammer-blows to defendants of the American education system.

Following a revue featuring male seniors dressed as cheerleaders (complete with huge false breasts) – a show that makes ritual mockery of the students still developing sexual identities – a smug gynaecologist speaks to an auditorium of boys, appealing to the more puerile facets of their nature by boasting of his professional access to women's vaginas ('I get paid to do it!'). 'Nature sets us up', he concludes, wagging his tightly framed finger, 'that the male is the aggressive, and the female the passive, in these circumstances … this is the nature of the beast.' The young men are continually suffused with the notion that a promiscuous appetite for sex is in their bestial make-up, a natural function of the id; for the young women, it is something that 'any society cannot tolerate', a transgression likely to lead to moral desolation and venereal disease. Suburban females were expected not to acquiesce to what they were told would be a barrage of hormonally-charged animals in thrall to nature; but men, as the supposedly progressive Bob Dylan sang in 1966, could plead, 'I want you, I want you … I want you so bad',[20] with no shame. Northeast's old-fashioned attitude towards gender formation and sexual behaviour demonstrates a patriarchal bent that Wiseman, by his inclusion of several scenes featuring sex education, seeks to make clear through his own, filmic inculcation: the manifesto of the school is not to nurture fresh thought but to propagate the mores of its catchment area.

High School's vignettes mostly concern the maintenance of Apollonian, conservative values by teachers who preserve the status quo and reflect the wishes of the wider, parental community; the vagaries of the libertine counter-culture and of rock 'n' roll, in an obviously sexually charged atmosphere, were not encouraged. If faculty in many schools were slow to take up the promotion of alternative values and radical thought, that too is hardly surprising. As we have seen, the Dionysian hippies only angered the older generation as 'rebels without a cause', and the New Left, which had focused its energies on stirring dissent on higher education campuses, was ineffective and already doomed. Patricia Cayo Sexton, writing in a 1967 report, notes that: 'Schools presumably extract the norms of the whole society for transmission to the young, but, in fact, school values represent a rather narrow band in the spectrum of social norms' (1967: 76). It is this blinkered socialisation that Wiseman seems most to abhor. When the narrator of the animated film about gonorrhea warns that, 'there is a danger that [the mother] may transmit the disease to the child when it passes out of her body', two messages concerning socially transmitted problems are imparted. The explicit meaning, of course, is that women should be wary of unprotected intercourse lest they become infectiously ill; this is the didactic point of the film-within-a-film. The implicit meaning, however, as Anderson and Benson point out, is a metaphorical device that exists only for those who are reading *High School* on a figurative level. It is a condensation of Wiseman's thesis; Northeast, we are invited to infer, is passing on a psychological 'disorder' to its students, whose values upon leaving are forever bound by strictures imposed at school (see Anderson & Benson 1991: 136).

The final scene, a culmination of the film's attack on Northeast, is indeed the 'climactic stroke in Wiseman's rhetorical design' (Benson & Anderson 1989: 138), and a comment on what is, on the school's part, an inability to judge how critics might perceive its declared goals. The principal reads, to a faculty meeting, a letter she has received from an 'academically sub-average' alumnus, Bob Walter, who is about to be dropped into service in Vietnam and wishes to bequeath his Army life insurance to the school:

> 'I have only a few hours before I go … I pray that I will make it back, but it is all in God's hands now. You see I am going with three other men; we are going to be dropped behind the DMZ. The reason for telling you this is that all my insurance money will be given, for that scholarship I once started, but never finished, if I don't make it back. I am only insured for ten thousand dollars – maybe it could help someone … My personal family usually doesn't understand me; they don't understand why I have to do what I do do [*sic*] … They say, 'Don't you value life? Are you crazy?' My answer is yes, but I value all the lives of South Vietnam, and the free world … Please don't say anything to Mrs C. – she would only worry over me. I am not worth it. I am only a body doing a job.'

The boy is off on what he sees as a grand American adventure; he is 'only a body doing a job', realising the legacy of JFK's commitment to the free world, and to the people of South Vietnam. Like the Project SPARC[21] astronauts earlier seen acting out another of Kennedy's aspirations (in which, through technological prowess, the Soviets are subdued), Bob must do his duty and prevent the spread of collectivism. Unlike the simulated space flight there is a risk of death, but Bob knows this – it is what his schooling has prepared him for. As *High School* begins with a dairy product, so it ends with a military product; the perfect tool of American imperialism has been moulded, 'just like a Chevrolet rolling off the GM line' (Wiseman quoted in Atkins 1976: 48). 'Now when you get a letter like this', concludes the teacher, beaming proudly, 'to me it means that we are very successful at Northeast High School. I think you will all agree with me.' Wiseman cuts to the credits, and his case rests.

In recent years Wiseman has become increasingly vehement in his abjuration of the potential for reform in documentaries:

> Documentaries are thought to have the same relation to social change as penicillin to syphilis. The importance of documentaries as instruments for change is stubbornly clung to, despite the total lack of any supporting evidence … Documentaries, like plays, novels, poems – are fictional in form and have no measurable social utility. (Quoted in MacDonald & Cousins 1998: 282)[22]

However non-reformist Wiseman may declare himself, it is worth noting that, as Raymond Aron said in 1965, 'If you study social organisations in detail, you will find something to improve everywhere. In order to seek a revolution – that is, a total upheaval – you must assume an overall viewpoint, take up a synthetic model, define the essence of a given society, and reject that essence' (1965: 5–6). It is doubtful that, at least subsequent to *Titicut Follies*, Wiseman has sought an upheaval. A theme of rejection, however, especially of authority, courses through *High School*, befitting an intellectually acute filmmaker emergent in the late 1960s, when despondency was overtaking optimism in the popular imagination and disillusionment with the 'machine' (Savio 1995: 111) of American society ran high. Students involved in the Free Speech Movement, as Dominick Cavallo notes, 'started to see themselves as fodder for an educational system – and a society – determined to mould them into efficient and compliant components' (Cavallo 1999: 109). University of California president Clark Kerr proudly called Berkeley a 'knowledge factory', but this metaphor provoked some collegiates, who 'saw it as proof that they were perceived by society as "products" and "resources" whose destiny was to serve the needs of an unidentified "national purpose" not of their choosing' (ibid.). Wiseman's functionalist hypothesis in *High School* is clear: teachers – the agents of ideological knowledge and power (Ginsberg's 'Moloch' personified) – suppress personal identity in their students to make way for the instillation of conservative values.

Kerr's 'national purpose' – which Wiseman questions and indicts in *High School* (and to a degree in most of his films) – and its implementation via a 'hypnotic' abuse of power by an institution acting *in loco parentis*, was of great concern not only to Wiseman, but to a great many of his more outspokenly reformist contemporaries. From Ken Kesey to SDS, egalitarians, artists and New Leftists believed in a danger inherent in modern America's 'assembly-line' ethos: homogenisation.[23] 'Beginning with school', wrote Charles A. Reich in *The Greening of America*, 'an individual is systematically stripped of his imagination, his creativity, his heritage, his dreams and his personal uniqueness, in order to style him into a productive unit for a mass technological society' (1970: 5). According to campus dissident Mark Kleiman, as expressed in an agitative SDS pamphlet:

> Both student and teacher are tool *and* product of administrative totalitarianism. The student comes out of high school a finished product to be consumed by either the agro-business or the war machine. He is by then also a tool, to be used to make others conform. The teacher, who began as a tool, in an Orwellian nightmare finally believes that he is helping his students to lead useful and moral lives. (1970: 320)

The condition of 'orderly, gentle, peaceful slavery' (de Tocqueville 1966: 693) that de Tocqueville saw underpinning nineteenth-century US democracy was, if Kleiman is to be believed, insidiously established at Northeast. As Wiseman – a polymath in his second major career – well knew by the time of *High School*, the opportunity for individualism and reinvention still existed at the heart of what America had always promised. But, for many, the American success story meant only regimentation and narrow expectations: a blinkered future founded upon the bounty of the post-war economy and the cautious, conservative wills of one's parents and mentors.

After completing *High School*, Wiseman turned his attention to the means by which the affluent society maintained its desired state of social removal from the other America and silenced those dissenters – Ivy League radicals and ghetto fighters alike – who might question its values too vigorously. Filmed in the autumn of 1968 (in the immediate aftermath of the anti-war riots that beset the Democratic Convention in Chicago),[24] Wiseman's *Law and Order*, its very title signifying a perspective critical of the Right's resurgence, examines the Kansas City police force's culpability and responds to that body's militaristic enforcement of consensus diktat. Although the film suggests that policemen are always close to losing their battle against anti-social menaces – and by no means are the officers the only physically threatening presence – Wiseman appears broadly to sympathise with the liberal-intellectual stance against the 'law and order' platform and its undertones of state-sponsored repression.

'Law and order', a phrase that conveyed a feeling of pervasive reluctance to jeopardise hard-won gains made in the years after World War Two, became in the late 1960s a mantra against so-called 'limousine liberals' and their policies aimed at tackling the root causes of crime rather than simply imprisoning every criminal. Johnson, upon declaring his 'war on crime' to Congress in March 1965, insisted that 'the long-run solution to crime is jobs, education, and hope' (quoted in Isserman & Kazin 2000: 202). This emphasis was, however, easily lambasted by Republicans looking to exploit domestic unrest. Gerald Ford, House minority leader in 1966, warned of what he saw as a 'soft social theory that the man who heaves a brick through your window or tosses a firebomb into your car is simply the misunderstood and underpriviliged product of a broken home' (quoted in Edsall & Edsall 1991: 51). By 1968, years of street crime, riots and aggressive protestation had embittered the majority of Americans' attitudes towards civil rectitude: public order was seen to be crumbling. 'Let the police run this country for a year or two', urged the now independent George Wallace on the campaign trail, 'and there wouldn't be any riots' (quoted in Isserman & Kazin 2000: 237). Although Wallace did not win the presidential election of November 1968 (the Alabamian governor's image was, at least above the Mason-Dixie line, tainted by unconcealed bigotry), Nixon would take the White House for the Republicans and symbolically demarcate the end of a political era. As he pledged during his second bid for office: 'This is a nation of laws and as Abraham Lincoln has said, "No one is above the law, no one is below the law", and we're going to enforce the law and Americans should remember that if we're going to have law and order.'[25] To most liberals and those on the Left, such rhetoric appealed to the worst in every citizen's nature.

As in *Titicut Follies* and *High School*, the majority of *Law and Order*'s scenes (as far as they can be so called) yield to the next; there are no resolutions – and no proposed solutions to what Wiseman ambivalently seems to concede are problematic issues. As he admits: 'I started off with the naïve idea of "getting the pigs," but realised that the police do not have a monopoly on brutality.'[26] The majority of *Law and Order*'s content, though, *is* undeniably pessimistic (and often appalling), as Wiseman focuses again on the plight of the other America following his despairing of suburban apathy at Northeast High. A prostitute, in the midst of a raid apparently carried out without a warrant, is held in a fierce armlock by a vice squad officer – 'Don't choke me no more', she pleads, as another cop says she is 'imagining it'; a drunk man is violently pushed to the ground as he yells 'you ain't got no guts'; an officer tells a young car thief (Howard) that he would 'like to break your god-damned head'; and a middle-aged woman despairs about being 'thrown into a paddy wagon bodily'. 'Jesus Christ, man – it's their way or none', she cries.

Law and Order constitutes an unfavourable illustration of the police of Kansas City and of the city itself. By his inclusion of so many physically confrontational scenes between the apparently belligerent police and exasperated poor, Wiseman engenders a disconcerting hypothesis: if, like the staff of Bridgewater, the police force had *carte blanche*, then perhaps its true nature as a modern-day 'Gestapo' would be exposed. (In Chicago the comparison was explicitly made, after police officers violently suppressed demonstrators.)[27] Indeed, Wiseman includes in *Law and Order* a series of projected mug shots that evoke the pseudo-scientific endeavours of nineteenth-century anthropologists to define a 'criminal type'. This stark sequence criticises the police's (unconscious yet perhaps real) continuation of a phrenological premise – the rogues' gallery – into modern times; we may even infer from this sequence that an unseen officer is 'reading' these physiognomies as might a genetic supremacist pursuing, in Miles Orvell's words, 'twisted theories of criminality that associated anti-social behaviour with a certain slant of the forehead or tilt of the nose' (2003: 31). Although the faces are diverse in character, and belong to people of disparate races, they share the same, hardened expression; these are countenances beaten down by life and its unending lack of real choices, both political and social. Consequently, when much later in the film we see and hear an electioneering Nixon's rancorous public address on the theme of criminal justice, it is with a sense of foreboding; poker-faced secret service men and police surround the podium, looking like Nazi agents and filmed in ominous close-up. When the eventual victor in the election of 1968 calls for 'respectful law and order', his words become, historically, a barometer of the shifting political climate. In the minds of liberals, notes William L. O'Neill, 'The Great Society was a marvellous idea', yet it became increasingly evident that most Americans would 'cheerfully have settled for a safe one' (1971: 148).

Law and Order's occasional glimmers of emotional relief come from pathos and a darkly comic inclination on the part of the filmmaker to join in the inured drollery of Kansas City's underclass. The despondency is leavened by some engaging and tender material: the abandoned black child in the care of the young, pipe-smoking officer, who buys her a candy bar and comforts her with toys as tears run down her face; the vulnerable husband who is close to crying because he thinks his wife has been abusing their daughter ('I ain't never been in trouble with the law'); the amiable teenage street informants chatting with their policeman friend as he leans out of his patrol car window. Moments like these serve to lend a balance to *Law and Order* that is arguably lacking in Wiseman's previously single-minded films; moreover, we are presented with the difficult question of how America should deal with violent and abusive recidivists like Howard, whom, we learn, gets away with only 'a slap on the wrist'. Gary Arnold notes that:

> Wiseman doesn't 'get' the cops, and he doesn't glorify them. What he does get is a vivid impression of their working lives and through this a complex sense of what it means to be in their position in a large American city. It's not an enviable position: much of the work is banal and repetitive and inconclusive, but there is the implicit threat of violence in any radio call. Moreover, the cops are expected to dispose of countless routine problems – drunks, accidents, family quarrels – that can't be 'solved' to anyone's satisfaction and that most 'decent' or privileged middle-class people don't want to touch. (1970: C6)

The police do indeed face a Sisyphean undertaking, but in *Law and Order* – a subtle but affecting plea for social justice – what matters more is the underlying, unspoken reason for the cyclical despondency, oppression, personal isolation and dread that allow the other America to exist. The overarching sense is one of a crippling societal failure: the fat woman in the station reminds us that the human spirit is hard to crush, but the tramp Bagsby's total inebriation proves that it all too often is. Confused as to its moral duty in world and home affairs, the 'decent', affluent society sought solace from a culture of fear – perpetuated in part by the mainstream media – in the subjugation of minorities, poor people, outspoken students and activists, and in the worship of a white, Anglo-Saxon Protestant God whose mercy did not extend to all of the nation under Him.

In *Hospital*, the dialogic content begins with a series of fractious exchanges between doctors and patients in the busy emergency room:[28] a distraught black woman is probed about her very recently dead mother's pathological history; a black, alcoholic man is questioned about the condition of his stools; a young, white, overdosing heroin user is barely able to respond to a doctor's vital queries; and a greatly disturbed black woman has to be carried to a bed by a policeman. These vignettes, as well as instantly establishing an atmosphere of uneasiness and panic, all concern the effects and uses of mollifying drugs, whether proscribed or prescribed: the grieving woman becomes frustrated with a physician's demands to know what colour pills her mother was taking, and is offered a sedative – an acceptable chemical remedy – as she becomes tearful. The alcoholic has sedated himself to the point of chronic illness with a legal substance, and ended up in care. Unable to rouse the heroin user from his stupor, the young doctor tries, with admirable patience, to ascertain how much his case has taken – the response is a mumbled request that no police be called. The urban poor of 1969 had a need for distraction through chemical means every bit as great as their middle-class, bohemian contemporaries; the crucial distinction between the hippies' and the New Yorkers' self-administering is that whilst the former viewed drug-taking as a 'mind-expanding' leisure pursuit, the latter sought soporiferous escape.[29]

A thematic undercurrent of disquiet runs through Wiseman's early work, but it is in *Hospital* that this motif – the modern condition and its bearing on lives in turmoil – most repeatedly surfaces. Inside the geometric, oppressive walls of functional institutions, superstructural manifestations of an attempt to conquer nature's cruellest territories, we see how humankind, to appropriate *Hospital*'s osteologist, 'is not born with disease [but] acquires these disorders when he tries to adapt to a certain level of civilisation'. Only the First World, with its promotion of structural care, can precipitate mass worry regarding long-term health and well-being in even its poorest citizens, and only in the industrialised West do we find regimes that have, rightly or wrongly, tried to screen their subjects from the reality of death. Wiseman does not shy away from depicting the failure of the world's richest country to eradicate mortality, madness and destitution, instead preferring to foreground these (metaphorical and literal) viscera in his films as a means of countering America's post-war assertion – based largely on faith in technology and science – of superiority.

In the late 1960s dissenting social critics and the wider left-wing public alike viewed large institutions of all kinds as fallible and manipulative, a critique with which Wiseman frequently concurs. Moreover, it is possibly as succinct an illustration of the filmmaker's convictions as can be found: the fundamental goodness of human beings under threat from misguided, domineering authority. This does not mean that Wiseman always disapproves of filmic subjects whose vocations apply the strictly disciplined American regime; he is often sympathetic to those who enforce an ideal, the 'humanity', as Morgan Miller observes, 'trapped within the technology'.[30] Many of the doctors in *Hospital* appear to be working hard to perform their function, and seem well aware of rising public expectations. In contrast to the warders of *Titicut Follies*, the teachers of *High School*, and the policemen of *Law and Order*, here the professionals are seen as diligent bearers of a national burden.

In this sense, *Hospital* marks Wiseman's depictive maturation; he no longer employs didactic editing or strives to realise a pre-conceived notion of slant or attack. Rather, it would seem that the once zealous reformist has finally settled upon a more balanced (or at least moderate) approach to filmic commentary; New York Metropolitan is not, like Bridgewater in *Titicut Follies*, an aberrant, modern-day Bedlam, but a typical example of a hard-pressed public healthcare unit (see Benson & Anderson 1989: 151). As a result, *Hospital* is not so much an indictment than a gradual, elegiac portrait: the different nature of the fourth institution in the series has necessarily led to the attenuation of Wiseman's methodology.

In one scene, an amiable psychiatrist speaks with a young, black, schizophrenic transvestite – Mr Vivas – who has come for a welfare assessment in a bid to cease prostituting himself. After interviewing Mr Vivas, the doctor makes an impassioned, telephoned plea to a bureaucrat, the farcically named Miss Hightower, for allowance. This lengthy exchange, with which Wiseman stays in an almost insufferably long take indicative of sympathy with the doctor, ends with the exasperated physician looking up (perhaps to Wiseman as he takes sound) and declaiming, 'She hung up on me!' As two links in a chain of approval – the remote official and the public interface – Miss Hightower and the doctor both try to do their jobs: hers conserving funds for judicious allocation; his providing immediate palliation of poverty. The impasse, however, proves too much: the system cannot cope, and Mr Vivas must remain forever (at least for the spectator) waiting, nervously smoking a cigarette in one of the hospital's uncongenial lobbies.

Repeatedly, we see this inability to accommodate made manifest, but Wiseman's film always presents it not as the fault of indoctrinated operatives but of a

Mr Vivas, stymied by the system in *Hospital* (1969)

malaise deeply rooted in America's political and societal mechanisms. Conservative politicians expediently blamed laziness and immigration for the 'monstrous, consuming outrage' of welfare (President Nixon quoted in Patterson 1996: 167). As Ronald Reagan exclaimed in 1967, 'We are not going to perpetuate poverty by substituting a permanent dole for a paycheck. There is no humanity or charity in destroying self-reliance, dignity, and self-respect ... the very substance of moral fibre' (ibid.). 'There is no question in anybody's mind', said Senator Russell Long, 'that the present welfare system is a mess' (quoted in Patterson 1996: 168). However, the patients in *Hospital* seem to want anything but permanent handouts – rather just a way back to health, work and pride. An elderly woman communicates her desire for support, 'when need comes'. 'You want to remain self-supporting, you don't want the government to support you all the time – don't you think so? Everybody has that', she maintains. America's shift to the Right with the imminent election of Nixon (an obvious concern for Wiseman in *Law and Order*, especially) did not entirely impede Lyndon Johnson's Great Society initiatives.[31] Medicare and Medicaid, two expensive packages aimed at relieving the old and very poor respectively, survived (and called into question the soundness of well-intentioned but unworkable liberal pronouncements).[32] In *Hospital*, no specific blame is apportioned, and no manifesto made plain; it is as though, for the first time in Wiseman's film career, cause (why is something happening?) is subordinate to consequence (what is happening). We care for these dispossessed American citizens precisely because they submit themselves in desperation, not because they are sectioned, arrested or legally required to attend classes.

Wiseman acknowledges the healthcare system's difficulties, but sees them as products of a wider, capitalist ethos in place since the end of feudalism, not as the end results of a legislature's particular policies. 'After all', as Michael Harrington has noted, 'St. Paul's injunction – he who does not work shall not eat – is the basis of the political economy of the West' (1985: 98). (A publicly funded system of comprehensive national health care, of course, would evoke for many affluent Americans the spectre of socialism, even though such provision finds funding in capitalist Europe through taxation.) Wiseman himself dilates:

> It's too much of a liberal's thing to say, 'If only we had more doctors...'. The problems are so much more complicated, so much more interesting ... And you see the staff trying to deal with them as best they can – but they can't correct the problems that led to these people walking through the hospital door in the first place. (Quoted in Levin 1971: 316)

'If', warned Harrington in 1962, 'there is to be a lasting assault on the shame of the other America, it must seek to root out of this society an entire environment, and not just the relief of individuals' (1962: 18). By the close of the 1960s, '"liberal" had become almost synonymous with "sellout,"' notes Mark Kurlansky: 'Phil Ochs amused young people with his song "Love Me, I'm a Liberal". The song's message was that liberals said the right things but could not be trusted to do them' (2005: 166). It is the metropolis – or so goes Wiseman's implied premise in *Hospital*

– that has engendered social disparity and the misery of the lower- and underclass, unable as they are to escape the echelon of the pariah by becoming 'functional', 'valued' components of the pervasive military-industrial complex.[33] In the words of Howard F. Stein, 'functionality is one of our most positively valued cultural symptoms and … any hint of dysfunction, and the dreaded dependency associated with it, is one of our most negatively valued cultural symptoms' (1990: 57). Throughout *Hospital*, New York, a 'dual city' of 'dreams and nightmares', a place in which the working class is estranged and the underclass swells, demonstrates its capacity to yield up incurable penury for the dependent.[34] The city, 'whose charity is inadequately financed, maddening in its slowness, and bureaucratically inexplicable to the uneducated poor' (Harrington 1985: 92), bears responsibility.[35]

Hospital's famous closing shot, as the sound of a dour religious service slowly fades, frames a highway down which endless cars – emblems of hollow, consumerist affluence – pass. It is a summation of Wiseman's outlook at the end of a supposed decade of revolution. The cars are standardised, sterile and carrying fully functioning advocates of the American Way back to suburbia, another bromidic, anaesthetising total institution 'inhabited by people from the same class, the same income, the same age group, witnessing the same television performances, eating the same tasteless pre-fabricated foods from the same freezers, conforming in every outward and inward respect to a common mould' (Lewis Mumford quoted in Diggins 1989: 183). By implication, they are fleeing the loci of anxiety (both in spirit and body) that Wiseman records and reconstitutes in his ongoing account of America's perpetual dichotomies.

CONCLUSION: AWAY FROM THE BROMIDES – BENDING THE RULES OF THE CHANGE GAME

> Any man who genuinely cares for his society will keep clear of any alignment of Right against Left or vice versa, just as a pacifist will have nothing to do with armies arrayed to slaughter one another.
> – Giovanni Baldelli (1971: 23)[36]

Titicut Follies has a distinct central theme – the cruelty of human nature when unchecked by rational authority and community; *High School*'s preoccupation is with the militaristic intellectual blinkering of students; *Law and Order*'s overriding message, regardless of concessions to the police, is that crime, though a symptom of deep social disparity, is not being addressed properly by either politicians or heavy-handed functionaries; *Hospital*'s premise is less clearly delineated (and less replete with 'liberal clichés' (Wiseman quoted in Atkins 1976: 56)) but the film is still concerned with social problems: poverty, inequality and the counter-productive machinations of officialdom. 'I'm not a pharmacist. I've had an opportunity to observe how middle-class reformers play the change game', Wiseman asserts; 'I guess I've gone very far away from the bromides that I started with, especially the simpleminded social work view of help and intervention' (ibid.). The failure of the system – that is to say the immutable capitalist system of the West – is the intangible cause of all the misery and terror on screen in *Hospital*, Wiseman's final work of the 1960s and his first 'mature' film. From the Byronic, middle-class art student who has taken poisoned mescaline to escape the boundaries of his creative despondency, to the underprivileged, black knife victim clinging on to life, everything is beyond an immediate human remedy, and beyond – as the director has realised – reform through schematic politics.

At the closing of the 1960s, pragmatic dissidents were coming to realise the impossibility of ending social injustice with passion and idealism alone.[37] Neither 'managerial liberals', who subscribed to the New Deal and Great Society model in which lobbying interest groups supposedly ensured ongoing democracy, nor activists who stressed the underlying unfairness of remote governance, would carry the day. Radicals who had split from organised New Left groups became more petulant, violent and nihilistic, ironically rendering even more internecine the domestic arguments Nixon had been chosen to assuage. As the 'permissive decade' gave way to the 1970s, it became obvious that one major casualty of the 1960s had been the liberalism that characterised its early gains in the way of civil rights. Fervent blue-collar and Middle-American backlash against oversold reform programmes, riots and 'sanctimonious do-gooders' (Patterson 1996: 677) would prove the nemesis of the increasingly unfocused Democratic Party, and of the hopes embodied by John Kennedy. 'A conservative, it was said, was a liberal who had been mugged; a liberal was a conservative who hadn't been mugged – yet', recalls James T. Patterson (ibid.). Washington could offer only varying degrees of palliation or suppression; America's moral incertitude, guaranteed by Vietnam's continuation, implicit in the speeches of Richard Nixon, and cast from the faces of the war-dead in *Life* magazine, hung heavily over a populace tired of sedition yet unsure of its destiny.

By the late 1960s direct cinema (away from the concert, the heroic protagonist or the dramatic crisis) already needed a new voice, but it would not be one of 'simpleminded' liberalism or formal imposition. Narrative has little place in Wiseman's films of the 1960s because those films are contrived in their anti-syntactical sequencing to operate outside of a reductive structural (or *institutional*) scheme.[38] Propitious was the time, argued the 'Class of 1968', to do away with 'all the orders of meaning and or reality that signs help maintain' (Rivkin & Ryan 1998: 334), and to avoid cultural assertions of axiomatic truth, rectitude and Symbolic Order. The then nascent Post-Structuralist disdain for such orders as 'strategies of power and social control' (ibid.) is arguably as manifest in Wiseman's early 'reality fictions' as it is in contemporaneous agitative or reflexive works (that could never, of course, have found funding from American public television).[39] Ultimately, Wiseman asks of his audience an understanding of how, to amend civilisation, one must *heuristically* question not so much the means of production, but the means by which our acculturation to non-didactic modes of reform may eventually preclude hegemonic influence on the civic realm also. Moreover, to forward a convincing critique of America's institutions that might supplement or supersede those of the transitorily influential New Left (with which Wiseman has much in common), the filmmaker distanced himself from schematic association of any kind, dismissing archetypes of both politics and culture as mutually inclusive, reductive institutions. Herbert Marcuse, perhaps the Sixties' most influential critic of corporate liberalism's disingenuous nature, warned that, 'Contemporary society seems to be capable of containing social change ... the struggle for the solution has outgrown traditional forms. The totalitarian tendencies of the one-dimensional society render the traditional ways and means of protest ineffective – perhaps even dangerous because they preserve the illusion of popular sovereignty' (1964: xii, 256).

Thoreau, in 1849, decried unchecked technological expansion as symbolised by the ever-extending railroad: 'Let your life be a counter friction to stop the machine' (1981: 92). By the middle of the next century, contended those on the Left, demand for compliant technicians was pervading the university and creating an environment in which intellectuality could be bent to the needs of the military-industrial complex; beyond a façade of epistemophilia, lamented Free Speech Movement leader Mario Savio, education served only the power elite's interlocking, all-pervasive network: 'There is a time when the operation of the machine becomes so odious, makes you so sick at heart, that you can't take part ... you've got to put your bodies upon the gears and upon the wheels, upon the levers, upon all the apparatus and you've got to make it stop' (Savio quoted in Lipsit & Wolin 1965: 163; see also Marx 1964: 63). Born at the beginning of both the Great Depression in the US and Nazism in Europe, Wiseman quickly learned that institutional authority could be a beguiling and insidious instrument of conformity. Coming to filmmaking thirty years later, when idealistically conceived non-violent reactions to the mechanisms of American society were already weakening, Wiseman naturally sought to convey a disavowal of commonplace or naïve political obligation. When asked to elaborate on the orientation of his social conscience, Wiseman is typically glib, appropriating a Situationist slogan that may well reveal more than intended: 'As the saying goes, the Marx is more Groucho than Karl' (quoted in Atkins 1976: vii).[40] Notwithstanding a reticence to bare his soul, the director paradoxically betrays a commitment to serious social commentary via his films' gradual abandonment of rhetorical fervency in favour of measured interpretation; all the more effective for an intellectuality beyond immediate interpretation, these films revel in a denial of all that is entrenched within systematised, post-industrial life.

Equality of societal franchise in modern America, since the affluent society had become so almost without realising it, was, for Wiseman, a fallacy maintained by establishment interests and promulgated by serfs of the apparatus: the prison warders, schoolteachers, policemen and bureaucrats who inhabit his oblique yet perceptibly timely *oeuvre*. 'A good filmmaker', said Wiseman, 'has to have some ideas in response to the world' (quoted in Feldman 1976: 68). It is this response, and the myriad contemporaneous rejoinders to the 'pseudopolitical burlesque[s]' (Cavallo 1999: 200) of the decade's end, which inform Wiseman's cinema of the 1960s.

In the film discussed in the final chapter, *Basic Training*, Wiseman recapitulated the anti-authoritarian themes of *High School* and lamented a more palpably destructive reality: the ongoing war for 'freedom' in Vietnam.

7 | THE SYSTEM FIGHTS BACK

Our arms must be mighty, ready for instant action, so that no potential aggressor may be tempted to risk his own destruction.
  – President Dwight D. Eisenhower[1]

It was like the fantasy life of a kid. I'd played cops and robbers as a kid, so when I saw what was happening in Nam, I really wanted to cash in on it. Why not? It was like being invited to play with the big kids … Nobody in the unit was over twenty-one.
  – Anonymous veteran (quoted in Baker 1982: 56)

In the summer of 1970, Frederick Wiseman visited the US Army Training Centre at Fort Knox, Kentucky, to film over the course of nine weeks – the entire duration of basic training from induction to graduation. What the filmmaker found during his days at the camp was a politically timely combination of human contrivance and feral atavism. Reminiscent in equal measure of *The Green Berets* (1968) and William Golding's *Lord of the Flies* (1954), *Basic Training*, completed in 1971, depicts an installation whose straightforward public remit – to turn boys into soldiers – belies disturbing paradoxes. Alumni numbering many thousands, from high schools like Northeast, graduated into the army in the late 1960s and found themselves in a world as familiar as it was strange; Fort Knox was not only a school, but also a rite of passage engineered by the necessities of a war in freefall.

DROPPING IN: JUST LIKE A MOVIE

The film begins with a sequence of initiation routines, as the recruits arrive at camp. This introduction evokes the customary 'arrival' prelude of the generic war film, and in this sense *Basic Training* is strikingly atypical of Wiseman's work. We see new trainees alighting from a bus, carrying their personal belongings in small luggage cases; they nervously dab their trousers and swipe their soon to be shaved hair with their hands. Vital statistics are taken; bunks are allocated by number; and the depersonalisation ritual is completed by the application of electric clippers to scalps. The troops receive inoculations, and pose for photographs against the Stars and Stripes, a globe (meant to intimate their potential or honorary kingship of the world upon joining the American forces) held in front of them by the photographer's assistant. 'Say something nice about George Wallace, huh?' says the white photographer to a black subject; the trainee does indeed smile at what is a refreshingly honest admission of political insidiousness. A drill sergeant asks, in the usual bellicose tones of an army trainer, if the assembled troops have their duffle bags and dog-tags ready and packed; the concerted reply is 'Yes, sergeant.' Already, the scene is set for a routine of drilled compliance.

Wiseman follows this montage with something equally redolent of generic narratives: the induction speech. An affable general takes the podium to the fanfare of 'The Caissons Go Rolling Along', and welcomes the young men to Fort Knox:

> I think you're gonna find that training here could be described as rigorous, probably also described as demanding, but you're gonna find that it's well within your capabilities ... What we are going to try and do, is give you the military training, which, backed up by your native instincts and native intelligence, is going to turn you into a soldier, so that your reactions in times of stress are going to be a combination of instinct, native ability and intelligence, reinforced by the military training that will give you the skills to react effectively.

So basic training is as much about instinct as it is discipline – at the camp, a contradictory, confusing sense of primal ordinance is instilled right away: a good soldier, so the recruits have been told, is an animal that obeys rules laid down by a distant elite to lay claim on territory. The inductees cannot know their own function within this new microcosm, and so are edged into submission through the familiar process of the double bind. If the young men are to fight, then they cannot at the same time ruminate; the nature and ethics of warfare regarding Vietnam were being questioned and highlighted by ubiquitous, arresting images and distressing testimony from the front line. 'There's nothing wrong', comments Susan Sontag in an essay on the emotional effects of war photography, 'with standing back and thinking' (2003: 106). In civilian life, this is observably true. In war without mandate, however, philosophical enquiry is insidious exactly because, as Sontag continues, 'Nobody can think and hit someone at the same time' (ibid.). Lt. Hoffman, 'your Company Commander', makes things plain in another speech aimed, as many (including Benson and Anderson (1989), and Barry Keith Grant (1992)) have noted, at pre-empting dissent in a similar manner to the teachers of *High School*: 'You start trying to fight the system, that's when you get in trouble. If you go along with the system, it's fine; it's when you buck it you come into the problems.' 'All we ask', continues Hoffman, 'is that you go along with it.' In contrast to the students of Northeast during their lessons in the liberal arts, however, the trainees seen in close-up appear rapt – perhaps unsurprisingly, given that they are doomed to stigmatisation or court-martial if they wish to escape.

Wiseman returns to certain recruits repeatedly in *Basic Training*, and, although there are no true protagonists, there is demonstrated within the film an empathetic regard for the institutionally subjected that is arguably lacking in *Titicut Follies*, *High School*, *Law and Order* and *Hospital*. Wiseman also abides by generic custom in *Basic Training* to the point of utilising dramatic stereotypes and narrative conventions for reasons other than simple formal or ideological subversion. As Grant writes, Wiseman evinces 'a greater interest in formal matters than [in] the earlier documentaries' (1992: 80), and this is a rhetorical strategy. The filmmaker wants the spectator to consider the relationship of notional fiction to notional reality, and to draw inference from a broad context of filmic representation. 'The essential concern of the [typical] war film', writes Grant, 'is to show the importance of a group working together to achieve a common goal; individuals must be welded together into a unit, a platoon, in which each works for the good of all and a clear, mutually accepted hierarchy is established' (1995: 118). Troops embroiled in the melee of Vietnam frequently declared, hinting at what was a psychologically protective (and thus necessary) sense of unreality, that the experience of fighting was 'just like a movie', because that was the frame of reference most beneficial to their coping strategies. Wiseman, by imposing generic conventions upon reality and highlighting popular mythology's appropriation of history, comments on and echoes this dubious means of comprehending, via the mental formulation of archetypes, an increasingly complex world. There was, in Vietnam, no unambiguous John Wayne figure to lead America's charge, but the trainees must still be shown moral examples, even when they do not properly exist. Despite the best efforts of generals and presidents to reiterate the need for victory, the methods and motives compelling the instructors – and, by extension, the war itself – were mired in confusion.

Throughout *Basic Training* (one of the earliest American films concerning Vietnam), we are invited by Wiseman's tessellation of a cinematic template to question the role of fantasy in the shaping of real life, and to consider what reality might ultimately entail for the often reluctant soldiers who we see being methodically 'welded together'. Active service is clearly more ruinous to potential than the conformist indoctrination evinced in *High School*, and, despite the numerous comparisons invited by *Basic Training*'s motifs, more scourging of innocence; Vietnam was a deadly destination, whether one was a draftee or volunteer. In *The Basic Training of Pavlo Hummel* (1969), playwright and veteran David Rabe's Sergeant Tower tells his recruits: 'Where you think you are? You think you in the movies? This here real life, gen'l'men. You actin' like there ain't never been a war in this world ... Don't you know what I'm sayin'? You got to want to put this steel in a man' (2002: 39). Tower, though, seems more honest and less equivocal in his intent than Fort Knox's instructors in *Basic Training* – Wiseman's 'war film' without heroes.

Wiseman, following the orientation speech, cuts to a film the trainees are being shown that demonstrates how one should clean one's teeth to 'avoid cavities while in the army'. Regimenting the most simple of individual ablutions to a surreal degree, this programmed enforcement of a particularly Western ritual is a diversion aimed at steering somatic attention towards the cosmetic and superficial. Despite Vietnam historian Mark Woodruff's claim that 'American troops are not trained to be mindless automatons' (1999: 239), it would nonetheless seem that they could not be trusted to carry out their own dental care regimen without group habituation effected by the screening of an indoctrinatory movie. Headed for an environment in which any kind of bathing was usually impossible, the troops would have little opportunity for tooth-brushing in the field of combat. After the students happily partake in the practical exercise, to the aural accompaniment of the educational film's jingoistic march, Wiseman offers his response to this method of filmic tutelage: holes in their teeth, so the filmmaker implies by apposition, were the least of their long-term worries.

MAKING PEACE WITH THE GUN

The gun is emblematically part of army training, and a longstanding totem of masculine endeavour in a world almost defined by precarious relationships of arms to counter-arms. An M-16-A1 was the combat soldier in Vietnam's standard tool, and the recruits in *Basic Training*, after their lesson on dental care, are ritualistically taught about its protective qualities by sergeants whose enthusiasm for the rifle is disconcertingly fetishistic:

> The M-16-A1 rifle ... Study it very carefully, nut-for-nut, screw-for-screw, rivet-for-rivet – and you will find very shortly that it is exactly, *exactly* my friends, the same as the one I have in my hand. Millimetre-for-millimetre, square inch-for-square inch, the weapon you have in your hand is exactly the same as I have in my hand.

A member of the assembled company asks if these mass-produced, identical (and hence 'perfect') 'guns' have been used before, worried about handling something that may have despatched Vietnamese soldiers. The sergeant, however, is more concerned about inappropriate terminology, and relishes again the chance to speak its name: 'Guns! Alright, this, is an M-16-A1 ... weapon; rifle; piece; or what-have-you. At no time, under any circumstances, will you refer to this piece of metal in my hands as a *gun*: a *gun* is a high-trajectory weapon.' Chastised, the recruit repeats his question, modifying his language: 'Have these weapons ever been used before? To kill people I mean.' 'Not yet', replies the sergeant. A muffled voice insists that, 'They never will, either', and a second senior officer intercedes to make the situation as clear as he feels is comfortable:

> We're getting pretty heavy on this discussion right here. It's like discussing religion: I don't discuss it with anybody because I don't believe I have any right to discuss whether you should kill a man or you should not kill a man.

He does, however, go on to do just that, incorporating, like his colleague, an ostensibly pointless list of synonymous terms:

> I do know one thing, gentlemen. If a man attempts to shoot me, kill me, slay me or murder me, I definitely will attempt to stop him in the fastest way possible. There's a lot going on about this nowadays, and I do believe you got a right to sound off about it, but what I'm saying is, when you get out in the jungles in Vietnam, I don't believe the thought of killing a man will enter your mind when you get hit from three sides ... You probably won't have anything on your mind but 'survive, survive, survive'. The man is out to kill you, gentlemen ... If you [think] he's not going to kill you, you're going to Cam Ranh Bay in a body bag ... If you want to get back from Vietnam, then you'd better learn how to use this black lickin' stick, and use it properly.

The truth about the M-16-A1, for all the discursive pedantry employed by military trainers to eulogise it as a triumph of engineering, is that it was not a reliable weapon in the arena of Vietnam; dirt, water and debris clogged its intricate mechanisms on many occasions, leaving troops vulnerable to attack by Viet Cong and NVA armed with the simpler, sturdier and easier to clean Kalashnikov provided by the Soviets. Far from being the American soldier's trusted friend – the venerated 'black lickin' stick' – the M-16 was, in the field, a despised liability, as noted by this anonymous veteran:

> [The M-16] was a piece of shit that never should have gone over there with all the malfunctions … I started hating the fucking government … There were times when we'd rather use [enemy] weapons than our own. I once took an AK-47 from a dead NVA and used it instead of my Mattel toy [M-16]. (Quoted in Shay 1994: 17)

Obviously, this man survived to tell his story; he was, however, understandably aggrieved and left permanently distrustful of hierarchical superiors. The soldier quoted above saw the provision of faulty weaponry as a betrayal by officers whose seniority meant that they themselves were not dependent on deficient rifles. The sergeants' 'black magic language'[2] when describing the M-16 in *Basic Training* might well be symptomatic of a desire to mask any doubts and interpolate any potentially undermining discourse by destroying the recruits' trust in their own linguistic ability; if the soldier loses faith in his weapon, something psychologist Jonathan Shay describes as 'more richly invested with emotion and symbolism than any other material objects he is likely to use' (1994: 141), then he is ineffectual as a military functionary. Tautology inculcates what the inexperienced troops will not be qualified to contradict until they arrive in the squalor of Vietnam: above all the M-16 must be trusted, loved and addressed correctly, because its owner's life, honour and success in combat depend on it.

After a short scene featuring men marching (*Basic Training* includes many such scenes, rightly construed by most critics as redolent of *High School*'s messages about 'keeping in step'),[3] Wiseman cuts to a rifle range, outdoors. A senior officer demonstrates the firing of an M-16, resting the butt on various parts of his body, to the amusement of the trainees:

> Next he will unlock the weapon, and put the butt on his thigh, and fire one round downrange [the demonstrator fires – there is impressively little recoil]. He will next put the butt of the weapon – this is the one I like – in his groin [there is laughter from the trainees]. Now if this hurts, let's face it, he's a married man, he's not going to do this [more laughter, and the demonstrator fires again, from a phallic angle]. And when I say now, he will fire all twenty rounds on automatic [the man fires a short burst, and the recruits (in inserted close-ups) gasp in awe].

Meaning, as is often the case in Wiseman's films, is imparted in this scene by both the pro-filmic content and Wiseman's textual selection and appropriation. The explicit aim of the pro-filmic event is to reassure the trainees that the M-16 is

The gun as mechanised phallus in *Basic Training* (1971)

comfortable and 'loyal', a miracle of the high-tech age that can only hurt the enemy; secondly, and maybe reflexively, the officer sexualises the rifle in the minds
of his adolescent audience – it becomes a potent machine capable of ejaculating
death, and a paradoxical, permanently readied lover and penis; thirdly, Wiseman,
in his insertion of facial and mechanical close-ups as the guns discharge, suggests
that we are indeed witnessing a ritual celebration of mechanised carnality: 'Why',
asks Richard Fuller in reviewing this scene and the one previous, 'would you ever
again need a woman?' (quoted in Atkins 1976: 106). The army, as poet Adrienne
Rich wrote in 'Caryatid: Two Columns' in 1973, empowers young trainees like they
have never been empowered before:

> The capacity for dehumanizing another which so corrodes male sexuality is carried
> over from sex into war. The chant of the basic training drill: 'This is my rifle, this is my
> gun [my penis]; this is for killing, this is for fun' is not a piece of bizarre brainwashing
> invented by some infantry sergeant's fertile imagination; it is a recognition of the
> fact that when you strike the chord of sexuality in the ... [male] psyche, the chord of
> violence is likely to vibrate in response; and vice versa. (1979: 114)

For the recruits, this jovially implied endowment of the weapon with sexual meaning is humorous, and exteriorisation of a shared response bonds them as 'mature'
cohorts; in the army's psychology of persuasion, though, it has a deeper purpose:
to reach and stimulate the primal psyches of the civilised 'gentlemen' whose nature is being denuded in order that they might become soldiers, men of strident

instinct. 'In retrospect', observes Barry Keith Grant of *Basic Training*'s gun scenes, 'Kaminsky's mad monologue in *Titicut Follies* about the connection between American military aggression and sexual pathology would seem to possess an unsettling quality of prophecy' (1992: 93). Rather than proposing a *direct* anthropological link between territorial assertion and male instinct, however, Wiseman, in *Basic Training*, chooses to expound upon the psychological means by which those who are susceptible can be manipulated.

One way to engage young men's interests is with base symbolism – visual similes appeal more directly to our cognitive faculty than relatively abstract political or ideological terms. Although the 'silent majority' of Americans at home still supported the war as a righteous crusade whose ends were essential to US interests, the anti-war voice, with its colourful slogans, brash films and rock music backing, was by far the loudest and most resonant in the young. Arthur Penn's *Bonnie and Clyde* (1967) was one of several fiction films released in the late 1960s to feature ballistomaniacal protagonists fighting authority figures. For Clyde, the gun – in lieu of intercourse – becomes an ersatz means of releasing sexual energy; for the boys at Fort Knox leaving their girls behind, it may yet come to take on similar import in rendering sex into aggression. It is not surprising, given the politically charged nature of the times and the militancy of domestic dissenters like the Black Panthers, that the US Army wished to reclaim the discourse of weaponry for itself and channel worship of the gun toward fighting faceless enemies overseas (see Hoberman 1998). In *The Basic Training of Pavlo Hummel*, Sergeant Tower tells his recruits: 'This an M-16 rifle ... You got to love this rifle, gen'l'men, like it you pecker and you love to make love' (Rabe 2002: 169). Rabe – in an unsubtle mode that Wiseman swiftly abandoned – juxtaposes action and sound to underscore the connection between sexual urges, technology and warfare: as we see and hear the sergeant, stage left, Pavlo, at stage right, is seen having sex with a prostitute. 'To some people', claims a veteran, 'carrying a gun constantly was like having a permanent hard-on. It was a pure sexual trip every time you got to pull the trigger' (Baker 1982: 146). In *Basic Training*, the officers both perpetuate this dangerous, unhealthy association and deftly exploit a perhaps natural, inextricable link between male concepts of sex and destruction. As Loren Baritz writes, 'The power of technology to convert boys into men, to bestow potency in the weak, caused many young American males to think of machinery and sex as the same thing' (1998: 52). More sinisterly, so Baritz hypothesises, such notions were not confined to hormonal youngsters in the lower military echelons: 'The war's leaders in Washington had similar, if vastly more sublimated, attitudes. It was partly the thrill of domination, but it was more than that. They loved weapons' (ibid.).

In one revealing scene, the M-16 is once again positioned as a phallic totem endowed with a protective aura. The parents and siblings of an eager recruit visit their prodigal kin, and lavish upon his gun an almost obscene veneration:

Mother: Don't touch it! Nobody touch it! Nobody touch it! Isn't it ... Ooh, it's a
         beauty – M-16. Don't touch it! It's so beautiful.
Older brother: How much does it weigh?

Recruit [proudly]: Six pounds ... Hundred and fifty-five dollars.

Mother: Is it clean?

Recruit: I'm almost done.

Father: You better do it right, gotta get it exact.

Mother: Spotless, it has to be spotless ...

Recruit: Twenty rounds, in three seconds; nine hundred rounds in less than a minute [the smiling younger boys look impressed, and inspect the weapon] ...

My elevation is fourteen and my windage is fourteen ... I feel good.

Father: The only thing is you do what you're supposed to do at all times.

Mother: If you don't come out of here and become a true man, by the time you're done here, you'll never be a man ... A true American soldier.

Recruit [kissing his little sister]: Happy birthday, tyke!

Evidently, as Wiseman communicates here, the boy is fitting in and is well on his way to manhood, via his conforming to the training programme and appreciation of the literal (if not the symbolic) power of his 'beautiful' M-16. The father seems keen that his son 'gets it exact', offering encouragement to the younger man so as he might better prove his commitment to what Baritz identifies as contemporary affinities of the 'masculine' American:

> The teenage boy cruising the streets in his tail-finned car in the '50s, or on his roaring motorcycle in the '60s, was training himself to love machinery, and to use the internal combustion engine as a surrogate for sex or as the means to make himself more sexually attractive. The more powerful the machine, the stronger the connection. The most manifestly powerful machines are those that kill. (1998: 52)

By turning the M-16 into something symbolically (if perversely) similar to Hendrix's guitar, an instrument of dramatic sexual potency, the army hoped to give its fledglings a sense of purpose and potential that was weakening rapidly for those engaged.

In 1966, years before de-escalation was at last effected (by Nixon), even Secretary of Defence Robert McNamara expressed his doubts in a speech that seemed less replete with political rhetoric than the guilty venting of emotion. '[Man has] a near-infinite capacity for folly ... the ambivalence of technology grows with its own complexity', he said. 'The real question is not whether we should have tools. But only whether we are becoming tools' (quoted in Hendrickson 1996: 244). By 1970, senior officers in the field had begun to question whether the war was viable anymore on an ethical basis, and Commander-in-Chief Nixon received letters from such dissenters in quantity. One communication to the president condemned 'a war in which few of us believe. This leaves us with nothing but survival – kill or be killed – as a motivation ... It seems very possible that if the war is allowed to continue much longer, young Americans in the military will simply refuse en masse to cooperate' (quoted in Hammond 1996: 370). Within the ranks, a crisis of faith was growing, and the problem of 'troublemaking' had to be addressed at an early stage in a soldier's career if he was to enter the arena with conviction.

HICKMAN: 'O FOR A MANLY LIFE IN THE CAMP'[4]

In the midst of several scenes featuring bayoneting and boxing – hand-to-hand tests of bodily prowess in combat – Wiseman introduces Private Hickman, a fresh-faced, skinny draftee who wears thick glasses. More so even than Vladimir in *Titicut Follies*, Hickman succinctly represents an embodiment of the processes at work in the institution under scrutiny; we feel – largely because of his physical unsuitability to an army career – that Fort Knox is forcing nature, corroding to create. The trainee fits the stereotype of a 'dork', and is far removed from the broad-shouldered military ideal, Whitman's 'strong man erect' (ibid.). As Grant opines, he is 'a real-life Sad Sack, in the tradition of Charlie in *Shoulder Arms* (1918) and Lou Costello in *Buck Privates* (1940) … He is, in short, a marvellous found example of the comic misfit' (1992: 91). Hickman is unable, or unwilling, to march in time with his colleagues during drill exercises (once more the theme of keeping 'in step' is revisited by Wiseman), but seems to take this 'deficiency' in good humour: the spectator warms to the incompetent Hickman because of his inability to conform to behavioural models imposed upon him by superordinates and their feral logic. 'Very quickly the situation becomes primitive', remarks an anonymous veteran, who gives a frightening, Darwinist description of life in boot camp as red in tooth and claw: 'The leaders are automatically the biggest … Everything is relegated to strength … Everybody understands brute force' (quoted in Baker 1982: 15). Such men as Hickman should not be going to their deaths in Vietnam, of course, but the training given at Fort Knox may convert even the weak into unquestioning stalwarts. As the cliché goes, the army breaks down a boy to make a man; to build a recruit to a new ideal, one must first excoriate the old from him.

'You better think about what you're doing, Hickman, or you'll never make it', says the drill sergeant, contradicting the induction speech about 'native intelligence'; 'Now go and join your chums.' Hickman continues his cakewalk, dragging his feet and grinning in either embarrassment, or bravado, or both. 'You're out of step, Hickman', inculcates the sergeant, enervating the boy in the process. When we next see Hickman, he is being taught how to tie his bootlaces by an officer who concernedly asks him, *in loco parentis*, if he has eaten breakfast that day. Wiseman cuts to another officer making a phone call to the chaplain explaining Hickman's 'motivational problems', and we learn that Hickman has 'suicidal tendencies' and comes from a broken home, a stigmatising provenence in the 1960s. In the chaplain's office, the diffident recruit is asked why he attempted to kill himself by 'swallowing a bunch of pills'. 'All the guys bug me constantly … Last night, about making the bed … They threatened to give me a blanket party if I didn't do everything right, ya know.'

So, it turns out, Hickman's smiles were defensive; he was not so much a comic misfit but a bullied child who needed a way out but could see no way of eliciting compassion other than to take a marginally excessive dose of tranquilisers. The common 'cry for help' of Western malcontents was the prevalent means of drawing attention to mental anguish in boot camp: in Rabe's 1969 play, the eponymous Private Hummel, after being attacked by his comrades, attempts something similar to Hickman. According to an unnamed veteran, 'We had one guy drink a can of Brasso ... I saw a couple of guys snap. But by the time you get to the end of [basic training], you feel like you're the baddest thing that ever walked the earth' (quoted in Baker 1982: 17). As the unnervingly sanguine chaplain (of whom, Benson and Anderson note, a 'bland acceptance of the army' (1989: 178)) says: 'If you fall down in the mud, you have to be willing to get up.' Hickman, the human centre of *Basic Training*, has been broken so that the readying for war may begin.

BENDING STEEL: THE PROCESS OF GETTING AHEAD

> Young males of all primate species engage in play fighting. Furthermore, this sort of play heightens imagination, teaches role taking, and affords the child an opportunity to come to terms with war, violence and death.
>   – Jeffrey Goldstein (1998: 53)

The trainees are seen enthusiastically play-boxing, crawling in the dust and receiving food. One young man is reprimanded by an officious officer for bringing a can of soda, concealed in his pocket, onto the range. 'You think you're real hot today, coming out here with a soda in your pocket trying to sneak one through ... If you don't wipe the smile off your face I'm gonna knock your God damn teeth out ... Get outta here.' After a recruit has bragged to his colleagues about an encounter with a $15 prostitute, three career soldiers, with reference to the then recently released *Patton* (1970), discuss reincarnation – a major theme of Franklin J. Schaffner's film – and the likelihood of Atlantians having infiltrated NASA. Again, as in *Titicut Follies*, we are encouraged by Wiseman to question the relative sanity of enforcers to their charges; does the army command, if its concerns are not in concert with its juniors', have a viable place in an American scheme of nominal pragmatism and practicality? Wiseman provokes incredulity at the sheer earnestness of a discussion that is not so much speculative as downright fanciful: a prostitute fulfils a basic need; wild imaginings and conspiratorial theories are a symptom of paranoia in the wake of assassinations, national guilt and civil unrest. A professional whose remit is to make war against others – the ideological enemy – must find justification wherever, or however, he can. Karma, for these men who view George Patton as a personification of nobility, is less a theoretical, nontheistic Buddhist tract than a game of tit-for-tat, a way of explaining an unfair and illogical world in the lexis of supernatural justice. They are coming to terms, in their own way, with the cruelty of human life. 'Nobody ever won a war by dying for his country', ran *Patton*'s tagline: 'He won it by making the other poor dumb bastard die for his country.' *Patton* was Richard Nixon's favourite film.

A generation previous to the baby-boomers' had fought a war for what was, by consensus, a noble cause. But things were now different for the more perspicacious and wealthy, who could see the illogic of comparing the two conflicts. One veteran, whose parents held the patriotic view, lamented this short-sightedness by authority figures and admitted his fears:

My old man, when the war came, he says, 'Oh, go. You'll learn something. You'll grow up to be a man. Go.' Shit, if my folks had to send their little poodle, they would have cried more tears over that than over me. But I'm supposed to go, because I'm a man. (Quoted in Baker 1982: 13)

Most blue-collar, rural and patriotic youngsters, however, were 'seduced by World War Two and John Wayne movies', and the notion that fighting for his country is 'what a man does with his life' (Baker 1982: 12). (John Wayne and Ray Kellogg's *The Green Berets* had instilled both training for and warfare in Vietnam with this sense of 'duty' and adventurous Americanism. Almost universally condemned by critics as a virtual recruitment advertisement, patriots see *The Green Berets* as a morally rightful tract against Communists.)[5] Successful trainees, like the boy with the M-16 in *Basic Training*, felt good with their new mission in life as 'true American soldiers' because they were sequacious products of the system; in other words, they were *High School*'s true success stories out to get 'the other dumb bastard' because that was what popular culture and their parents had told them was right. Tough, white, all-American movie star John Wayne was a role model for many GIs; as he killed marauding 'Injuns', so his idolaters slew 'gooks' in a real-life movie of their own. Blacks, however, still marginalised as they were in many ways (if not as hated by whites as the Vietnamese), had no such idol to whom they might look – America had not created one.

Wiseman follows the M-16-worshipping vignette by cutting to Lt. Hoffman's office, and to the first of two similar scenes featuring black recruits who, in contrast to the white trainee we have just seen flaunting his gun, are not keeping in step, and not accepting easily their military remit. Hoffman says to a private: 'I understand that this morning you failed to make reveille [bugle] formation with the rest of the company. It is my intention as your commanding officer to give you an article 15 for failing to make reveille. Now, I inform you that you do not have to accept this article. You may, if you wish, request a trial by court martial; this is up to you.' Against the wishes of the lieutenant, the recruit opts for the court martial, and to 'go to jail, period'. It would appear that the soldier would prefer anything – even incarceration – to continuation of his military service. The second scene reiterates and expands upon this theme; this time, though, the private is eloquent and persuasive, drawing attention to uneasy truths about race relations in the US Army of the late 1960s.

Private:	I'm takin' the court martial. Actually, the thing that I did, it's minor, it's less than minor…
Sergeant:	You slept on fire guard, right?
Private:	No, I just … I just refused fire guard … To each his own…
Sergeant:	In a combat situation, if you don't do what you're told sometimes, you can be shot, too.
Private #2:	He might be a good soldier.
Private:	But we're not in war. You're talking about being in war. I don't want no medals. I don't want to be here, period. I don't want no medals.

> I want my life. That's my medal, and my heart. I want to function, out in
> society, not in here. Outside.

Sergeant: This is your country, too.

Private: No, it's not. No, it's not. Now you, now let's be frank with each other.
Now you know it's not my country …

Sergeant: A man without a country, huh?

Private: Right.

The private has not 'made his peace with war' (Benson & Anderson 1989: 191), and sees no reason why he should go along with the army's intentions. 'He's trying to break me', says the resilient recruit, '[but] that's just like trying to bend steel. He's gonna wear his own self out.'

Washington Star journalist Paul Hathaway spent several months interviewing black soldiers in South Vietnam, concluding that the vast majority were unhappy with the military's treatment of them, and with the attitudes of 'hicks' – uneducated and economically lower-class whites – who constituted a high proportion of America's troops. Many black people understandably decided that they were fighting 'a white man's war', 'and wondered whether they should be home fighting for their own people' (Hammond 1996: 175–6). By early 1970, a subcommittee of the House Armed Services Committee had begun investigating inter-racial disturbances; the delay was attributed, by black columnist Carl Rowan, to 'arrogance on the part of white liberals within the Johnson administration who believed they knew more about black problems than did blacks themselves' (quoted in Hammond 1996: 177). Denial was in itself exacerbating the problem:

> Information officers, for their part, often found themselves caught between the fact
> of continuing racial tension and their superiors' apparent inability to define the scope
> of the problem … Learning of an increase in the number of racial incidents during the
> summer of 1970, the chief of information for U.S. Army forces in South Vietnam, Col.
> Alfred J. Mock, thus argued vehemently against any announcements to the press.
> (Hammond 1996: 181)

'The mere acknowledgement of a rise in racial incidents would serve no useful purpose and be self-defeating', Mock told the deputy commanding general, in an effort to quell public doubts about the army's supposedly good record in the way of race equality (quoted in ibid.). Wiseman, ever cynical about media representation, seeks redress here: by his inclusion of the lengthy, taut dialogue between the black trainee and his sergeant, he gives voice to the black soldier in Vietnam ('a man without a country') and asks if it really is their America, too. 'Leaders avoid talking about a war which is being fought every night in barracks and other places where our soldiers gather', said Lt. Col. James White during a February 1970 briefing (quoted in ibid.). Likewise, the sergeant in *Basic Training* is unwilling to continue this 'self-defeating' discourse, and leaves the room having changed the subject and asked the now chagrined private to wax a floor. Jonathan Shay puts it in simple terms: 'Men segregated themselves rigidly along racial lines in the rear … Racially motivated killings and riots were common in Vietnam. American soldiers in the rear were not safe *from each other.*' (Shay 1994: 60)[6]

Hoffman, however, is clearly getting along well in the army. He is promoted, in the subsequent scene, from lieutenant to captain, while his family look on (or at least this is Wiseman's editorial implication) proudly. 'You have equal opportunity now', declares the officer conducting the ceremony, and, by phrasal conversance, Wiseman refers us to the black soldier in the previous scene: Lt. Hoffman, unlike the trainee, is a man *with* a country, who will go 'all the way down the line' as a true American soldier, a man of provision and virility. As Hoffman's mother says, holding his baby, 'I think he's found his niche in the world!' We cannot disagree. Another natural warrior, the sergeant and veteran who has just told the black trainee that it was his country, too, addresses the company in a bid to instil some national pride with mention of the boys' 'forefathers, and theirs before them':

They fought to keep this country free. They got your independence; it all started back, way back then about the Boston Tea Party, and it kept working up, we fought many a hard battle … No matter where they put me over there, I'll do my best. And if some of you men come over there, I'll risk my life to save yours if you're in a spot. And I expect the same of you, 'cause that's the way I was trained, and that's the way I'm trying to train you. We take care of our people over there, believe you me. I know. I've seen a lot of young men like you that didn't make it … They went out there to do a job. I've seen some of them try to save another life, and they got it. This is part of combat – the part we don't like.

Benson and Anderson, though acknowledging the absurdity of the sergeant's final words ('what part of combat *do* we like?') (1989: 194) note that the speech is a sincere means of conveying the idea of the army as arcane brotherhood, the fraternal nature of which demands that lives are offered up: 'I am only a body doing a job', 'I am not worth it'; Bob Walters' words resonate through the scene, a reminder that all must be subsumed to the greater good of the army if one is to be an effective soldier.

Once more the trainees march, before they are subjected to a simulated gas attack. They wear masks until they are told to remove them, and then choke, vomit, cry and expectorate as quietly as they can manage.[7] Yet another scene of marching follows, including a low-angle shot of legs, boots, arms and fists as they seem to merge into one like the limbs of a centipede, totally in sync as an organ of one organism. 'Left, right, left', chants the sergeant, as the young men – a unit now – move towards a huge American flag and its emblematic potency. The recruits, still synchronised, are seen massed in an auditorium to watch two didactic films (which we do not see) that are introduced by a portly officer:

Our first one is an old one, but it stars some of your favourite characters such as Robert E. Lee and, urr, General Andrew Jackson – it's on the achievements and traditions of the United States Army. Our second one, which I know you're looking forward to, in which some of you may play a part in the next one, is on Vietnam – the reasons why we're there, and how we got there.

The legendary forefathers ('your favourite characters') are invoked as the exceptional soldiers they were, even though Jackson was a slaveholder who sent three thousand Native Americans to their deaths during the Trail of Tears, and Lee a Confederate whose loyalty lay with Virginia and not Lincoln. By now, we may sense an Orwellian purpose in the army's jingoistic melding of domestic history to a uniquely modern, overseas war – a conflict pursued not in the name of change, but for the furtherance of a regime pleasing to America's elite. 'Our dead revolutionaries', as Carl Oglesby mused to an anti-war Washington crowd in 1965, 'would [today] wonder why their country was fighting against what appeared to be a revolution' (Oglesby 1970: 183).[8] The announcer continues:

> The objectives of these two movies are first of all, for the first one, to find out the winning tradition we have in the United States Army. If you think about some of the teams in sports – which I know you follow – either amateur or professional, all the great champions that you can ever thought of [sic] never went undefeated the whole time. The United States Army has never lost a war: it is undefeated. Think about that. That's quite a record and you're part of this army at this time; it's up to you to carry on this tradition.

Yet in a few years, the great champion America, whose endemic hatred of losing is epitomised in *High School* via 'Casey at the Bat', would 'strike out' in Indochina.

Basic Training's closing scenes depict the trainees' physical practice for what awaits them, and are less dependent on dialogue than is usual for Wiseman. After they are lectured about the offensive potential of a Claymore mine, and how many casualties they inflict ('eight per cent of US kills'), the film follows the final few steps of the recruits' progress from placid boys to fighting men. Hickman reappears as a volunteer in a demonstration of how to kill a man by strangulation or bludgeoning; he is by now assimilated, and welcomed back into the fold with hearty applause. We see Hickman having camouflage paint applied, ready for an exercise, and realise that, without his glasses, he is as his comrades: no more or less a handsome potential hero ('PAVLO MOTHERHUMPIN' HUMMEL!') (Rabe 2002: 53). At night, the boys patrol the forest, feeling for imagined mines and ducking under barbed wire. Guns are fired, obstacles are surmounted, and there is no doubt that the course has almost run because the recruits are obviously *enjoying* it. On the infiltration field, the trainees move in concert; in the forest, they move together as a pack of hunters, the memories of nine weeks ago wiped by highly effective schooling.

GRADUATION

Basic Training culminates in a ritual whose typically Wisemanian function – for both the film and Fort Knox – is to demonstrate the training process's perfection as a 'mechanism of assimilation' (Janowitz 1972: 167). Heralded by a bugle call, the graduation ceremony begins with a brass band-led parade. Wiseman employs a montage technique here that conveys, through rhythm and selection, the pomp, uniformity and pride on display. First we see the lone bugler in close-up, his polished, fixedly horizontal instrument shining in the sun; a drummer then raps his snare, again shot in close-up; a conductor keeps time with suitably vigorous precision; and the Stars and Stripes is held aloft at the front of the assembly, as Wiseman zooms in on a flag-bearer's bumptious expression. The physical mechanics of generating a percussive prompt – a regular beat to which all the recruits are now happily marching – become important for Wiseman here; in its metronomic rigidity, this music (with which Wiseman synchronises his cuts) urges the troops towards their collective destiny, guided by a tradition passed down through generations of American militarism. If through circumstance or upbringing one had either no alternative or no inclination to offer defiance, then the army, as always, offered a more concretely graspable objective: acceptance into the fraternity of the warrior.

Lt. Hoffman introduces the winner of the American Spirit of Honour Award, 'in recognition of outstanding qualities of leadership, best expression of the American spirit, honour, initiative [and] loyalty'. The square-jawed recipient takes the stage to give his acceptance speech, and he is, as Benson and Anderson opine and as we must expect, a 'blandly handsome ideal soldier', who delivers a succession of clichés imbued with predictable, 'earnest wholesomeness' (1989: 198).

> Whether one prefers to call today's exercises 'graduation' or 'commencement', it matters not. But may I suggest to you keep both words in their individual connotative and denotative meanings in mind today. 'Graduation' signifies an end, while 'commencement' is of course a beginning … We came here from different places with different backgrounds … we arrived in blue jeans, sandals, tennis shoes, and t-shirts. We are now emerging as trained fighting men in the uniform of the US Army.

Wiseman inserts a shot of assembled graduands, all of whom look nearly identical at even a short distance. The director then moves in to frame their faces, but we do not see anyone we recognise from earlier scenes – Hickman, for example, or the good son with the M-16. We do, though, realise that although the soldiers' faces are still disparate, their fixedly severe countenances are not. The private continues:

> We are now at the end of basic training. We leave the classes we've had, the weapons we've fired, the friends we've made, and the officers and drill sergeants who've gained our respect … For some [the army] may be a sojourn of a year or two, for others a way of life. However, it is now up to each of us to carry on in the tradition of those who have gone before.
>
> The award which I have the honour and pleasure to receive today is entitled 'The American Spirit of Honour Award'. This is what we are now entrusted with and must carry forth: the American spirit of honour. It was born in the snow of Valley Forge, nurtured midst the smoke of Gettysburg and San Juan Hill … When fascism reared

its ugly head, the American spirit came forth and slew the dragon … And now South-east Asia. Laying aside the political controversy surrounding this conflict, we see once again displayed that American spirit of honour: fighting men dying for their na-tion and democracy … Lord, give us the strength to meet the challenge. I thank you.

The audience claps with a reverential lack of verve, and the commanding general thanks the speaker – presumably for his appropriate 'expression of the American spirit' – by shaking his hand and saying, 'Well said, son.'

American 'honour' is evoked and any pertinent meditation dismissed in favour of rhetorical comparisons to entirely different campaigns. The phrase 'the weap-ons we've fired', nestled as it is between terms such as 'friends' and 'respect', is indicative of the private's conditioned attitude to firearms and their new place in his life, as is his romanticising of Gettysburg, the bloodiest battle ever fought on American soil. Our 'favourite characters', heroes of what Walter A. McDougal calls the 'victory culture' (1997: 86), again are summoned to validate new actions by evoking old deeds (which more fiery historians have argued were essentially predi-cated on 'Indian hating and empire building' (ibid.)). It is at least acknowledged that some of the recruits (now 'fighting men') will be killed, but their lives will be lost not for their nation's security, unity or sovereignty, but for a cause that was, for most, more obscured by the passing of a decade than Valley Forge's was by a lapse of nearly two centuries.

Stanley Hoffman argues that Americans commonly use history as a 'grabbag from which each advocate pulls out a "lesson" to prove his point' (quoted in Jervis 1976: 217), and this is frequently borne out in *Basic Training*.[9] If fascist Germany was a 'dragon', a dehumanised catchall of mythically evil proportions, then Viet-namese Communists could not be so labelled for fear of 'controversy', false ac-cusation or improper professional conduct along racial lines (in the field they re-mained for the Westerner exotic, wily 'gooks' – the mysterious Other; see McDou-gal 1997: 205).[10] The recruits' civilian clothing – 'blue jeans, sandals, tennis shoes and t-shirts' – has been stripped away; they are commencing a new life away from the discourses and paradigms of what they know, and away from an environment of relatively cosseted safety. During 1970, a period of supposed 'de-Americanisa-tion … with all deliberate speed', 6,065 Americans were killed in Vietnam (Nixon 1978: 741). When these fresh-faced adolescents get to Cam Ranh Bay (the real point of 'commencement'), they will forever be ruined; if they make it back, the traumas of a nightmarish 'sojourn' will never leave them.

CONCLUSION: CAM RANH BAY IN A BODY BAG

The same revolutionary belief for which our forebears fought is still at issue around the globe, the belief that the rights of man come not from the generosity of the state but from the hand of God … Let every nation know, whether it wishes us well or ill, that we shall pay any price, bear any burden, meet any hardship, support any friend, oppose any foe to assure the survival and the success of liberty.

– President John F. Kennedy (1962: 7)[11]

You must either make a tool of the creature, or a man of him. You cannot make both.
    – John Ruskin (2004: 14)

Basic Training, like so many of Wiseman's films, is about a (or *the*) 'system', a force so powerful and relentless that it can send naïfs like Hickman to Vietnam and show no compunction in so doing. *Basic Training*'s conclusion implies a beginning of sorts; as witnessed in this ritual 'commencement', the graduands are expertly transmogrified, and the hopes of the early 1960s similarly become, at decade's end, disintegrating memories of misguided idealism and illusory political progressiveness. As the Right resurged to fill the vacuum created by the New Left's implosion and the undeclared war went on, Wiseman criticised not just functionaries, but the broader issues that lay behind self-interested US policies of military containment.

The senior officers, of course, are only themselves components, politically impotent and gagged by a duty to serve the interests of their employers – successive and mostly liberal presidents who feared embarrassing Cold War defeats and heeded 'domino theory''s ominous prophecies.[12] Wiseman duly does not scapegoat the army for strategies begun by Truman in response to multifarious global events; indeed, sharing James Alden Barber's opinion that to 'blame all that is bad in our foreign policy on the man in uniform ... is an evasion of the real issues, and no more likely to contribute to a solution to our problems than is any other form of scapegoating' (1972: 309), the filmmaker orchestrates his narrative around a central premise of inexorability. 'This film', remark Benson and Anderson of *Basic Training*, 'is not about Hickman, or the rifle-rack soldier, or the man who hired a prostitute in Louisville. It is about a system of basic training that, whatever happens to those particular men, will continue' (1989: 200). We may or may not remember the many faces Wiseman has shown us, but we can be sure that they will not be the last victims of the American system's methods.

Television networks in the late 1960s began to breach Department of Defense vetoes and broadcast material critical of US conduct and 'imperialist' motives. Although always denounced as disreputable or seditious by patriots and government representatives, these films (that were frequently shot in the field of combat) nonetheless exposed disingenuous falsehoods perpetuated by State Department spokesmen.[13] Overt anti-war rhetoric was becoming commonplace, and an almost *de rigueur* tactic employed by fervent documentarists working in territories both hostile and friendly.[14] Characteristically, Wiseman did not make an unequivocal case for cessation of engagement, instead looking beneath specific iniquities to the causal malaise within not the Pentagon but the unnamed 'system' at play. The chaplain in *Basic Training* asks for God's help, as if America's aspirations to govern and police the world were a divine right; 'Lord, give us the strength to meet the challenge', echoes the Spirit of Honour Award-winner, evoking an assumption held by his ancestors that Nature and God concurred in their endorsement of proselytising and territoriality. Jefferson envisaged a future in which 'our rapid multiplication will ... cover the whole northern if not southern continent, with people speaking the same language, governed by similar forms, and by similar laws' (quoted in Perkins 1993: 170), a longing common to early American statesmen that would later be crystallised in John O'Sullivan's phrase 'manifest destiny'.[15] As the 'empty' continent was filled – and the natives subdued by gunpowder – a politico-economic ethos based on capital security grew to encompass an isolated, insular nation suspicious of most revolutions or insurgencies despite its own heritage.

As John Quincy Adams said in his Fourth of July address of 1821: 'America does not go abroad in search of monsters to destroy … she might become the dictatress of the world. She would be no longer the ruler of her own spirit' (quoted in McDougal 1997: 36). Pearl Harbor, of course, forced America to abandon its isolationist stance that reached a crest in the 1930s; after World War Two, the 'welfare-warfare state'[16] began a campaign of global meliorism that would become the ostensibly benevolent motivation for the Vietnam War, a conflict Harry G. Summers describes as

> the international version of our domestic Great Society programs where we presumed that we knew what was best for the world in terms of social, political, and economic development and saw it as our duty to force the world into the American mould – to act not so much as the World's Policemen as the World's Nanny. (1984: 229)

Kennedy's inaugural boast that Americans would 'pay any price, bear any burden', is well known; but, he elaborated further:

> To those people in the huts and villages of half the globe struggling to break the bonds of mass misery, we pledge our best efforts to help them help themselves, for whatever period is required – not because the Communists might be doing it, not because we seek their votes, but because it is right. If a free society cannot help the many who are poor, it cannot save the few who are rich. (1962: 7–8; see also Riddell 1987: 6)

Wiseman's core contention in *Basic Training* is that a country such as America, despite good intentions, has no God-given right to assume control of other countries, or its own young men's destinies, because the great 'City on the Hill' is riddled with contradictions, folly, hypocrisy and an overwhelming sense of its own divine duty to 'truly light the world' (Kennedy 1962: 10). Sermons like Kennedy's were basically well-meaning, but invited intellectual criticisms aimed at problems within the United States of crime, civil disorder, inequality, extensive bureaucracy, drugs and injustice – valid complaints that find a voice in Wiseman's early films. As Carl Oglesby of SDS iterated in 1965: 'This country, with its thirty-some years of liberalism, can send 200,000 young men to Vietnam to kill and die in the most dubious of wars, but it cannot get 100 voter registrars to go into Mississippi' (quoted in Teodori 1970: 184). By 1970, the social revolution proposed by the New Left and the wider Movement had not yet been realised: the system, gradually and surely, prevailed.

The processes revealed in *Basic Training* reflect the larger society's functions and maintain a ceaseless, insidious momentum that drives the officers towards their own, selfish fulfilment whilst compelling the recruits to acquiesce. Hoffman sacrifices his right to a political voice for the chance to climb a career ladder and achieve status amongst his colleagues;[17] the chaplain sacrifices his morality to play a part in the desolation of his captive flock and, with no less hypocrisy than a television evangelist, denounces materialism and then 'offers salvation in exchange for a full collection plate' (Benson & Anderson 1989: 195). The majority of recruits, fighting as they were for the interests of richer men (whose own lives and sons were never in danger), were being used by a state that so cherished 'freedom' and detested poverty that it was willing to send thousands of its own poor to their deaths to establish American ideals in a small, ex-French colony in Indochina.

Unlike the Hollywood and Office of War Information films the film frequently evokes, the putative rite-of-passage narrative of *Basic Training* ends in a confounding suggestion of cyclical and inevitable subsumption; the viewer is not offered a satisfying resolution or even the certainty that any of the film's until-now prioritised subjects do eventually graduate. We are left wondering, 'What happened to Hickman, or the man "without a country"?' Wiseman followed the recruits for the full nine weeks, but chose not to focus on familiar individuals at the film's end, as to do so would imply that *Basic Training* is centrally about individuals, and less about an unstoppable process by which America fights to proliferate values that Wiseman deplores. When the soldiers we expect (or hope) to see do not appear, we infer that they have been, as Wiseman insinuates, perfectly effaced by the system, and are no more important in the scheme of things than any other graduands of boot camp during this or any war. The implication here is not, as the National Mobilization Committee asserted in 1968, that America then possessed 'one of the most reluctant armies in histories [*sic*].' Wiseman's contrary illustration of basic training is that, after nine weeks of 'bullying and blinding', its outcome is successful and the soldiers proud and ready. Paul Potter asked the March on Washington:

> What kind of system is it that justifies the United States or any other country seizing the destinies of the Vietnamese people and using them callously for its own purpose? What kind of system is it that disenfranchises people in the South, leaves millions upon millions of people throughout the country impoverished and excluded from the mainstream and promise of American society, that creates faceless and terrible bureaucracies and makes those the place where people spend their lives and do their work, that consistently puts material values before human values – and still persists in finding itself fit to police the world? What place is there for ordinary men in that system and how are they to control it, make it bend itself to their wills rather than bending them to its? (1985: 220)

Answers to these questions, as Wiseman suggests in *Basic Training*, might be found in the paradoxes of the American Way: the timeless need to impose prescribed stability on disorder, make a garden out of a wilderness, and trade freely at whatever cost to moral integrity; the Promised Land was also a Crusader State, and the Garden a seedbed for industrialisation. 'We embrace contradictory principles with equal fervour and cling to them with equal tenacity', writes Eugene V. Rostow. 'Should our foreign policy be based on power or morality? Realism or idealism? Pragmatism or principle? Should its goal be the protection of interests or the promotion of values? Should we be nationalists or internationalists? Liberals or conservatives? We blithely answer, "All of the above"' (1993: 22). In 1972, Democrat George McGovern would fight the presidential election on a platform of total and immediate withdrawal from Vietnam; he subsequently garnered the lowest share of the popular vote ever achieved in a two-way contest.

Frederick Wiseman, perhaps the most sagacious of American documentarists, continues, like so many commentators and artists first emergent in the 1960s, to query the machinations of the system in his own, less than blithe but never less than extraordinary rejoinders to Samuel Smith's hymn:

> My country, 'tis of thee,
> Sweet land of liberty,
>   Of thee we sing:
> Land where our fathers died,
> Land of the pilgrims' pride,
> From ev'ry mountainside
>   Let freedom ring![17]

CONCLUSION

Culture-Bound

American film does not merely have a history – it also *is* history. Movies are a continuous inscription and interpretation of American experience through time and in the world. Films are traces of specific moments in specific spaces mediated by human beings who are always culture-bound.

– Vivian Sobchack (1980: 293)

The true revolution of the Sixties – more powerful and decisive for Western society than any of its external by-products – was an inner one of feeling and assumption: a revolution in the head.

– Ian MacDonald (1994: 24)

This book's rhetorical design is three-tiered. It has been my intention to explicate the content of the films under discussion by providing immediate socio-cultural context; to posit the direct cinema filmmakers within their epoch's most salient political and intellectual imperatives; and to trace the roots from which direct cinema emerged as extending further into American thought than technological, dramaturgical or anthropological analysis has so far allowed. The transformative bearing of the 1960s on documentary form was catalysed by factors other than an urge for aesthetic probity, and beyond a response to didacticism and television's lacklustre treatment of actuality. Had reactive observationalism come to fruition outside the United States, it would have been quite different in intention and scope; indeed, it is possible that the direct cinema movement *could not* have sprung from any other time and place than the American Sixties. The fibre of direct cinema, it follows, is predicated as much on a philosophical reawakening as on the portability of equipment: roving camera-sound systems, developed at first to assist orthodox journalistic or anthropological endeavour, eventually became totems of a new-found cinematic transcendence.

The films I have appraised are canonical works. They comprise a broad, chronological sample of direct cinema's most cherished and remembered records not because of a disregard for Robert Drew's post-*Crisis* achievements, but in order to contemplate why some direct cinema productions of the 1960s abide, whilst others do not. The Maysles brothers, D. A. Pennebaker, Richard Leacock, Michael Wadleigh and Frederick Wiseman attenuated their modes of expression to incorporate and comment upon what mattered about their nation as it entered a period of discursive change and existential craving; they outgrew the Living Camera template because they saw *themselves* as alive and creatively more central to a true understanding of the world than a belief in the power of lightweight equipment to go anywhere – to show everything. The objectivity/subjectivity argument here-after becomes redundant, a notion perhaps as bogus as Drew's faith in 'real life coming out of the film'. As Peter Graham insightfully observed in 1964, shortly af-ter Drew's Associates had dissolved: '[The Maysles brothers, Drew and Leacock] present not *the* truth, but *their* truth. The term *cinéma vérité*, by postulating some absolute truth, is only a monumental red herring. The sooner it is buried and forgot-ten, the better' (1964: 36). After its gestation under network control, direct cinema broke free: *cinéma vérité* became a term loaded with callow implications, raising more questions about empiricism than ontology. What is apparent is an abjura-tion of the pseudo-scientific study of modernity in favour of transcendent, musical and oblique commentaries on Western humanity and its struggles against fear in a wealthy yet confusing age of proliferating information. To paraphrase Dylan, America did not need a weatherman, but a turnabout in and a revivification of its national consciousness that could effect a renaissance of compassionate, com-munity politics.

Despite David E. James' assertion that direct cinema of the late 1960s 'failed to engage the most pressing social issues of the day' (1989: 213) and therefore represented a less valid form than the more obviously confrontational avant-garde, there is bountiful evidence that suggests a modus operandi in keeping with preva-lent counter-cultural hopes. Charles A. Reich, responding in 1970 to the apparently stymied circumstances of political momentum on the Left, proposed a 'revolu-tion through consciousness' as a substitute for entrenched methods of dissent: 'Must we wait for fascism before we realise that political activism has failed?' he asked (1970: 252).[1] Concurring with Reich, Theodore Roszak was circumspect but still hopeful that the nation's youth would 'strike beyond ideology to the level of consciousness ... building the good society is not primarily a social, but a psychic task' (1971: 49). Correspondingly, the direct cinema filmmakers were not attracted to either combative or liberalist advocacy; rather, they occupied a sagacious politi-cal province that Todd Gitlin, in his more moderate and reflective phase, shared: 'Right now it is a question of whether the living consciousness that a new world is possible – free of material misery, hierarchy and useless work – can encounter the more traditional needs of the rest of the American people without abandoning its integrity' (1987: 457). This, as the 1960s wore on, was a quandary increasingly vital to reformers. Traditional liberals prosecuted the war in Vietnam as vigorously as the war on poverty; both gave higher taxpayers a reason to elect Nixon, who sum-moned no victory in either crusade, but had plenty of hard-line rhetoric against 'the deterioration of respect for the rule of law' (Nixon quoted in Gitlin 1987: 338). New Deal and Great Society principles, for Drew's alumni, were thus too contentiously illusory, too sweetened a placebo to countenance as a way of ending endemic ha-tred, distrust of others and the abject despair sustained by corporate-government relations. The post-Old Left, post-industrial *milieu* called for a contrapuntal cine-matic art, one that might make evident the unshackled potential – the essential joy – of life lived beyond submission to anger, or to clichés of reportage or resistance;

what Leacock, Pennebaker, the Maysles brothers and Wiseman bespoke was a desire for the realisation of multi-dimensional thinking: a revolution in the head.

Inevitably, what was once a manifesto for a new artistic attitude in documentary has, since its brief domination of the genre, been vitiated. Hand-held footage now serves as a shorthand cipher for candid honesty, appearing in television 'docu-soaps' and dramas, 'reality' shows, feature films and advertisements to lend a semblance of Robert Drew's avid vision. There is promise, beyond these chimeras, still left in direct cinema's aesthetic tradition. Numerous high-profile filmmakers, including Michael Moore, Nick Broomfield, Morgan Spurlock, Ric Burns, Barbara Kopple and Molly Dineen, have lucratively appropriated the candid method by incorporating its visual immediacy into engaging stories, polemics and character studies; moreover, with the ever-proliferating abundance of cheap, digital cameras further democratising the practice of reality filmmaking, everybody with an interest can emulate what took years to develop at Time-Life. Yet, as Leacock notes, 'Anyone can use a pen, but how many people can write great novels?'[2]

As of May 2007, Leacock, Pennebaker, Albert Maysles, Frederick Wiseman, Michael Wadleigh and Robert Drew continue sporadically to create (with varying degrees of commercial interest) according to their own ideals. But, or so it would appear, the times are not as ripe as they once were. 'I had a sense that we had really opened up a whole new world, and that the horizons were limitless', said Leacock in 1984. 'Somehow it ran out of steam ... I still don't understand. It seemed to run into a vacuum. Maybe that's my problem' (quoted in O'Connell 1992: 209). Perhaps, as the moribund dream of a new consciousness gave way to the penitent 'vacuum' of the 1970s, so direct cinema correspondingly subsided as a cohesive proposition; certainly, a mantle of sorts was passed to the New Hollywood's recalcitrant young auteurs, who profitably absorbed (among myriad cinematic influences of chiefly European and Japanese provenance) American reactive observationalism's disavowal of 'the tyranny of technical correctness' (Biskind 1998: 17).[3] Adroitly cynical projections of post-1960s trauma, often upon allegorical or fantastical situations, largely superseded – at least in terms of public profile – the candid recording and restrained presentation of reality. Hollywood's short-lived rebirth represented a brashly invigorating purge: in a violent and morally culpable climate, the baby-boomers again brought market forces to bear upon channels of expression, rendering direct cinema's ongoing, understated critique obsolete. What is more, notes Jeanne Hall, 'the movement quickly fell out of fashion as contemporary film theory called into question the apparently obvious nature of the cinematic sign ... by the end of the decade, film studies programmes were teaching ideology, interpellation and subjectivity ... Cinéma-vérité filmmakers ... became easy targets indeed' (Hall 1991: 27). Although it traced the Sixties' high-rising arc of political upheaval and cultural dynamism with unusual acuity, the observational movement was, by 1970, once more largely relegated to television and diminishing returns.

Leacock, his muse apparently deserted and his innovations subsumed, lapsed into ennui before embarking on a high-profile teaching career and the supervision of avant-garde theatrical productions; Pennebaker devoted himself almost exclusively to filming performers, who, since *Dont Look Back*, have proved his natural subjects; Wiseman's annually released films generate much discussion to this day, though they have lost intensity in recent years; Albert and David Maysles produced one more masterpiece, *Grey Gardens* (1975), before David's premature death; and Robert Drew entered the 1970s with a film about Mariner IV, thereafter continuing to make edifying, sponsored television programmes such as *Saving Energy: It Begins at Home* (1974), *Men of the Tall Ships* (1976) and *Build the Fusion Power Machine* (1984). 'The flower of art blooms', wrote Henry James, 'only where the soil is deep' (1984: 320). For the filmmakers discussed herein, the seedbed of the long, strange Sixties was fertile indeed.

NOTES

INTRODUCTION

1 Extract from the commentary of *Crisis: Behind a Presidential Commitment* (Robert Drew, 1963).

2 Toni A. Perrine (1998) *Film and the Nuclear Age: Representing Cultural Anxiety* and David E. James (1989) *Allegories of Cinema: American Film in the Sixties* are just two amongst many volumes concerning cinema of the 1960s in its cultural context. Both, as do most similar studies, all but ignore contemporaneous documentaries.

CHAPTER 1

1 Drew speaking in the British television film *Arena: Theatre Without Actors* (tx: BBC2, 12 March 1994).

2 'America's photography', writes Sean Wilentz, 'has been this country's greatest single contribution to the visual arts. Photography is the jazz of the visual arts' (quoted in Miles Orvell 2003: 13).

3 O'Connell here gives an exhaustive account of Drew's tenure at Time-Life and a series of lengthy quotes that elucidate the burgeoning producer's views regarding mid-twentieth-century television programming. See also Stephen Mamber 1974: 23–30.

4 See also John Grierson 1966; and Frances Hubbard Flaherty 1960.

5 Drew speaking in *Arena: Theatre Without Actors*.

6 *Cinéma vérité*, a term often – if improperly – employed with respect to observational documentary in the US, is a literal translation of Vertov's *Kino-Pravda*, or 'Cinema Truth'. The most famous exponent of *cinéma vérité* was Jean Rouch, who opposed what he saw as a fundamental denial on the part of direct cinema artists, documentarists who shun self-reflexivity and obvious pro-activity in their own films, preferring instead to remain off camera. This lack of interaction, in Rouch's view, reduces these films' merit as works of empirically sound anthropology or sociology. As Rouch declares in the introduction to his and Edgar Morin's *Chronique d'un été* (*Chronicle of a Summer*, 1960), 'This film was not played by actors, but lived by men and women who gave moments from their lives to a new experience of cinema truth' (see Kevin Macdonald & Mark Cousins 1998: 250). See also Rouch's *Chronique d'un été*, fellow Frenchman Chris Marker's *La Joli Mai* (1963), directed with Pierre Lhomme, and Dziga Vertov's *Chelovek s kino-apparatom* (*Man With a Movie Camera*, 1928), the pre-eminent exemplar of the influential *Kino-Pravda* movement. For a summary of general criticisms aimed at direct cinema, see Alan Rosenthal 2002: 274.

7 Drew, transcribed from archive footage featured in *Arena: Theatre Without Actors*.

8   Parallels are often drawn between direct cinema and the fleeting 'Free Cinema' move-
     ment in the UK, which evinced similar interest in unplanned quotidian material in the
     1950s but quickly gave way to the scripted, 'kitchen-sink' drama. Leacock flatly denies
     any useful genealogical connection, saying that 'the Brits had no influence on us and they
     never ever lost control', and that he made *Jazz Dance* 'long before it was mimicked [in
     1956, by Karel Reisz and Tony Richardson] as *Momma Don't Allow*'; quoted in O'Connell
     1992: 237.

9   Leacock interviewed in Peter Wintonick's film *Cinéma Vérité: Defining the Moment*
     (2001).

10   For an expatiation on the 'crisis structure' evident in Drew's early work, see Mamber
     1974: 115–40.

11   When Luce's *Fortune* attempted to expose Joseph Kennedy's affair with Gloria Swanson
     in 1936, Kennedy threatened to mount a raid that would buy out *Time* magazine, and the
     piece was pulled. Numerous accounts of press blackmailing, mafia courting and vote-
     buying by the Kennedys, including the successful suppression of JFK's extra-marital af-
     fairs (with, among others, Marilyn Monroe) in the mid-1950s, can be found in Seymour
     Hersh's 1997 exposé, and in Nigel Hamilton 1992.

12   Photographer Robert Frank's book *The Americans* (1959), though it did not serve any
     governmentally dictated purpose, functions as a despondent echo of Walker Evans' ear-
     lier work, revealing the conformity and aimlessness of affluent, urban life. 'He sucked a
     sad poem right out of America onto film', wrote Jack Kerouac in the book's introduction
     (1959: 9).

13   See, for instance, Nixon's infamous, 30-minute 'Checkers' speech of 1952, once thought
     lost to posterity, but restored to the public domain by Emile de Antonio in *Millhouse: A
     White Comedy* (1971). For a discussion of Nixon's self-conscious performance see Stella
     Bruzzi 2000: 134–7.

14   Kennedy used his private family jet, bought in 1957, to take his campaign to the voters
     (see Theodore C. Sorensen 1965: 100, 135). Drew's preliminary insinuation is germane
     to actual circumstances, as Humphrey lamented in his memoir: 'Nothing so well symbol-
     ises the difference in the two campaigns as modes of transportation … The Kennedys
     flew in their private Convair, the Caroline. We chugged about in an old, slow, and cold
     rented bus … Once, as we started into the darkness of the rural countryside, I heard a
     plane overhead. On my cot, bundled in layers of uncomfortable clothes, both chilled and
     sweaty, I yelled, "Come down here, Jack, and play fair"'; Humphrey 1991: 151.

15   Only one cameraman, Leacock, was shooting synchronised sound; added to this, the
     team's equipment was constantly breaking down.

16   See, for references and examples, Mamber 1974: 40. White later called Kennedy 'an en-
     chanting man, who … believed that the hero is a man who masters the circumstances',
     (1979: 455).

17   White was a friend of Henry Luce, until the two fell out over White's unfavourable cover-
     age of non-communist Chinese factions. White was subsequently employed again by
     Time-Life on a less frequent basis.

18   Follow-tracks such as this are now of course commonplace, but it is understandable that
     Drew and his cohorts would wish to revel in their ability to go where few had gone be-
     fore, especially given their privileged access and (roughly) synchronised-sound capability.

19   Drew, in the director's commentary accompanying the Docurama DVD release of *Pri-
     mary*.

20   Leacock quoted at: www.popped.com/articles98/cinemaverite/veriteleacock.html, ac-
     cessed on 23 March 2004.

21 A missile gap did indeed exist, but the imbalance, it would transpire, favoured America.

22 Leacock quoted at: www.popped.com/articles98/cinemaverite/vertieleacock.html, accessed on 14 March 2004.

23 Kennedy and Humphrey, observed the *New York Times'* Cabell Phillips, are 'as like as two peas in what they think and as unlike as carrots and onions in how they say it' (1959a: 24).

CHAPTER 2

1 For a discussion of the mid-1950s' 'Crisis of American Masculinity', as christened by Arthur Schlesinger Jr in his 1958 *Esquire* article of the same name, see Miriam Reumann 2005: 54–85.

2 As Michael Curtin writes: 'Throughout the program, one senses the heavy hand of ABC management molding the documentary to make the case for a more active foreign policy to take on the challenge from Fidel and make Latin American markets safe for American free enterprise' (1995: 141).

3 'The film', notes Richard M. Barsam, 'takes it [*sic*] stand on the matter of rehabilitation, not on the merits of the capital punishment argument' (1992: 307). For an analysis of *The Chair*, see Monika Beyerle 1997: 138–72. William Friedkin's documentary on the same subject, *The People Versus Paul Crump* (1962), argued for Crump's exoneration.

4 This initiative pushed Fidel Castro towards a lasting and more ideologically grounded bond with Khrushchev (see Aleksandr Fursenko & Timothy Naftali 1999: 99.

5 Medgar Evers tried to cast his vote in Jackson, Mississippi, despite threats from whites (which proved tragically genuine) that they would kill him if he tried: he died on the way to hospital. Byron de la Beckwith was charged, but escaped conviction when juries deadlocked. Later, he boasted to a Ku Klux Klan meeting, 'Killing that nigger gave me no more inner discomfort than our wives endure when they give birth to our children. We ask them to do that for us. We should do just as much.' Evers' perceived martyrdom threatened Kennedy's hopes for a peaceful resolution to racial conflict (see Carter 1995: 154; Patterson 1996: 25 and 481–2).

6 Gould had earlier exalted *Yanki No!*, calling it 'an arresting and fascinating study of Communist infiltration of Latin America, a presentation greatly expanding the techniques of visual reportage' (1960: 71).

7 'A lot of imitations appeared that tarnished the name [of our films]' (Drew: 1988: 400).

8 Many still photographers, including Daniel Budnik, traded on this fairly obvious image.

9 *Faces of November* won the Venice Film Festival's Short Subject category.

10 See Drew 1998: 400–1, for his own account of his frustrations; see also Barsam 1992: 305.

11 Drew would twice revisit footage from his early works featuring Kennedy in order to satisfy growing public nostalgia for the early 1960s; see *Being With John F. Kennedy* (1984) and *Kennedy versus Wallace* (1988).

12 Women did not figure prominently in the original direct cinema movement, a reflection, perhaps, of entrenched attitudes. As Chopra recalled: 'The women were all hired for their attractiveness. I was at a conference recently with Pennebaker and he was describing to a group of sociologists how you make a film and he said, "you know, a cameraman goes out and his girlfriend takes sound." And that sums up that mentality' (quoted in Hall 1991: 50).

13 See W. James Potter 1998: 118, for a discussion of the media's traditional ennobling of rural communities.

14 'In 1963, 43 percent of America's 3.1 million farm families, almost 5 million people, lived in poverty' (Patterson 2000: 78).

15 'Normally you'd be furious that it had started to rain', commented Jean Rouch, 'but Leacock is certainly very happy about it and continues shooting that shabby disaster. This is Leacock's commentary'; Pennebaker called *Happy Mother's Day* a 'fantastic insight by an Englishman into America, and it's horrifying' (both quoted in Levin 1971: 138, 261).

16 Basil Wright derided the ABC cut as 'buggered-up' (quoted in Levin 1971: 50).

17 Thomas Waugh takes the view that 'contempt was probably the predominant tone of the entire *cinéma vérité* movement (probably since contempt is the stance which comes most easily to Eastern liberalism when it interacts with middle America)' (1985: 235). This is a severe position, almost irrespective of the fallaciousness of Waugh's claim that direct cinema, beyond its first forays under Drew, maintained a 'posture of objectivity'. Waugh also chides Leacock and his contemporaries for failing in what he sees as a duty to 'support the momentum of alternative politics' and provoke the 'potentially activist, liberal audience they addressed' into action (1985: 236). Waugh's preference for Emile de Antonio's politically fervent, Eisensteinian effects is understandable. Yet his essay bluntly seeks to devalue Leacock's subversive critique of American placebos, by somewhat inapposite comparison with de Antonio's methods, as futile swiping (see Waugh 1985: 233–58).

18 The two had previously made *Showman* (1964), about entertainment promoter Joe Levine. Though it is a highly regarded work, *Showman* is today an obscurity.

19 The Freedom Riders were participants in several anti-segregation civil disobedience campaigns organised by the Congress for Racial Equality (CORE).

20 *The Goon Show*, featuring Michael Bentine, Peter Sellers, Harry Secombe and Spike Milligan, was a popular, irreverently surreal British radio programme of the 1950s.

21 Unscrupulous manufacturers circumvented copyright laws by spelling the band's name 'The Beetles'.

22 Maysles, in the director's commentary accompanying the Apple DVD release of *What's Happening!* (Re-titled *The Beatles: The First U.S. Visit*, the DVD includes all the *Ed Sullivan Show* appearances and footage of the band, rendered inaudible by screams, playing the Washington Coliseum.)

23 No original source or name is given.

24 As Errol Morris has opined: 'I believe *cinema verité* set back documentary filmmaking twenty or thirty years. It sees documentary as a sub-species of journalism' (quoted in Arthur 1993: 127).

25 As documentarist Nick Broomfield enthuses: 'Leacock, Pennebaker, the Maysles ... They're so young at heart. And this is, obviously, really appealing. It's like everything is a delicacy to be savoured and understood' (quoted in Wood 2005: 238).

26 Daniel Bell, in evaluating the 1950s' prosperity, consensus and renunciation of Old-Left thought, heralded the 'end of ideology', or the 'end of chiliastic hopes [and] apocalyptic thinking ... the old ideologies have lost their "truth" and their power to persuade' (1962: 393, 402).

27 Accounts differ regarding the date of the Beatles' psychedelic initiation. Peter Brown and Steven Gaines (1983: 157) assert that this took place on 28 August 1964 in New York City. Says Paul McCartney: 'It was Bob Dylan that turned us all on to pot in America and it opened a different kind of sensibility really; more like jazz musicians ... I kind of liked marijuana. I didn't have a hard time with it and to me it was mind-expanding, literally mind-expanding' (quoted in Miles 1998: 185, 190).

CHAPTER 3

1 In 1961, Dylan travelled to New York to sit by the dying Guthrie's bedside and play him some songs, both traditional and self-authored (see Sounes 2002: 104).

2 King's original speech was made on 23 June 1963, at the Great March for Freedom in Detroit.

3 F. O. Matthiessen conceived the appellation 'American Renaissance,' meaning the pre-Civil War period, in his landmark 1941 study *American Renaissance: Art and Expression in the Age of Emerson and Whitman.*

4 Walt Whitman in a self-penned review of his *Leaves of Grass* (1855 edition) (1998: xvi–xvii).

5 'It was my attempt to simplify the language' (Pennebaker in Sounes 2002: 208). Dylan, as had George Bernard Shaw throughout a number of plays, made the same extraction in his book *Tarantula* (written in 1966): 'i really dont care what you think of my work as i now know you dont understand it anyway' (1971: 93). A short history of American linguistic inventiveness can be found in Bryson 1994: 77–98.

6 Neuwirth was on the payroll, but his exact job remains mysterious.

7 A reference to a lyric in the Beatles' recently released 'I Feel Fine', a 1965 hit single in America.

8 In his 1849 essay 'Dissertation on Language', Horace Bushnell argued that words are only 'inexact representations of thought'. An inherently American philosophy, Bushnell's theories stemmed from the restive democratic literary culture within which multiple meanings proliferated and unambiguousness was critically invalidated (1849: 55).

9 For an interpretive essay, see Bert Cartwright 1985.

10 Eisenhower later made the ill-considered statement, 'Our government makes no sense unless it is founded on a deeply-felt religious faith – and I don't care what it is.' In 1955, congress added 'In God We Trust' to US currency (see Patterson 1996: 329).

11 Billy Graham publicly denounced Communism as 'a great sinister anti-Christian movement masterminded by Satan' (see Patterson 1996: 329–30).

12 In a 1991 interview, Dylan said, 'I believe in everything the Bible says. My favourite books are Leviticus and Deuteronomy … I read it all the time … [The next Apocalypse] will be by fire next time. It's what's written' (quoted in Williams 1993: 85).

13 They had been special guests at each other's concerts since 1963 (see Williams 1994: 140).

14 Masques or carnivals appear often in antebellum writing: Edgar Allan Poe's 'Masque of the Red Death' (1838), George Lippard's *The Quaker City* (1845), Herman Melville's *Moby-Dick* (1851) and Nathaniel Hawthorne's *The Marble Farm* (1860) all combine the 'high' and the 'low' in carnival scenes that celebrate the democratisation of style.

15 'You will hardly know who I am or what I mean, But I shall be good health to you nevertheless, And filter and fibre your blood' (Whitman 1998: 79).

16 See Chapter 2, page 30.

17 The song helped make Medgar Evers posthumously famous, much more so than his living brother, a moderate civil rights activist and locally prominent politician who nearly made it to government (see Denselow 1990: 39).

18 The John Birch Society was a right-wing extremist group established in 1958 by confectioner Robert Welch (John Birch was a missionary who became an American spy).

19 Harold Macmillan, from a speech in Bedford, England, 20 July 1957 (see Sampson 1967: 159).

20 Ginsberg called Dylan's songs 'the culmination of Poetry-music as dreamt of in the 1950s

and early 1960s' (quoted in Ricks 2004: 11).

21 As the *New York Times'* Robert Shelton remarked: 'The racial crisis in the South has become a theme of major importance for folk singers of the North. New songs on this theme are not only weapons in the civil rights arsenal, but are also developing into valuable commodities in the music industry' (1963: 7).

22 'He did it, and he did it well, because it was expected of him and he was being paid and his pride was on the line and so forth … but the magic was gone' (Williams 1994: 141).

23 'how come youre so afraid of things that dont make any sense to you,' wrote Dylan (calling himself 'your valve cleaner, Tubber', in 1966); 'how come youre so afraid to stop talking?' (1971: 39–40).

24 In 1967 Terry Ellis, with his friend Chris Wright, formed Chrysalis Records.

25 A scene memorably parodied, in reverse, by Rob Reiner in *This is Spinal Tap* (1982).

26 The 'British Invasion' by guitar groups like the Beatles, the Animals and the Rolling Stones had begun to redress this deficiency. These bands were surprised at how readily stateside record-buyers took to their blues-based material, fearing at first that 'taking the coals to Newcastle' could not be a propitious career move. In reality, due to popular radio stations' embargos on records by black musicians, most white music fans had not been exposed to original black music.

27 Donovan would soon carve a career niche for himself as an idealist songwriter, more suited, as his character was, to inoffensive 'flower power' eulogies drawing on Tolkienesque imagery. George Melly calls him 'the Fairy Prince of Pop', and the 'precursor of Love' (1970: 101).

28 Other fabrications include stories of joining a travelling circus and recording with Gene Vincent and Elvis Presley as a teenager (see Melly 1970: 38).

29 See the *Subterranean*, 9 September 1843 and 24 January 1846.

30 'Tomorrow Never Knows' was the first attempt to convey the hallucinogenic experience of LSD through song: 'Turn off your mind, relax and float downstream…' See Ian MacDonald 1994: 164–70, for an expert dissection of this hallowed non-single's musical and cultural implications.

31 Judson later told writer Howard Sounes: 'I went to the concert. My opinion then and now was that the music was unpleasant, the lyrics inflated, and Dylan a self-indulgent, whining show-off' (see Sounes 2002: 213).

32 San Franciscan hippie activists the Diggers, from a 1966 bulletin quoted in Dominick Cavallo 1999: 97. The Diggers were iconoclastic luminaries with a distaste for authoritarian control, who drew inspiration from the English, seventeenth-century utopian group of the same name. In effect, they were a libertine answer to the Salvation Army (see O'Neill 1971: 252).

33 By scholastic convention, the 1798 publication of William Wordsworth and Samuel Taylor Coleridge's *Lyrical Ballads* marks the beginning of the Romantic period. Characteristically Romantic works have in common the fact that they model themselves upon existing folk ballads and nursery rhymes. Blake, Wordsworth and Coleridge rejected elitist, neoclassical ideals in their poetry; 1960s artists like Dylan (in his early phase) drew upon similarly traditional influences for comparable reasons.

34 Hall makes the same point in an earlier essay, citing the derision of 'one reporter after another' as *Dont Look Back*'s '*raison d'être*', but again stopping short of placing the film's double-edged attack on journalistic tradition in tension with Drew and his own methods (1991: 45–6).

35 A few direct cinema artists, although they were mostly unaffiliated with specific political groups and disinclined toward protest or activism, had personal links to the counter-cul-

ture that motivated career choices in the way of subjects. Pennebaker (and by extension Leacock) was introduced to Albert Grossman and Bob Dylan by Sara Lownds of Drew Associates; Michael Wadleigh was a hippie working on the East Coast as a cinematographer on and some-time actor in counter-cultural film productions (such as Jim McBride's *David Holzman's Diary* (1967)) before getting the *Woodstock* commission.

CHAPTER 4

1 'Dancing on the Brink of the World' is a Native American (Costanoan) chant.

2 Extract from the lyric of 'San Francisco (Be Sure to Wear Some Flowers in Your Hair)' (1967), written by John Phillips for Scott McKenzie.

3 The term 'love-in' simply referred to any gathering or exposition of this kind. The most famous love-in until Monterey Pop was the Human Be-In, held in San Francisco's Golden Gate Park on 14 January 1967: 'The air seemed heady and mystical. Dogs and children pranced around in blissful abandon…' (Swick-Perry 1995: 314).

4 Michael Fallon coined the term 'hippie' in a piece for the *San Francisco Examiner* of 5 September 1965 (see Cook 1971: 200).

5 The May 1970 Kent and Jackson State killings of six student protestors (by National Guardsmen and the police respectively) would end any illusions.

6 The festival poster urged, 'be happy, be free; wear flowers, bring bells'. Or, as journalist Robert Christgau cynically put it, 'act like hippies, mingle with hippies, and hear hippie music' (quoted in Echols 1999: 163). In the main a purely aesthetic statement drawn from pre-Raphaelite and Art Nouveau sources, the hippies' frequent wearing of flowers also symbolised a harking back to pagan notions of mankind's symbiosis with nature (and the related worship of fertility deities), and, by historical association, a rejection of Christian doctrine.

7 The British photographers David Bailey and Terence Donovan, and the fashion designer (of the miniskirt) Mary Quant, helped define the era's notions of glamour, shifting emphasis away from the chest to the less maternally symbolic legs.

8 George Melly disparages Burdon as 'a bearable shouter within the blues idiom, [he] was only ever able to produce pseudo-mystic rubbish … as empty as the mumbling of a drunk who thinks he's stumbled upon the secret of the universe' (1970: 122). Never in the vanguard, the group's (now renamed Eric Burdon's Animals, for legal reasons) time in the limelight was effectively over.

9 The English had already been exposed to Hendrix by his manager, former Animals bassist Chas Chandler, who discovered him in America whilst playing the 'chitlin'' (slang for the small intestines of a pig, commonly eaten by poor musicians) circuit of music clubs as a backup guitarist, and exported him to Britain in 1966.

10 The Black Panthers, a hardline 'Black Power' organisation set up in Oakland, in 1966, by Bobby Seale and Huey Newton, would later attempt to secure Hendrix's endorsement, with some success, although he remained uninterested in outspoken advocacy (see McDermott & Kramer 1992: 340).

11 Townshend asked Hendrix for a piece of the Monterey guitar. Hendrix's retort, 'Oh yeah? I'll autograph it for you, honkie', shocked the Who's leader, who 'just crawled away' (see Murray 1989: 91).

12 Extract from the lyric of '59th Street Bridge Song (Feelin' Groovy)', by Paul Simon.

13 William Rothman also makes a comparison between *Monterey Pop* and *Triumph of the Will*; (1997: 29); Riefenstahl's Nazi documentary, 'masterfully fed the German population an image of themselves, their history and their destiny, that reinforced the state and the

power of the Fuhrer' (Macdonald & Cousins 1998: 126).

14 One CBS marketing campaign proclaimed, 'The Man Can't Bust Our Music'. Charles Shaar Murray comments that, 'This equated buying a Big Brother, Electric Flag or Moby Grape album with burning a draft card, marching in solidarity with the Black Panthers or demonstrating against the decision of the Democratic party to withhold political legitimacy from opponents of the Vietnam war' (1989: 20).

CHAPTER 5

1 CBS presenter Walter Cronkite exclaimed, 'What the hell is going on? I thought we were winning this war!' The media, in growing disillusionment, began to question their own pro-America bias in reporting the war (see Patterson 1996: 680).

2 'Tet' is a Vietnamese holiday celebrating the start of the lunar year, upon which was expected to fall a diminution of hostility (see O'Neill 1971: 346).

3 The story was suppressed for twenty months before it entered the public domain via a leak to the American press (see Hammond 1996: 217–35).

4 David Maysles allegedly punched Wadleigh, realising he'd been 'bested by a junior' (Jeanne Field quoted in Bell 1999: 32).

5 The festival was originally supposed to take place in Woodstock, but moved to Bethel under protest, retaining the name; the town of Woodstock had great counter-cultural cachet, as it was the home of Bob Dylan and Albert Grossman among other 'hip' luminaries (see Roberts 1999: 55). Dylan (of course not himself a hippie, or willing to be seen as such) refused to take part, viewing Woodstock as, 'the sum total of all this [hippie] bullshit' (quoted in Sounes 2002: 296).

6 'I did shoot … with a bug-eyed lens which distorted it, but we all felt distorted. We felt we'd been put in an emotionally different place by the whole experience'; cameraman David Myers (1999: 128).

7 Camerman Don Lenzer conceded that *Monterey Pop* was an influence on *Woodstock* (1999: 142).

8 *Woodstock* was edited by, among others, a young Martin Scorsese and his colleague, Thelma Schoonmaker, who would go on to edit all Scorsese's films. Although few documentaries had used split-screen cutting, *The Boston Strangler* (1968), starring Tony Curtis, features multi-image sequences that are unquestionably analogous to *Woodstock*'s.

9 In order to lessen public unrest, the police decided not to enforce drug laws (see O'Neill 1971: 260).

10 The first battle of the American Revolution took place in Concord, MA, on 19 April 1775. (Ralph Waldo Emerson, Henry David Thoreau and Louisa May Alcott all lived there.) Havens also sings a verse about the racial conflicts in Birmingham, Alabama, of the early 1960s (see Carter 1995: 479).

11 *One Flew Over the Cuckoo's Nest* author Ken Kesey's hallucinogen-inspired collective, the Merry Pranksters, travelled the country in a decorated school bus. For a comprehensive and much celebrated account of the Pranksters' activities, see Tom Wolfe 1971.

12 The Hog Farm operated in the utopian tradition of experimental groups such as Brook Farm, a secular community near Boston that briefly flourished in the early nineteenth century. Brook Farm attracted some of America's brightest progressive intellectuals, including Emerson and Hawthorne (see Maier *et al.* 2003: 419).

13 Security was provided, to good effect, by a group of unarmed civilians trained by the Hog Farm (see O'Neill 1971: 262).

14 Folk revivalist Hardin (who would die of a drugs overdose at the age of 39) played a set

at Woodstock, but his performance is not featured in Wadleigh's film.

15 Baez was inspired to take up protest music upon hearing Bob Dylan perform his 'The Death of Emmett Till', in 1962. 'When I heard "Emmett Till" I was knocked out. It was my first political song. That song turned me into a political folk singer' (quoted in Hood 1986: 72).

16 'She [the Earth Mother] is a symbol of nature, she is the earth, sexual but protective, always there for the masculine ego to inhabit when he wants to escape from the realities of life' (Whiteley 1998: 165).

17 Townshend hated Woodstock, and has made it widely known that the Who only played for the substantial payment (see Marsh 1986: 346). Early in the Who's set, 'Yippie' provocateur Abbie Hoffman invaded the stage in the hope of using the festival as a vehicle; Townshend hit him hard over the head with his guitar, knocking him to the ground (see Perry 1999: 140).

18 'Woodstock was really a tremendous amount of editing – editing made the film. The performances made the film originally [but] if Wadleigh hadn't shot them against all odds as beautifully as he did we would have had nothing' (co-editor Thelma Schoonmaker interviewed at http://members.aol.com/morgands1/closeup/text/cfthelm2.htm; accessed 20 August 2002).

19 Wadleigh, too, was on the receiving end of Townshend's rage. When the director got too close, his subject kicked him away, shouting, 'The next person that walks across this stage is going to get fucking killed!' (see http://www.thewho.net/whostory/augold.html; accessed 18 August 2002).

20 The post-war 'baby boom' saw the youth demographic surge dramatically in the 1960s. Those aged 15–24 numbered 24 million in 1960; by 1970, they were 35.3 million strong, an increase of 47 per cent (see Patterson 1996: 451).

21 Charles Fourier had argued, in the 1830s, that 'only when man gives free expression to his natural impulses (including sexual ones) could civilisation's deceits and interests be overcome' (quoted in Reynolds 1988: 80–1).

22 Jesse Slokum in an e-mail to the author of 18 August 2002 (punctuation is as in original text). Slokum appears briefly in Woodstock, leading an audience handclap during Richie Havens' set.

23 In his Woodstock address, Satchidananda also broadcasts the statement, 'America is becoming a whole.' Such an erroneous announcement, in the politically divergent, divided climate of mid-1969, betrays not a little short-sightedness. Two months after Woodstock, a record half a million anti-war protesters would gather in Washington, D.C., a city described by national security adviser Henry Kissinger at the time as 'a besieged city', with 'the very fabric of government … falling apart' (1979: 511, 513–14).

24 Lyric by Arthur Singer, John L. Medora and David White. The song was originally performed, in 1958, by Danny and the Juniors.

25 The hippies' hankering for alternative beliefs was a recapitulation (like much of the counter-culture's philosophy) of American Renaissance themes. Every important writer of the antebellum period paid homage to Oriental tales; Edgar Allan Poe and Emily Dickinson saw Oriental fiction as symbolic of free, creative imagination; Herman Melville and Nathaniel Hawthorne employed Eastern motifs to engender greater philosophical flexibility and question the strict doctrines of Puritan Calvinism; and one of Walt Whitman's goals (stated in 'Passage to India') was to 'Eclaircise the myths Asiatic, the primitive fables … The daring plots of the poets, the elder religions … eluding the hold of the known, mounting to heaven!' (1998: 316) (see also Reynolds 1988: 41–53).

26 'Why Take Life So Seriously, Anyway?' proclaimed the popular 1920s magazine Success.

Amid the short-lived economic growth of the period, prominent sociologist E. A. Ross wrote that the nation was in transition – from a 'pain' to a 'pleasure' economy (see Patterson 1996: 19).

27 The Age of Aquarius is the supposed end of the age of Jesus Christ.

28 The original hippies of the early 1960s, who strived for effective communal living, had long since decamped (in disgust at the deluge of interlopers) to scattered, dissipating cooperatives in the country.

29 James Russell Lowe fiercely indicted Thoreau for hypocrisy in *Walden*: 'He squatted on another man's land; he borrows an ax; his boards, his nails, his bricks, his mortar, his books, his lamp, his fishhooks, his plough, his hoe, all turn state's evidence against him as an accomplice in the sin of that artificial civilization' (quoted in Conn 1990: 177).

30 McDonald saw Dylan play at the Hollywood Bowl in 1964, stating afterwards that he 'wanted to be that' (see Denselow 1990: 66–7).

31 SDS's demise is detailed in Sale 1973. The Weathermen planned a bombing campaign to 'fight the pigs', but, farcically, succeeded only in accidentally blowing-up three of their own (see Patterson 1996: 716–17).

32 Chuck Nyren at www.suite101.com/article.cfm/227/2914; accessed 20 August 2002.

33 'The "F-U-C-K Cheer" always makes things a lot funnier and still is hated by the conservatives – and that's good reason for me to enjoy doing it.' MacDonald at: www.freetimes.com/issues/935/music-soundcheck.php3; accessed 20 August 2002.

34 As Richard Howells avers, 'Che has become, in many instances, a fashion statement from which history has been removed', or 'a left-wing myth *par excellence*' (2003: 108).

35 Henry David Thoreau, *Walden* (1961: 150).

36 Nudist films, although made to titillate, were presented as serious documentaries in order to overcome obscenity laws. *The Nude World* (1955) is an exemplar of this short-lived genre, which became redundant after the watershed 1961 publication of D. H. Lawrence's *Lady Chatterley's Lover* (1928) in unabridged form. Succeeding 'nudie-cutie' films (the most popular were by pioneering soft-porn director Russ Meyer) explored more risqué territory.

37 The Motion Picture Association of America (MPAA) introduced its voluntary rating system in November 1968; this measure, which served to avert potential federal regulation following the 1964 abolition of the Production Code of America, was a response to citizens' complaints of escalating cinematic nudity, profanity and violence. Well-produced erotica was valuable to the industry, and it was, for the MPAA, essential to prevent backlash against 'grind-house' pornography putting an end to lucrative films such as *Blow-up* (1966), *Belle de Jour* (1967) and *Barbarella* (1968) (see O'Neill 1971: 220).

38 See Patterson 1996: 448. The producers of *Hair* paid those employees who undressed on stage more than those who did not, thus tacitly recognising the stigma of public bareness in the 'permissive' age. Artie Kornfeld signed novelty family act The Cowsills (who later had a hit with *Hair*'s theme tune) to MGM in 1967.

39 Fleming Van der Goes' 'Adam and Eve' (1470) is perhaps the most famous pictorial depiction of The Fall; the painter rather awkwardly obscures the still innocent couple's genitalia (see Clark 1956: 311–13).

40 The Demilitarised Zone in Central Vietnam.

41 For the film, Taggart is a blessing; there is, however, a disheartening coda to the Port-O-San scene. The beloved American proletarian who had received a standing ovation at a preview screening, decided, in 1970, to sue for defamation of character, claiming that the makers had shown him 'in a demeaning occupation, and that to add insult to injury, [they] had used subtitles to convey his words, as though he could not talk clearly and be

understood'. Though Taggart lost his case (as did everyone who filed suit against *Woodstock*), his litigation upset the filmmakers and cast a shadow over an otherwise sublime role. The reality was that heaven could wait for the hereafter, at least for Taggart, a child of the Great Depression whose off-screen humanity, perhaps reasonably, did not extend to restraint in the face of a potential dividend.

42 Michael Wadleigh in an e-mail to the author of 20 August 2002.

43 In 1967, anxious about possible subversive fomentation, Congress passed a bill making it illegal to desecrate the flag. Millions of patriotic Americans decorated their cars with Stars and Stripes bumper stickers proclaiming, 'One Country, One Flag', and 'Love It or Leave It' (see Anderson 1995: 165).

44 The celebrated, epoch-marking lyric, 'Lately it occurs to me, what a long, strange trip it's been', is an extract from the Grateful Dead's 1970 song 'Truckin'', which can be found on the same year's *American Beauty* LP.

45 This comes from a description of Hieronymus Bosch's fifteenth-century moralistic triptych, 'The Garden of Earthly Delights', in Peter Beagle's book on the subject.

46 'Many', note David Ehrenstein and Bill Reed, likened the festival to a 'Nuremburg rally for teendom', and Ehrenstein and Reed themselves call *Woodstock* a '*Triumph of the Will* of youth culture' (1982: 79, 271) (see also Rosenbaum 1997: 8). Albert Maysles still vituperates *Woodstock*, calling it a 'stupid piece of shit', and criticising its 'propagandising' stance (see www.popped.com/articles98/cinemaverite/veritemaysles.html; accessed 12 April 2003).

47 See Wadleigh's website, www.gritty.org.

48 Lyric from 'Big Yellow Taxi' (1970).

49 It is a measure of *Woodstock*'s impact that Joni Mitchell, despite not even being at the festival, still felt compelled to write a song about it.

50 'When I saw Woodstock at the Cannes film festival', recalls Jonathan Rosenbaum, 'Wadleigh dedicated the film to the four students killed by National Guardsmen at Kent State … when the screening was over, he stood by the exit doors and passed out black armbands. I took one myself, but two days later some boutiques in Cannes started selling similar armbands. What had seemed political on Saturday had become a sort of marketing device by Monday' (1997: 8).

CHAPTER 6

1 Lyric from the song 'Gimme Shelter' (1970), by Mick Jagger and Keith Richards.

2 Barger recalls in his autobiography: 'I took all the cocaine we had in the front room with me into the bedroom and called the station. They gave me the runaround until I convinced them I was actually who I said I was … I was loaded. "Flower people ain't a bit better than the worst of us," I said. "It's about time people started realising that"' (2001: 167).

3 Belli was known as 'The King of Torts', having represented many high-profile clients, including Jack Ruby, Lee Harvey Oswald's killer. At the time of *Gimme Shelter*, Belli was involved in the Charles Manson murder trial – witnesses were waiting outside his office as the Maysles filmed (see Norman 1993: 382).

4 Zwerin in an extract from the audio commentary accompanying the Criterion DVD release of *Gimme Shelter*.

5 Albert Maysles, ibid.

6 John Milton, *Paradise Lost* (2005: 17).

7 For a comprehensive account of Grogan's life in activism, see Cavallo 1999: 98–144.

8 Sonny Barger refutes claims that the Hell's Angels used pool cues as weapons ('they break too easily' (2001: 168)). The makeshift bludgeons are, however, visible throughout *Gimme Shelter*'s Altamont footage and numerous photographs of the event.

9 Upon witnessing the violence and sensing the 'bad vibes', Garcia retreated to his trailer and refused to perform: 'No way am I playing, man, no fucking way am I going out there … The inmates have taken over the asylum … This show is like some runaway train, and we best get the fuck out of here before it runs into us' (quoted in Scully & Dalton 1996: 212–13.

10 Stanley Booth, in the booklet accompanying the Criterion DVD release of *Gimme Shelter*, roundly blames the lateness of the Stones' performance on bassist Bill Wyman's refusal to get out of bed.

11 Jagger and Richards had been dabbling facetiously in Satanism since they had met film-maker and Aleister Crowley devotee Kenneth Anger. Anger's diabolical allegiance was rather more serious and unsettling than the Stones', but Jagger nevertheless would score (on his recently acquired Moog synthesiser) one of the besotted Anger's films, *Invocation of my Demon Brother* (1969) (see Norman 1993: 312–13).

12 'We're the one percenters, man – the one percent that don't fit and don't care'; an anony-mous biker quoted in Thompson 1967: 14.

13 'Keith Richards leaned over to me and said, "Man, I'm sure it doesn't take three or four great big Hell's Angels to get that bird off the stage." I just walked over and kicked her in the head. "How's that?"' (Barger 2001: 164).

14 'Some of what [the Rolling Stones] were writing was just plain nasty', writes Ian Mac-Donald, 'like, for example, the appalling misogyny of "Under My Thumb", a despicable song from an age prior to the concept of sexism' (2002: 70).

15 We see Hunter earlier in the film, very briefly, in a medium close-up.

16 'Street Fighting Man', concerning the militant protests of 1968, was construed by many to be an incitement to further violence and banned by every radio station in the Chicago area. In its ironic context at Altamont, its purpose was to placate the crowd. 'We knew that if we stopped', says Stones guitarist Mick Taylor, 'there really would have been a riot' (quoted in Norman 1993: 397).

17 'The revolutionary youth of the world hears your music', wrote a group of extreme Cali-fornian radicals to the Stones during the band's 1969 tour, 'and is inspired to even more deadly acts' (quoted in Cavallo 1999: 148).

18 As seen in Robert Frank's unreleased but widely bootlegged film *Cocksucker Blues* (1972).

19 According to William L. O'Neill: '*Rolling Stone* said that a cameraman was recording a fat, naked girl freaking out backstage when the director stopped him. "Don't shoot that. That's ugly. We only want beautiful things." The cameraman made the obvious re-sponse. "How can you possibly say that? Everything here is so ugly"' (1971: 262). In the light of *Gimme Shelter*'s final content, either the directors were blind to events around them, later to adapt their slant, or (as seems much more likely) this purported exchange is shamelessly yellow journalism.

20 This is from an open letter from David Maysles, Albert Maysles and Charlotte Zwerin to the *New Yorker* republished in Macdonald & Cousins.

CHAPTER 7

1 Although he firmly belongs to the Drew school, Wiseman has never worked with the original direct cinema practitioners, preferring always to operate independently of edito-

rial control (and freely of journalistic obligation). For an account of Wiseman's early life, see Anderson & Benson 1991: 8–9.

2   See Anderson & Benson 1991: 1. Carolyn Benson and Thomas W. Anderson's *Reality Fictions: The Films of Frederick Wiseman* (1989) is a detailed study of Wiseman's work that, unlike this contextual preface, expatiates on Wiseman's rhetorical methodology, and 'how the films construct an implied author and an implied audience and how audiences might respond' (1989: xvi).

3   'My films are totally subjective. The objective/subjective argument is from my point of view, at least in film terms, a lot of nonsense. The films are my response to a certain experience' (Wiseman quoted in Winston 1993: 49).

4   Sinclair, most famously, wrote *The Jungle* (1906), a 'muckraking' look at a meat-packing plant in Chicago. Wiseman would go on to tackle the same subject in *Meat* (1976).

5   I tentatively use the term 'slide-puzzle' here because, although Nichols rightly sees a scenic tessellation in Wiseman's rejection of conventionally progressive narratives, 'mosaic' implies a naturalistic or logical whole that becomes visible when viewed from a certain distance. In Wiseman's work (as Nichols again points out), though narrative logic is not entirely absent, no obvious, fixed 'picture' is ever apparent (see Nichols 1981: 211).

6   'One of the failings of documentary theory', writes Stella Bruzzi, 'has been to sideline the dissenting or questioning [voice] of Fred Wiseman' (2000: 68).

7   Said as a member of Students for a Democratic Society, 1961.

8   'What is wanted is men, not of policy but of probity, who recognise a higher law than the Constitution, or the decision of the majority' (Thoreau quoted in Conn 1990: 180).

9   Amos Vogel calls *Titicut Follies* 'a major work of subversive cinema' (2005: 187). The *New York Times* claimed that the film 'makes *Marat/Sade* look like *Holiday on Ice*' (quoted in Anderson & Benson 1991: 64).

10 See Anderson & Benson 1991 for a book-length discussion of the Commonwealth of Massachusetts' twenty-year battle to suppress the film.

11 This act was the Mental Retardation Facilities and Community Mental Health Act (see Maier *et al.* 2003: 932–63).

12 Agee worked with Walker Evans on an account of the lives of Depression sharecroppers, *Let Us Now Praise Famous Men* (1941); *The Snake Pit* (1955), by Mary Jane Ward, is a fictionalised record of an actual residence in an asylum.

13 'The asylum', writes Dominick Cavallo, 'reflected what Kesey saw as the banality, conformity and violence at the core of American culture' (1999: 111). Kesey's book was adapted for the screen by Milos Forman in 1975.

14 Thomas R. Atkins, whilst correctly describing *Titicut Follies* as 'one of the strongest condemnations of an institution and its governing officials', writes also that this 'condemnation, of course, is implicit in the existing material and not the result of any editorializing or manipulation by the director' (1976: 5). This view is not only naïve, but plainly wrong.

15 The teacher is not being lascivious; it is, in fact, an entirely different door through which he is looking. Wiseman also overdubs and fades up the dance-class music as the teacher approaches, making this a highly devious insinuation.

16 'Baseball', notes J. Ronald Oakley, is 'as essential to American culture and Americanism as the flag, apple pie, and motherhood' (1986: 17).

17 See Diggins 1989: 211–12, and Anderson 1995: 310–12. 'The feminine mystique says that the highest value and the only commitment for women is the fulfilment of their own femininity' (Friedan 1992: 38).

18 Boys, so spake a Kimberley-Clark pamphlet (*Your Years of Self-Discovery*) in 1969, were forbidden fruit for any morally upright young lady: 'The instant gratification of your sens-

es, at the expense of your feelings of self-worth, can only lead to deep unhappiness' (see Wolf 1997: 67).

19 Rings appear continually in *High School*, usually filmed in close-up, and constitute a motif playing on the Northeasters' endearing but essentially meaningless attempts at being different while still abiding by the school's dress code.

20 Lyric from 'I Want You' (1966).

21 SPARC is an acronym for Space Research Capsule.

22 Earlier, however, Wiseman had proclaimed himself 'a consultant on social problems' (see Benson & Anderson 1989: 332).

23 SDS's Port Huron Statement of 1962 defined their aims: 'Men have unrealised potential for self-cultivation, self-direction, self-understanding and creativity ... The goal of man and society should be human independence [and] finding a meaning in life that is personally authentic' (see Isserman & Kazin 2000: 169). Most SDS members were, like the older and non-affiliated Wiseman, high-achieving scholars and researchers who were eloquent, expert in debate, intellectually poised and 'trained in the ways of competition' (Gitlin 1987: 109).

24 During which police, chanting 'Kill, kill, kill', beat anti-war protesters and even McCarthy delegates. One criticism of Stephen Mamber's otherwise diligent *Cinéma Vérité in America* (1974) is that Mamber, throughout his discussion of Wiseman (pp. 216–49), wrongly describes *Law and Order* as Wiseman's second film; this chronological error denies the film its heated and specific political context and skews what is the most significant early exegesis of Wiseman's work.

25 Richard Nixon, quoted at: http://www.gprep.org/~sjochs/nixonelection1968.htm; accessed on 21 July 2003.

26 From Wiseman's introduction to the only British broadcast of *Law and Order* (tx: Channel 4, 25 August 1986).

27 Senator Abraham Ribicoff publicly denounced the police's aggressive behaviour at the Democratic Convention of August 1968, and likened them to the Gestapo (much to the chagrin of Chicagoan mayor Richard J. Daley, who hit back with a tirade of anti-Semitic abuse). Wiseman's images of forceful arrest bring to mind Danny Lyon's dramatic coverage of civil rights demonstrations. His most famous photograph, *Atlanta* (1963–64), became the cover of SNCC's (Student Nonviolent Coordinating Committee) book, *The Movement*; in the Soviet Union, it was printed in *Pravda*, above the caption, 'Police Brutality, USA'.

28 'In low income areas', noted Professor Eli Ginzberg in a 1971 report, 'the emergency room substitutes for the private physician. A 1965 study of four New York City hospitals showed that emergency rooms located in middle- and high-income areas treat patients who, facing an emergency and unable to make contact with their regular physician, seek stopgap help ... Thus, the emergency room has become, in the absence of any effective alternative, the primary source of medical care for a significant proportion of New York City's population' (1971: 122).

29 Doctors wrote 150 million prescriptions per year in the late 1960s for tranquilisers and amphetamines (see Anderson 1995: 250).

30 Morgan Miller, quoted at www.24framespersecond.com/writings/writings/wiseman.html; accessed 16 May 2003.

31 These were upheld by Congressional Democrats, with whom Nixon mostly went along.

32 Medicare (for which Kennedy had unsuccessfully campaigned) and Medicaid were introduced on 30 July 1965; the latter also outlawed racial segregation in hospitals (see Patterson 1996: 153–66, for a discussion of the welfare boom under Johnson).

33 President Eisenhower, in his farewell address of 1961, warned of the growing 'military industrial complex'. His inspiration was dissident 1950s critic C. Wright Mills, who 'questioned the cherished faiths of American democracy by proposing that the Republic had come to be ruled by an interconnected network of "establishments" consisting of big business, the military, and the government bureaucracy' (Diggins 1989: 249); see also Mills 1958: 6).

34 New York's per capita health expenditure was, in 1969, $38; overall municipal expenditure reached $6 billion by the end of the decade (see Ginzberg 1971: 2).

35 For a discussion of historical and modern 'American nervousness' about urbanisation, see White & White 1969.

36 Giovanni Baldelli was Secretary of the International Anarchist Commission.

37 As former SDS president Todd Gitlin conceded in 1969: 'The Left must be conscious of its visionary prerogative as well as of its privilege; it must find ways of working on the other side of both hope and despair because there is no other way to live and because Americans must be confronted with the practicality of a new way of life' (1995: 458).

38 As Adrian Tilley says: 'Narratives are about the survival of particular social orders rather than their transformation. They suggest that certain systems of values can transcend social unrest and instability by making a particular notion of "order out of chaos". This may be regarded as the ideological work of narrative' (quoted in Watson 1998: 144).

39 Paul Séban indicted television for showing 'the sordid picturesque', but not the 'imperialism which is the cause of it' (quoted in Harvey 1978: 29).

40 'Je suis Marxist – tendance Groucho', was a slogan first used at the Nanterre branch of the University of Paris in May 1968.

CHAPTER 8

1 This quote is from his 'Farewell Address to the Nation' of 17 January 1961 (ee Eisenhower 1972: 62).

2 'Black magic language' is Allen Ginsberg's phrase to describe discursive appropriation for reasons of control; Barry Keith Grant makes this connection in Voyages of Discovery (1992: 96) (see also Ginsberg 1969).

3 This inference as we watch the marching is perhaps inevitable, and has been elucidated by others. Again, I point the reader towards the work of Grant, Anderson and Benson, and Mamber. Grant highlights the ideological inversion, by Wiseman, of marching imagery beloved of John Ford and featuring most frequently in the director's 'cavalry trilogy': Fort Apache (1948), She Wore a Yellow Ribbon (1949) and Rio Grande (1950) (1992: 80).

4 Walt Whitman, Leaves of Grass (1998: 221).

5 'Liberals should love this movie', wrote Dan Bates, 'for it makes John Wayne's kind of hawk look incredibly stupid' (1968: 73). Renata Adler called The Green Berets 'so unspeakable, so stupid, so rotten and false in every detail' (1968: 49).

6 Mark Woodruff takes an alternative stance in his polemic Unheralded Victory, arguing that racial tensions were much lesser in the army than in civilian life (1999: 244–5).

7 'American military culture in Vietnam regarded tears as dangerous but above all as demeaning, the sign of a weakling, a loser. To weep was to lose one's dignity' (Shay 1994: 63).

8 Oglesby's speech, usually called 'Trapped in a System', has become a classic amongst New Left rhetoric for its intelligent indictment of corporate liberalism. As Martin Luther King commented of the Vietnam War, 'The greatest irony and tragedy of all is that our

nation, which initiated so much of the revolutionary spirit of the modern world, is now cast in the mold of being an arch antirevolutionary' (quoted in Scott King 1985: 87).

9   Further, Dominick Cavallo notes that John Kennedy 'wrapped his Cold War rhetoric around the idea of a new frontier', and that 'Lyndon Johnson compared the American stake in winning the war in Vietnam to the struggle at the Alamo' (1999: 78). Edward W. Said observes that an 'alarming defensiveness has crept into America's image of itself, especially in its representations of the national past' (1994: 380). Wiseman fulfils Said's desire that a 'cultural intellectual' should 'show how all representations are constructed, for what purpose, by whom, and with what components' (ibid.).

10 Walter A. McDougal notes that 'Some radical critics have made this fear and disdain for the Other the drivewheel of all American history' (1997: 205).

11 Theodore Sorensen, although not always credited, wrote this Inaugural Address and the majority of Kennedy's speeches.

12 Truman first used the 'domino' metaphor to justify support for Greece and Turkey because, he felt, countries neighbouring those that had 'toppled' into communist rule were liable to follow suit.

13 See Erik Barnouw 1993: 269–83, for a summary of these films' impact and some responses to domestic propaganda.

14 See, for instance, Emile de Antonio's *Vietnam: In the Year of the Pig* (1968).

15 O'Sullivan, the editor of the *Democratic Review*, claimed in 1845 that it was 'our manifest destiny to overspread the continent allotted by Providence for the free development of our yearly multiplying million' (quoted in Zinn 1990: 149).

16 For a definition and discussion of corporate liberalism under its foremost exponents, Presidents Kennedy and Johnson, see Teodori 1970: 42–3.

17 As C. Wright Mills says, 'Prestige to the point of honour, and all that this involves has, as it were, been the pay-off for the military's renunciation of political power' (1958: 174).

18 Extract from 'America' (1832), by Samuel Francis Smith.

CONCLUSION

1   Reich described a tertiary level of awareness that was, he thought, arising as a response to a need for community values and a rejection of acquisitive goals: 'One quality unites all aspects of the Consciousness III way of life: energy. It is the energy of enthusiasm, of happiness, of hope ... Consciousness III draws energy from new sources: from the group, the community, from Eros, from the freedom of technology, from the uninhibited self' (1970: 251).

2   Leacock speaking in 'The Originators', a filmed press conference included on the Docurama DVD re-release of *Primary*.

3   See also King 2001: 41–2, for a discussion of direct cinema's influences on the New Hollywood.

FILMOGRAPHY

SELECT CHRONOLOGICAL FILMOGRAPHY
Distribution companies are current at the time of writing. Some films remain without an officially listed distributor, though may be available for rent or viewing via archives or the principal filmmakers.

Daybreak Express (USA 1953: 5 mins, colour)
Dir. D. A. Pennebaker. Distributed by Pennebaker-Hegedus films.

Jazz Dance (USA 1954: 22 mins, black and white)
Dir. Roger Tilton; camera: Richard Leacock.

Baby (USA 1955: 5 mins, black and white)
Dir. D. A. Pennebaker. Distributed by Pennebaker-Hegedus Films.

Primary (USA 1960: 60 mins, black and white)
Conceived and produced by Robert Drew for Time-Life Broadcasting. Photographers: Richard Leacock, D. A. Pennebaker, Terence McCartney-Filgate and Albert Maysles. Managing editor: Robert Drew. Writer: Robert Drew. Distributed by Direct Cinema.

Yanki No! (USA 1960: 60 mins, black and white)
Producer: Robert Drew. Filmmaker: Richard Leacock, with Albert Maysles and D. A. Pennebaker. Reporters: William Worthy and Quinera King. Co-produced by Time, Inc., ABC-TV and Drew Associates.

The Children Were Watching (USA 1961: 25 mins, black and white)
Executive producer: Robert Drew. Filmmaker-producer: Richard Leacock. Photographer: Kenneth Snelson. Correspondents: Lee Hall and Gregory Shuker. Co-produced by Time, Inc., ABC-TV and Drew Associates.

Adventures on the New Frontier (USA 1961: 51 mins, black and white)
Executive producer: Robert Drew. Filmmakers: Richard Leacock, D. A. Pennebaker, Albert Maysles and Kenneth Snelson. Correspondents: Lee Hall, Gregory Shuker and David Maysles. Co-produced by Time, Inc. and Drew Associates.

The Chair (USA 1962: 59 mins, black and white)
Executive producer: Robert Drew. Filmmakers: Gregory Shuker, Richard Leacock and D. A. Pennebaker. Correspondents: Gregory Shuker, Robert Drew, John MacDonald and Sam Adams. Co-produced by Time-Life Broadcasting and Drew Associates.

Crisis: Behind a Presidential Commitment (USA 1963: 52 mins, black and white)
Executive producer: Robert Drew. Producer: Gregory Shuker. Filmmakers: Richard Leacock, James Lipscomb and D. A. Pennebaker. Produced by ABC News in association with Drew Associates. Distributed by Direct Cinema.

Faces of November (USA 1963: 20 mins, black and white)
Executive producer: Robert Drew. Producer: Gregory Shuker. Photographers: James Lipscomb, Sidney Reichman and Al Wertheimer. Correspondent: Tom Johnston. Produced by ABC News in association with Drew Associates.

Happy Mother's Day (USA 1963: 26 mins, black and white)
Directors/editors: Richard Leacock/Joyce Chopra. Produced by Leacock-Pennebaker Films. Distributed by Pennebaker-Hegedus Films.

What's Happening! The Beatles in the USA (USA 1964: 54 mins, black and white)
Directors/editors: Albert Maysles/David Maysles. Produced and distributed by Maysles Films.

You're Nobody 'Til Somebody Loves You (USA 1964: 12 mins, black and white)
Director/editor: D. A. Pennebaker. Co-filmmakers include: Michael Blackwood and Jim Desmond. Produced by Leacock-Pennebaker Films. Distributed by Pennebaker-Hegedus Films.

Meet Marlon Brando (USA 1965: 28 mins, black and white)
Directors: Albert Maysles/David Maysles. Editor: Charlotte Zwerin. Produced and distributed by Maysles Films.

Dont Look Back (USA 1965: 96 mins, black and white)
Director/editor: D. A. Pennebaker. Co-filmmakers include: Howard Alk, Jones Alk and Ed Emschwiller (Greenwood sequence). Produced by Leacock-Pennebaker Films. Distributed by Pennebaker-Hegedus Films.

Monterey Pop (USA 1967: 78 mins, colour)
Director/editor: D. A. Pennebaker. Co-filmmakers include: Richard Leacock, Albert Maysles, James Desmond and Roger Murphy. Produced by Leacock-Pennebaker Films. Distributed by Pennebaker-Hegedus Films.

Salesman (USA 1968: 85 mins, black and white)
Directors/editors: Albert Maysles/David Maysles/Charlotte Zwerin. Produced and distributed by Maysles Films.

Woodstock (USA 1970: 184 mins, colour)
Director: Michael Wadleigh. Co-filmmakers include: Al Wertheimer, Martin Scorsese, Thelma Schoonmaker and Don Lenzer. Produced by Bob Maurice for Warner Bros. Distributed by Warners Films.

Gimme Shelter (USA 1970: 91 mins, colour)
Directors/editors: Albert Maysles/David Maysles/Charlotte Zwerin. Co-filmmakers include: Ellen Giffard, Robert Farren, Joanne Burke, Kent McKinney and George Lucas. Produced and distributed by Maysles Films.

Titicut Follies (USA 1966: 84 mins, black and white)
Director/editor/producer: Frederick Wiseman. Camera: John Marshall. Distributed by Zipporah Films.

High School (USA 1968: 75 mins, black and white)
Director/editor/producer: Frederick Wiseman. Camera: Richard Leiterman. Distributed by Zipporah Films.

Law and Order (USA 1969: 81 mins, black and white)
Director/editor/producer: Frederick Wiseman. Camera: William Brayne. Distributed by Zipporah Films.

Hospital (USA 1970: 84 mins, black and white)
Director/editor/producer: Frederick Wiseman. Camera: William Brayne. Distributed by Zipporah Films.

Basic Training (USA 1971: 80 mins, black and white)
Director/editor/producer: Frederick Wiseman. Camera: William Brayne. Distributed by Zipporah Films.

BIBLIOGRAPHY

Adair, Gilbert (1981) *Vietnam on Film: From The Green Berets to Apocalypse Now*. New York: Proteus.

Adams, Sam (2001), 'Music to his Eyes', www.citypaper.net/articles/110801/mov.mountain.shtml; accessed 14 March 2002 and 4 July 2005.

Adams, Val (1963) 'Satire on Birch Society Barred from Ed Sullivan's TV Show', *New York Times*, 14 May, 61.

Adler, Renata (1968) '"Green Berets" as Viewed by John Wayne', *New York Times*, 20 June, 49.

Adorno, Theodor W. and Max Horkheimer (1997 [1944]) *Dialectic of Enlightenment*, trans. John Cumming. London: Verso.

Albanese, Catherine (1975) 'The Kinetic Revolution: Transformation in the Language of the Transcendentalists', *New England Quarterly*, 48, 3, September, 319–40.

Albert, Judith and Stewart (eds) (1985) *The Sixties Papers: Documents of a Rebellious Decade*. New York: Praeger.

Albrow, Martin (1970) *Bureaucracy*. London: Pall Mall Press.

Aldgate, Anthony, James Chapman and Arthur Marwick (eds) (2000) *Windows on the Sixties: Exploring Key Texts of Media and Culture*. London: I. B. Tauris.

Allen, Robert C. and Douglas Gomery (1985) 'Case Study: The Beginnings of American *Cinéma Vérité*', in Robert C. Allen and Douglas Gomery *Film History: Theory and Practice*. New York: Knopf, 213–41.

Alvarado, Manuel, Ed Buscombe, Tanya Krzywinska, Michael Newton, Alan Stanbrook, Adam Stevens, Catherine Surowiec and Emma Widdis (eds) (2000) *The Movie Book*, London: Phaidon.

Anderson, Carolyn and Thomas W. Benson (1991) *Documentary Dilemmas: Frederick Wiseman's Titicut Follies*. Carbondale, IL: Southern Illinois University Press.

Anderson, David L. (ed.) (1993) *Shadow on the White House: Presidents and the Vietnam War 1945–1975*. Lawrence, KS: University Press of Kansas.

Anderson, Terry (1995) *The Movement and the Sixties: Protest in America from Greensboro to Wounded Knee*. New York: Oxford University Press.

Andrew, Dudley (1997) *The Image in Dispute: Art and Cinema in the Age of Photography*. Austin: University of Texas Press.

Andrew, John A. III (1998) *Lyndon Johnson and the Great Society*. Chicago: Ivan R. Dee.

Anon. (n.d.) 'The Woodstock Generation', www.britannica.com/psychedelic/textonly/woodstockgeneration.html; accessed 5 February 2002.

____ (1960) 'Those Rush Hour Blues', *Time*, 18 January, 75–6.

____ (1988) 'Untitled Donovan Interview', *Q*, 24 September, 25.

____ (1996/97) 'Blocking the Schoolhouse Door: George Wallace Clears his Conscience',

Journal of Blacks in Higher Education, 14, Winter 1996–97, 67–8.

Aristotle (1996) *Poetics* (trans. Malcolm Heath). London: Penguin.

Armstrong, Dan (1989) 'Wiseman's Realm of Transgression: *Titicut Follies*, the Symbolic Father, and the Spectacle of Confinement', *Cinema Journal*, 29, 1, Autumn, 20–35.

Arnold, Gary (1969a) *'Salesman'*, *Washington Post*, 6 June, C1.

_____ (1969b) *'High School* a "Fine Film"', *Washington Post*, 12 November, B10.

_____ (1969c) 'Wiseman's "Depressing Movies"', *Washington Post*, 23 November, 177–8.

_____ (1970) *'Law and Order'*, *Washington Post*, 7 March, C6.

Arnold, Gina (2001) 'Pop Perfect', online at:www.metroactive.com/papers/metro/06.14.01/montereypop-0124.html; accessed 12 December 2004.

Aron, Raymond (1965) *Main Currents in Sociological Thought*, trans. Richard Howard and Helen Weaver. New York: Basic Books.

Arthur, Paul (1993) 'Jargons of Authenticity (Three American Moments)', in Michael Renov (ed.) *Theorizing Documentary*. New York: Routledge, 108–34.

Atkins, Thomas R. (ed.) (1976) *Frederick Wiseman*. New York: Simon & Schuster.

Bachman, Gideon (1961) 'The Frontiers of Realist Cinema: The Work of Ricky Leacock', *Film Culture*, 22, Summer, 12–33.

Bailey, Thomas A. (1968) 'The Mythmakers of American History', *Journal of American History*, 55, 1, June, 5–21.

Baker, Mark (1982) *Nam*. London: Abacus.

Bakhtin, Mikhail (1984) *Rabelais and his World* (trans. Hélène Iswolsky). Bloomington: Indiana University Press.

Baldelli, Giovanni (1971) *Social Anarchism*. Harmondsworth: Penguin.

Barber, James Alden Jr (1972), 'The Military Services and American Society: Relationships and Attitudes', in Stephen E. Ambrose and James A. Barber Jr (eds) *The Military and American Society*. New York: Macmillan, 299–310.

Barger, Ralph 'Sonny' (2001) *Hell's Angel*. London: Fourth Estate.

Baritz, Loren (1998) *Backfire: A History of How American Culture Led Us into Vietnam and Made Us Fight the Way We Did*. Baltimore: Johns Hopkins University Press.

Barnouw, Erik (1964) 'Films of Social Comment', *Film Comment*, 2, 1, Winter, 16–17.

_____ (1990) *Tube of Plenty: The Evolution of American Television* (second edition). New York: Oxford University Press.

_____ (1993) *Documentary: A History of the Non-Fiction Film* (second edition). New York: Oxford University Press.

Barsam, Richard M. (1986) 'American Direct Cinema: The Re-Presentation of Reality', *Persistence of Vision*, 3, 4, 131–57.

_____ (1992) *Non-Fiction Film: A Critical History*. Bloomington, IN: Indiana University Press.

Barthes, Roland (1972) *Mythologies*. London: Vintage.

_____ (1977) *Image Music Text*. London: Fontana Press.

_____ (1981) *Camera Lucida*. London: Vintage.

_____ (1990) *S/Z*. Oxford: Basil Blackwell.

Bates, Dan (1968) *'The Green Berets'*, *Film Quarterly*, 22, 1, Autumn, 73–4.

Baughman, James L. (2001) 'Who Read *Life*?', in Erika Doss (ed.) *Looking at Life Magazine*. Washington, D.C.: Smithsonian Institution Press, 41–51.

Bazin, André (1971) *What is Cinema?* (trans. Hugh Gray). Berkeley: University of California Press.

Beagle, Peter S. (1982) *The Garden of Earthly Delights*. London: Pan.

Beattie, Keith (1998) *The Scar That Binds: American Culture and the Vietnam War*. New York: New York University Press.

Becker, Howard S. (1963) *Outsiders: Studies in the Sociology of Deviance*. New York: The Free Press.

____ (1997) 'The Culture of a Deviant Group: The "Jazz" Musician', in Ken Gelder and Sarah Thornton (eds) *The Subcultures Reader*. New York: Routledge, 55–65.

Beecher, Jonathan and Richard Bienvenu (eds) (1971) *The Utopian Vision of Charles Fourier*. Boston: Beacon Press.

Bell, Dale (ed.) (1999) *Woodstock: An Inside Look at the Movie that Shook up the World and Defined a Generation*. Studio City, CA: Michael Wiese Productions.

Bell, Daniel (1962) *The End of Ideology: On the Exhaustion of Political Ideas in the Fifties*. New York: The Free Press.

Bellah, Robert N., Richard Madsen, William M. Sullivan and Ann Swidler (eds) (1985) *Habits of the Heart*. Berkeley, CA: University of California Press.

Belz, Carl I. (1967) 'Popular Music and the Folk Tradition', *Journal of American Folklore*, 80, 316, April–June, 130–42.

Benjamin, Walter (1975) *Illuminations*. New York: Schocken Books.

Bennett, William (1982) '*Dont Look Back*', *Boston Phoenix*, 14 September, 4.

Benson, Thomas W. and Carolyn Anderson (1989) *Reality Fictions: The Films of Frederick Wiseman*. Carbondale, IL: Southern Illinois University Press.

Bercovitch, Sacvan and Myra Jehlen (eds) (1986) *Ideology and Classic American Literature*. New York: Cambridge University Press.

Berg, Beatrice (1970) 'I Was Fed Up With Hollywood Fantasies', *New York Times*, 1 February, D25.

Berg, Stephen and Robert Mezey (eds) (1969) *Naked Poetry*. Indianapolis and New York: Bobbs-Merrill.

Berger, John (1972) *Ways of Seeing*. London: Penguin.

Berki, R. N. (1972) 'Marcuse and the Crisis of the New Radicalism: From Politics to Religion?', *Journal of Politics*, 34, 1, February, 56–92.

Berkowitz, Edward (ed.) (1991) *America's Welfare State from Roosevelt to Reagan*. London: Johns Hopkins Press.

Bernstein, Irving (1991) *Promises Kept: John F. Kennedy's New Frontier*. New York: Oxford University Press.

Beyerle, Monika (1997) *Authentisierungsstrategien im Documentarfilm: Das americanische Direct Cinema der 60er Jahre*. Frankfurt am Main: WVT Wissenchaftlicher Verlag Trier.

Bigsby, Christopher (1990) *Arthur Miller and Company*. London: Methuen.

Biskind, Peter (1998) *Easy Riders, Raging Bulls: How the Sex 'n' Drugs 'n' Rock 'n' Roll Generation Saved Hollywood*. London: Bloomsbury.

Bloodworth, William A., Jr (1977) *Upton Sinclair*. Boston: Twain.

Bloom, Alexander and Wini Breines (eds) (1995) *Takin' it to the Streets: A Sixties Reader*. New York: Oxford University Press.

Blue, James (1965) 'One Man's Truth: An Interview with Richard Leacock', *Film Comment*, 3, Spring, 16–22.

Bode, Carl (ed.) (1947) *The Portable Thoreau*. New York: Viking.

Bodroghkozy, Aniko (2001) *Groove Tube: Sixties Television and the Youth Rebellion*. Durham NC: Duke University Press.

Booker, Christopher (1969) *The Neophiliacs*. London: Collins.

Bordwell, David and Kristin Thompson (1997) *Film Art: An Introduction* (Fifth Edition). New York: McGraw-Hill.

____ (2002) *Film History: An Introduction*. New York: McGraw-Hill.

Booth, William (1995–96) 'James Hood's One Man March', *Journal of Blacks in Higher Edu-*

cation, 10, Winter, 96–7.

Bradford, Sarah (2001) *America's Queen: The Life of Jacqueline Kennedy Onassis*. London: Penguin.

Braudy, Leo and Marshall Cohen (eds) (1999) *Film Theory and Criticism: Introductory Readings* (Fifth Edition). New York: Oxford University Press.

Breitrose, Henry (1964) 'On the Search for the Real Nitty-Gritty: Problems and Possibilities in *Cinéma Vérité*', *Film Quarterly*, 17, 4, Summer, 36–40.

Brinkley, Alan (2000) *Liberalism and its Discontents*. Cambridge MA: Harvard University Press.

Brogan, Hugh (1996) *Profiles in Power: Kennedy*. New York: Longman.

Bronner, Stephen Eric (1983/84) 'Reconstructing the Experiment: Politics, Ideology, and the American New Left', *Social Text*, 8, Winter, 127–41.

Brown, Joe David (ed.) (1967) *The Hippies*. New York: Time-Life.

Brown, Norman O. (1959) *Life Against Death: The Psychoanalytical Meaning of History*. Wesleyan, CT: Wesleyan University Press.

Brown, Peter and Steven Gaines (1983) *The Love You Make: An Insider's Story of The Beatles*. New York: McGraw-Hill.

Brustein, Robert (1994) *Dumbocracy in America: Studies in the Theatre of Guilt (1987–1994*. Chicago: Ivan R. Dee.

Bruzzi, Stella (2000) *New Documentary: A Critical Introduction*. London: Routledge.

Bryson, Bill (1990) *Mother Tongue*. London: Hamish Hamilton.

_____ (1994) *Made in America*. London: Secker & Warburg.

Buck, Chris (n.d.), 'An Interview with Richard Leacock', online at: www.popped.com/articles98/cinemaverite/veriteleacock.html; accessed 3 March and 11 May 2003.

_____ (n.d.) 'An Interview with Albert Maysles', online at: www.popped.com/articles98/cinemaverite/veritemaysles.html; accessed 7 July 2004.

Bulgakov, Mikhail (1967) *The Master and Margarita*. London: Harwell & Collins.

Bunyan, John (1987 [1678]) *The Pilgrim's Progress*. London: Penguin.

Burroughs, William (1993) *Naked Lunch*. London: Flamingo.

Burr, Vivien (1995) *An Introduction to Social Constructionism*. London: Routledge.

Bushnell, Horace (1849) *God in Christ. Three Discourses, Delivered at New Haven, Cambridge and Andover, with a Preliminary Dissertation on Language*. Hartford: Brown and Parsons.

Buzzanco, Robert (1999) *Vietnam and the Transformation of American Life*. Malden MA: Blackwell.

Callenbach, Ernest (1961) 'Going Out to the Subject: II', *Film Quarterly*, 14, 3, Spring, 38–40.

_____ (1967) '*Dont Look Back*', *Film Quarterly*, 20, 4, Summer, 78.

_____ (1969) '*Monterey Pop*', *Film Quarterly*, 23, 1, Autumn, 52.

Callow, Alexander B. (ed.) (1969) *American Urban History: An Interpretive Reader with Commentaries*. New York: Oxford University Press.

Cameron, Ian and Mark Shivas (1963) 'New Methods, New Approach', *Movie*, 8, April, 12–15.

Canby, Vincent (1970a) 'Woodstock Ecstasy Caught on Film', *New York Times*, 27 March, 22.

_____ (1970b) 'Of Sticks and Stones and Blood at Altamont', *New York Times*, 7 December, 60.

Carlin, M. M. (1964) 'Love on Film', *Transition*, 17, 34–8.

Carter, Dan T. (1995) *The Politics of Rage: George Wallace, The Origins of the New Conserva-*

tism, and the Transformation of American Politics. New York: Simon & Schuster.

Cartwright, Bert (1985) *The Bible in the Lyrics of Bob Dylan*. Bury: Wanted Man.

Cashmore, Ellis (1994) *... And Then There Was Television*. London: Routledge.

Cavallo, Dominick (1999) *A Fiction of the Past: The Sixties in American History*. New York: Palgrave.

Cavell, Stanley (1972) *The Senses of Walden*. New York: Viking.

Cayo Sexton, Patricia (1967) *The American School: A Sociological Analysis*. Englewood Cliffs, NJ: Prentice-Hall.

Chalmers, David (1996) *And the Crooked Places Made Straight: The Struggle for Social Change in the 1960s* (second edition). Baltimore: Johns Hopkins University Press.

Chenoweth, Lawrence (1971) 'The Rhetoric of Hope and Despair: A Study of the Jimi Hendrix Experience and the Jefferson Airplane', *American Quarterly*, 23, 1, Spring, 25–45.

Chomsky, Noam (2004) *Hegemony or Survival: America's Quest for Global Dominance*. London: Penguin.

Christgau, Robert (1970) 'Leacock Pennebaker: The MGM of the Underground?', *Show*, 1, 1, January, 92–6.

Chunovic, Louis (2004) *Why Do People Love America?: A Supersized Analysis of US Cultural Influences*. London: Sanctuary.

Clark, Kenneth (1956) *The Nude: A Study in Ideal Art*. Harmondsworth: Penguin.

Cohen, Bernard (1963) *The Press and Foreign Policy*. Princeton, NJ: Princeton University Press.

Coles, Robert (1997) *Doing Documentary Work*. New York: Oxford University Press.

Collins, Robert M. (1994) 'Growth Liberalism in the Sixties: Great Societies at Home and Grand Designs Abroad', in David Farber (ed.) *The Sixties: From Memory to History*. Chapel Hill NC: University of North Carolina Press, 11–44.

Comfort, Alex (1963) *Sex in Society*. London: Pelican.

Comolli, Jean-Louis and Jean Narboni (1976) 'Cinema/Ideology/Criticism', in Bill Nichols (ed.) *Movies and Methods*. Berkeley and Los Angeles: University of California Press, 22–30.

Conn, Peter (1990) *The Cambridge Illustrated History of American Literature*. New York: Guild.

Conover, Patrick W. (1975) 'An Analysis of Communes and International Communities with Particular Attention to Sexual and Genderal Relations', *Family Coordinator*, 24, 4, October, 453–64.

Cook, Bruce (1971) *The Beat Generation*. New York: Charles Scribner.

Cook, Pam (ed.) (1998) *The Cinema Book*. London: British Film Institute.

Corcoran, Neil (ed.) (2002) *'Do you, Mr Jones?' Bob Dylan with the Poets and Professors*. London: Chatto & Windus.

Corner, John (1996) *The Art of Record: A Critical Introduction to Documentary*. Manchester: Manchester University Press.

Curry, Timothy Jon (1985) 'Frederick Wiseman: Sociological Filmmaker?', *Contemporary Sociology*, 14, 1, January, 35–9.

Curtin, Michael (1995) *Redeeming the Wasteland: Television Documentary and Cold War Politics*. New Brunswick, NJ: Rutgers University Press.

Dallek, Robert (1998) *Flawed Giant: Lyndon Johnson and His Times (1961–1973)*. New York: Oxford University Press.

____ (2004) *John F. Kennedy: An Unfinished Life*. London: Penguin.

De Tocqueville, Alexis (1966 [1835]) *Democracy in America*, trans. George Lawrence. New York: Harper & Row.

Debord, Guy (1970) *The Society of the Spectacle*. Detroit: Black and Red.

Denselow, Robin (1990) *When the Music's Over: The Story of Political Pop*. London: Faber & Faber.

DeRogatis, Jim (2000) *Let it Blurt: The Life and Times of Lester Bangs*. London: Bloomsbury.

Didion, Joan (2001) *Slouching Towards Bethlehem*. London: Flamingo.

Diggins, John (1989) *The Proud Decades: America in War and Peace (1941–1960)*. New York: W.W. Norton.

____ (1992) *The Rise and Fall of the American Left*. New York: Norton.

Docker, John (1994) *Postmodernism and Pop Culture*. Cambridge: Cambridge University Press.

Doss, Erika (ed.) (2001) *Looking at Life Magazine*. Washington, D.C.: Smithsonian Institution Press.

Drew, Robert (1946) 'The Fliers', *Life*, 9 December, 104.

____ (1988) 'An Independent with the Networks', in Alan Rosenthal (ed.) *New Challenges for Documetary*. Berkeley, CA: University of California Press, 389–401.

Dylan, Bob (1971 [1966]) *Tarantula*. New York: Macmillan.

____ (2004) *Chronicles: Volume One*. New York: Simon & Schuster.

Echols, Alice (1999) *Scars of Sweet Paradise: The Life and Times of Janis Joplin*. New York: Henry Holt.

The Editors of Time-Life Books (1970) *Documentary Photography*. Netherlands: Time-Life International.

Edsall, Thomas B. and Mary D. Edsall (1991) *Chain Reaction: The Impact of Race, Rights and Taxes on American Politics*. New York: Norton.

Ehrenreich, Barbara, Elizabeth Hess and Gloria Jacobs (1997) 'Beatlemania: A Sexually Defiant Consumer Culture?', in Ken Gelder and Sarah Thornton (eds) *The Subcultures Reader*. New York: Routledge, 523–36.

Ehrenstein, David and Bill Reed (1982) *Rock on Film*. London: Virgin.

Eisen, Jonathan (1969) *The Age of Rock*. New York: Vintage.

Eisenhower, Dwight D. (1972) 'Farewell Address to the Nation, Jan. 17, 1961', in Stephen E. Ambrose and James A. Barber Jr (eds) *The Military and American Society*. New York: Macmillan, 61–3.

Eitzen, Dirk (1995) 'When is Documentary? Documentary as a Mode of Reception', *Cinema Journal*, 35, 1, Autumn, 81–102.

Ellis, Jack C. (1989) *The Documentary Idea: A Critical History of English-Language Documentary and Video*. Englewood Cliffs NJ, Prentice-Hall.

Elson, Robert T. (1968) *Time, Inc.: The Intimate History of a Publishing Enterprise (1923–1941)*. New York: Atheneum.

Emerson, Ralph Waldo (1882) *Society and Solitude*. Boston: Houghton, Mifflin.

____ (1983) *Essays and Lectures*. New York: Library of America.

____ (n.d.) *The Works of Ralph Waldo Emerson in One Volume*. New York: Black's Readers Service Company.

Evans, Harold (1997) *Pictures on a Page: Photo-Journalism, Graphics and Picture Editing*. London: Pimlico.

Fairclough, Norman (1993) *Discourse and Social Change*. Cambridge: Blackwell.

Faithfull, Marianne and David Dalton (1995) *Faithfull*. London: Penguin.

Farber, David (ed.) (1994) *The Sixties: From Memory to History*. Chapel Hill, NC: University of North Carolina Press.

Feinberg, Lawrence (1969) 'High Schools More Complex than Presented in New Film', *Washington Post*, 25 October, B1.

Feldman, Silvia (1976) 'The Wiseman Documentary', *Human Behaviour*, 5, 2, 64–9.

Feuer, Lewis S. (1972) 'Student Unrest in the United States', *Annals of the American Academy of Political and Social Science*, vol. 404: *Higher Education: Prospects and Choices*, November, 64–72.

Flaherty, Frances Hubbard (1960) *The Odyssey of a Film Maker*. Urbana: Beta Phi Mui.

Fong-Torres, Ben (ed.) (1972) *Rolling Stone Interviews 2*. New York: Warner Books.

Fowler, Roger (1991) *A Dictionary of Modern Critical Terms*. London: Routledge.

Frank, Robert (1959) *The Americans*. New York: Grove Press.

Frascina, Francis (1999) *Art, Politics and Dissent: Aspects of the Art Left in Sixties America*. Manchester: Manchester University Press.

Friedan, Betty (1992 [1963]) *The Feminine Mystique*. London: Penguin.

Friedenberg, Edgar Z. (1971) 'The High School as a Focus of Student Unrest', *Annals of the American Academy of Political and Social Science*, vol. 395: *Students' Protest*, May, 117–26.

Frith, Simon (1981) '"The Magic That Can Set You Free": The Ideology of Folk and the Myth of the Rock Community', *Popular Music, vol. 1: Folk or Popular? Distinctions, Influences, Continuities*, 159–68 .

_____ (1983) *Sound Effects: Youth, Leisure, and the Politics of Rock 'n' Roll*. London: Constable.

Frith, Simon and Howard Horne (1989) *Art Into Pop*. London: Routledge.

Fursenko, Aleksandr and Timothy Naftali (1999) *One Hell of a Gamble: Khrushchev, Castro, Kennedy and the Cuban Missile Crisis (1958–1964)*. London: Pimlico.

Galanti, Geri-Ann (1997) *Caring for Patients from Different Cultures: Case Studies from American Hospitals*. Philadelphia: University of Pennsylvania Press.

Galbraith, John Kenneth (1958) *The Affluent Society*. Boston: Houghton Mifflin.

Gardner, Paul (1964a) '3000 Fans Greet British Beatles', *New York Times*, 8 February, 25–6.

_____ (1964b) 'TV Series Joins Search for Truth: *Cinéma Vérité* Technique is Used in Documentaries', *New York Times*, 5 October, 67.

Garrow, David (1986) *Bearing the Cross: Martin Luther King Jr and the Southern Christian Leadership Conference*. New York: Morrow.

Gaylin, Ned L. (1970) 'The Woodstock Generation. Frankenstein or Golem', *Family Coordinator*, 19, 1, January, 3–10.

Gelder, Ken and Sarah Thornton (eds) (1997) *The Subcultures Reader*. New York: Routledge.

George, Nelson (1988) *The Death of Rhythm and Blues*. New York: Plume.

Geller, Debbie (2000) *The Brian Epstein Story*, ed. Anthony Wall. London: Faber & Faber.

Giddens, Anthony (ed.) (1986) *Durkheim, Politics and the State*. Cambridge: Polity Press.

Ginsberg, Allen (1956) *Howl and Other Poems*. San Francisco: City Light Books.

_____ (1969) 'Wichita Vortex Sutra, Part II', in Stephen Berg and Robert Mezey (eds) *Naked Poetry*. Indianapolis and New York: Bobbs-Merrill, 207–20.

Ginzberg, Eli (1971) *Urban Health Services: The Case of New York*. New York: Columbia University Press.

Gitlin, Todd (1987) *The Sixties: Years of Hope, Days of Rage*. New York: Bantam.

_____ (1995 [1969]) 'New Left, Old Traps', in Alexander Bloom and Wini Breines (eds) *Takin' it to the Streets: A Sixties Reader*. New York: Oxford University Press, 454–58.

Green, Jonathon (1999) *All Dressed Up: The Sixties and the Counterculture*. London: Random House.

Goffman, Irving (1991) *Asylums: Essays on the Social Situation of Mental Patients and Other Inmates*. London: Penguin.

Goldman, Albert (1988) *The Lives of John Lennon*. New York: Bantam.

Goldsmith, Martin (2004) *The Beatles Come to America*. Hoboken, NJ: John Wiley & Sons.

Goldstein, Jeffrey H. (ed.) (1998) *Why We Watch: The Attractions of Violent Entertainment*. New York: Oxford University Press.

Gonzalez, Nancie L. (1972) 'Happy Mother's Day', *American Anthropologist*, 74, 6, December, 1572–3.

Goodman, Fred (1997) *The Mansion on the Hill: Dylan, Young, Geffen, Springsteen and the Head-On Collision of Rock and Commerce*. London: Jonathan Cape.

Gosse, Van and Richard R. Moser (2003) *The World the Sixties Made: Politics and Culture in Recent America*. Philadelphia: Temple University Press.

Gould, Jack (1960) 'Yanki, No!', *New York Times*, 8 December, 71.

_____ (1963a) 'Too Many Cameras: Documentary on the Segregation Crisis Termed "Just a Peep Show"', *New York Times*, 22 October, 75.

_____ (1963b) 'Behind Closed Doors: Television Coverage of Matters Involving Executive Decision Can Tarnish National Dignity', *New York Times*, 27 October, B13.

Gower Price, Charles (1997) 'Sources of American Styles in the Music of The Beatles', *American Music*, 15, 2, Summer, 208–32.

Graham, Peter (1964) '*Cinéma Vérité* in France', *Film Quarterly*, 17, 4, Summer, 30–6.

Grant, Barry Keith (1992) *Voyages of Discovery: The Cinema of Frederick Wiseman*. Chicago: University of Illinois Press.

_____ (ed.) (1995) *Film Genre Reader II*. Austin: University of Texas Press.

_____ (1998) 'Ethnography in the first person: Frederick Wiseman's *Titicut Follies*', in Barry Keith Grant and Jeannette Sloniowski (eds) *Documenting the Documentary: Close Readings of Documentary Film and Video*. Detroit: Wayne State University Press, 238–53.

Green, Jonathon (1999) *All Dressed Up: The Sixties and the Counterculture*. London: Random House.

Greer, Germaine (1970) *The Female Eunuch*. London: MacGibbon & Kee.

Grierson, John (1966) *Grierson on Documentary*, ed. Forsyth Hardy. London: Faber & Faber.

Griffith, Thomas (1995) *Harry & Teddy: The Turbulent Friendship of Press Lord Henry R. Luce and his Favorite Reporter, Theodore H. White*. New York: Random House.

Guiliano, Geoffrey (1986) *The Beatles: A Celebration*. London: Sidgwick & Jackson.

Guillory, Ferrel (1969) 'Camera Catch', *Washington Post*, 11 July, B9.

Guralnick, Peter (1994) *Last Train to Memphis: The Rise of Elvis Presley*. London: Little, Brown.

Haavio-Mannila, Elina (2002) *Sexual Lifestyles in the Twentieth Century: A Research Study*. London: Palgrave.

Hainley, Bruce (1995) 'Nan Goldin at the Matthew Marks Gallery', *Artforum*, 33, May, 95–9.

Hajdu, David (2002) *Positively 4ᵗʰ Street: The Lives and Times of Bob Dylan, Joan Baez, Mimi Baez and Richard Fariña*. London: Bloomsbury.

Halberstadt, Ira (1974) 'An interview with Frederick Wiseman', *Filmmakers' Newsletter*, 7, 4, February, 19–25.

Halberstam, David (1979) *The Powers That Be*. New York: Knopf.

Hall, Jeanne (1991) 'Realism as a Style in *Cinéma Vérité*: A Critical Analysis of *Primary*', *Cinema Journal*, 30, 4, Summer, 24–50.

_____ (1998) 'Don't You Ever Just Watch? American *Cinéma Vérité* and *Dont Look Back*', in Barry Keith Grant and Jeannette Sloniowski (eds) *Documenting the Documentary: Close Readings of Documentary Film and Video*. Detroit: Wayne State University Press, 223–37.

Hall, Stuart (1997) *Representation: Cultural Representations and Signifying Practices*. London: Open University.

Hallin, Daniel C. (1984) 'The Media, the War in Vietnam and Political Support: A Critique of the Thesis of an Oppostional Media', *Journal of Politics*, 46, 1, February, 2–24.

Hamilton, Nigel (1992) *JFK: Reckless Youth*. London: Arrow.

Hammond, William M. (1996) *The U.S. Army in Vietnam: Public Affairs – The Military and the Media 1968–1973*. Washington, D.C.: US Army Center of Military History.

Hanlin, Oscar (1954) *The American People in the Twentieth Century*. Cambridge MA: Harvard University Press.

Hardy, Phil and Dave Laing (1995) *The Faber Companion to 20th Century Popular Music*. London: Faber & Faber.

Harker, Dave (1980) *One for the Money: Politics and Popular Song*. London: Hutchinson.

Harrington, Michael (1962) *The Other America*. Harmondsworth: Penguin.

____ (1985) *The New American Poverty*. London: Firethorn.

Hart, James D. (1986) *The Concise Oxford Guide to American Literature*. New York: Oxford University Press.

Harvey, Sylvia (1978) *May '68 and Film Culture*. London: British Film Institute.

Haycock, Joel (1971) 'Gimme Shelter', *Film Quarterly*, 24, 4, Summer, 56–60.

Henderson, David (1978) *'Scuse Me While I Kiss the Sky: The Life of Jimi Hendrix*. London: Omnibus.

Hendrickson, Paul (1996) *The Living and the Dead: Robert MacNamara and Five Lives of a Lost War*. London: Macmillan.

Henrickson, Margot A. (1997) *Dr Strangelove's America*. Berkeley, CA: University of California Press.

Hersh, Seymour M. (1983) *The Price of Power: Kissinger in the Nixon White House*. New York: Summit Books.

____ (1997) *The Dark Side of Camelot*. London: HarperCollins.

Hicks, Jack, James D. Houston, Maxine Hong Kingston and Al Young (eds) (2000) *The Literature of California: Writings from the Golden State*. Berkeley, CA: University of California Press.

Hiatt, Howard H. (1987) *America's Health in the Balance*. New York: Harper & Row.

Hill, Gladwin (1968) 'Marcuse Returns as Storm Center on Campus', *New York Times*, 29 September, 71.

Hill, Lee (2001) *A Grand Guy: The Life and Times of Terry Southern*. London: Bloomsbury.

Hillier, Jim (ed.) (1986) *Cahiers du Cinéma: 1960–1968: New Wave, New Cinema, Reevaluating Hollywood*. Cambridge MA: Harvard University Press.

Hirsh, Foster (1971) 'Woodstock', *Film Quarterly*, 24, 3, Spring, 54–6.

Hoberman, J. (1998) 'A Test for the Individual Viewer: Bonnie and Clyde's Violent Reception', in Jeffrey H. Goldstein (ed.) *Why We Watch: The Attractions of Violent Entertainment*. New York: Oxford University Press, 116–43.

Hodgson, Godfrey (1973) 'The Politics of American Health Care: What is it Costing You?', *Atlantic Monthly*, October, 60–70.

Hoffman, Joyce (1995) *Theodore White and Journalism as Illusion*. Columbia, MO: University of Missouri Press.

Hogenson, Barbara (1984) 'D. A. Pennebaker on the Filming of *Dont Look Back*', *Film Library Quarterly*, 17, 2–4.

Holland, Patricia (1997) *The Television Handbook*. London: Routledge.

Hollister, Leo E. (1968) *Chemical Psychoses: LSD and Other Drugs*. Springfield IL: Charles C. Thomas.

Holmes, Oliver Wendell (1859) 'The Stereoscope and the Stereograph', *Atlantic Monthly*, 3, 20, June, 738–48.

Hood, Phil (ed.) (1986) *Artists of American Folk Music*. New York: GPI Books.

Hopkins, Jerry and Danny Sugerman (1980) *No One Here Gets Out Alive*. London: Plexus.

Horn, Barbara Lee (1991) *The Age of Hair: Evolution and Impact of Broadway's First Rock Musical*. New York: Greenwood.

Horn, John (1963) 'Kennedy Documentary', *New York Herald Tribune*, 28 November, 19.

Howells, Richard (2003) *Visual Culture*. Malden MA: Polity.

Hughes, Robert (1997) *American Visions: The Epic History of Art in America*. London: The Harvill Press.

Humphrey, Hubert H. (1991) *The Education of a Public Man: My Life and Politics*. Minneapolis: University of Minnesota Press.

Huxley, Aldous (1959) *The Doors of Perception*. Harmondsworth: Penguin.

Iser, Wolfgang (1987) *Walter Pater: The Aesthetic Moment*. Cambridge: Cambridge University Press.

Issari, M. Ali (1971) *Cinéma Vérité*. East Lansing: Michigan State University Press.

Isserman, Maurice and Michael Kazin (2000) *America Divided – The Civil War of the 1960s*. New York: Oxford University Press.

Izod, John (1988) *Hollywood and the Box Office, 1895–1986*. London: Macmillan.

Jackson, Bruce (1988) 'What People Like Us Are Saying When We Say We're Saying the Truth', *Journal of American Folklore*, 101, 401, July–September, 276–92.

Jacobs, Diane (1977) *Hollywood Renaissance*. Cranbury NJ: A. S. Barnes & Co.

Jacobs, Lewis (ed.) (1979) *The Documentary Tradition* (Second Edition). New York: W. W. Norton.

Jacobs, Paul and Saul Landau (1966) *The New Radicals*. New York: Vintage.

Jaffe, Patricia (1965) 'Editing *Cinéma Vérité*', *Film Comment*, 3, 3, Summer, 43–7.

James, David E. (1989) *Allegories of Cinema: American Film in the Sixties*. Princeton, NJ: Princeton University Press.

James, Henry (1984 [1879]) 'Hawthorne', in *Literary Criticism Volume 1*. New York: Library of America, 315–457.

Janowitz, Morris (1972 [1969]) 'Characteristics of the Military Environment', in Stephen E. Ambrose and James A. Barber Jr (eds) *The Military and American Society*. New York: Macmillan, 166–73.

Jappe, Anselm (1999) *Guy Debord*, trans. Donald Nicholson-Smith. Berkeley, CA: University of California Press.

Jeffreys, Sheila (1990) *Anticlimax: A Feminist Perspective on the Sexual Revolution*. London: The Women's Press.

Jeffries, John W. (1978) 'The "Quest for National Purpose" of 1960', *American Quarterly*, 30, 4, Autumn, 451–70.

Jervis, Robert (1976) *Perception and Misperception in International Politics*. Princeton, NJ: Princeton University Press.

Johnston, Ian (1997) 'God Rides a Harley in the Land of the Free', online at: www.mala.bc.ca/~johnstoi/introser/adam.htm; accessed 5 June 2004.

Joseph, Peter (1973) *Good Times: An Oral History of America in the Nineteen Sixties*, New York: Morrow.

Kael, Pauline (1969) '*High School*', *New Yorker*, 45, 18 October, 202–3.

Kahana, Jonathan (1999) 'The Reception of Politics: Publicity and its Parasites', *Social Text*, 58, Spring, 92–109.

Kampelman, Max M. (1978) 'Hubert H. Humphrey: Political Scientist', *PS*, 11, 2, Spring, 228–36.

Keil, Charlie (1998) 'American Documentary Finds Its Voice: Persuasion and Expression in

The Plow That Broke the Plains and The City', in Barry Keith Grant and Jeannette Sloniowski (eds) *Documenting the Documentary: Close Readings of Documentary Film and
Video*. Detroit: Wayne State University Press, 119–35.

Kellner, Douglas (1990) *Television and the Crisis of Democracy*. Oxford: Westview.

Kelly, Kitty (1979) *Jackie Oh!* London: Mayflower.

Kennedy, John F. (1962) *To Turn the Tide*, ed. John W. Gardner. London: Hamish Hamilton.

Kenney, Richard L. (1971) 'American Cinematic Form', *Film Quarterly*, 25, 2, Winter, 9–19.

Kesey, Ken (1973) *One Flew Over the Cuckoo's Nest*. London: Picador.

Kilborn, Richard and John Izod (1997) *Confronting Reality: An Introduction to Television Documentary*. Manchester: Manchester University Press.

King, Geoff (2001) *New Hollywood Cinema: An Introduction*. London: I.B. Tauris.

Kissinger, Henry (1979) *White House Years*. Boston: Little, Brown.

Kleiman, Mark (1970) 'High School Reform: Toward a Student Movement', in Massimo Teodori (ed.) *The New Left: A Documentary History*. London: Jonathan Cape, 318–323.

Knight, Curtis (1974) *Jimi: An Intimate Biography*. London: W. H. Allen.

Koestenbaum, Wayne (1995) *Jackie Under My Skin: Interpreting An Icon*. London: Fourth
Estate.

Kolker, Robert Phillip (1971) 'Circumstantial Evidence: An Interview with David and Albert
Maysles', *Sight and Sound*, 40, 4, 183–6.

Kuhn, Annette (1978) 'The Camera-I: Observations on Documentary', *Screen*, 19, 2, Summer, 73.

Kurlansky, Mark (2005) *1968: The Year That Rocked the World*. London: Vantage.

Lacayo, Richard (1983) 'Why are Documentaries So Dull?', *New York Times*, 20 February,
29.

Laing, R. D. (1961) *Self and Others*. London: Tavistock.

____ (1967) *The Politics of Experience and The Bird of Paradise*. Harmondsworth: Penguin.

Leary, Timothy (1999 [1967]) *Turn On, Tune In, Drop Out*, ed. Beverly Potter. Berkeley, CA:
Ronin.

Lee, Martin A. and Bruce Shlain (1985) *Acid Dreams: The Complete Social History of LSD:
The CIA, the Sixties, and Beyond*. New York: Grove Press.

Lenzer, Don (1999) 'A Vision for Antonia', in Dale Bell (ed.) *Woodstock: An Inside Look at
the Movie that Shook up the World and Defined a Generation*. Studio City, CA: Michael
Wiese Productions, 141–4.

Levin, G. Roy (1971) *Documentary Explorations: 15 Interviews with Film-Makers*. New York:
Doubleday.

Lewis, Roger (1972) *Outlaws of America: The Underground Press and its Context*. London:
Heinrich Hanau.

Lhamon, W. T., Jr. (1990) *Deliberate Speed: The Origins of a Cultural Style in the American
1950s*. Washington: Smithsonian Institution Press.

Lipscomb, James C. (1964) 'Correspondence and Controversy: *Cinéma vérité*', *Film Quarterly*, 18, 2, Winter, 62–3.

Lipsit, Seymour M. and Sheldon S. Wolin (eds) (1965) *The Berkley Student Revolt*. New York:
Doubleday.

Lucie-Smith, Edward (2001) *Movements in Art Since 1945*. London: Thames & Hudson.

Luel, S. A. and P. Marcus (eds) (1984) *Psychoanalytic Reflections on the Holocaust: Selected
Essays*. New York: KTAV.

Lukács, Georg (1967) *History and Class Consciousness*. New York: Merlin Press.

Luns, Jend and R. Serge Denisoff (1971) 'The Folk-Music Revival and the Counter-Culture:
Contributions and Contradictions', *Journal of American Folklore*, 84, 334, October–De-

cember, 394–405.

Lynd, Staughton (1969) 'The New Left', in *Annals of the American Academy of Political and Social Science*, vol. 382: *Protest in the Sixties*, March, 64–72.

MacDonald, Dwight (ed.) (1974) *Discriminations: Essays and Afterthoughts (1938–1974)*. New York: Grossman.

MacDonald, Ian (1994) *Revolution in the Head: The Beatles' Records and the Sixties*. London: Pimlico.

_____ (2002) 'Play With Fire', *Uncut*, 66, November, 70.

Macdonald, Kevin and Mark Cousins (1998) *Imagining Reality: The Faber Book of Documentary*. London: Faber & Faber.

_____ (1998) 'The Grain of Truth', in Kevin Macdonald and Mark Cousins, *Imagining Reality: The Faber Book of Documentary*. London: Faber & Faber, 249–282.

Macedo, Stephen (ed.) (1997) *Reassessing the Sixties: Debating the Political and Cultural Legacy*. New York: W. W. Norton.

Maier, Pauline, Merritt Rose Smith, Alexander Keysarr and Daniel J. Kelves (2003) *Inventing America: A History of the United States*. New York: Norton.

Mailer, Norman (1963) *The Presidential Papers*. Harmondsworth: Penguin.

_____ (1968) *The Armies of the Night*. London: Weidenfeld and Nicholson.

_____ (1969) *Why Are We In Vietnam? A Novel*. London: Weidenfeld and Nicholson.

Maitland, Sarah (ed.) (1988) *Very Heaven: Looking Back at the 1960s*. London: Virago Press.

Mamber, Stephen (1970) 'High School', *Film Quarterly*, 23, 3, Spring, 48–51.

_____ (1973) '*Cinéma Vérité* and Social Concerns', *Film Comment*, 9, 6, 8–15.

_____ (1974) *Cinéma Vérité in America: Studies in Uncontrolled Documentary*. Cambridge, MA: MIT Press.

Marcorelles, Louis (1963) 'The Leacock Experiment', reprinted in Jim Hillier (ed.) (1986) *Cahiers du Cinéma 1960–1968: New Wave, New Cinema, Reevaluating Hollywood*. Cambridge MA: Harvard University Press, 264–70.

_____ (1973) *The Living Cinema*. New York: Praeger.

Marcus, Greil (1991) *Mystery Train*. London: Penguin.

_____ (1989) *Lipstick Traces: A Secret History of the Twentieth Century*. Cambridge MA: Harvard University Press.

Marcuse, Herbert (1964) *One-Dimensional Man: Studies in the Ideology of Advanced Industrial Society*. London: Routledge & Kegan Paul.

Margolis, Jon (1999) *The Last Innocent Year: America in 1964 (The Beginning of the 'Sixties')*. New York: William Murrow.

Marsh, Dave (1986) *Before I Get Old*. New York: St. Martin's.

Marwick, Arthur (2000) 'Introduction: Locating Key Texts amid the Distinctive Landscape of the Sixties', in Anthony Aldgate, James Chapman and Arthur Marwick (eds) *Windows on the Sixties: Exploring Key Texts of Media and Culture*. London: I.B. Tauris, xi–xxi.

Marx, Leo (1964) *The Machine in the Garden: Technology and the Pastoral Ideal in America*. New York: Oxford University Press.

Matthiessen, F. O. (1941) *American Renaissance: Art and Expression in the Age of Emerson and Whitman*. New York: Oxford University Press.

May, Lary (ed.) (1989) *Recasting America: Culture and Politics in the Age of Cold War*. Chicago: University of Chicago Press.

Mazower, Mark (1999) *Dark Continent: Europe's Twentieth Century*. London: Penguin.

McDermott, John, with Eddie Kramer (1992) *Hendrix: Setting the Record Straight*. New York: Warner Books.

McDougal, Walter A. (1997) *Promised Land, Crusader State: The American Encounter with* the World Since 1776. New York: Mariner.

McHoul, Alec (1996) Semiotic Investigations: Towards an Effective Semiotics. Lincoln and London: University of Nebraska Press.

McLuhan, Marshall (1987) Understanding Media: The Extensions of Man. London: Ark.

McWilliams, Donald E. (1970) 'Frederick Wiseman', Film Quarterly, 24, 1, Autumn, 17–26.

Mellers, Wilfrid (1984) A Darker Shade of Pale: A Backdrop to Bob Dylan. London: Faber & Faber.

Melly, George (1970) Revolt Into Style: The Pop Arts in the 50s and 60s. Harmondsworth: Penguin.

Melville, Herman (1966 [1850]) White-Jacket; or The World in a Man-of-War. Oxford: Oxford University Press.

____ (1992 [1851]) Moby-Dick; or The Whale. Harmondsworth: Penguin.

Metz, Christian (1994) The Imaginary Signifier. London: Macmillan.

Miles, Barry (1998) Paul McCartney: Many Years From Now. New York: Henry Holt.

____ (2002) In the Sixties. London: Jonathan Cape.

Miller, Arthur (1949) Death of a Salesman. London: Penguin Plays.

Mills, C. Wright (1958) The Power Elite. New York: Oxford University Press.

Milton, John (2005 [1667]) Paradise Lost. Cambridge MA: Hackett Publishing Company.

Minow, Newton M. (1964) Equal Time: The Private Broadcaster and the Public Interest. New York: Atheneum.

Morgan, David (1997) 'An Interview with Thelma Schoonmaker', online at: www.members. aol.com/morgands1/closeup/text/cfthelm2.htm; accessed 1 March 2005.

____ (2001) 'The Image of Religion in American Life, 1936–1951', in Erika Doss (ed.) Looking at Life Magazine. Washington, D.C.: Smithsonian Institution Press, 139–57.

Murray, Peter and Linda Murray (1980) The Penguin Dictionary of Art and Artists. Harmondsworth: Penguin.

Myers, David (1999) 'Our Mentor Speaks', in Dale Bell (ed.) Woodstock: An Inside Look at the Movie that Shook up the World and Defined a Generation. Studio City, CA: Michael Wiese Productions, 123–9.

Naficy, Hamid (1982) 'Richard Leacock: A Personal Perspective', Literature Film Quarterly, 10, 4, 234–53.

Neaverson, Bob (1997) The Beatles Movies. London: Cassell.

Nichols, Bill (1981) Ideology and the Image. Bloomington, IN: Indiana University Press.

____ (ed.) (1985) Movies and Methods Volume 2. Berkeley, CA: University of California Press.

____ (1991) Representing Reality. Bloomington, IN: Indiana University Press.

Nixon, Richard (1978) The Memoirs of Richard Nixon. London: Arrow.

Norman, Philip (1993) The Stones. London: Pan.

Nuttall, Jeff (1968) Bomb Culture. London: MacGibbon & Kee.

Oakley, J. Ronald (1986) God's Country: America in the Fifties. New York: Dembner.

O'Brien, James P. (1971) 'The Development of the New Left', Annals of the American Academy of Political and Social Science, vol. 395: Students Protest, May, 15–25.

O'Connell, P. J. (1992) Robert Drew and the Development of Cinéma Vérité in America. Carbondale, IL: Southern Illinois University Press.

O'Neill, William L. (1971) Coming Apart: An Informal History of America in the 1960s. Chicago: Quadrangle Books.

Oglesby, Carl (1970 [1965]) 'Trapped in a System', in Massimo Teodori (ed.) The New Left: A Documentary History. London: Jonathan Cape, 182–88.

Orvell, Miles (2003) American Photography. Oxford: Oxford University Press.

Parmet, Herbert S. (1971) *'Gimme Shelter', Sight and Sound*, Autumn, 226–7.

_____ (1990) 'The Kennedy Myth and American Politics', *History Teacher*, 24, 1, November, 31–9.

Partridge, William L. (1973) *The Hippie Ghetto: The Natural History of a Subculture*. New York: Holt, Rinhart and Winston.

Patterson, James T. (1996) *Grand Expectations: The United States 1945–1974*. New York: Oxford University Press.

_____ (2000) *America's Struggle Against Poverty in the Twentieth Century*. Cambridge, MA: Harvard University Press .

Penley, Constance (ed.) (1988) *Feminism and Film Theory*. London: Routledge.

Perkins, Bradford (1993) *The Cambridge History of American Foreign Relations, Vol. 1: The Creation of a Republican Empire, 1776–1865*. Cambridge: Cambridge University Press.

Perrine, Toni A. (1998) *Film and the Nuclear Age: Representing Cultural Anxiety*. New York: Garland.

Perry, Hart (1999) 'One Very Additional Camera', in Dale Bell (ed.) *Woodstock: An Inside Look at the Movie that Shook up the World and Defined a Generation*. Studio City, CA: Michael Wiese Productions, 139–40.

Perry, John (2004) *Electric Ladyland*. New York: Continuum.

Peterson, Merrill D. (ed.) (1984) *Jefferson: Writings*. New York: Library of America.

Phillips, Cabell (1959a) 'Democrats Divided on Party's Image for '60', *New York Times*, 28 June, E3.

_____ (1959b) 'Two Candidates on the Road', *New York Times Magazine*, 25 October, 24–9.

Phillips, John (1985) *It Happened in Our Lifetime: A Memoir in Words and Pictures*. London: Michael Joseph.

Pirie, David (1970) *'Woodstock* and *Monterey Pop', Sight and Sound*, Summer, 159–60.

_____ (1971) *'Gimme Shelter', Sight and Sound*, Autumn, 226–7.

Pomper, Gerald (1966) 'The Nomination of Hubert Humphrey for Vice-President', *Journal of Politics*, 28, 3, August, 639–59.

Ponech, Trevor (1999) *What is Non-Fiction Cinema? On the Very Idea of Motion Picture Communication*. Boulder CO: Westview.

Potter, Paul (1985) 'Speech to the April 17 1965 March on Washington', in Judith and Stewart Albert (eds) *The Sixties Papers: Documents of a Rebellious Decade*. New York: Praeger, 218–25.

Potter, W. James (1998) *Media Literacy*. Thousand Oaks, CA: Sage.

Quart, Leonard and Albert Auster (1984) *American Film and Society Since 1945*. London: Macmillan.

Rabe, David (2002) *Plays: 1*. London: Methuen.

Ramsey, Paul (1970) *The Patient as Person*. New Haven: Yale University Press.

Reeves, Richard (1994) *President Kennedy: Profile of Power*. New York: Simon & Schuster.

Rees, A. L. (1999) *A History of Experimental Film and Video*. London: British Film Institute.

Reich, Charles A. (1970) *The Greening of America*. New York: Random House.

Reidhead, Julia (ed.) (1998) *The Norton Anthology of American Literature: Fifth Edition*. London: Norton.

Renov, Michael (ed.) (1993) *Theorizing Documentary*. New York: Routledge.

Reumann, Miriam G. (2005) *American Sexual Character: Sex, Gender, and National Identity in the Kinsey Reports*. Berkeley, CA: University of California Press.

Reynolds, David S. (1988) *Beneath the American Renaissance: The Subversive Imagination in the Age of Emerson and Melville*. Cambridge, MA: Harvard University Press.

Rice, William (1968) 'Real Horror Movie at Janus', *Washington Post*, 7 December 7, D6.

Rich, Adrienne (1979) *On Lies, Secrets, and Silence: Selected Prose 1966–1978*. New York: Norton.

Ricks, Christopher (2004) *Dylan's Visions of Sin*. London: Penguin.

Riddell, Roger C. (1987) *Foreign Aid Reconsidered*. Baltimore: Johns Hopkins University Press.

Riis, Jacob (1980) *How the Other Half Lives*. London: Penguin Classics.

Rivkin, Julie and Michael Ryan (eds) (1998) *Literary Theory: An Anthology*. Malden, MA: Blackwell.

____ (1998) 'The Class of 1968 – Post-Structuralism *par liu-même*', in Julie Rivkin and Michael Ryan (eds) *Literary Theory: An Anthology*. Malden, MA: Blackwell, 333–57.

Roberts, John (1999) 'Reminiscences', in Dale Bell (ed.) *Woodstock: An Inside Look at the Movie that Shook up the World and Defined a Generation*. Studio City, CA: Michael Wiese Productions, 52–5.

Robertson, Nan (1967) 'The Student Scene: Angry Militants', *New York Times*, 20 November, 1–2.

Robinson, Paul (1972) *The Sexual Radicals*. London: Paladin.

Rollins, Peter C. (1991) 'Vietnam and American Culture', *Journal of American Culture*, 14, 4, Winter, 77–84.

Romanowski, Patricia (ed.) (1995) *The New Rolling Stone Encyclopedia of Rock & Roll*. New York: Simon & Schuster.

Rosenbaum, Jonathan (1997) *Movies as Politics*. Berkeley, CA: University of California Press.

Rosenstone, Robert A. (1969) '"The Times They Are A-Changin'"': The Music of Protest', *Annals of the American Academy of Political and Social Science, vol. 382: Protest in the Sixties*, March, 131–44.

Rosenthal, Alan (1971) *The New Documentary in Action: A Casebook in Film Making*. New York and Berkeley, University of California Press

____ (1978/79) 'Ellen Hovde: An Interview', *Film Quarterly*, 32, 2, Winter, 8–17.

____ (ed.) (1988) *New Challenges for Documentary*. Berkeley, CA: University of California Press.

____ (2002) *Writing, Directing and Producing Documentary Films and Videos*. Carbondale, IL: Southern Illinois University Press.

Rosenthal, Alan and John Corner (eds) (2005) *New Challenges for Documentary: Second Edition*. Manchester: Manchester University Press.

Rostow, Eugene V. (1993) *A Breakfast for Bonaparte: U.S. National Security Interests from the Heights of Abraham to the Nuclear Age*. Washington, D.C.: National Defense University Press.

Roszak, Thedore (1971) *The Making of a Counter Culture: Reflections on the Technocratic Society and Its Youthful Opposition*. London: Faber & Faber.

Roth, Wilhelm (1982) *Der Dokumentarfilm seit 1960*. Munich: C.J. Butcher.

Rothman, William (1997) *Documentary Film Classics*. New York: Cambridge University Press.

Ruby, Jay (2005) 'The Ethics of Image Making', in Alan Rosenthal and John Corner (eds) *New Challenges for Documentary: Second Edition*. Manchester: Manchester University Press, 209–19.

Ruskin, John (2004) *On Art and Life*. London: Penguin.

Russell, Bertrand (1996 [1945]) *History of Western Philosophy*. London: Routledge.

Sadkin, David (1972) '*Gimme Shelter*: A Corkscrew or a Cathedral?', *Filmmakers Newsletter*, 5, 2, December, 20–8.

Said, Edward W. (1994) *Culture and Imperialism*. London: Vintage.

Sale, Kirkpatrick (1973) *SDS*. New York: Vintage.

Sampson, Anthony (1967) *Macmillan: A Study in Ambiguity*. London: The Penguin Press.

Sarris, Andrew (1968) '*Dont Look Back*: Digging Dylan', *Film*, 67, 68, 248–53.

Savio, Mario (1995) 'An End to History', in Alexander Bloom and Wini Breines (eds) *Takin' it to the Streets: A Sixties Reader*. New York: Oxford University Press, 111–15.

Scaduto, Anthony (1973) *Bob Dylan*. London: Sphere.

Scott King, Coretta (1985) *The Words of Martin Luther King*. London: Fount.

Schiff, Martin (1973) 'Neo-Transcendentalism in the New Left Counter-Culture: A Vision of the Future Looking Back', *Comparitive Studies in Society and History*, 15, 2, March, 130–42.

Schlesinger, Arthur M., Jr (1965) *A Thousand Days: John F. Kennedy in the White House*. London: Andre Deutsch.

Scully, Rock with David Dalton (1996) *Living with the Dead: Twenty Years on the Bus With The Grateful Dead*. London: Little, Brown.

Selig, Michael (1993) 'Genre, Gender, and the Discourse of War: The A/Historical and Vietnam Films', *Screen* 34, 1, 1–18.

Shaar Murray, Charles (1989) *Crosstown Traffic: Jimi Hendrix and the Post-War Rock 'n' Roll Revolution*. New York: St. Martin's.

Shankar, Ravi (1999) 'While My Sitar Gently Weeps', online at: www.guardian.co.uk/Archive/Article/0%2C4273%2C3905479%2C00.html; accessed 9 February 2003.

Shapiro, Michael (ed.) (1984) *Language and Politics*. Oxford: Basil Blackwell.

Shay, Jonathan (1994) *Achilles in Vietnam: Combat Trauma and the Undoing of Character*. New York: Simon & Schuster.

Sheehan, Neil (1998) *A Bright Shining Lie: John Paul Vann and America in Vietnam*. London: Pimlico.

Shelton, Robert (1963) 'Freedom Songs Sweep North', *New York Times*, 6 July, 7.

____ (1964) 'This Long-Haired Singer is No Beatle', *New York Times*, 2 February, 64.

____ (1965) 'New Pop-Folk Formulas', *New York Times*, 21 February, 23.

Sherman, Norman (1991) 'Afterword', in Hubert H. Humphrey, *The Education of a Public Man: My Life and Politics*. Minneapolis: University of Minnesota Press, 331–40.

Shipman, David (1994) *Cinema – The First Hundred Years*. London: Phoenix.

Sinclair, Andrew (1999) *A Concise History of the United States*. Stroud: Sutton Ltd.

Skipper, James K., Jr. and Robert C. Leonard (1965) *Social Interaction and Patient Care*. Philadelphia: J. B. Lippincott.

Smith, Edward Lucie (1994) *The Thames and Hudson Dictionary of Art Terms*. London: Thames and Hudson.

Smith, Huston (1964) 'Do Drugs Have Religious Import?', *Journal of Philosophy*, 61, 8, October, 517–30.

Smith, Terry (2001) '*Life*-Style Modernity', in Erika Doss (ed.) *Looking at Life Magazine*. Washington, D.C.: Smithsonian Institution Press, 25–39.

Smith, Tom W. (1986) 'The Polls: The Most Admired Man and Woman', *Public Opinion Quarterly*, 50, 4, Winter, 573–83.

Sobchack, Vivian C. (1980) 'Beyond Visual Aids: American Film as American Culture', *American Quarterly*, 32, 3, 280–300.

Solinger, Rickie (2001) 'The Smutty Side of *Life*', in Erika Doss (ed.) *Looking at Life Magazine*. Washington, D.C.: Smithsonian Institution Press, 201–19.

Sontag, Susan (2001) *Against Interpretation*. London: Vintage.

____ (2002) *On Photography*. London: Penguin Classics.

____ (2003) *Regarding the Pain of Others*. London: Penguin.

Sorensen, Theodore C. (1965) *Kennedy*. London: Hodder and Stoughton.

Sounes, Howard (2002) *Down the Highway: The Life of Bob Dylan*. London: Black Swan.

Souster, Tim (1968/69) 'Notes on Pop Music', *Tempo*, 87, Winter, 2–6.

Spates, James L. (1976) 'Counterculture and Dominant Culture Values: A Cross-National Analysis of the Underground Press and Dominant Culture Magazines', *American Sociological Review*, 41, 5, October, 868–83.

Spears, Timothy B. (1995) *100 Years on the Road: The Travelling Salesman in American Culture*. New Haven, CT: Yale University Press.

Spiegel, Alan (1976) *Fiction and the Camera Eye: Visual Consciousness in Film and the Modern Novel*. Charlottesville: University Press of Virginia.

Spigel, Lynn and Michael Curtin (1997) *The Revolution Wasn't Televised: Sixties Television and Social Conflict*. London: Routledge.

Spiller, Robert E. (1955) *The Cycle of American Literature*. New York: Macmillan.

Spiller, Robert E. and Thomas E. Crawley (eds) (1976) *Four Makers of the American Mind: Emerson, Thoreau, Whitman and Melville*. Durham, NC: Duke University Press.

Spitz, Bob (1989) *Bob Dylan: A Biography*. New York: Norton.

Sragow, Michael (1961) 'Politics and Film for Beginners: *Gimme Shelter*, Godard and Others with a Little Introduction', *Harvard Crimson*, 17 June.

Stannard, David E. (1992) *American Holocaust: The Conquest of the New World*. New York: Oxford University Press.

Steigerwald, David (1995) *The Sixties and the End of Modern America*. New York: St. Martin's.

Stein, Howard F. (1990) *American Medicine as Culture*. London: Westview.

Stephenson, Ralph and Guy Phelps (1989) *The Cinema as Art (Revised Edition)*. London: Penguin.

Stowe, Harriet Beecher (1967 [1852]) *Uncle Tom's Cabin; or, Life Among the Lowly*. New York: Collier.

Stratton, Jon (1983) 'Capitalism and Romantic Ideology in the Record Business', in *Popular Music, vol. 3: Producers and Markets*, 143–56.

Street, John (1986) *Rebel Rock*. New York: Basil Blackwell.

Stubbs, Liz (2002) *Documentary Filmmakers Speak*. New York: Allworth Press.

Students for a Democratic Society (1970) 'The Port Huron Statement', in Massimo Teodori (ed.) *The New Left: A Documentary History*. London: Jonathan Cape, 163–72.

Sugerman, Danny (1991) *Wonderland Avenue: Tales of Glamour and Excess*. London: Abacus.

Summers, Harry G. Jr (1984) *On Strategy: A Critical Analysis of the Vietnam War*. New York: Dell.

Swick-Perry, Helen (1995 [1967]) 'The Human Be-In', in Alexander Bloom and Wini Breines (eds) *Takin' it to the Streets: A Sixties Reader*. New York: Oxford University Press, 313–16.

Swiss, Thomas, Andrew Herman and John M.Sloop (eds) (1998) *Mapping the Beat: Popular Music and Contemporary Theory*. Malden MA: Blackwell.

Tanner, Tony (1971) *City of Words: American Fiction 1950–1970*. London: Jonathan Cape.

Taylor, Charles (1998) '*Titicut Follies*', *Sight and Sound*, 57, 2, 98–103.

Teodori, Massimo (ed.) (1970) *The New Left: A Documentary History*. London: Jonathan Cape.

Terkel, Studs (1982) *American Dreams: Lost and Found*. London: Paladin.

Thompson, David (2003) 'Crazy About the Weather', *Sight and Sound*, 13, 12, 18–19.

Thompson, Hunter S. (1967) *Hell's Angels*. Harmondsworth: Penguin.

Thompson, Peter (2000) *Cassell's Dictionary of Modern American History*. London: Cassell & Co.

Thoreau, Henry David (1961 [1854]) *Walden*. New York: Holt, Rinehart and Winston.

_____ (1981 [1849]) 'Civil Disobedience', in *Walden and Other Writings*. New York: Bantam Classics, 85–104.

Thurschwell, Pamela (2002) 'A Different Baby Blue', in Neil Corcoran (ed.) *'Do you, Mr Jones?' Bob Dylan with the Poets and Professors*. London: Chatto & Windus, 253–73.

Tiber, Elliot (1994) *The Times Herald-Record: Woodstock Commemorative Edition*.

Tobias, Michael (ed.) (1998) *The Search For Reality: The Art of Documentary Filmmaking*. Studio City, CA: Michael Wiese Productions.

Trachtenberg, Alan (ed.) (1980) *Classic Essays on Photography*. New Haven: Leete's Island Books.

Turner, Steve (1995) *Hungry for Heaven: Rock and Roll and the Search for Redemption*. London: Hodder and Stoughton.

Twain, Mark (1984 [1884]) *The Innocents Abroad & Roughing It* (single volume). New York: The Library of America.

Unger, Irwin (1974) *The Movement: A History of the American New Left 1959–1972*. New York: Dodd, Mead.

Uyeki, Eugene S. (1960) 'Draftee Behaviour in the Cold-War Army', *Social Problems*, 8, 2, Autumn, 151–8.

Various (1994) *The Times Herald-Record: Woodstock Commemorative Edition*.

Vogel, Amos (2005) *Film as a Subversive Art* (revised second edition). London: C.T.Editions.

Wadleigh, Michael (2004) 'The Woodstock Generation, online at: www.britannica.com/psychedelic/textonly/woodstockgeneration.html; accessed 10 April 2004.

Waldman, Anne (1996) *The Beat Book*. Boston: Shambhala.

Warhol, Andy and Pat Hackett (1980) *POPism: The Warhol Sixties*. San Diego, CA: Harcourt Brace.

Warren, Charles (ed.) (1996) *Beyond Document: Essays on Nonfiction Film*. Hanover NH, Wesleyan Unversity Press.

Watson James (1998) *Media Communication*. London: Macmillan.

Waugh, Thomas (1985) 'Beyond Vérité: Emile de Antonio and the New Documentary of the Seventies', in Bill Nichols (ed.) *Movies and Methods, Volume 2*. Berkeley, CA: University of California Press, 233–58.

Webster, Duncan (1988) *Looka Yonder! The Imaginary America of Populist Culture*. London: Routledge.

Webster, Frank (1995) *Theories of the Information Society*. London: Routledge.

Westin, Alan (1974) '"You Start Off with a Bromide": Wiseman on Film and Civil Liberties', *Civil Liberties Review*, 1, 52–67.

White, Morton and Lucia White (1969) 'The American Intellectual versus the American City', in Alexander B. Callow (ed.) *American Urban History: An Interpretive Reader with Commentaries*. New York: Oxford University Press, 333–43.

White, Theodore H. (1962) *The Making of the President 1960*. London: Jonathan Cape.

_____ (1979) *In Search of History: A Personal Adventure*. New York: Warner Books.

Whiteley, Sheila (1998) 'Repressive Representations', in Thomas Swiss, Andrew Herman and John M.Sloop (eds) *Mapping the Beat: Popular Music and Contemporary Theory*. Malden, MA: Blackwell, 160–86.

Whitfield, Stephen J. (1996) *Cold War Culture* (second edition). Baltimore: Johns Hopkins University Press.

Whitman, Walt (1982) *Complete Poetry and Collected Prose*. New York: Library of America.

____ (1998 [1855]) *Leaves of Grass*. Oxford: Oxford University Press.

____ (1964) *Prose Works, Vol. 2: Collect and Other Prose*, ed. Floyd Stovall. New York: New York University Press.

Williams, Chris (1993) *Bob Dylan in his Own Words*. London: Omnibus Press.

Williams, Paul (1994) *Bob Dylan: Performing Artist 1960–1973, The Early Years*. London: Omnibus Press.

Williams, Raymond (1974) *Television: Technology and Cultural Form*. London: Fontana.

____ (1981) *Culture*. London: Collins.

Wilson, Robert N. (1972) 'Hospital', *Social Forces*, 51, 2, December, 254–5.

Winston, Brian (1993) 'The Documentary Film as Scientific Inscription', in Michael Renov (ed.) *Theorizing Documentary*. New York: Routledge, 37–57.

____ (1995) *Claiming the Real: Documentary Film Revisited*. London: British Film Institute.

Wolf, Naomi (1990) *The Beauty Myth*. London: Vintage.

____ (1998) *Promiscuities: A Secret History of Female Desire*. London: Vintage.

Wolfe, Tom (1966) *The Kandy-Kolored Tangerine-Flake Streamline Baby*. London: Jonathan Cape.

____ (1971) *The Electric Kool-Aid Acid Test*. London: Bantam.

Wolff, Janet (1993) *The Social Production of Art* (Second Edition). London: Macmillan.

Wollen, Peter (1998) *Signs and Meaning in the Cinema – Expanded Edition*. London: British Film Institute.

Wood, Jason (2005) *Nick Broomfield: Documenting Icons*. London: Faber & Faber.

Woodruff, Mark W. (1999) *Unheralded Victory: Who Won the Vietnam War?* London: Harper-Collins.

Yablonksy, Lewis (1968) *The Hippie Trip*. New York: Pegasus.

Young, Colin (1964) 'Three Views on *Cinéma Vérité*: Cinema of Common Sense', *Film Quarterly*, 17, 4, Summer, 26–9.

____ (!975) 'Observational Cinema', in Paul Hockings (ed.) *Principles of Visual Anthropology*. The Hague and Paris: Mouton, 65–79.

Young, Jock (1971) *The Drugtakers: The Social Meaning of Drug Use*. London: Paladin.

____ (1997) 'The Subterranean World of Play', in Ken Gelder and Sarah Thornton (eds) *The Subcultures Reader*. New York: Routledge, 71–80.

Zinn, Howard A. (1990) *A People's History of the United States*. New York: HarperPerennial.

INDEX

Nonfictions is dedicated to expanding and deepening
the range of contemporary documentary studies.
It aims to engage in the theoretical conversation
about documentaries, open new areas of scholarship,
and recover lost or marginalised histories.

General Editor, Professor Brian Winston